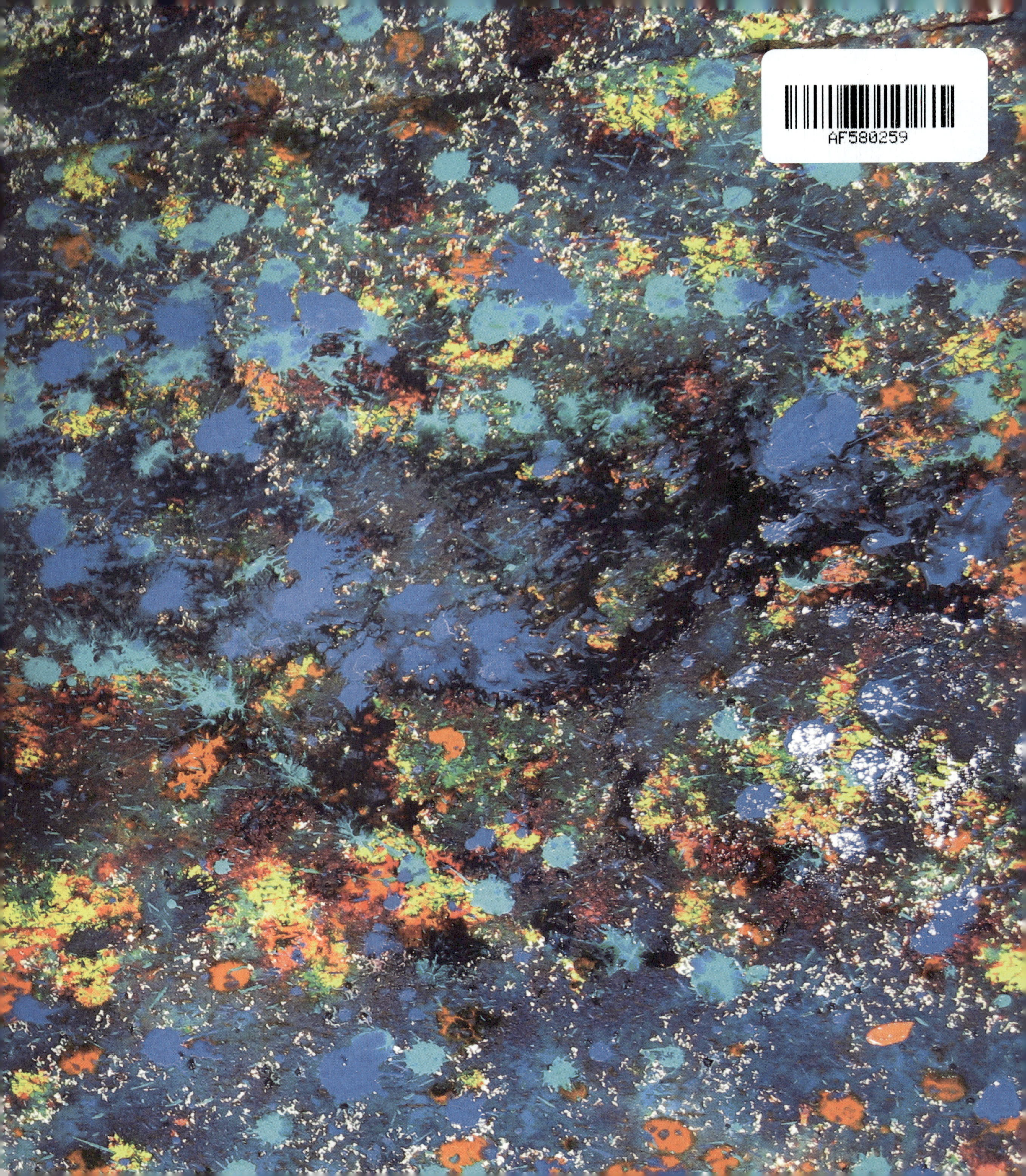

To Jack Aloha

THE ART AND LIFE OF WYLAND

Wyland 2014

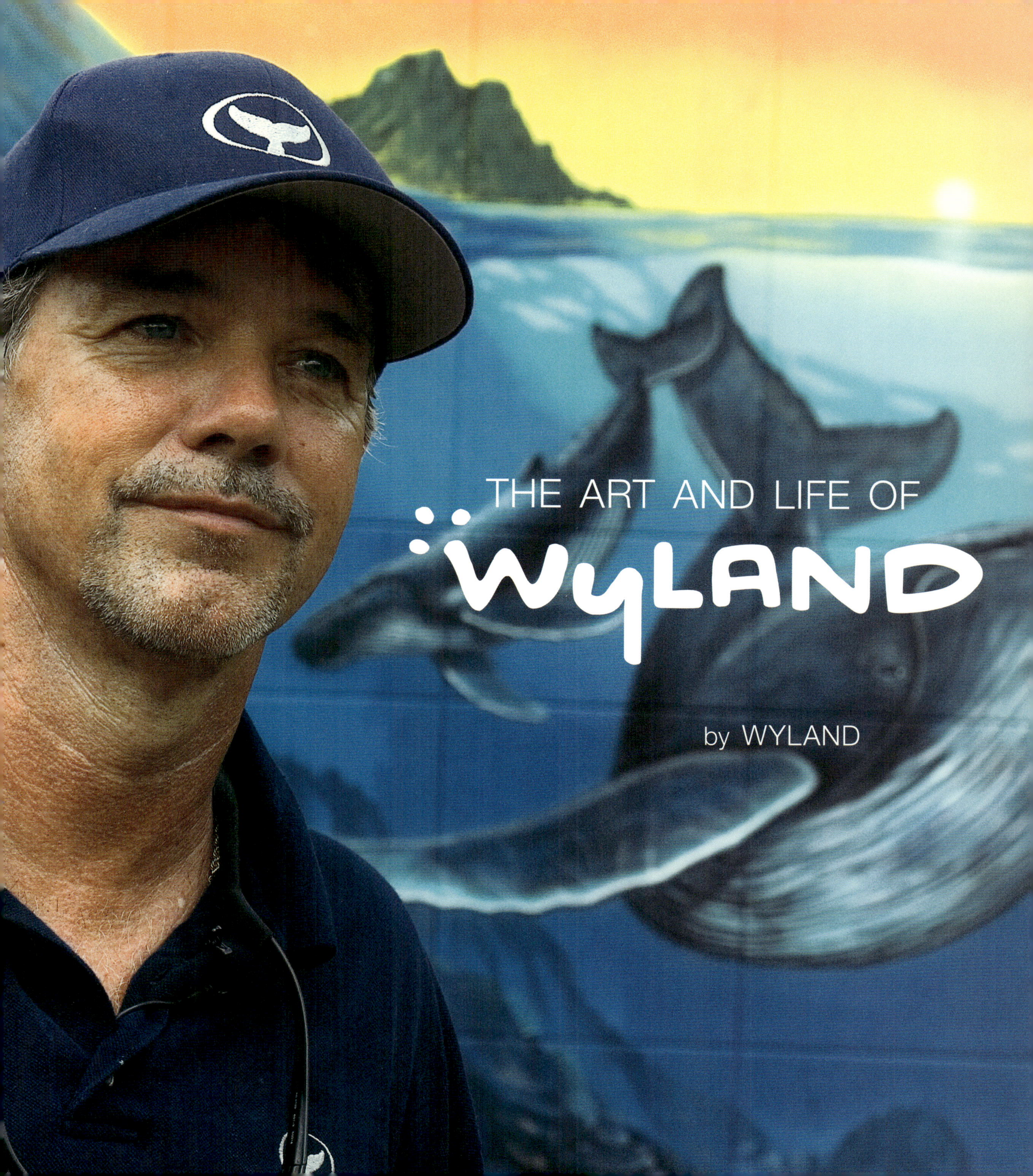
THE ART AND LIFE OF
WYLAND
by WYLAND

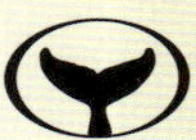

Wyland Worldwide, LLC
5 Columbia, Aliso Viejo, CA 92656
Phone 949-643-7070, Fax 949-643-7099
www.wyland.com, customerservice@wyland.com

Official photographer; Gary Firstenberg
Photos by: Gino Beltran, Kim Tayor Reece, Stephen Frink, Chris Bangs, Michael Aw, Jim Abernathy, Bob Torrez, and Jeff Pantukhoff

Thank you to all who have picked up the camera to help me document the journey over the years.

Printed in China using vegetable based inks and bound in 2009

Produced by:
Wyland Worldwide, LLC
5 Columbia, Aliso Viejo, CA 92656

1 3 5 7 9 10 8 6 4 2

Library of Congress Cataloging-in-Publication Data

Wyland, 1956

Wyland: Visions of the Sea

ISBN 978-1884840043(Limited Edition)
ISBN 978-1884840036(Standard Edition)

Special thanks to Wyland Design, Gregg Hamby, Steve Creech, Gino Beltran, Karla Kipp, and Jennifer Martin

Creative Production: Wyland Design
Printing: 2009 Everbest Printing Co.,Ltd

This book of my art
and life is dedicated
to my mother
Darlene Wyland

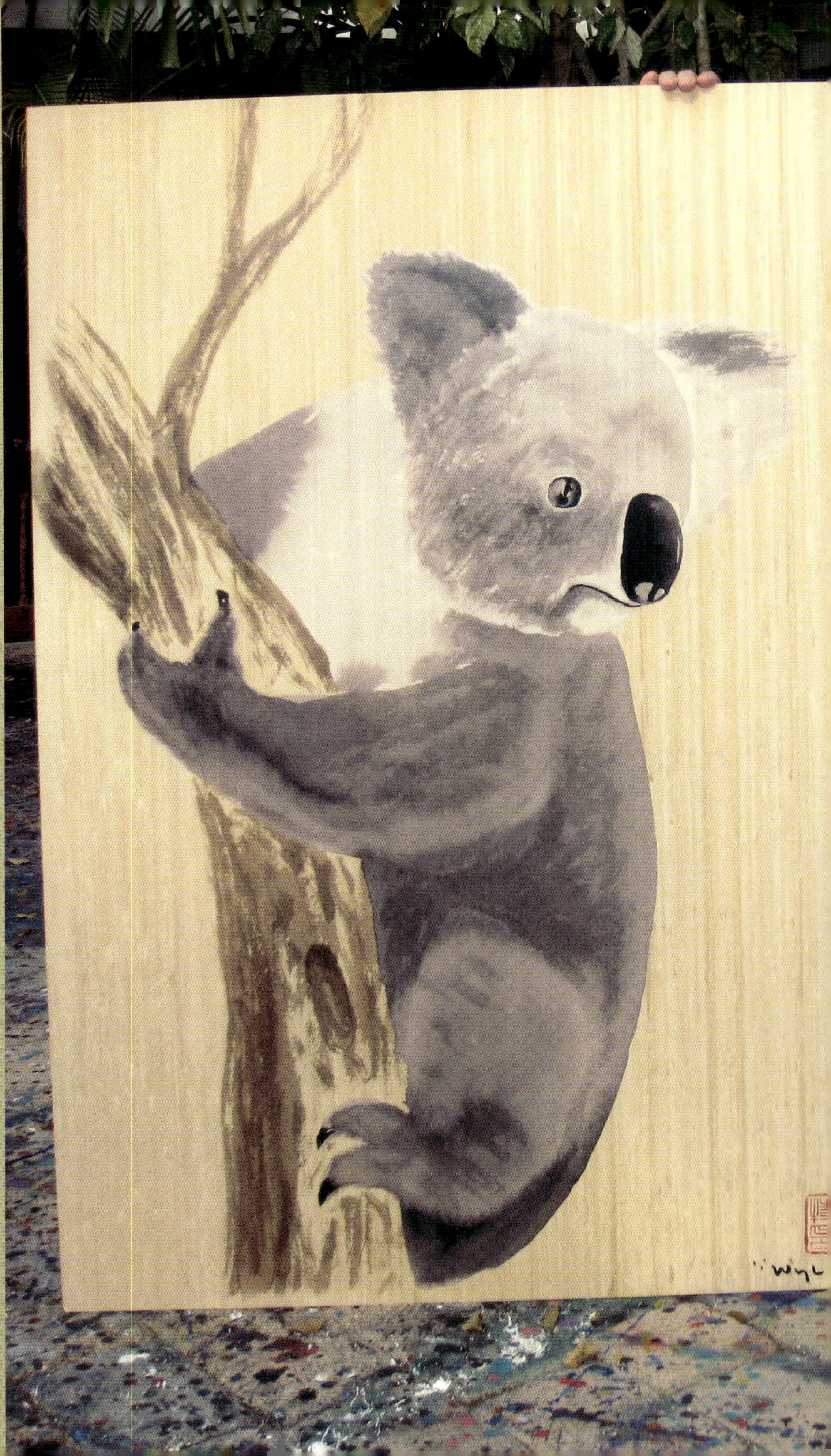

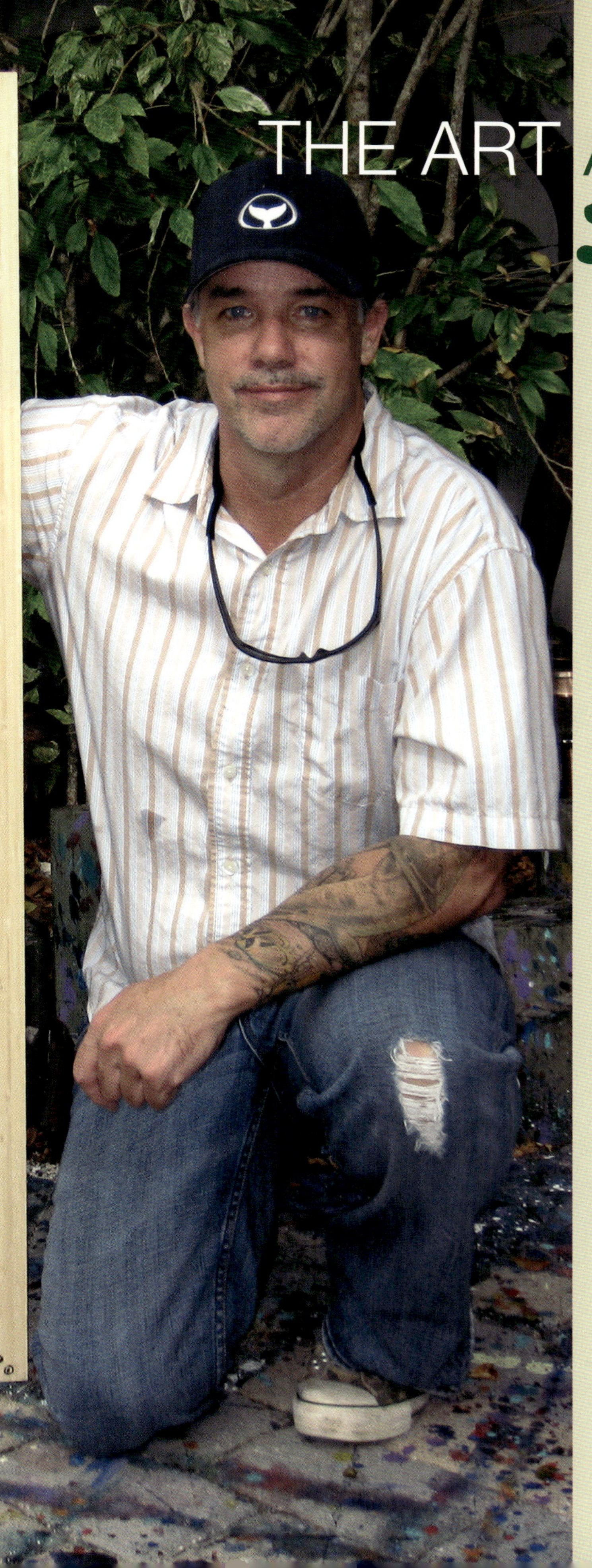

THE ART AND LIFE OF WYLAND®

CONTENTS

...The message is to learn everything we can about our environment and use art to educate and inspire people to get involved...

:: WYLAND

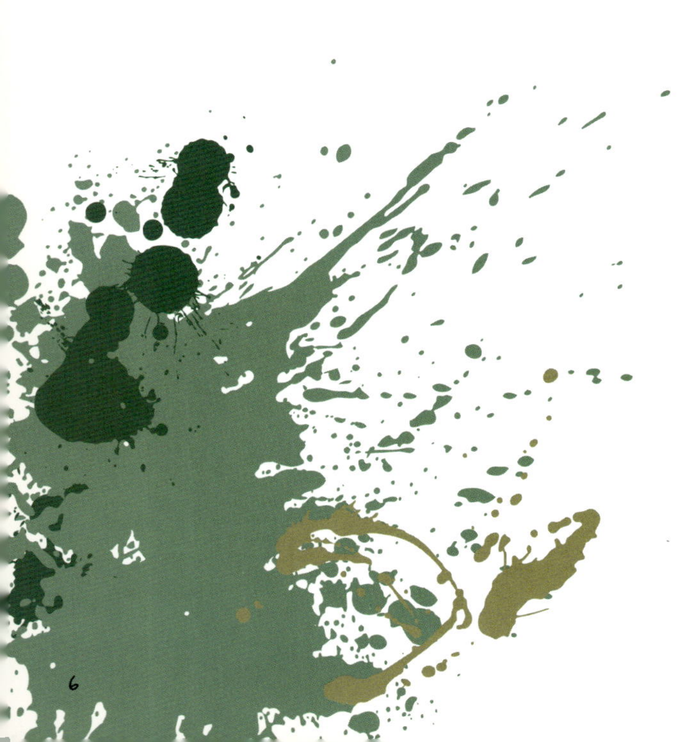

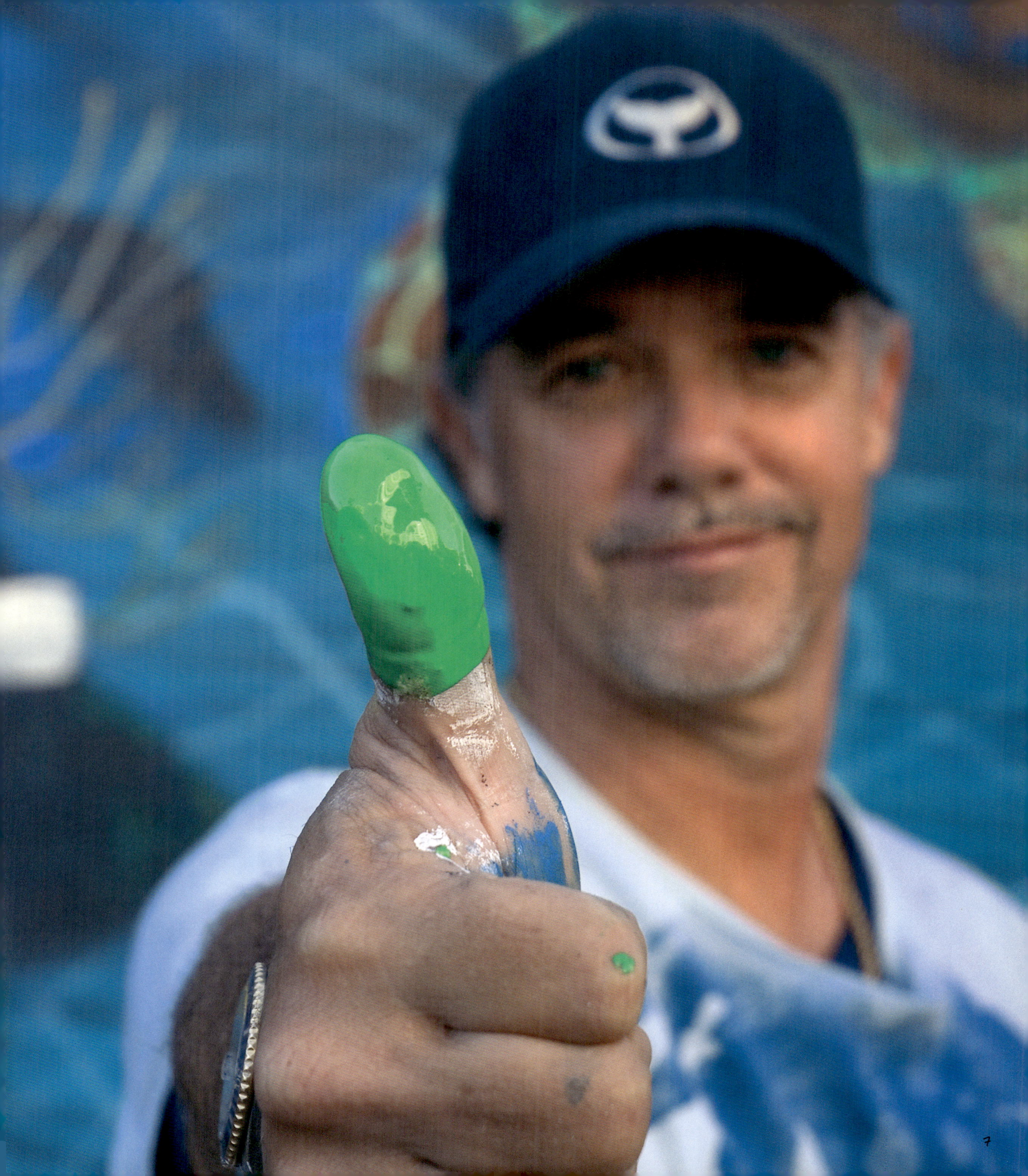

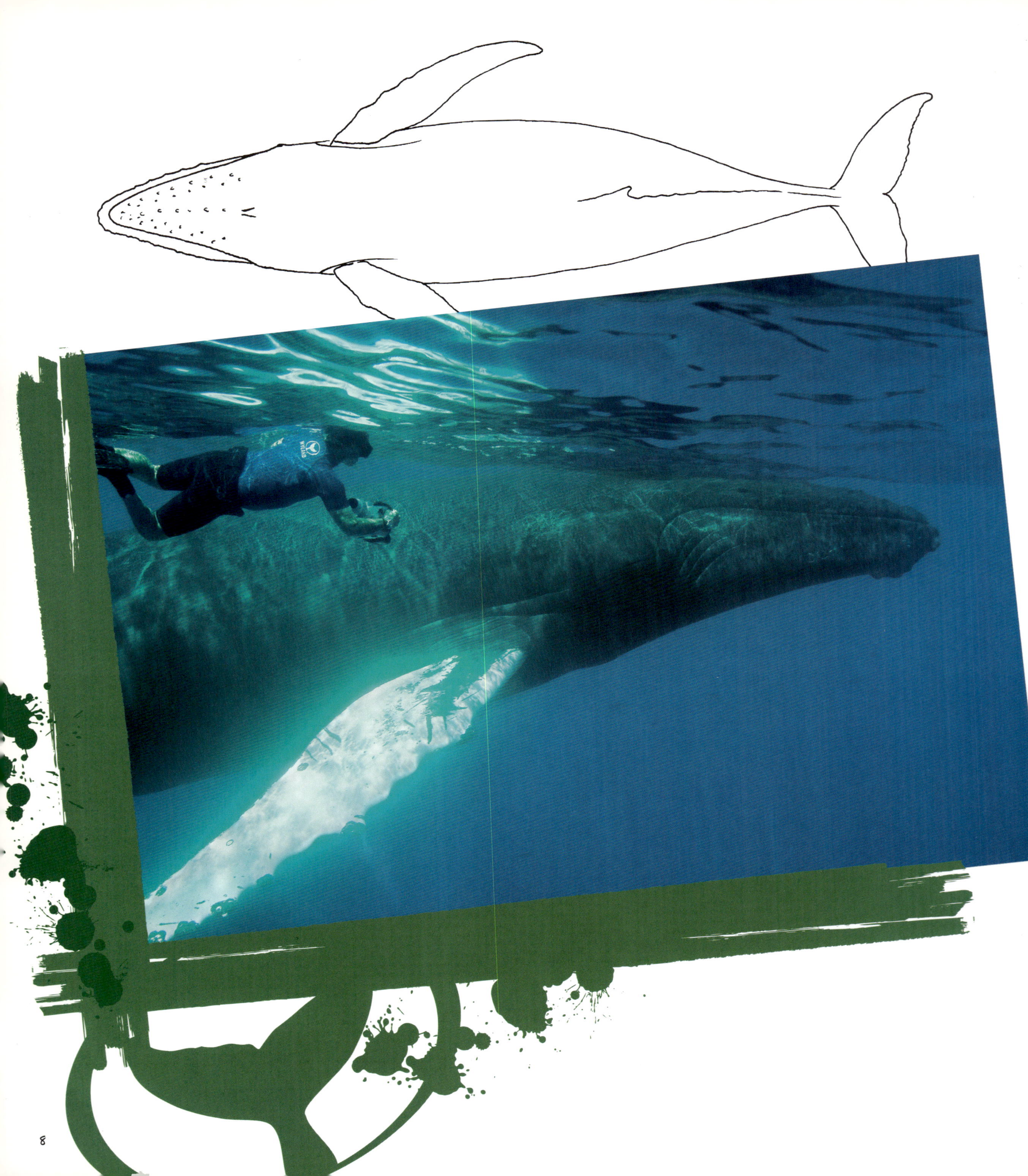

THE FIRST EARTH DAY BACK IN 1970 FOREVER CHANGED THE WAY WE THINK...

Introduction

The first Earth Day back in 1970 forever changed the way we think about the environment. Before that, it seemed, only a small handful of activists expressed any concern about the state of our air, water, and natural resources. The politicians at the time certainly weren't doing anything. But thanks to the encouragement of a few dedicated individuals, millions of ordinary people suddenly stepped forward to acknowledge what was obviously a global environmental crisis. I was fourteen years old then and heard the call with resounding clarity. I was amazed to think that so many people were interested in our planet and wanted to do their part.

At the same time, new, incredible visions of our undersea world were appearing regularly on television thanks to the astonishing underwater documentary work of Jacques Cousteau. These images encouraged even more people to think about the global impact humans were having on the environment, as did the work of small groups like Greenpeace, who boldly challenged industries responsible for the wholesale slaughter of marine species. I remember news photos of Greenpeace volunteers positioning their small Zodiac boats between the harpoons of massive Japanese whaling ships.

All these events resonated in my young consciousness. They instilled me with a passion to use my budding artistic ability as a way to further the environmental cause and engage people not only to see the beauty in nature, but to actively work toward protecting it.

Today is Earth Day, and I am standing on the eleven-story-high Long Beach Arena roof preparing to put the finishing touches on the largest "portrait" of Earth in history. The nearly three-acre mural celebrates Earth Day thirty-nine years after I heard the call. In a twenty-four-hour marathon, I hope not only to paint our water planet, as it would be seen from space, suspended against the backdrop of our vast, dark universe, but to share the idea that this beautiful, fragile place is the only home we've ever had – and will ever have.

I have always tried to use my art as a way of engaging people throughout the world about environmental issues regarding clean water and healthy oceans. I believe art will continue to play an important role in conservation and may very well be the one element that inspires people to become better caretakers of the legacy we've been given. You don't have to look hard at this gigantic mural of Earth to notice that our planet is mostly covered by water – and it is water that sustains us. It certainly is the one element that has sustained my passion for painting, sculpture, murals, nature photography, and all the outreach and community service work that my foundation and I have been doing over the years. Our ultimate goal is to bridge the world of art and science and share our message forward with young people throughout the world.

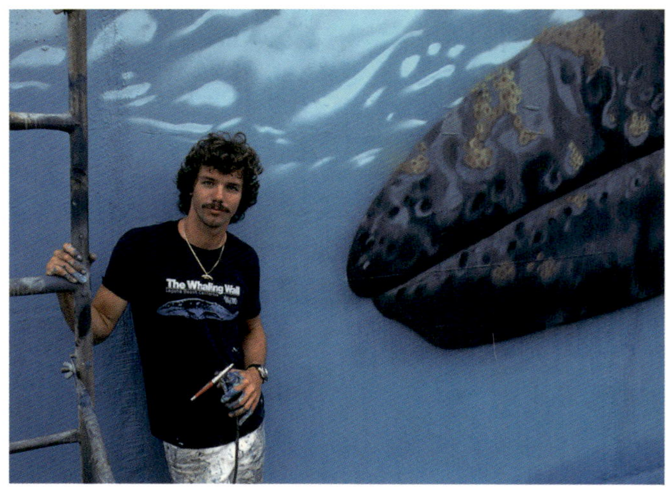

Working with great institutions, like the Scripps Institution of Oceanography (UCSD), UNEP, AZA, the Ocean Institute, and scientists like Dr. Sylvia Earle and Bob Ballard, has given me the motivation to continue sharing the green message forward – particularly with kids.

I'm most proud to say that in the last thirty years I've painted with more than one million kids in all fifty states and many countries around the world. I am continually learning from kids. If you spend any time talking with them, you can see they have a natural curiosity and concern for all living things. You're also immediately taken by how much better informed they are than my generation ever was.

In 2008, I had the opportunity to paint my last Whaling Wall in Beijing for the Green Olympics. We titled the effort "Hands Across the Oceans", an international movement to bring together children around the world to show their love for the environment through the depiction of our ocean, lakes, rivers, streams, and wetlands. The project launched in Norway at the United Nations Environment Programme's International Children's Conference, then continued on as part of the Beijing Olympic Cultural Festival in Chaoyang Park, site of the Olympic volleyball event. In total, young people from more than 110 countries took part in this landmark project, all joining in the effort to paint habitats – salt water and fresh – from regions around the world. The idea was simple: water connects us all, regardless of geographic or political boundaries – and every drop counts. Our goal was to empower these international kids to be youth ambassadors for the planet. In the spirit of the Olympic games, each was given a Wyland Foundation medal

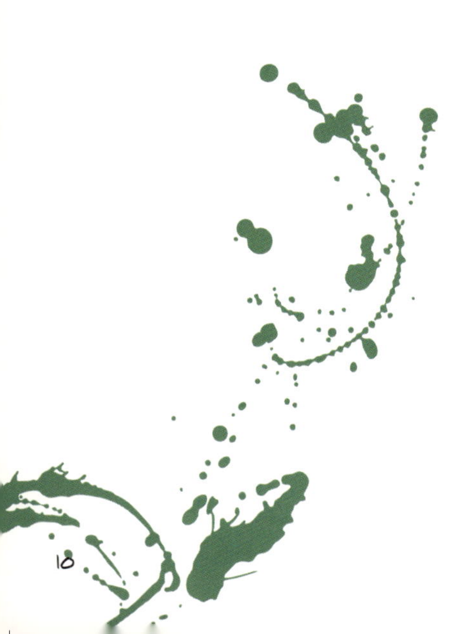

and inspired to go back to their country and share the message of conservation through art and science. Whaling Wall 100, "Hands Across the Oceans" as this project was known, was dedicated with all the giant canvases the children and I created placed around Chaoyang Park's famous lake. In the end, kids throughout China and other nations joined hands to conclude our efforts over the years to create one of the largest public art projects in history.

The very next day, I began my quest to again use public art in the service of environmental awareness. This time I plan to create one hundred monumental sculptures with water elements for one hundred official cities over the course of the next twenty-five years. My goal is to sculpt all the great whale species and other aquatic life at a scale of life-size or larger than life. Such art on a grand scale in public places engages our senses and allows us to see the natural world differently. It plays an important role in how we view not only the great whales and other species, but how we perceive our place in nature's grand scheme. Not everyone is going to get a chance to swim with a blue whale like I did in the Sea of Cortez, but art gives us the opportunity to experience nature in an emotional, engaging way – one that can leave a lifelong impression and cause awareness and hopefully action.

We've come a long way since that first Earth Day. It's no longer just the activists who are going green. It's everybody, and it's global. I'm very proud to be an artist who can make a difference and inspire a generation of people to get involved. On this special day, I have to smile and think about all the goodwill from around the world for the Earth and this generation's moment to change the world and bring the planet back to its pristine state. I can think of no better legacy for all us to leave behind.

– Wyland
Earth Day, 2009
Long Beach, California

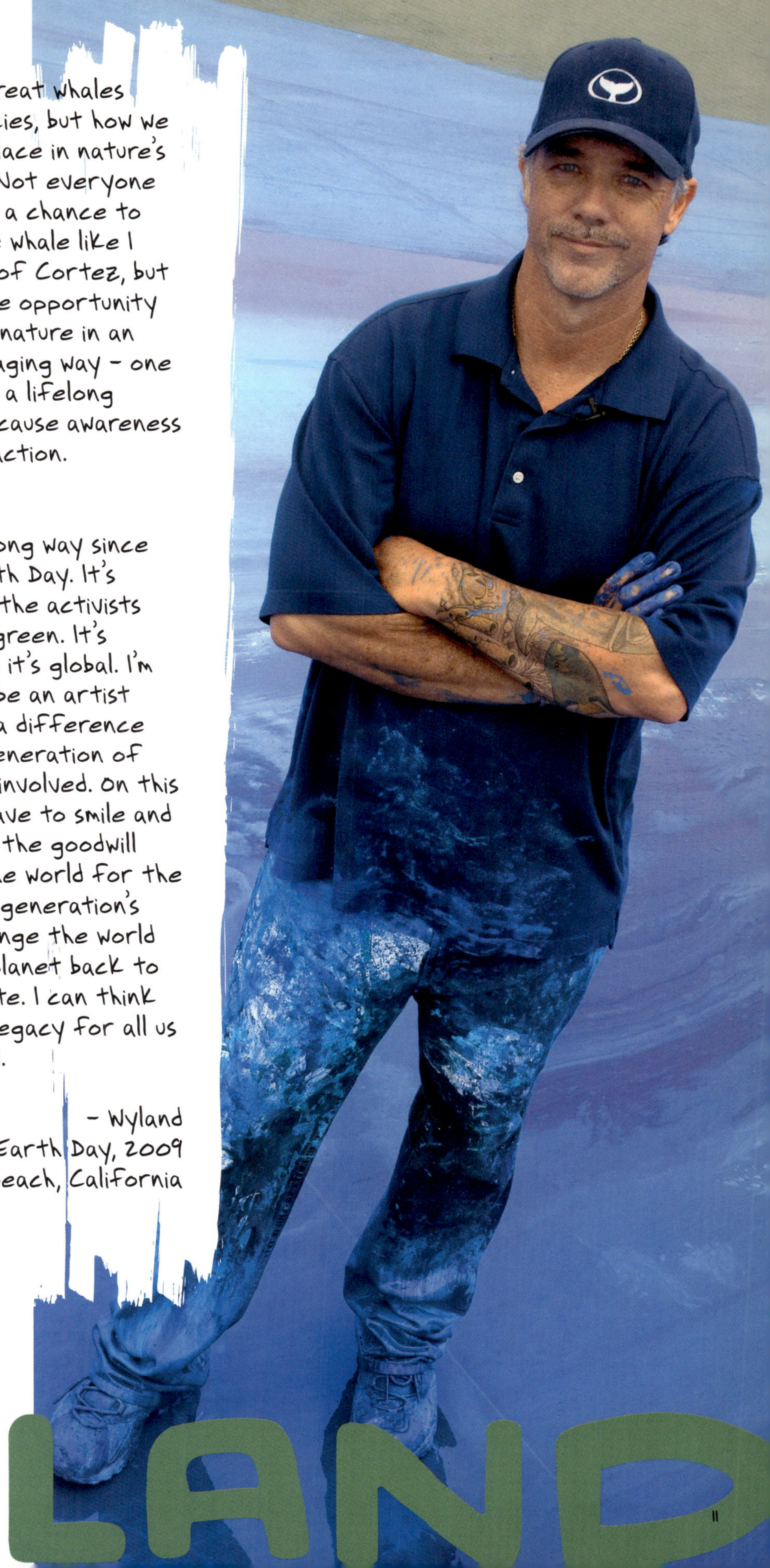

WyLAND

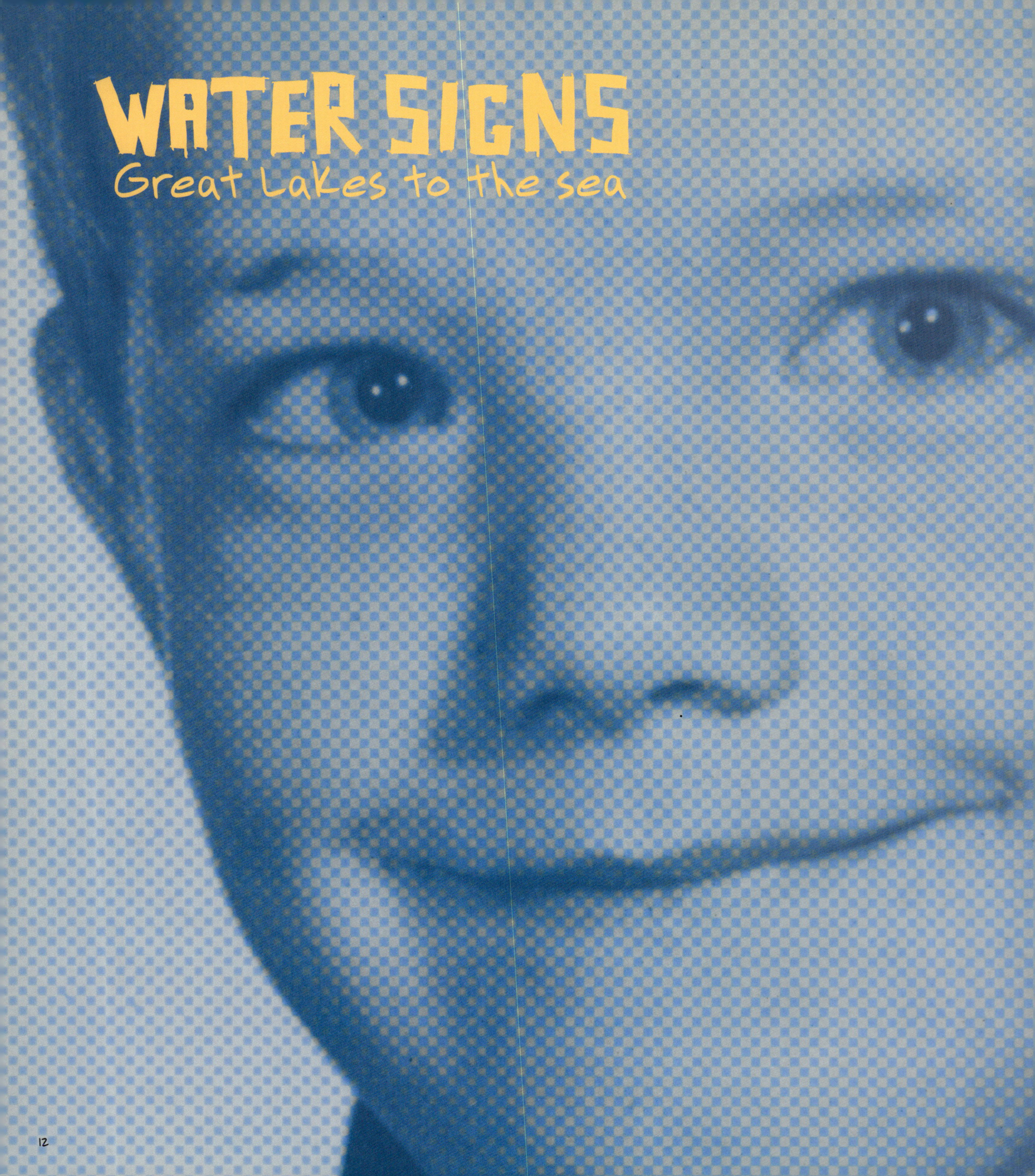

WATER SIGNS

Great Lakes to the sea

When I'm immersed in water,

I am most at home. It has been the inspiration for everything I do, and perhaps it's not a coincidence that I am a water sign or that I was born at a time when water issues were starting to take shape.

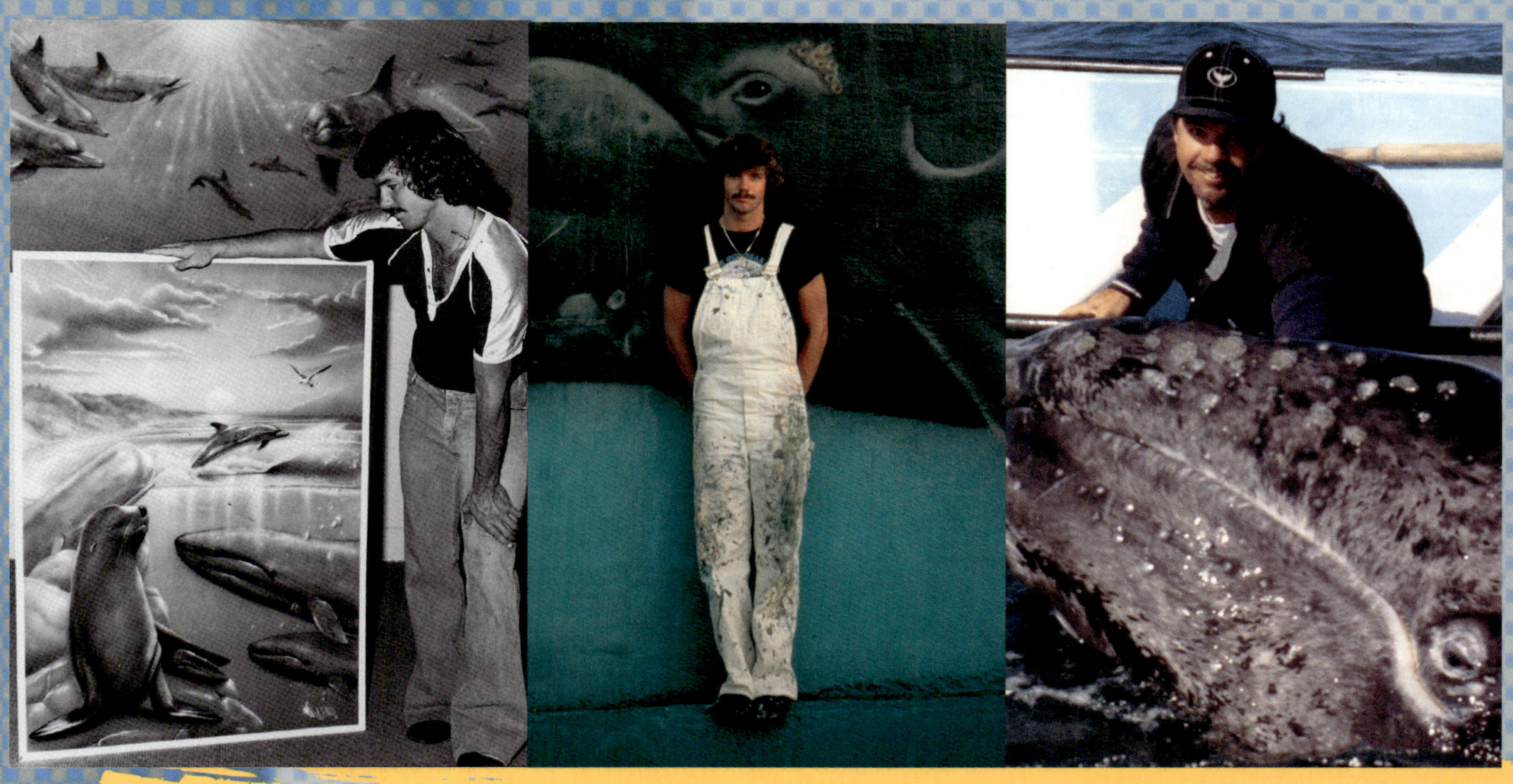

"In my mind's eye, I see whales out there large and small, all spyhopping and craning their necks, trying to get a glimpse of Wyland's work."

Dr. Roger Payne,
Introduction of *"Celebrating 50 Wyland Whaling Walls"*

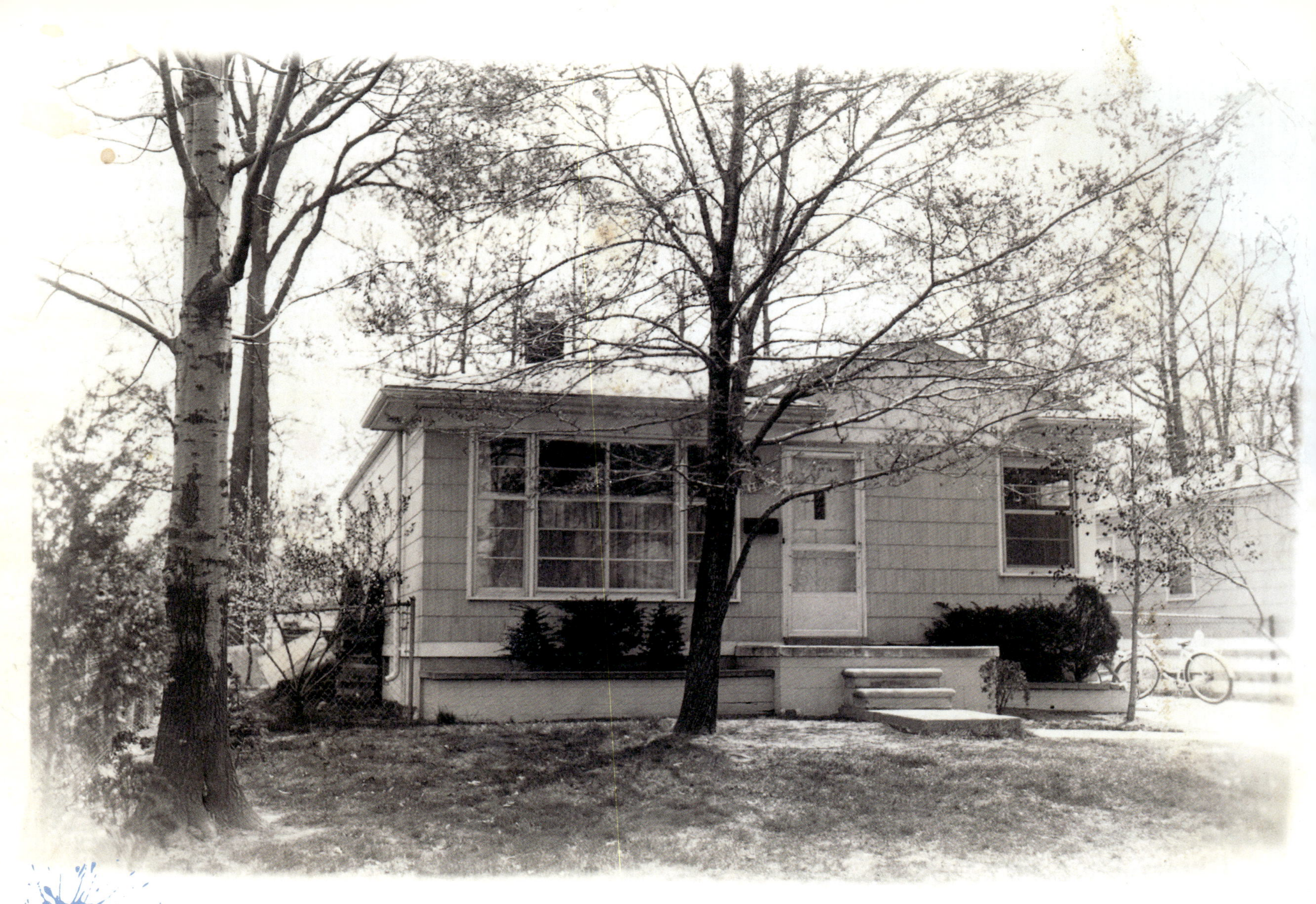

Of course when you're a kid growing up in the Midwest,

the idea of spending twenty-seven years painting monumental murals of great whales and ocean life on the sides of buildings seems impossible. As I look back on the seeds that were planted long ago, the old saying that everything happens for a reason is true. Everything in my life led to where I am today – an artist sharing his art and message with the world.

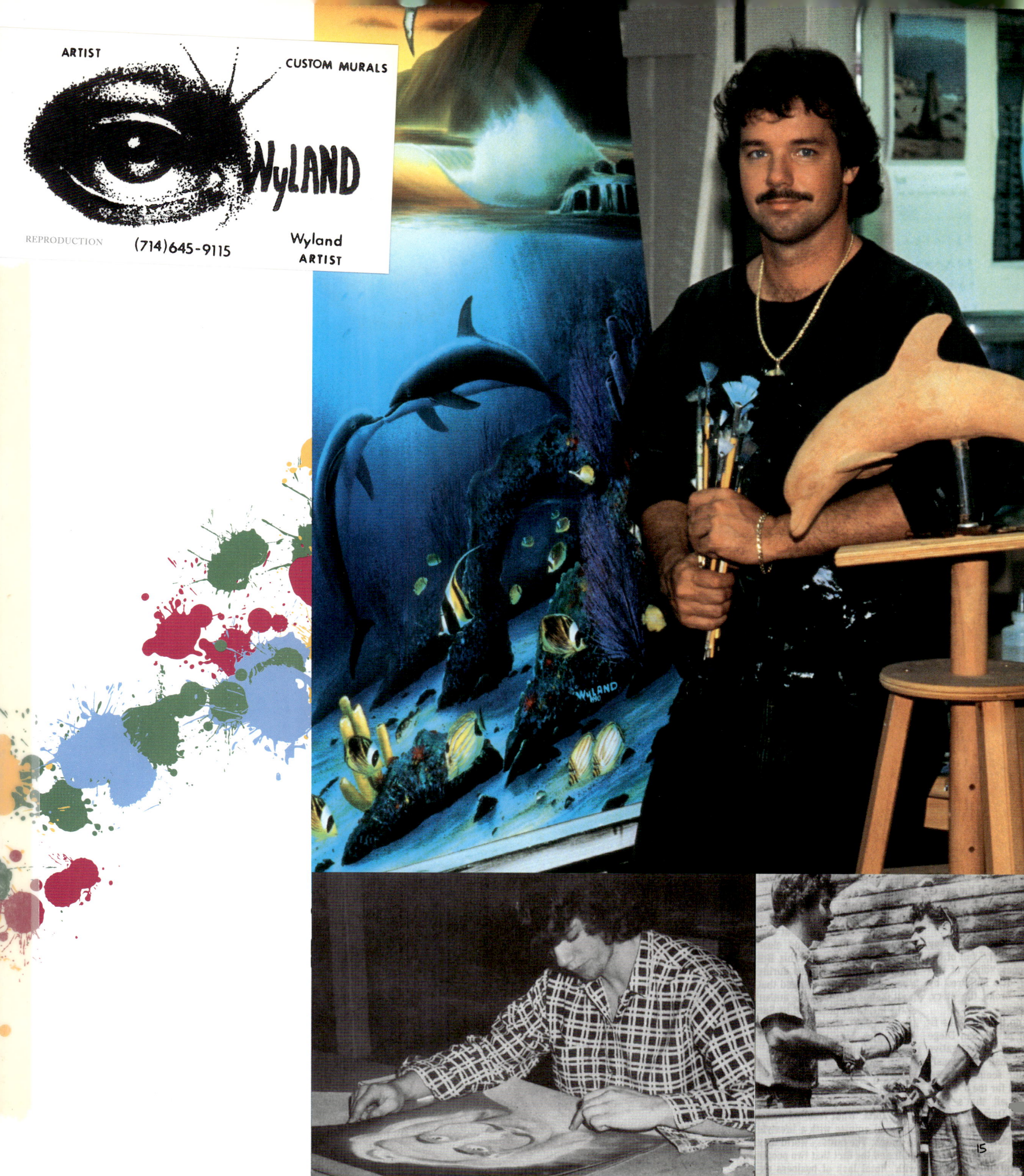
ARTIST
CUSTOM MURALS
WyLAND
REPRODUCTION
(714)645-9115
Wyland
ARTIST
WYLAND

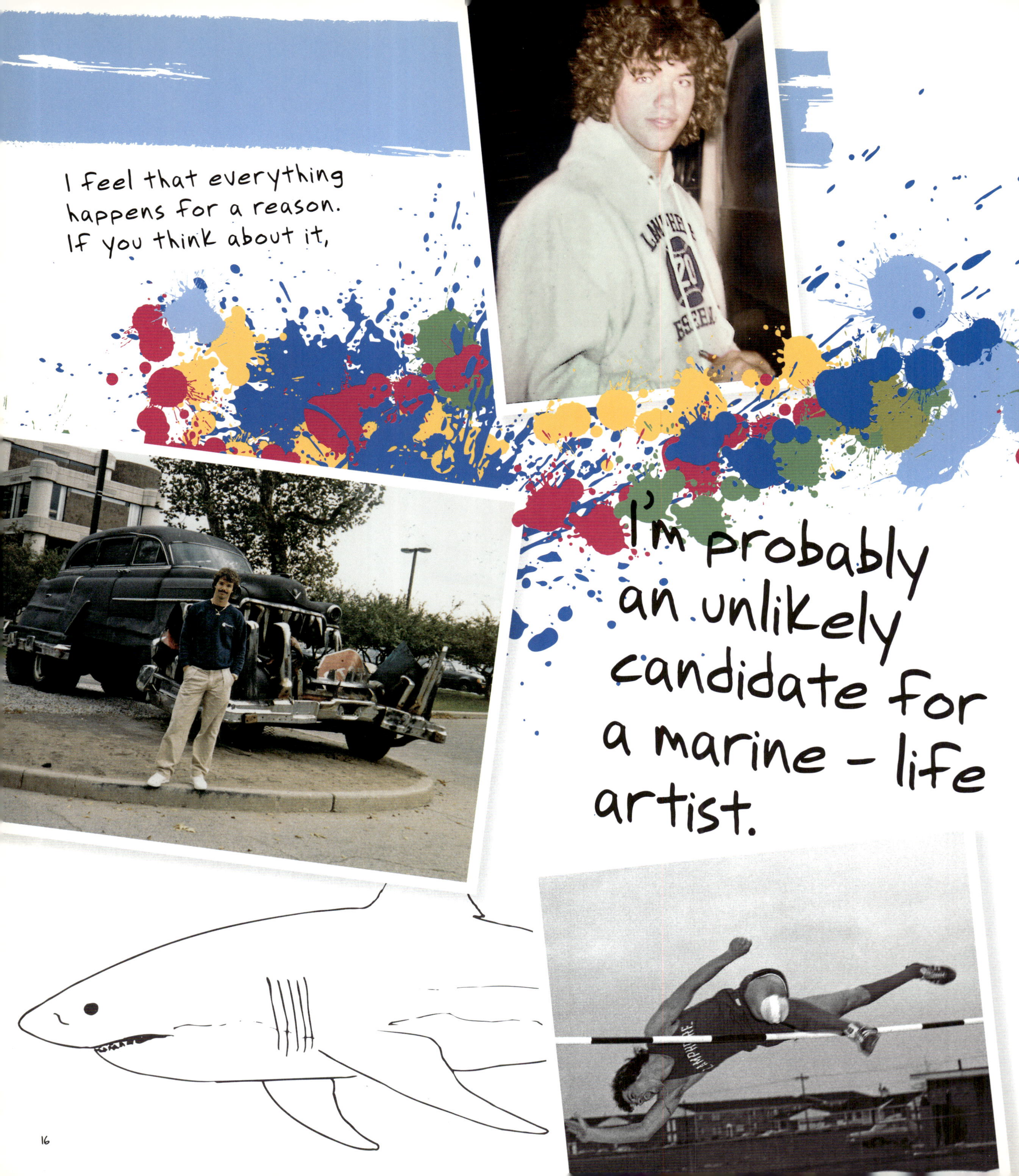

I feel that everything happens for a reason. If you think about it,

I'm probably an unlikely candidate for a marine-life artist.

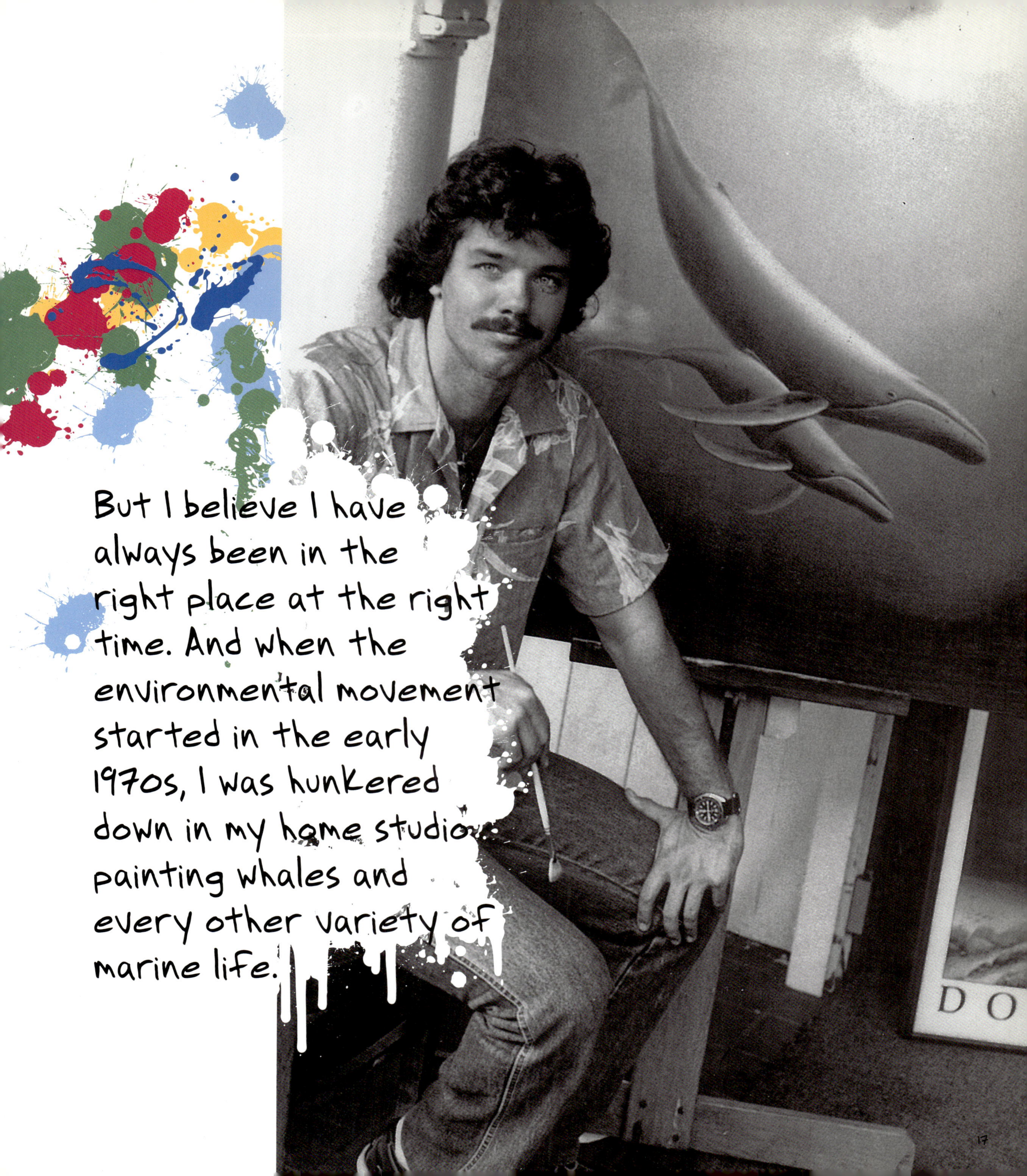

But I believe I have always been in the right place at the right time. And when the environmental movement started in the early 1970s, I was hunkered down in my home studio painting whales and every other variety of marine life.

By painting the whales, I began to understand them. And one day it occurred to me that I could paint these amazing animals in true-to-life proportions. My smaller paintings of whales on canvas were developing nicely, but I felt compelled to paint them in giant murals.

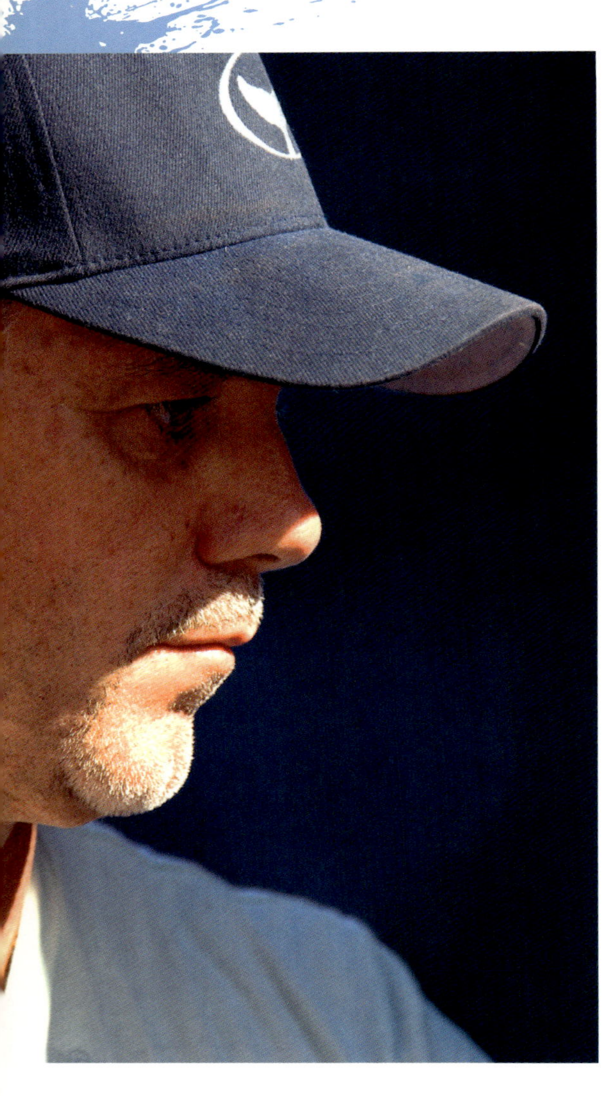

I felt that art could play an important role in the efforts to preserve the environment and the animals in the sea.

WyLAND

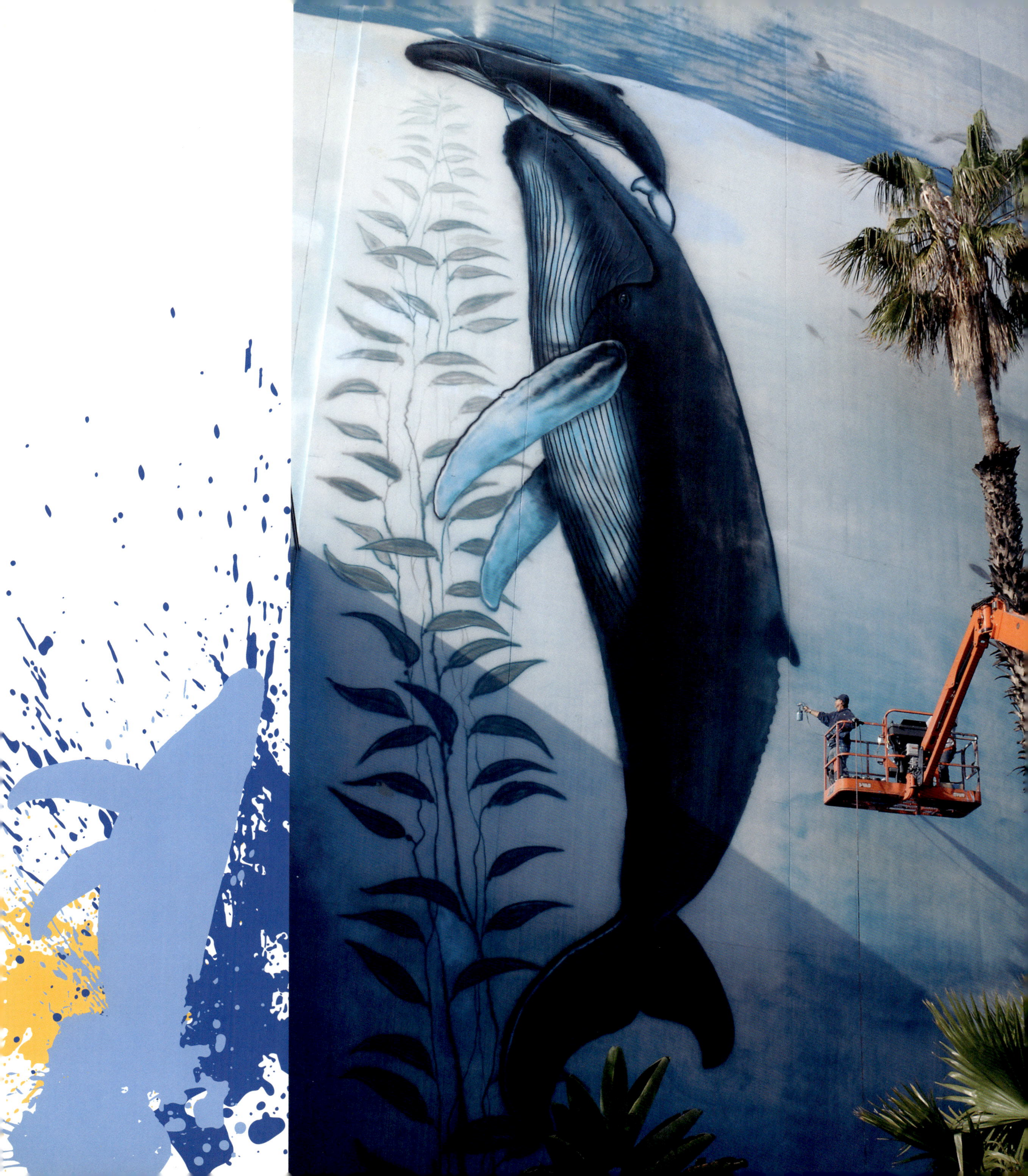

I started the Wyland Foundation

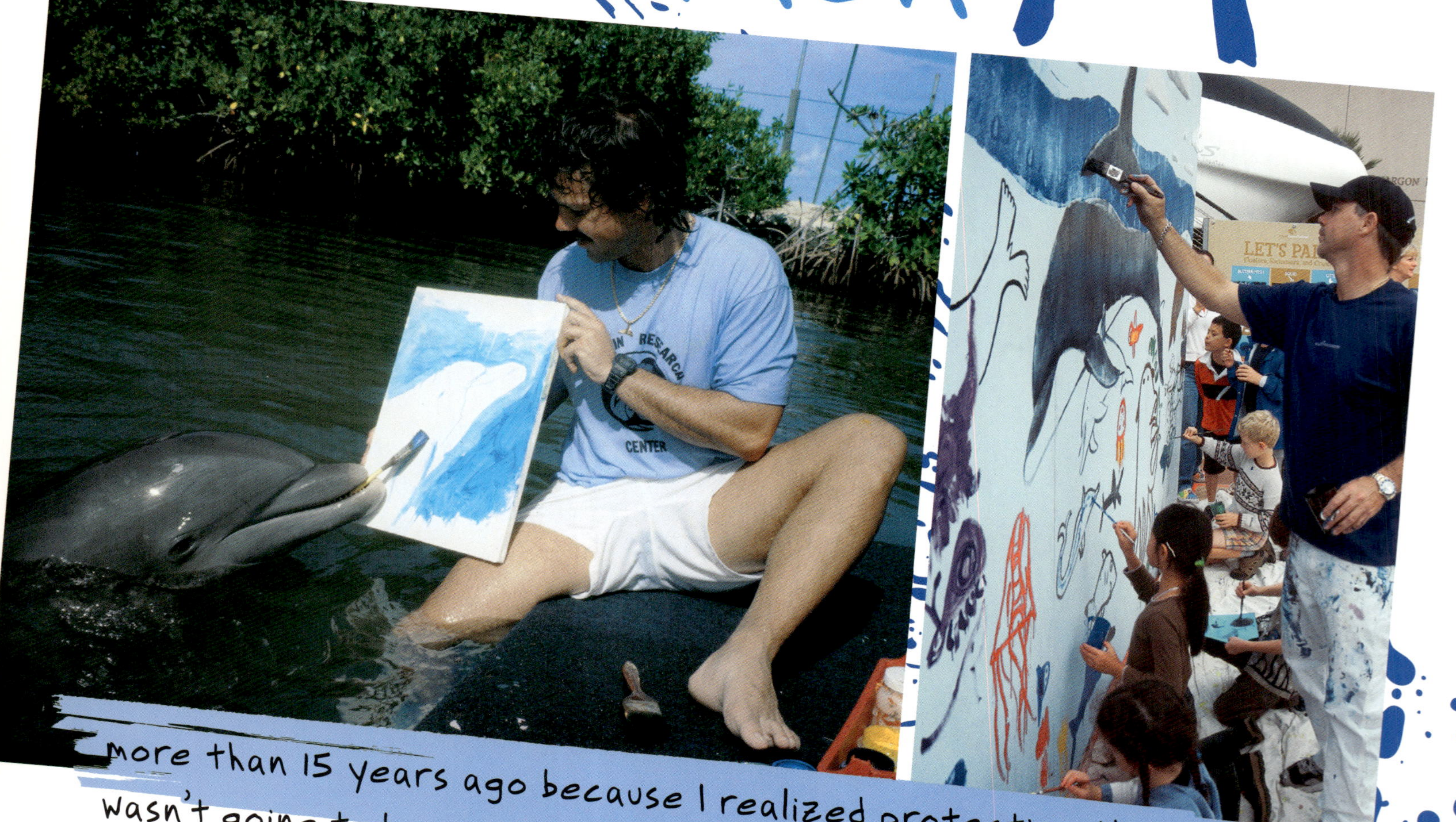

more than 15 years ago because I realized protecting the ocean wasn't going to be enough. It became clear to me that the future of our ocean, lakes, rivers, streams, wetlands, and estuaries would depend on everyone.

The role of young people in saving our planet

can't be overstated.

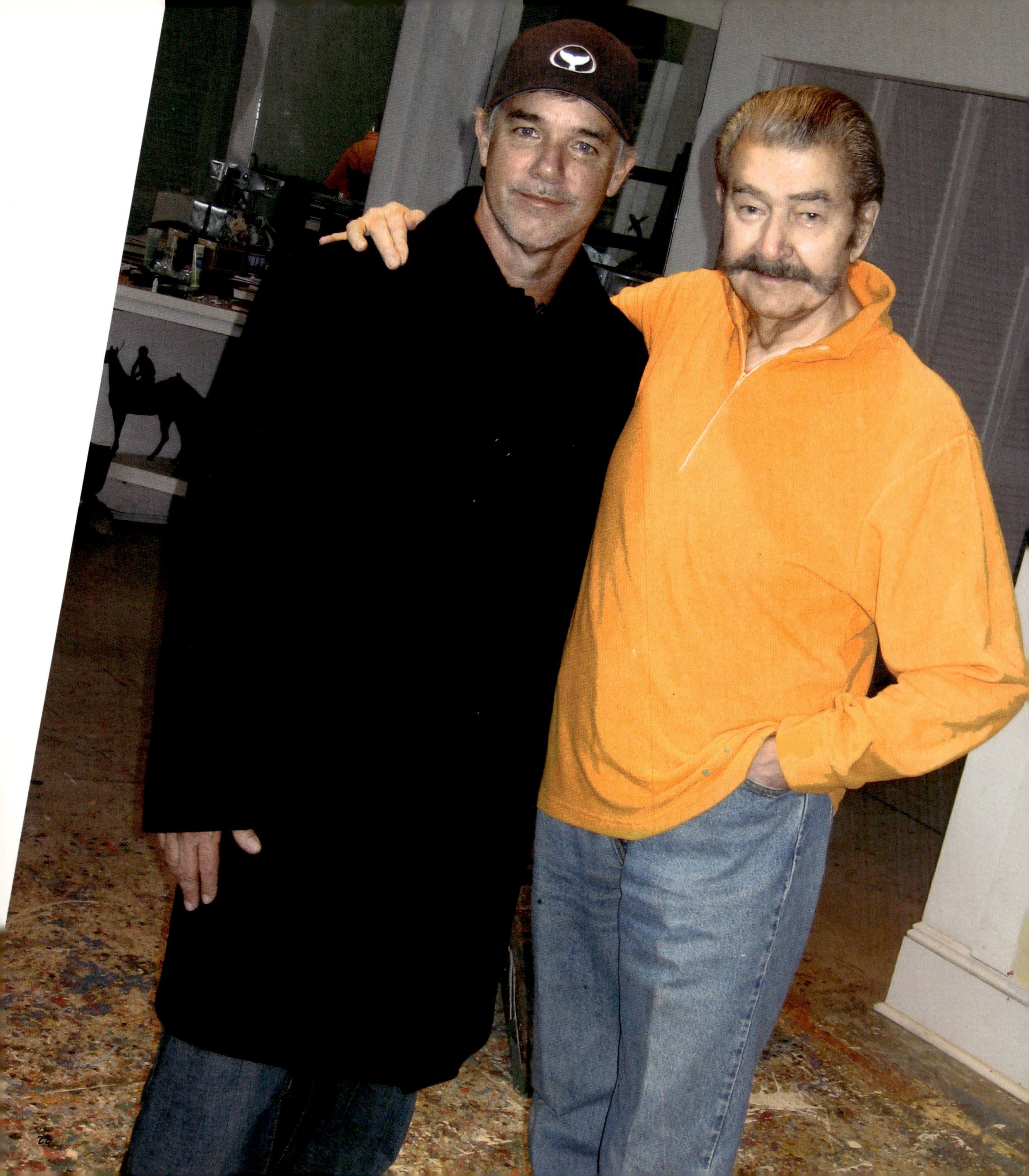

I'm proud to say that my journey to become a fine artist and realize my dream has taken me around the world.

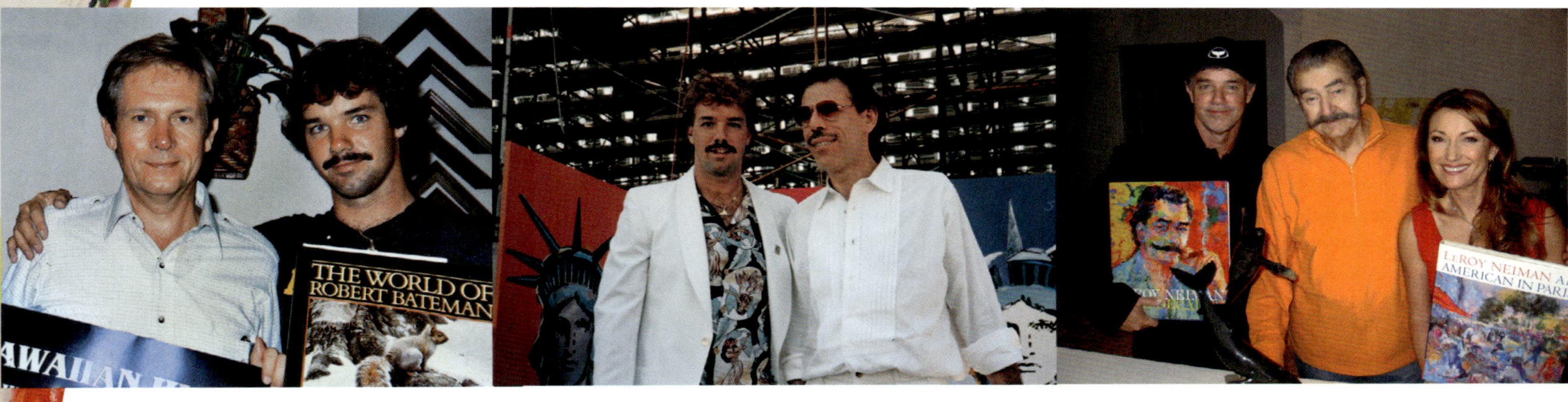

I have met some of the great artists of the 21st century and even become friends with quite a few of them. Robert Bateman, the wonderful wildlife artist in Canada, whom I have admired for many years, wrote the foreword to my first book, "The Art of Wyland." We both remain advocates for the environment, using our art to raise money and awareness for conservation. I have also had the pleasure of knowing LeRoy Neiman, Peter Max, Ed Ruscha, John Pitre, and recently, Romero Britto, who painted with me and thousands of kids at the White House in celebration of ocean conservation. I always knew I would be an artist. But I didn't realize how much fun I would have sharing it with the world.

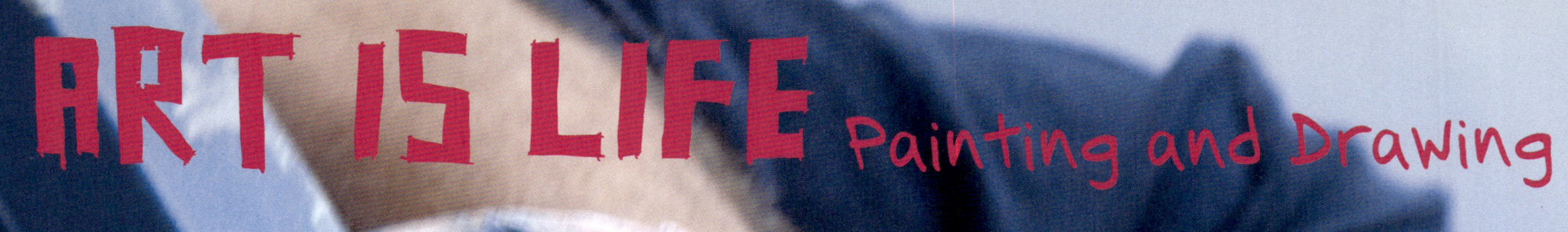

ART IS LIFE Painting and Drawing

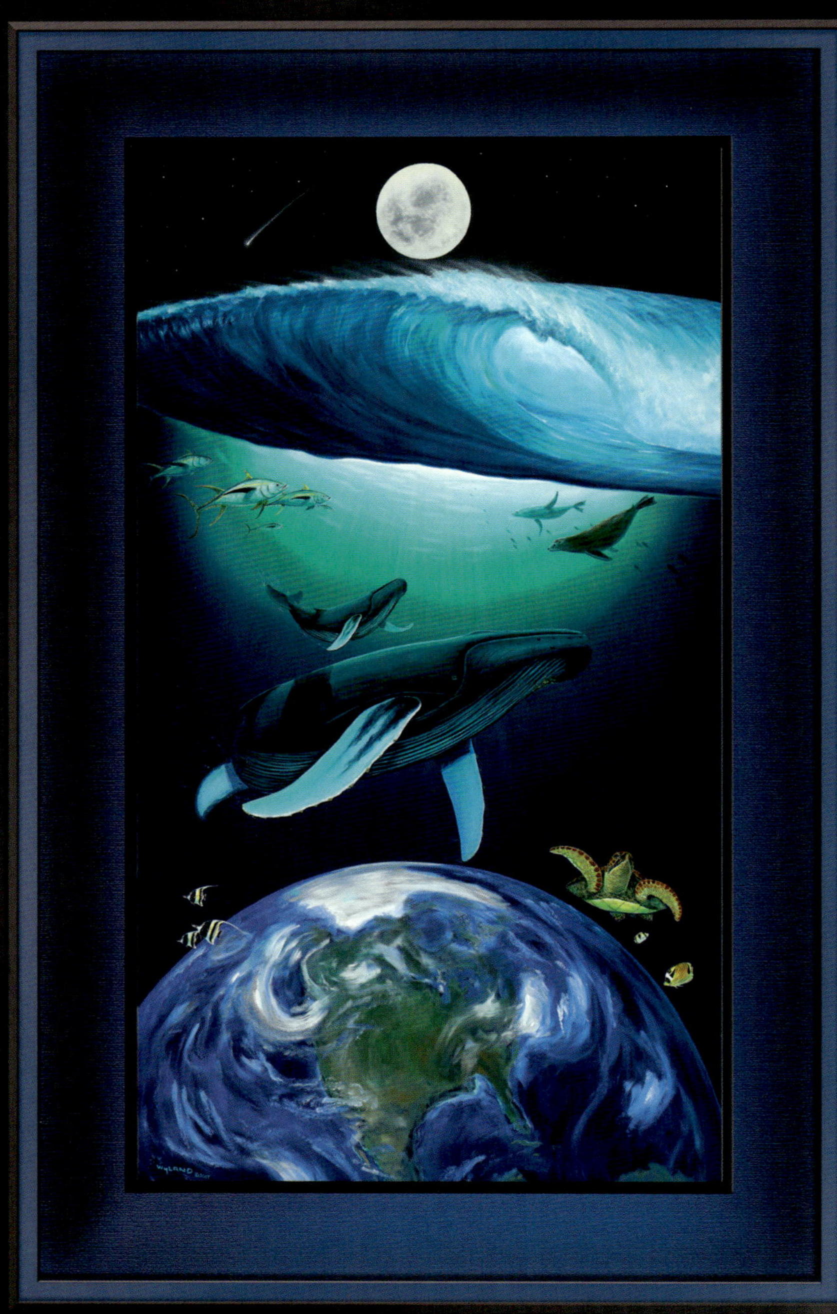

we live in a world of art.

Companies build their products with it — and people surround their lives with it. Wyland has been at the center of these worlds for years. Inspired by the art of nature, he's built an international reputation not only because of his art, but his emphasis on education and inspiration for a broader view of our relationship with the beauty of our entire blue planet.

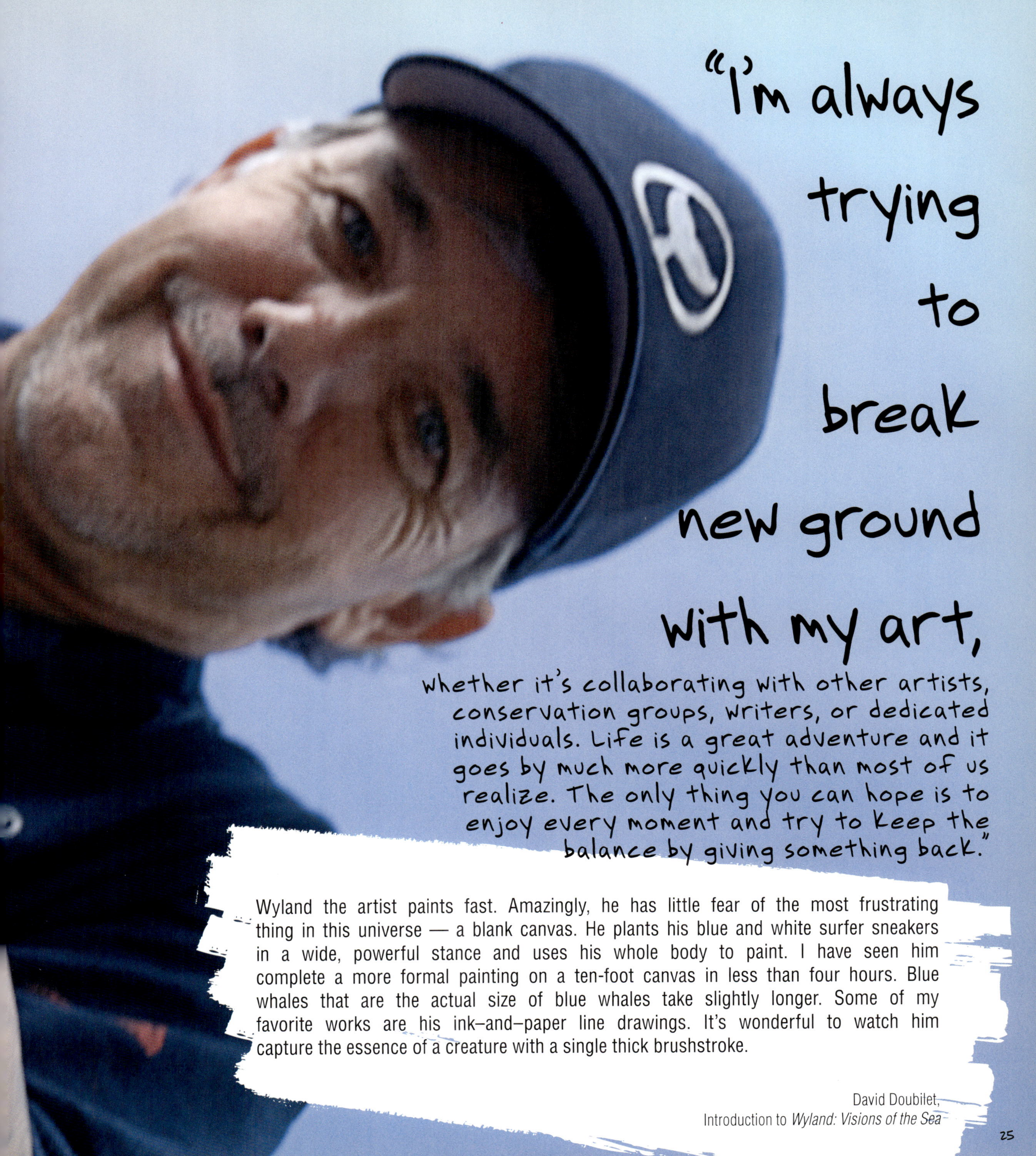

"I'm always trying to break new ground with my art,

whether it's collaborating with other artists, conservation groups, writers, or dedicated individuals. Life is a great adventure and it goes by much more quickly than most of us realize. The only thing you can hope is to enjoy every moment and try to keep the balance by giving something back."

Wyland the artist paints fast. Amazingly, he has little fear of the most frustrating thing in this universe — a blank canvas. He plants his blue and white surfer sneakers in a wide, powerful stance and uses his whole body to paint. I have seen him complete a more formal painting on a ten-foot canvas in less than four hours. Blue whales that are the actual size of blue whales take slightly longer. Some of my favorite works are his ink–and–paper line drawings. It's wonderful to watch him capture the essence of a creature with a single thick brushstroke.

David Doubilet,
Introduction to *Wyland: Visions of the Sea*

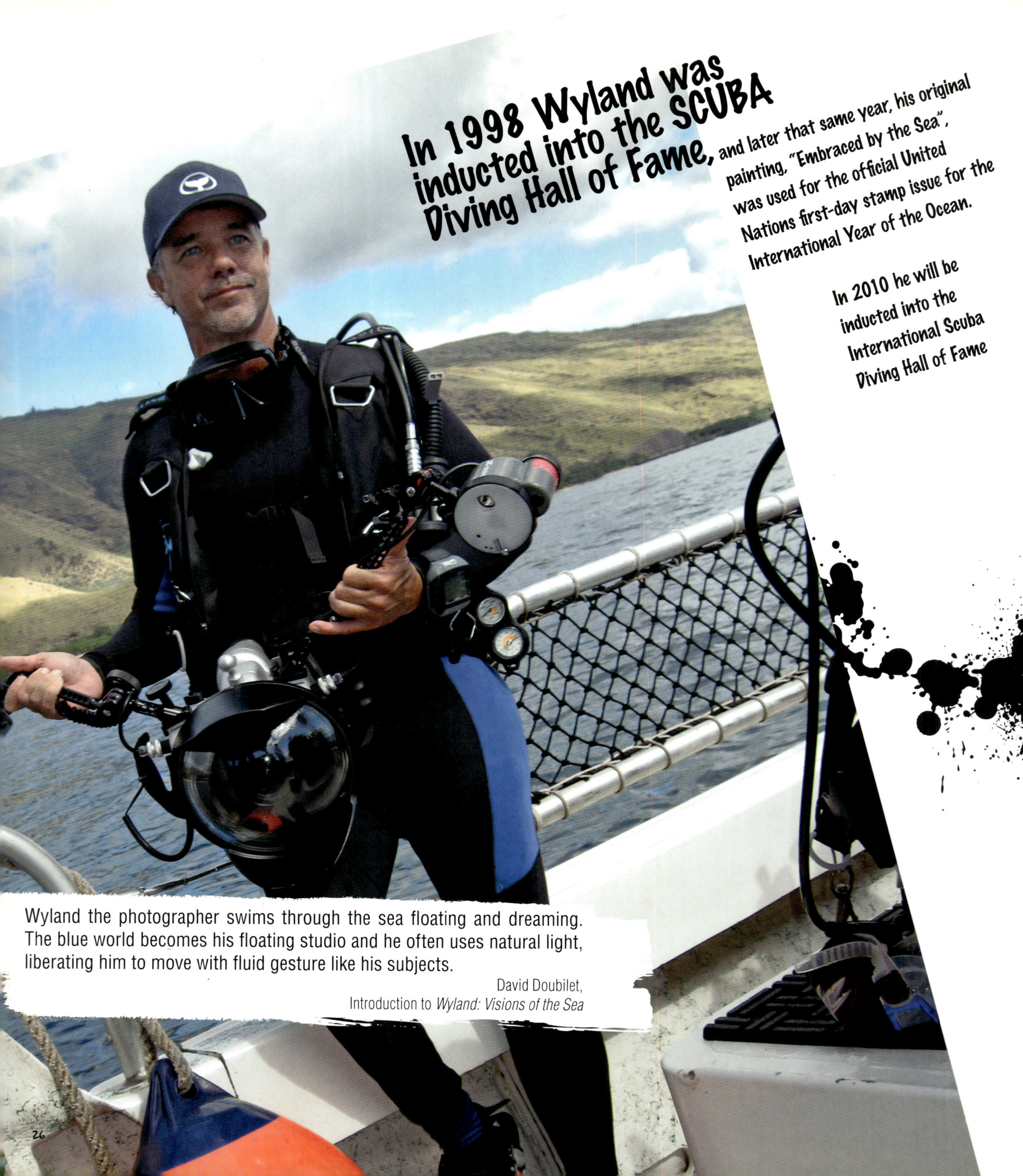

In 1998 Wyland was inducted into the SCUBA Diving Hall of Fame,

and later that same year, his original painting, "Embraced by the Sea", was used for the official United Nations first-day stamp issue for the International Year of the Ocean.

In 2010 he will be inducted into the International Scuba Diving Hall of Fame

Wyland the photographer swims through the sea floating and dreaming. The blue world becomes his floating studio and he often uses natural light, liberating him to move with fluid gesture like his subjects.

David Doubilet,
Introduction to *Wyland: Visions of the Sea*

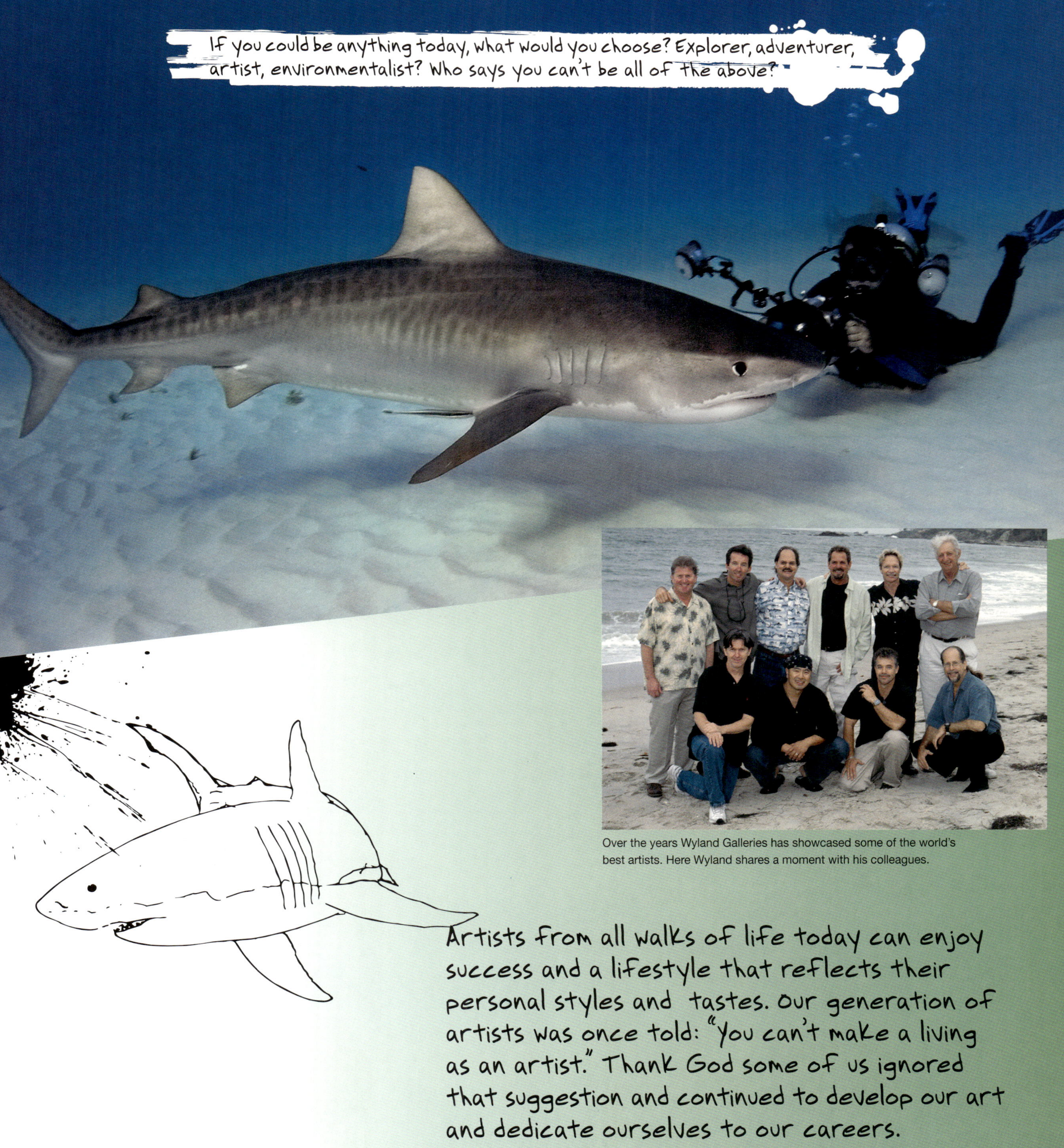

If you could be anything today, what would you choose? Explorer, adventurer, artist, environmentalist? Who says you can't be all of the above?

Over the years Wyland Galleries has showcased some of the world's best artists. Here Wyland shares a moment with his colleagues.

Artists from all walks of life today can enjoy success and a lifestyle that reflects their personal styles and tastes. Our generation of artists was once told: "You can't make a living as an artist." Thank God some of us ignored that suggestion and continued to develop our art and dedicate ourselves to our careers.

...If people see the beauty in nature, they will work to protect it...

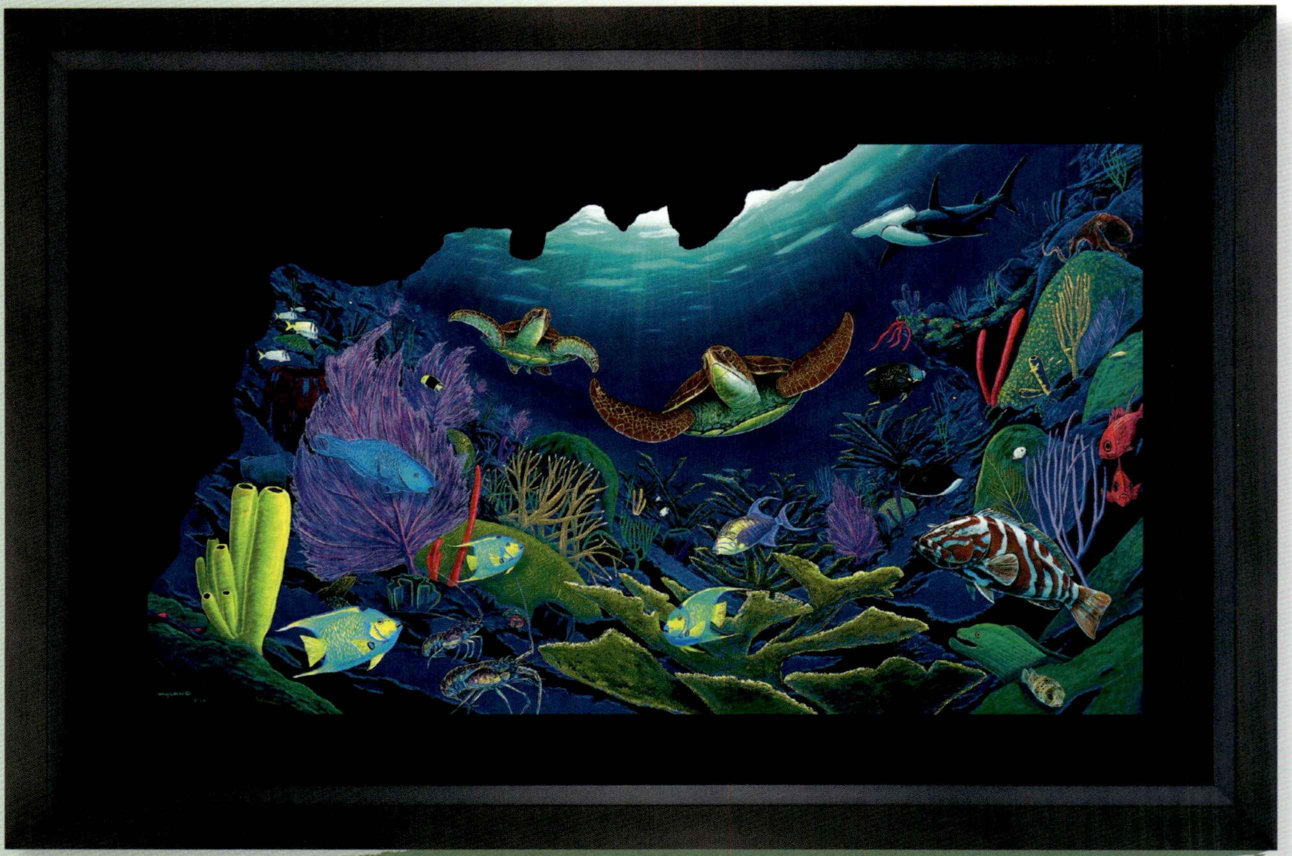

Few artists in history can match the influence of Wyland.

Renowned for his incomparable 100 Whaling Walls in more than 75 cities in 14 countries, Wyland's artwork and community outreach over the last 30 years have had a lasting impact that can be seen in today's global "green" movement.

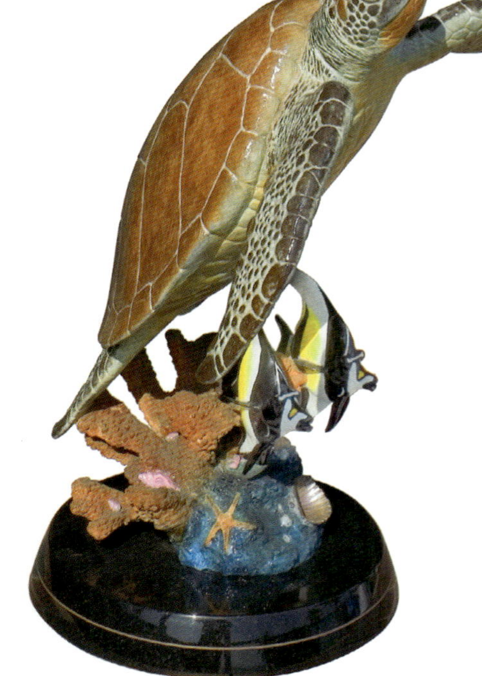

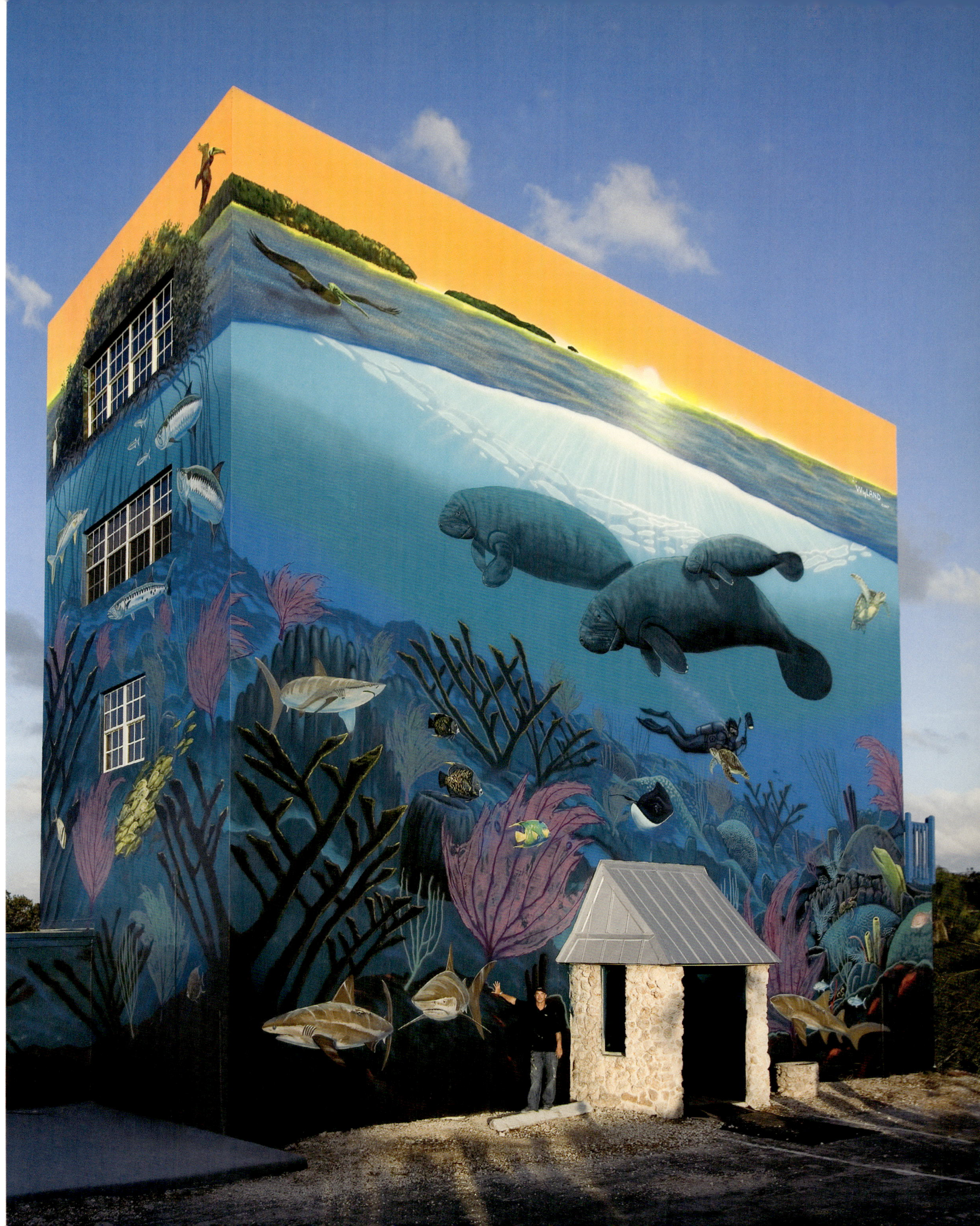
WyLAND

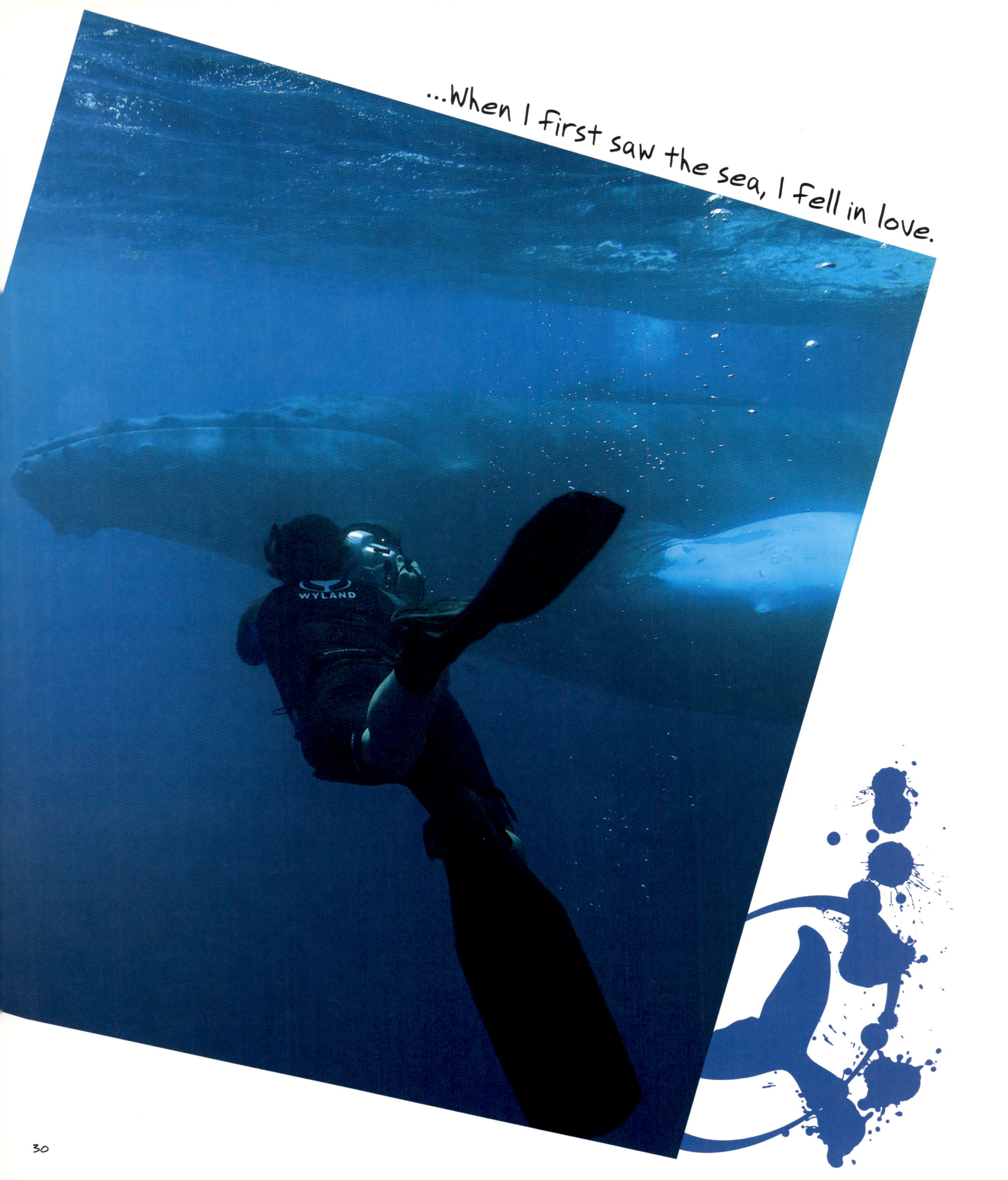

...When I first saw the sea, I fell in love.

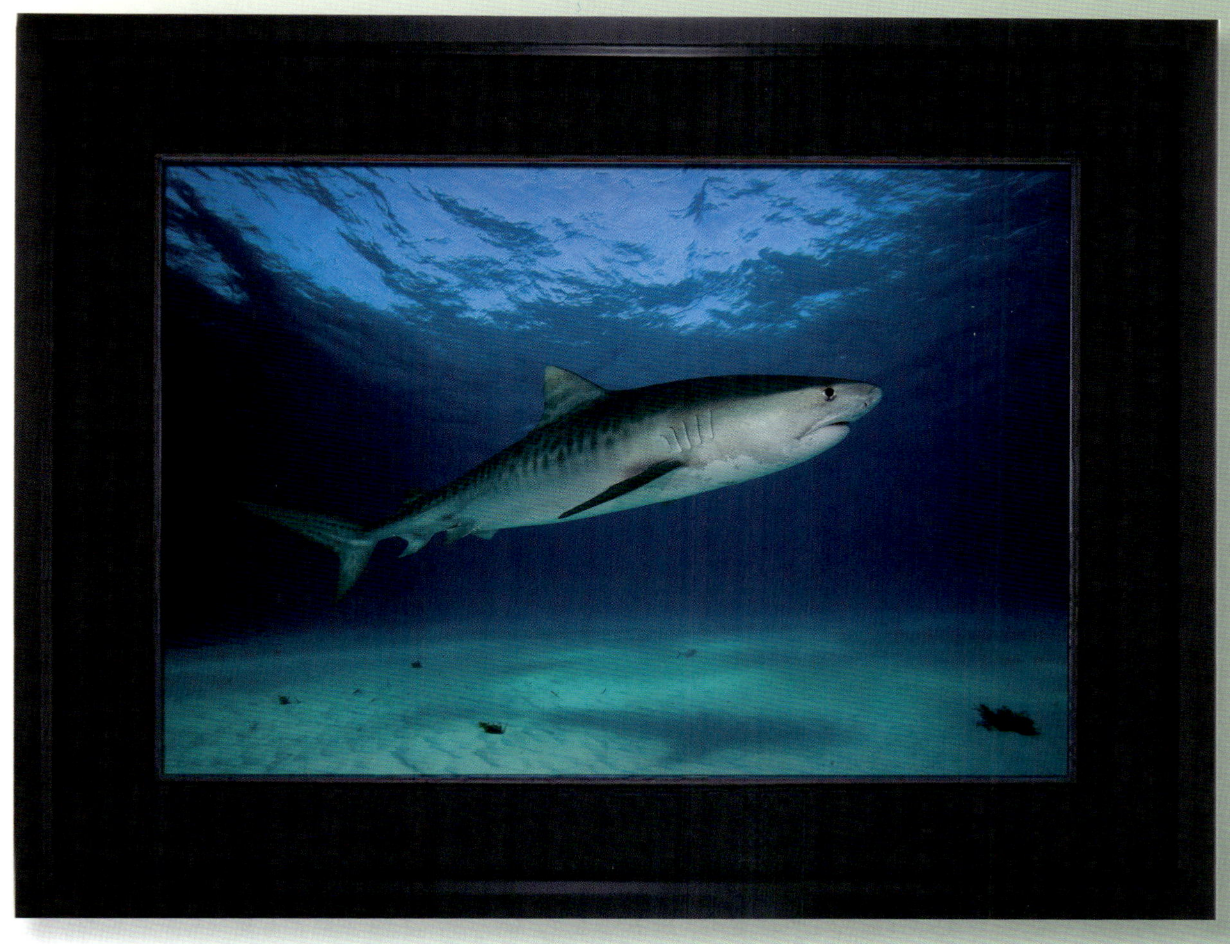

Wyland's first encounter with the ocean at age 14 had a profound influence on his life.

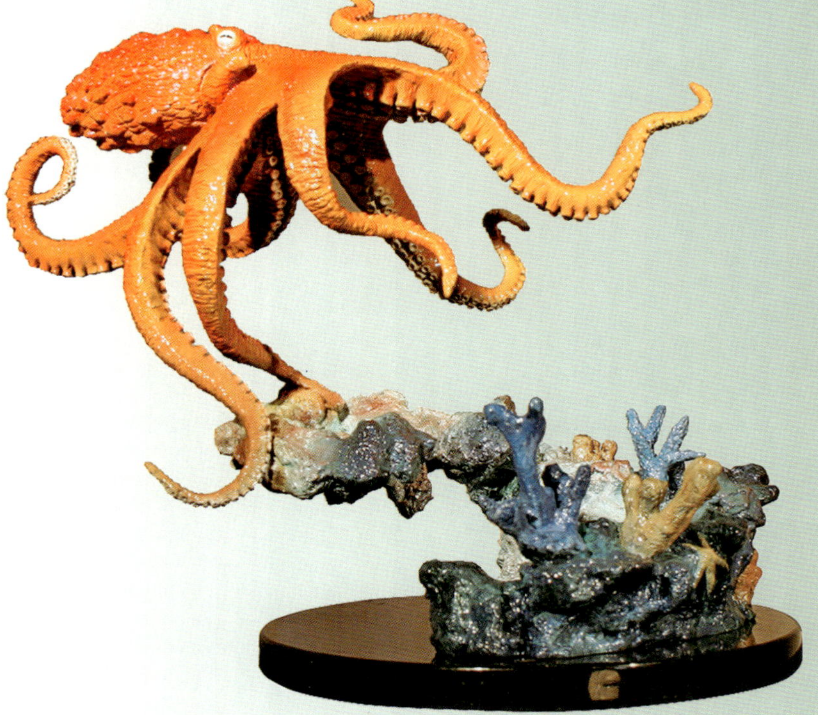

Later, he began SCUBA diving, photographing a world of blue whales, giant mantas, sea turtles, sharks, and living reefs. Today, he is recognized as one of the most influential artists of the 21st century. His work is praised by marine biologists, authors, educators, and artists. And his name has become synonymous with conservation of clean water and healthy oceans.

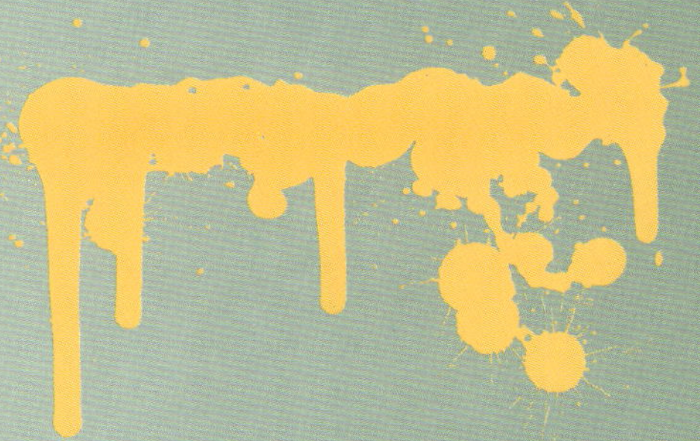

OIL PAINTING

...Today Wyland's art is collected by over 500,000 people in 100 countries...

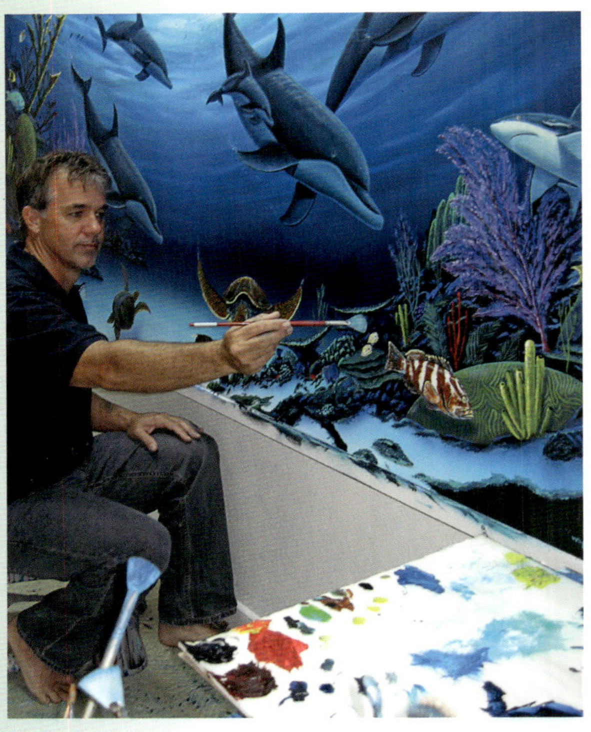

Wyland's oil paintings are celebrated the world over

by corporations, celebrities, museums, and individual collectors who share the artist's commitment for conservation of the world's oceans, lakes, rivers, streams, and wetlands. "The ocean can be an indescribable place," the artist says, "yet through oil painting, I can communicate in a way that transcends words, using color, movement, emotion, and light."

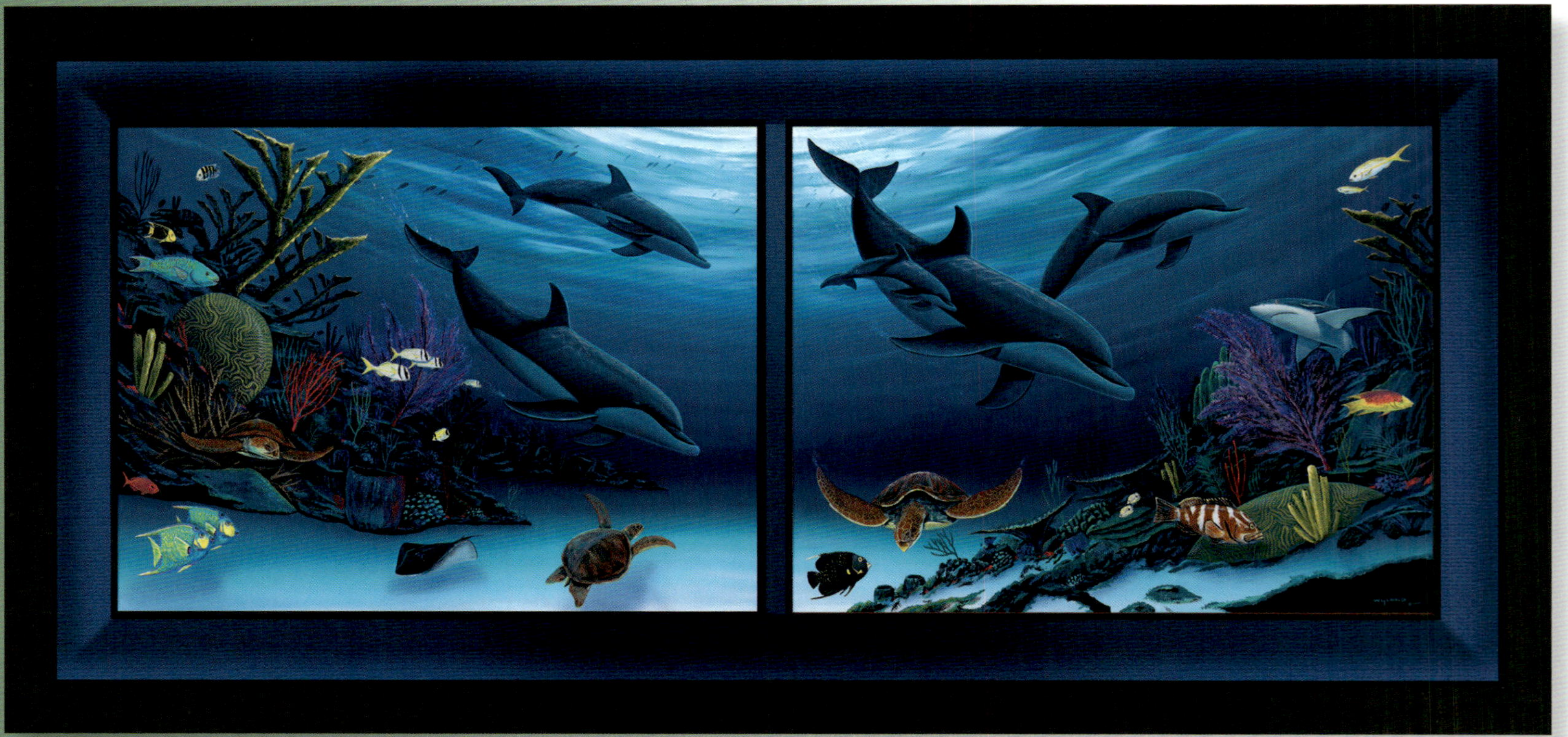

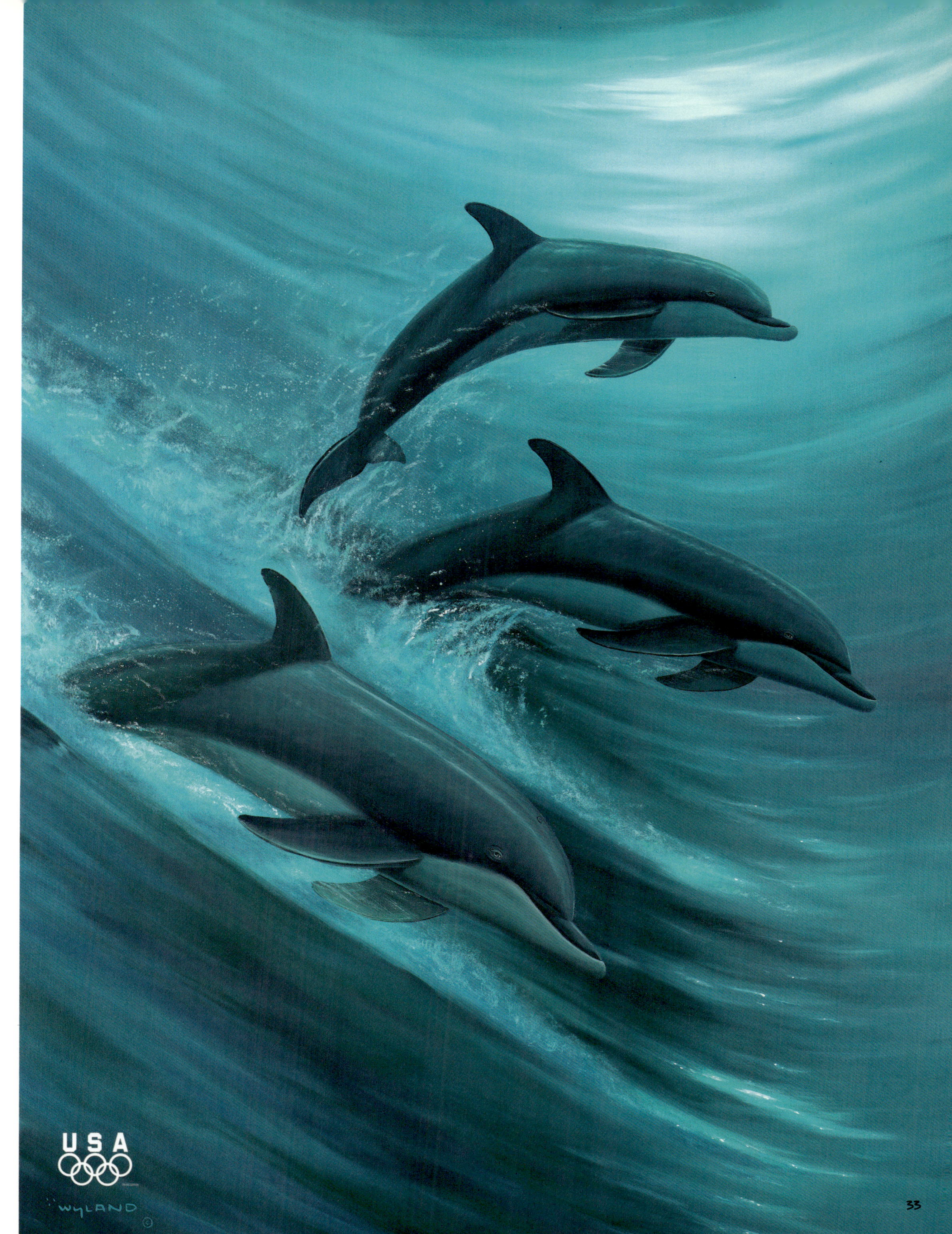
USA
WYLAND

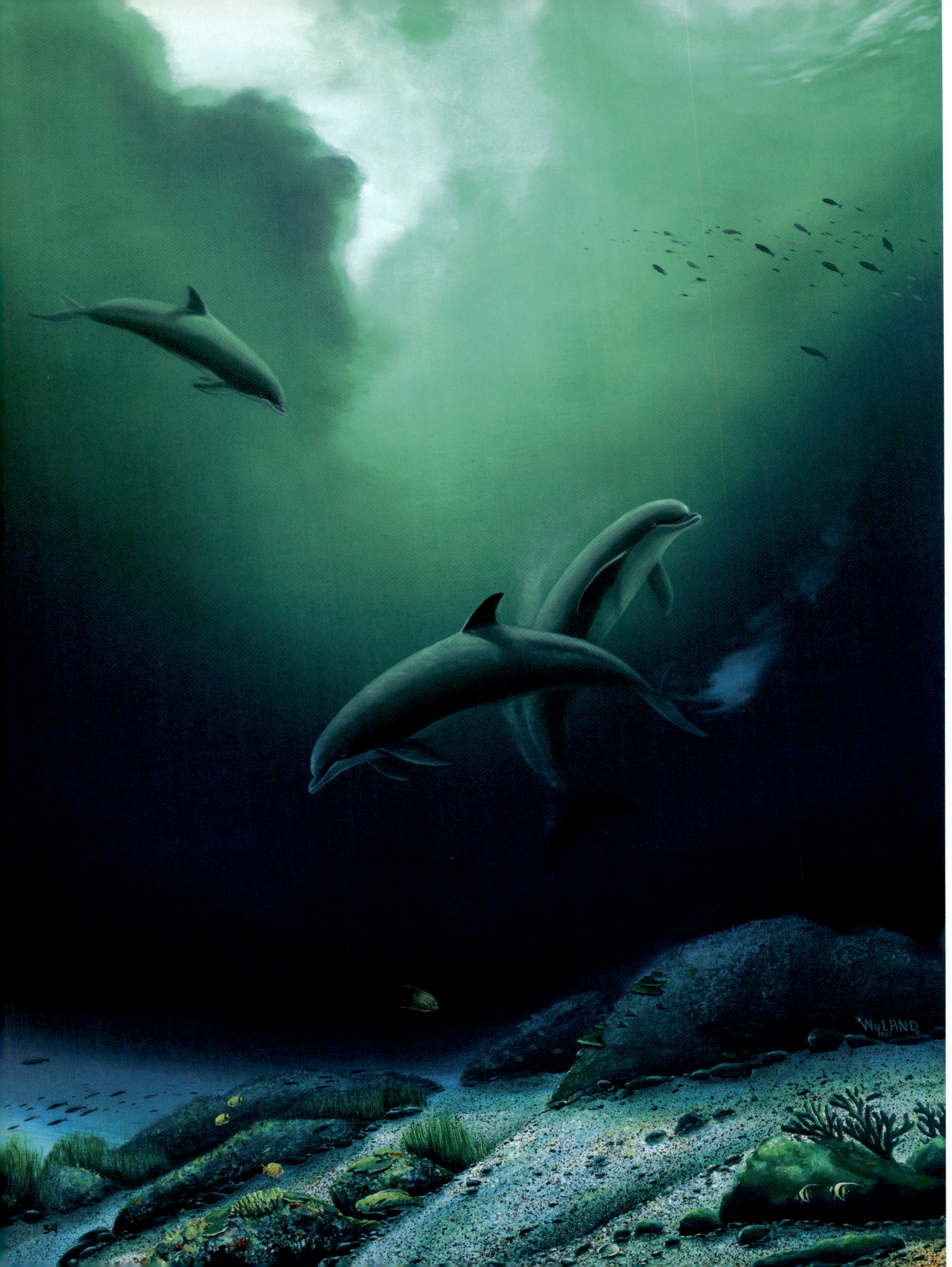
WyLAND
1983 ©

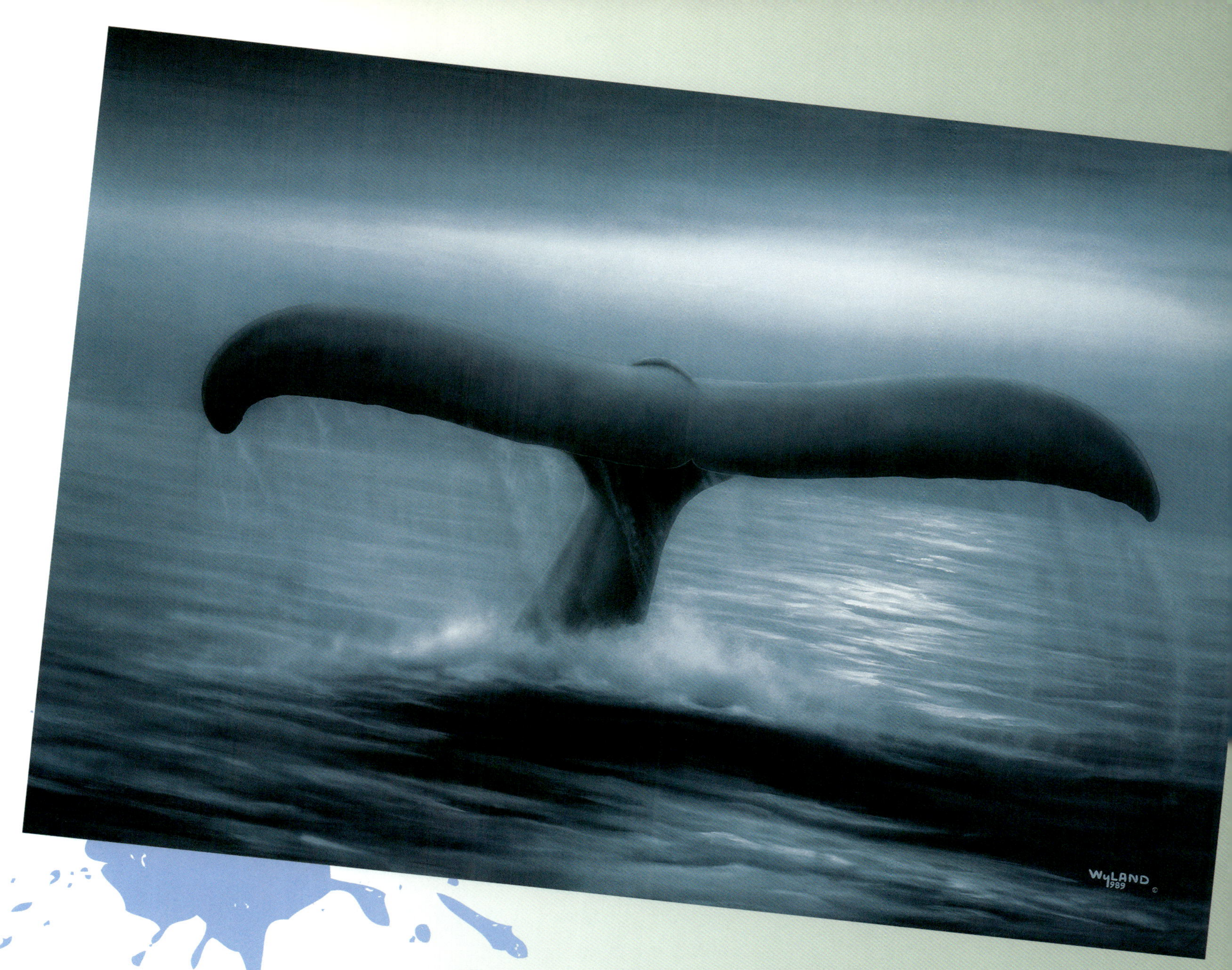

Several years later, as the environmental movement began with Greenpeace,

the artist was compelled to paint the mammals of the sea, his favorite subjects. "I was in the right place at the right time, and as the appreciation for the environment grew, so did appreciation for my art," Wyland said. "The public's interest had evolved from man's conquest of the sea into marine life art, which celebrated life in the sea and the message of conservation."

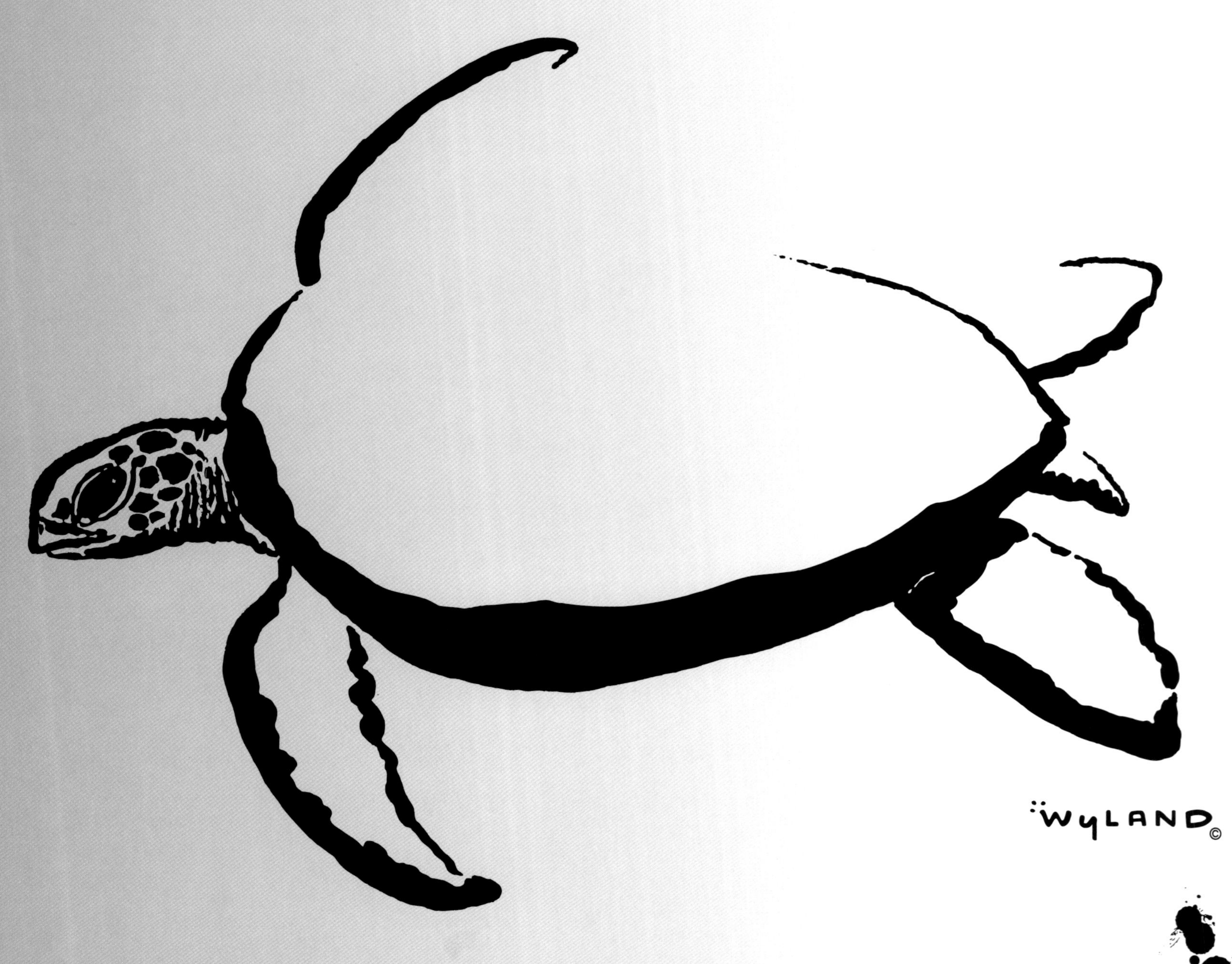
WYLAND ©

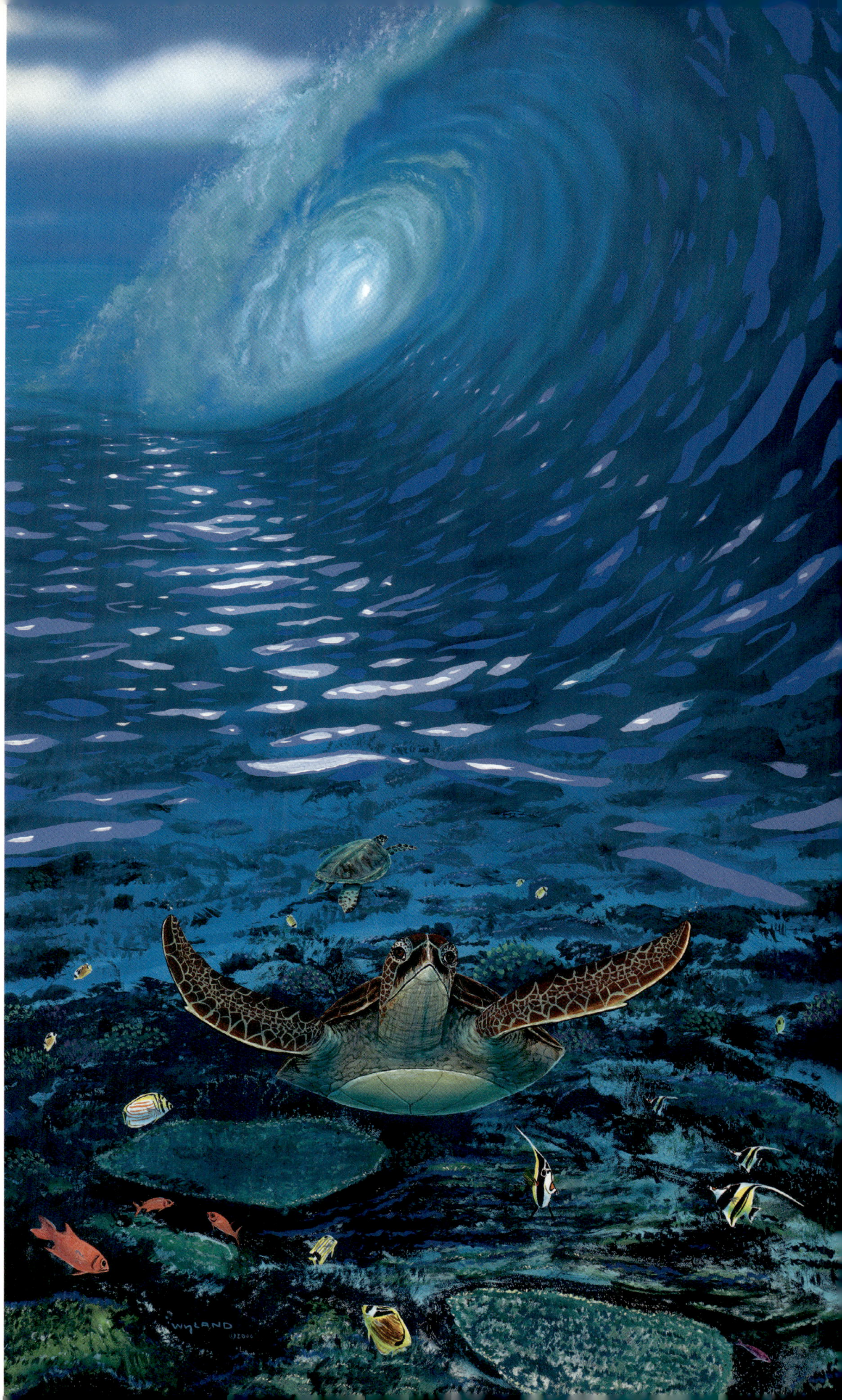

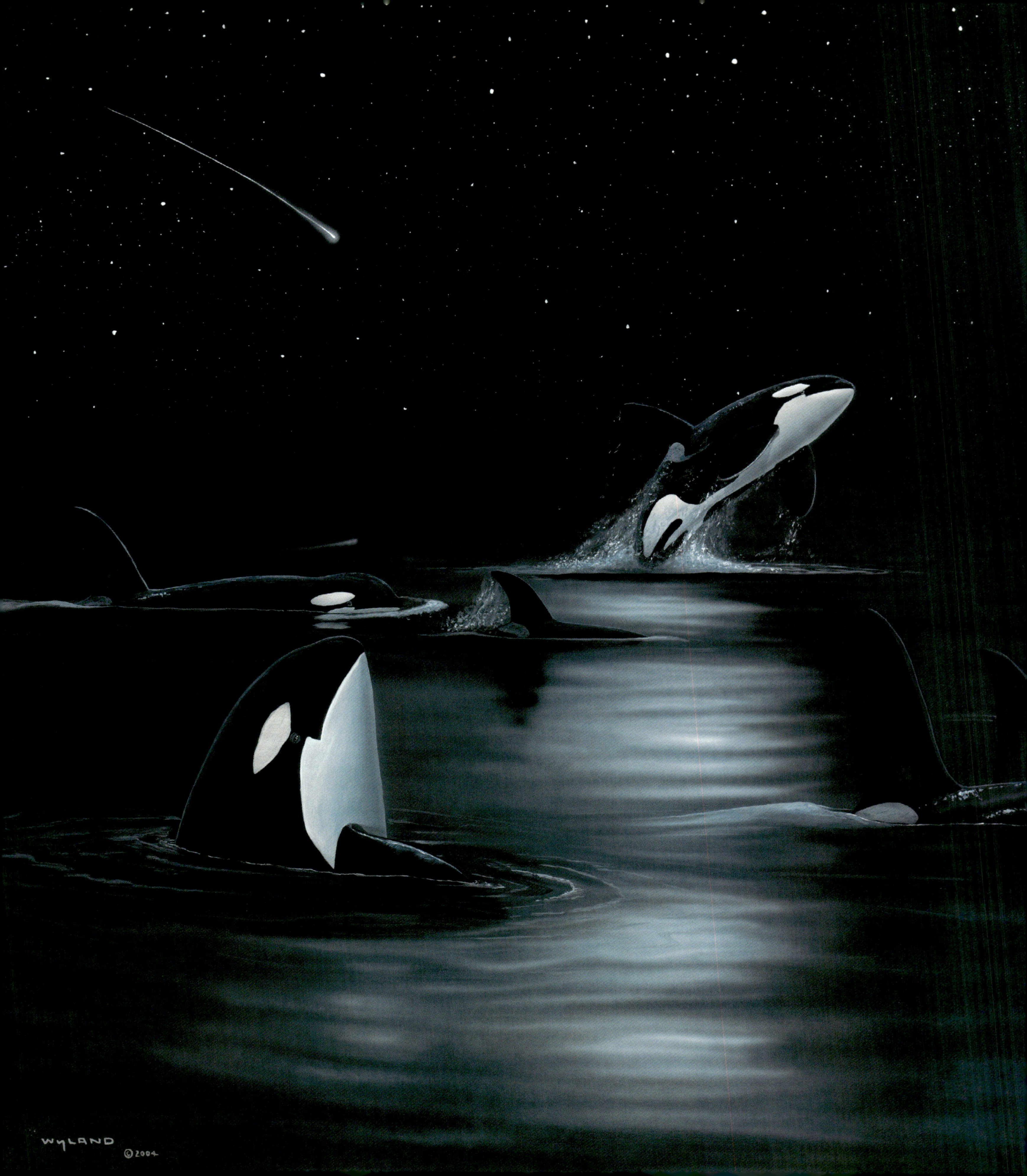
WYLAND
©2004

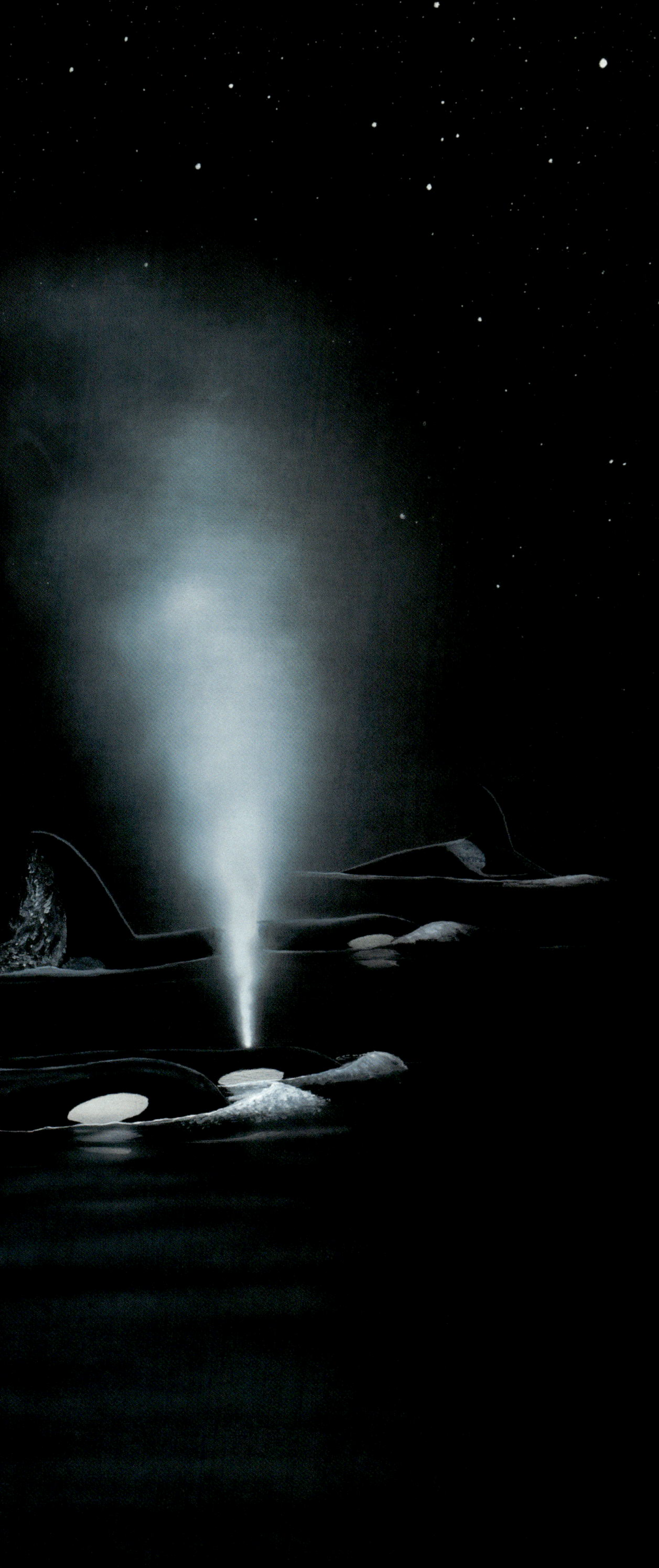

Today people always ask me how I got so successful. I have a simple answer:

I worked hard, every single day, with a singular focus to evolve my work.

Like many artists, I experimented with different mediums and found the unique ability to express different aspects of my subjects in oils, watercolors, acrylics, Chinese brush art, drawings, photography, and, of course, murals.

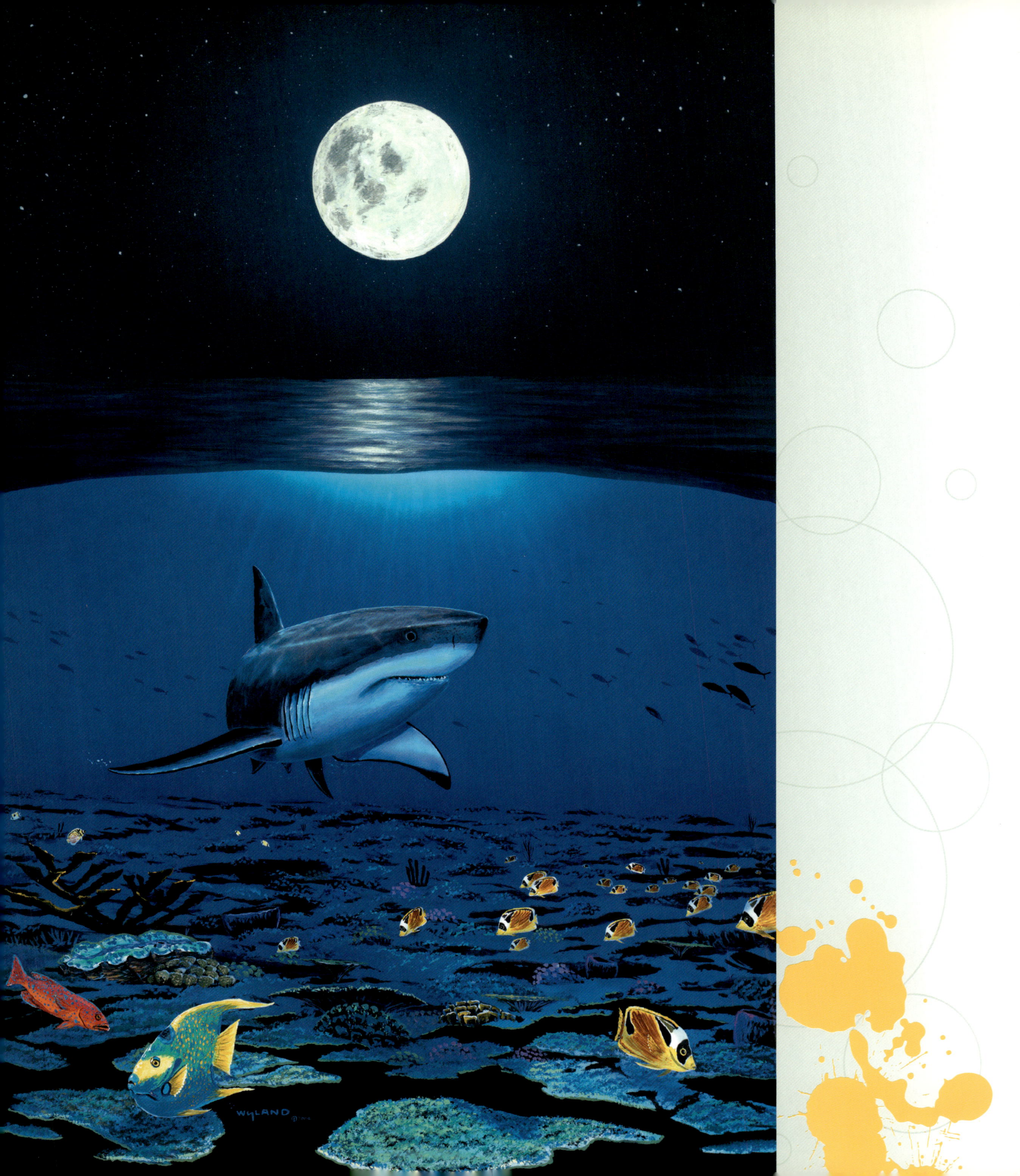
WYLAND

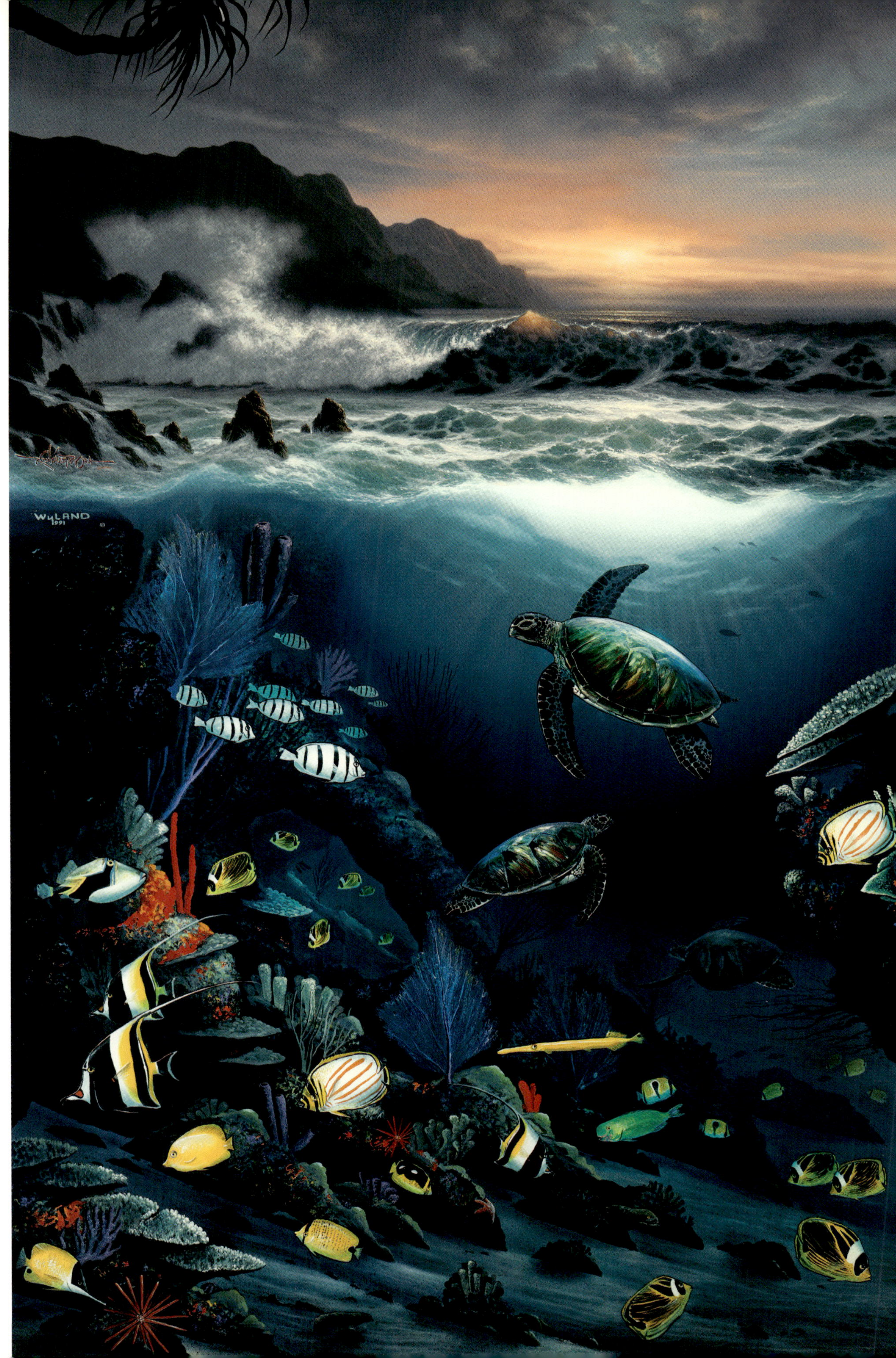
WYLAND
1991 ©

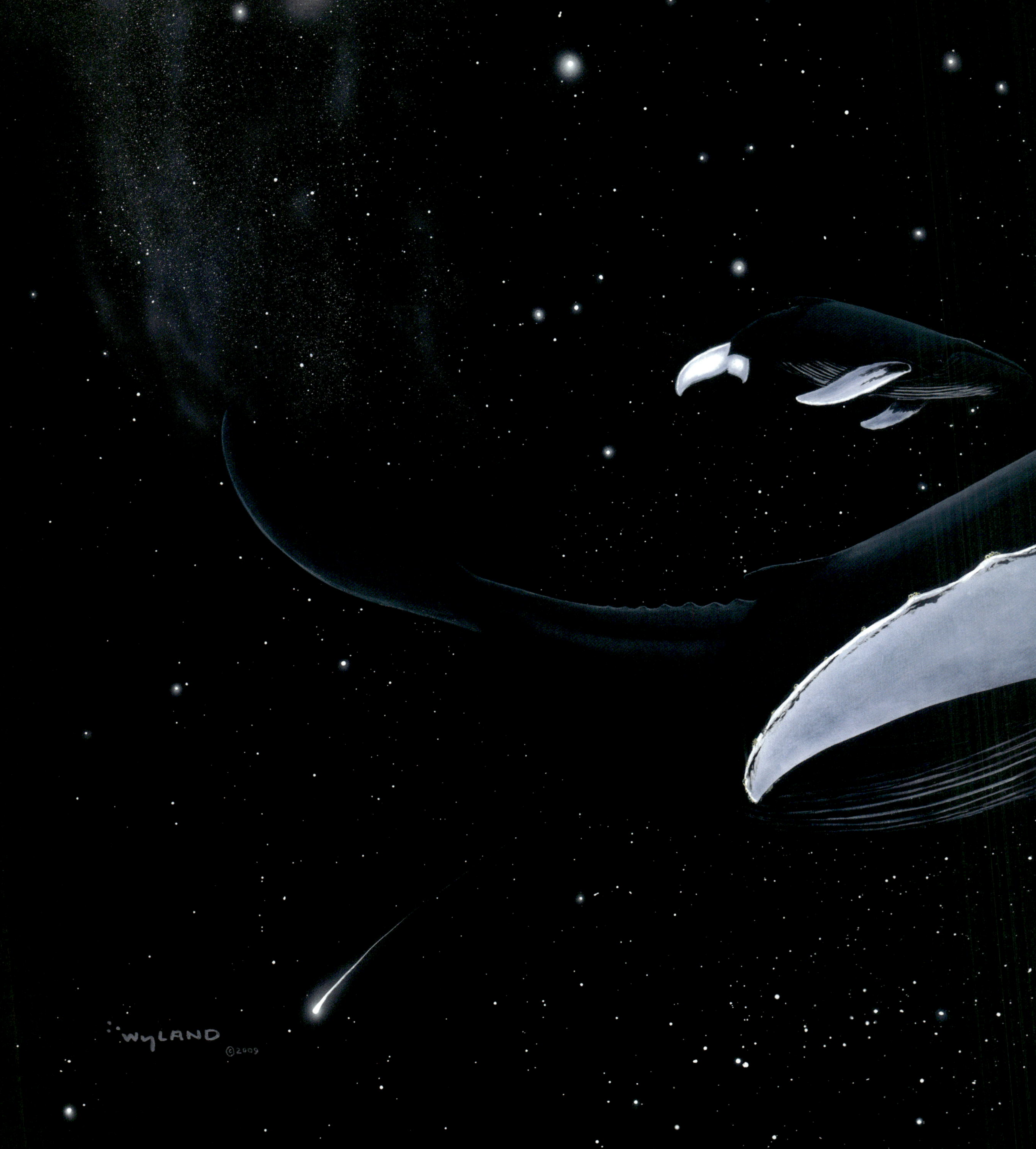
WYLAND
©2009

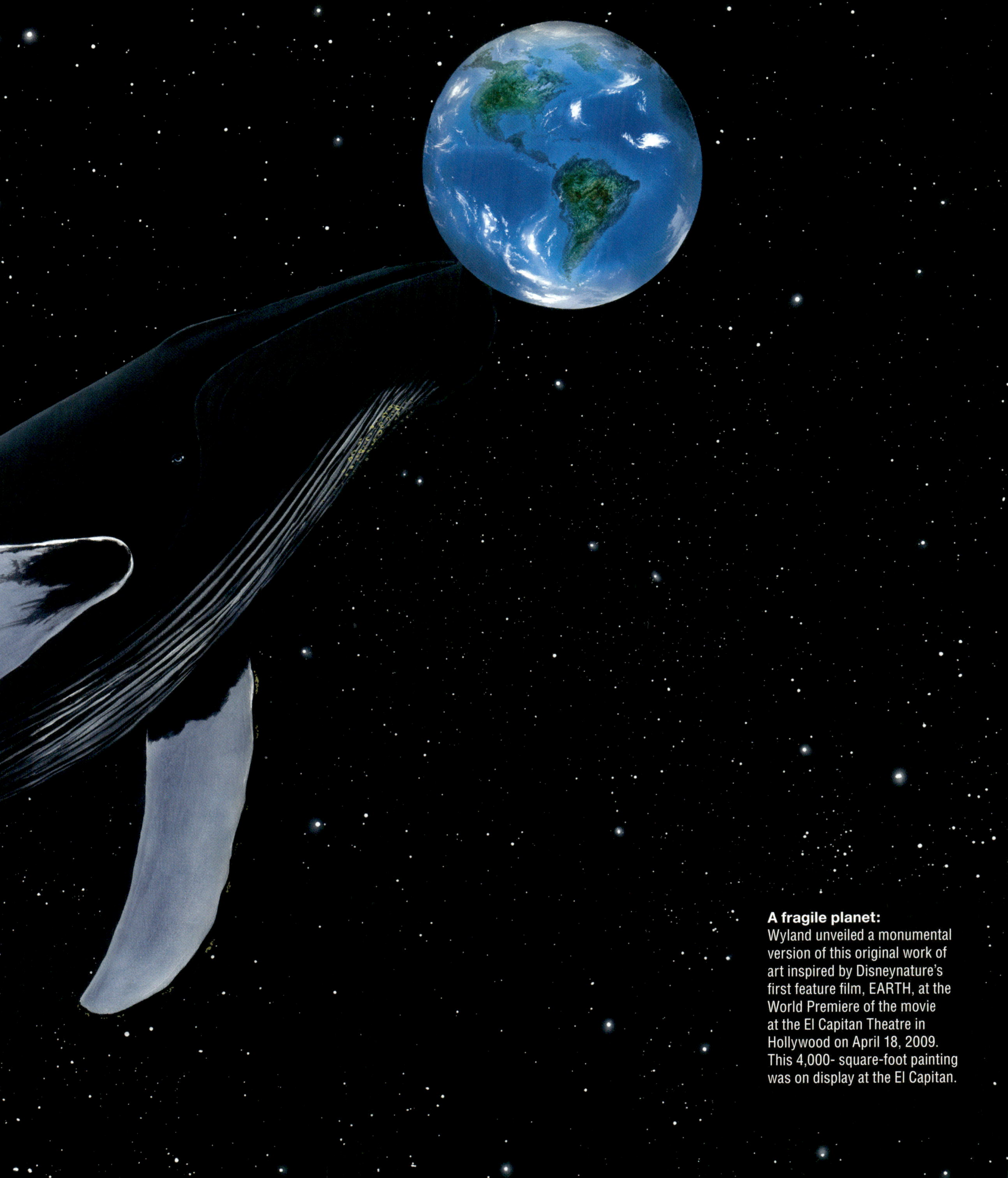

A fragile planet:
Wyland unveiled a monumental version of this original work of art inspired by Disneynature's first feature film, EARTH, at the World Premiere of the movie at the El Capitan Theatre in Hollywood on April 18, 2009. This 4,000- square-foot painting was on display at the El Capitan.

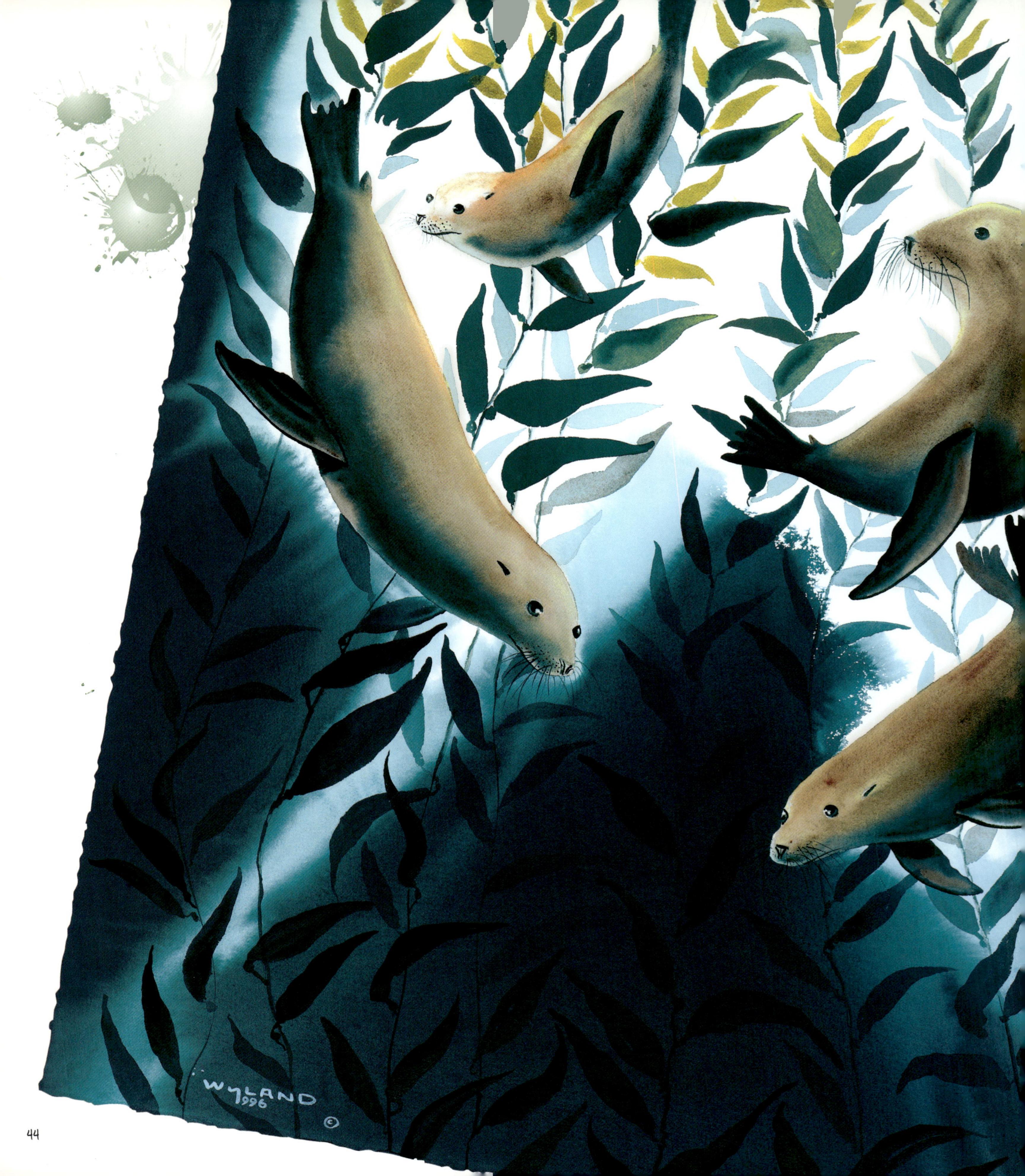
WYLAND
1996
©

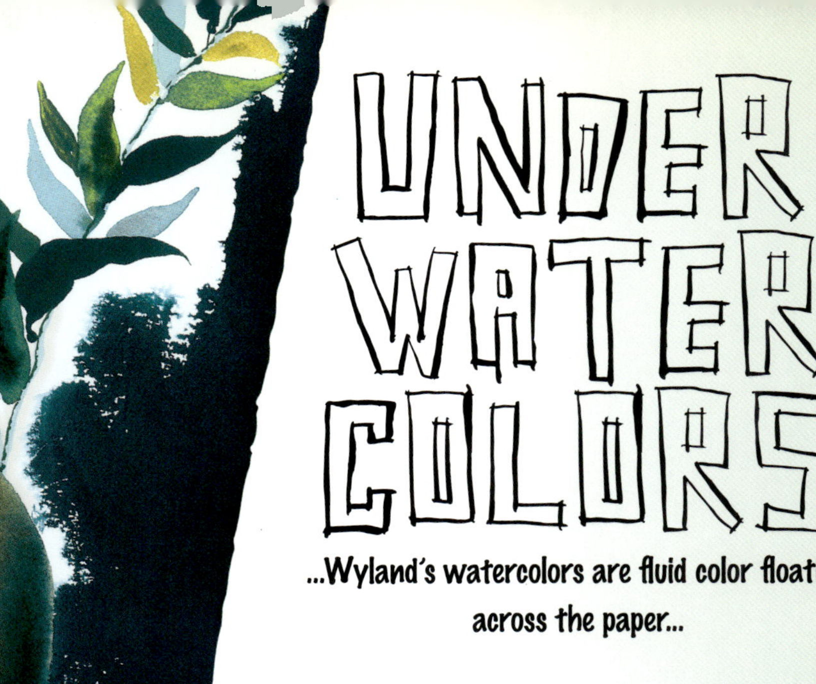

UNDER WATER COLORS

...Wyland's watercolors are fluid color floating across the paper...

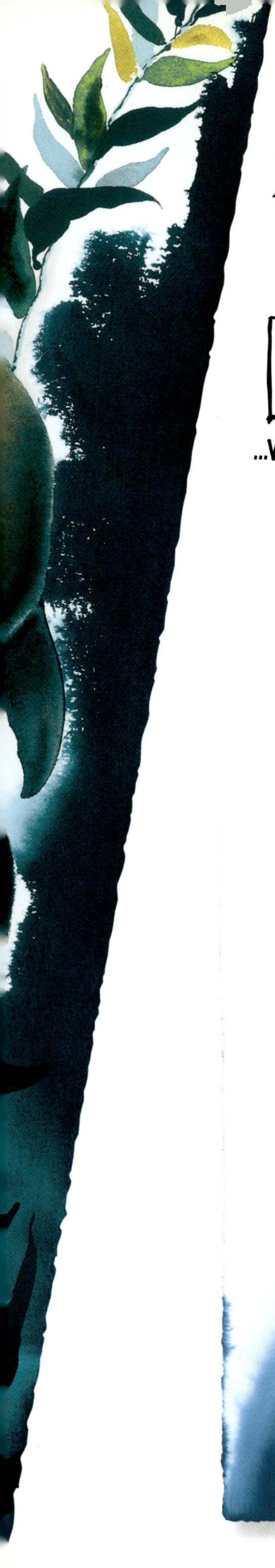

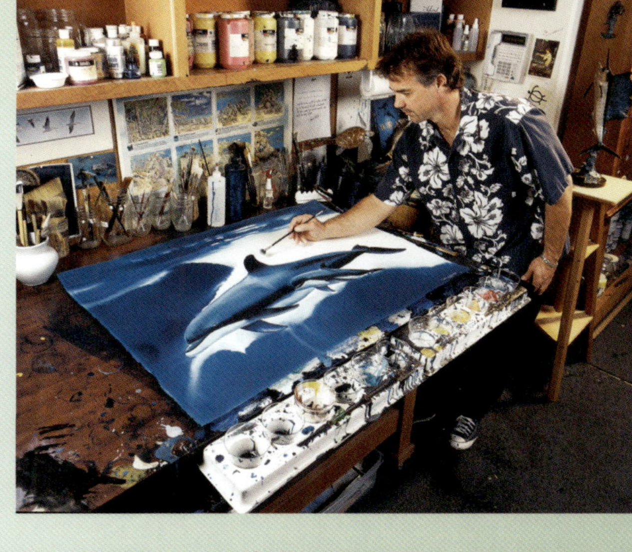

Wyland brings to life some of the world's most unique images using the natural spontaneity of watercolor. The near-abstract effects of his "Underwater Colors" are created using a wet process that summons energy and motion to his turtles, dolphins, whales, and other amazing sea life. The effect is lively, fluid, colorful, and indisputably Wyland.

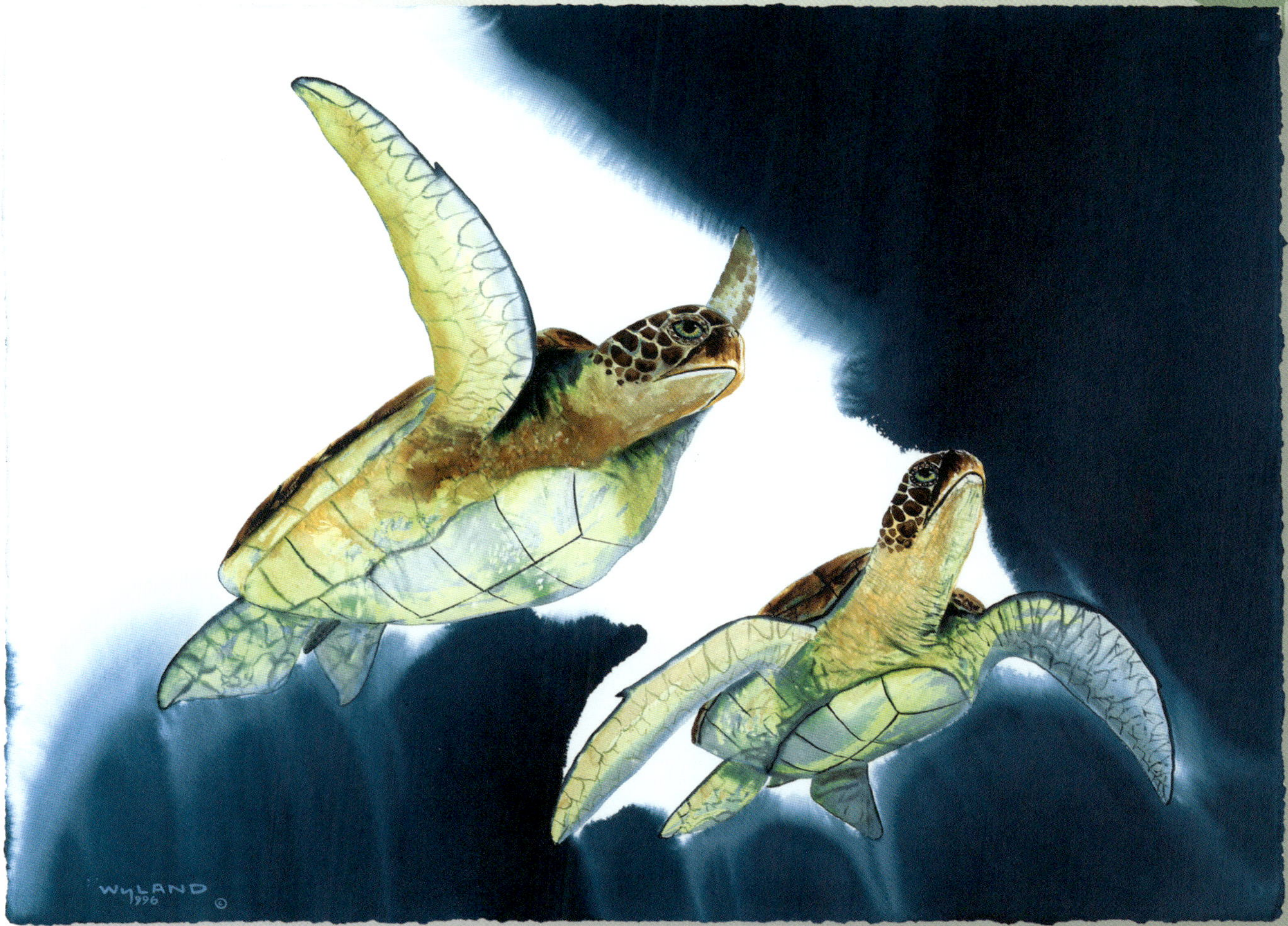

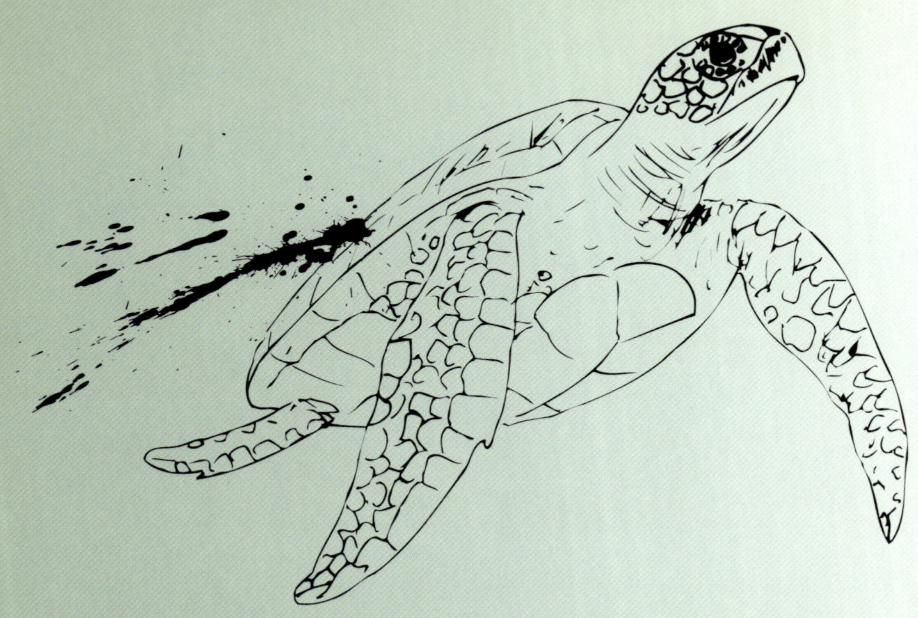

"Surprisingly,

art

has

come

full

circle.

The first art was created by prehistoric man in the form of cave paintings, and told stories that depicted man and animals against a backdrop of the natural world. Now, it seems, nature is back in a big way."

WYLAND

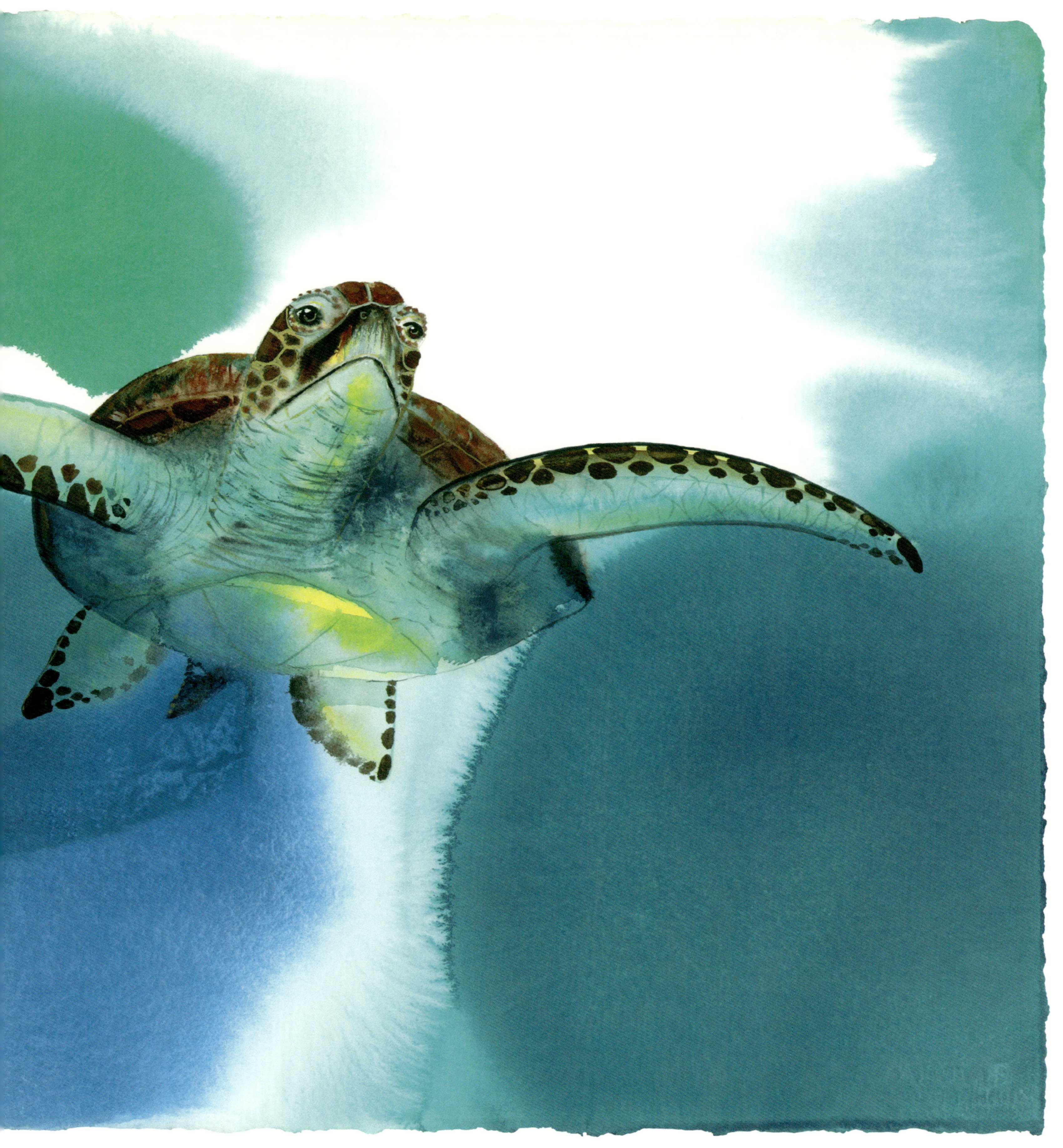

ABSTRACT EXPRESSIONISM

...Wyland's newest abstracts reflect nature's radiance...

Inspired by California, the Florida Keys, and Oahu's beautiful North Shore sunsets and the sea,

Wyland's soulful marine art often combines abstract expressionism with contemporary art to reflect the radiant colors and organic shapes reflected in our natural world.

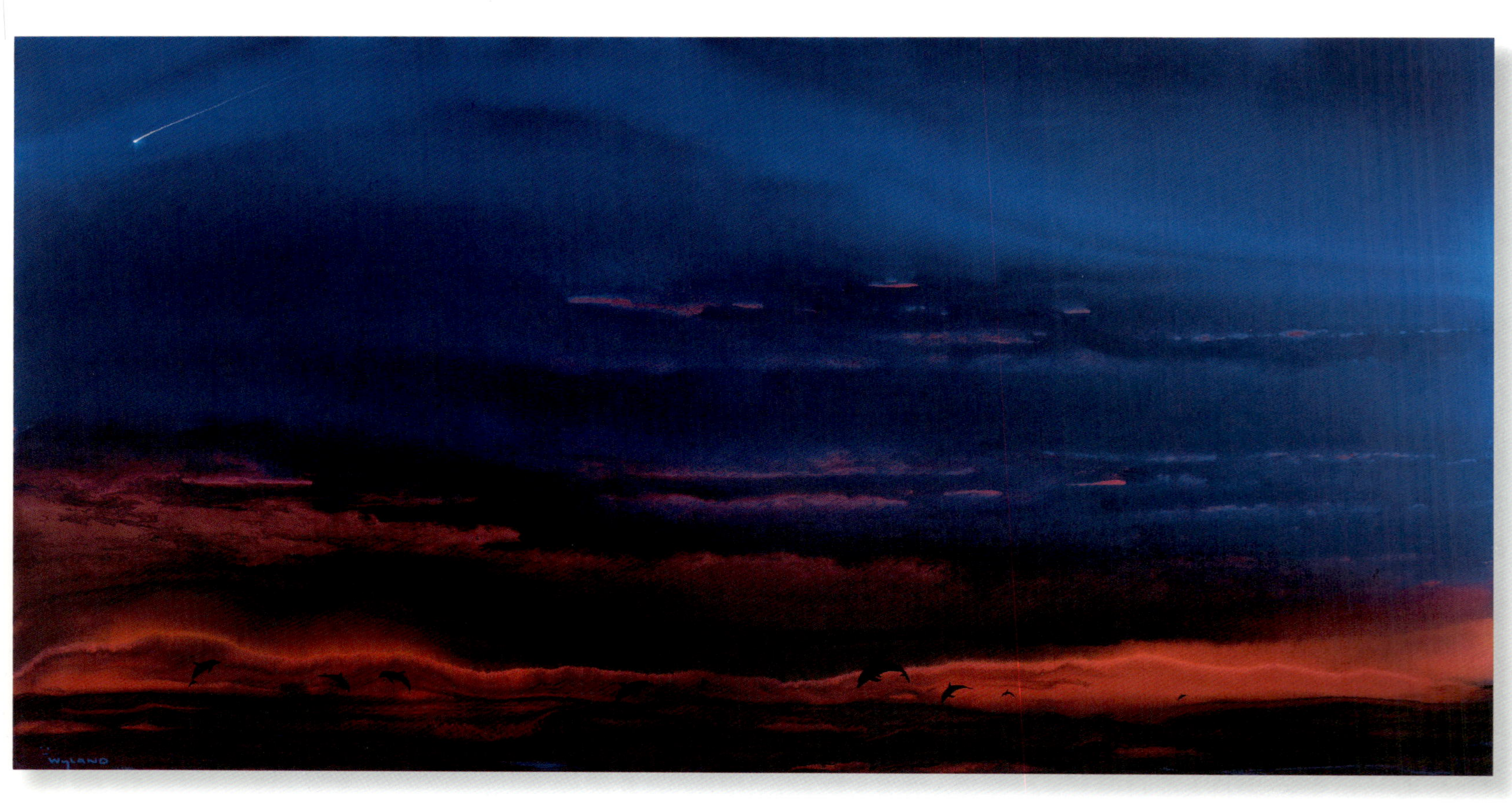

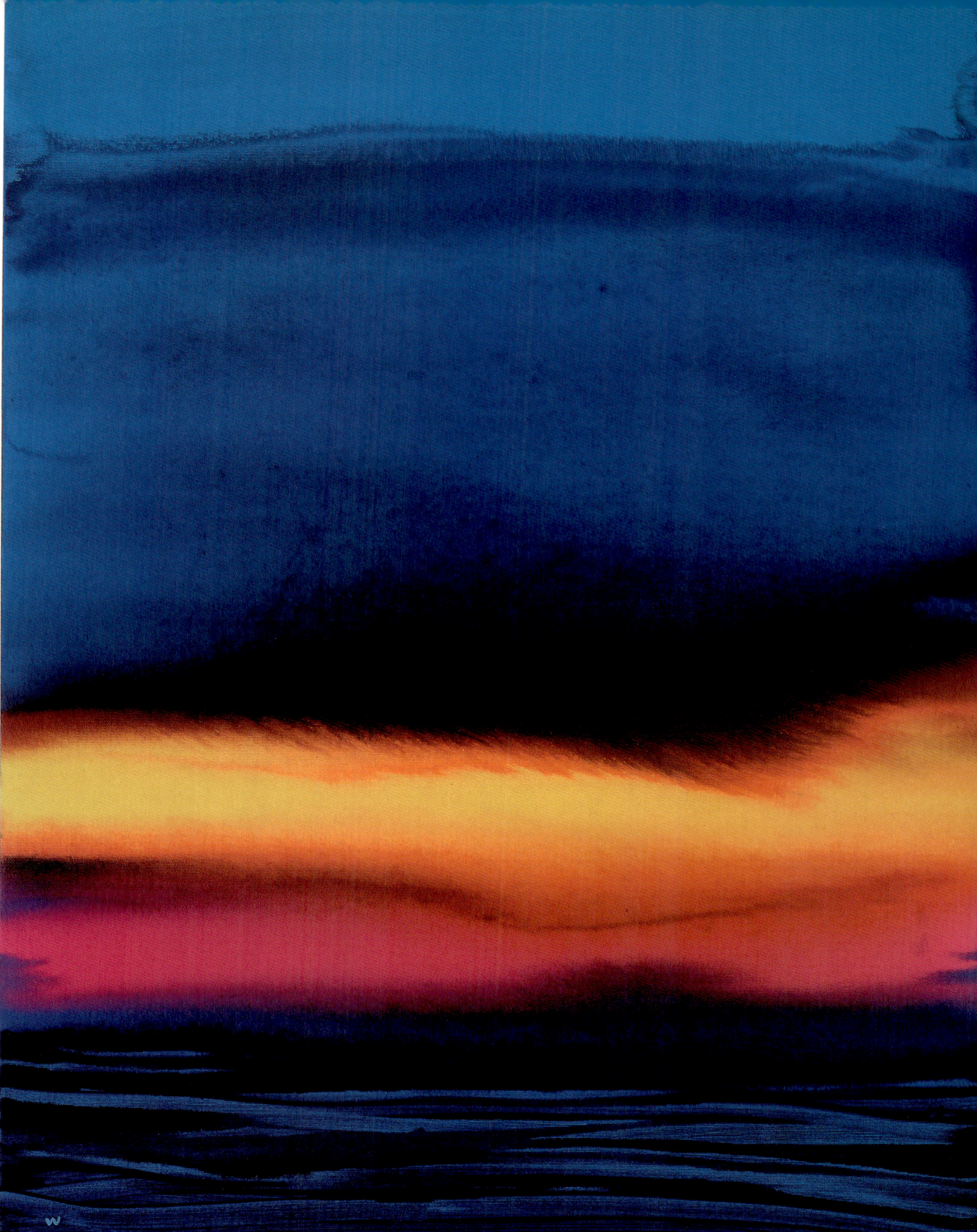

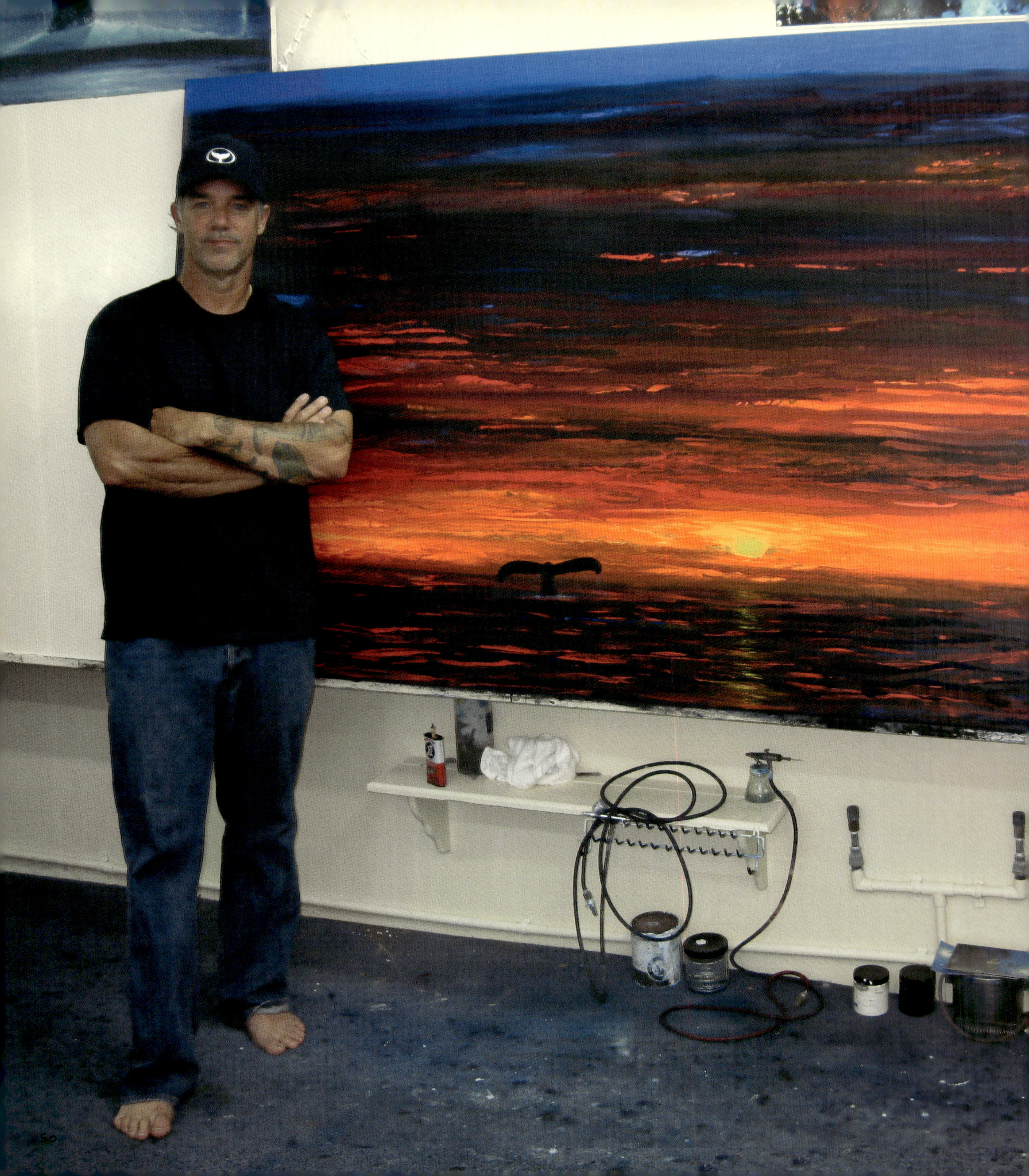

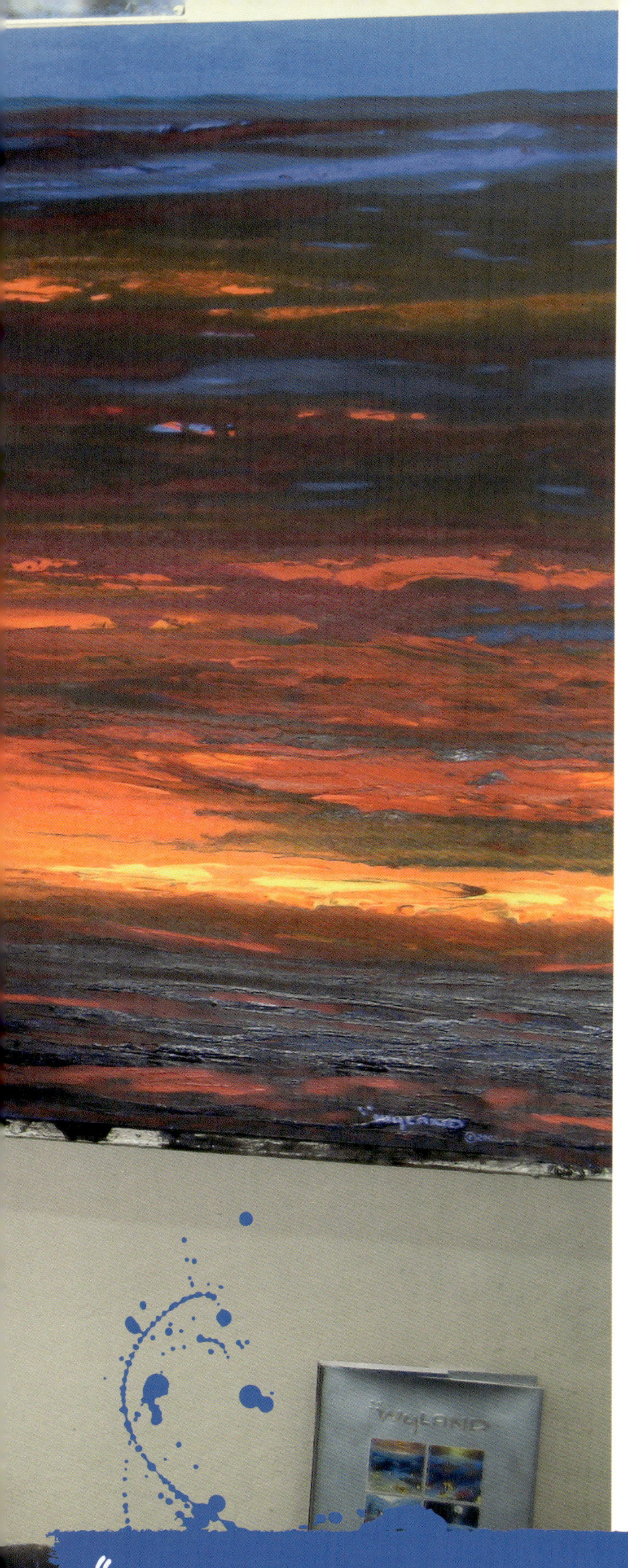

"L'art pour l'art," insisted the French avant-garde at the end of the 19th century. "Art for art's sake." But here is Wyland — painter, sculptor, muralist, writer, photographer **— not just using all these media but pushing them, stretching them, and wringing from them a truth much larger than the works themselves. Pursuing that truth** — that the earth is what matters, and the waters that sustain it — Wyland has produced a body of work that staggers the imagination and that places him, according to many, among the most important artists of the 21st century.

"There is no rest when you're on planetary duty."

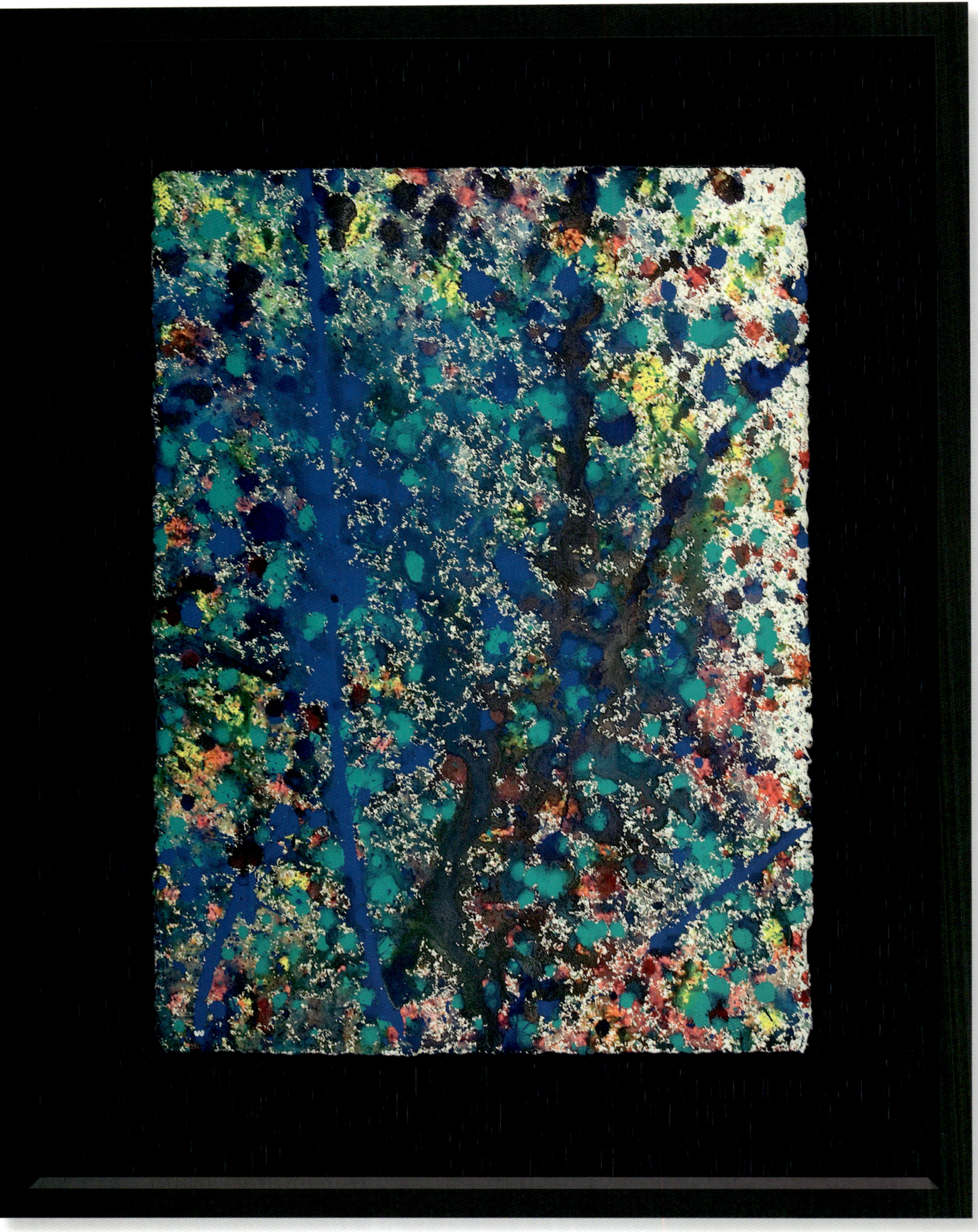

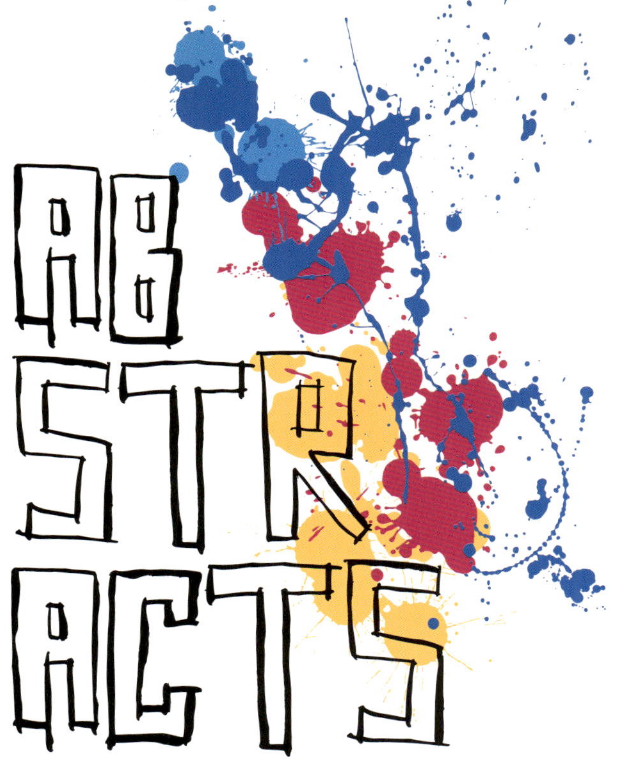

"... imagine Wyland meets Jackson Pollock in contemporary abstract action paintings..."

Wyland has dived living reefs the world over for more than twenty-five years. At the National Aquarium in Washington, D.C., he unveiled the official painting for the International Year of the Reef 2008. In keeping with his passion for reef conservation, **Wyland created a dazzling series of new abstracts inspired by these amazing underwater worlds.**

These original abstract paintings capture the vibrant colors and form of coral reefs on canvas and watercolor paper with hand-torn deckle edges.

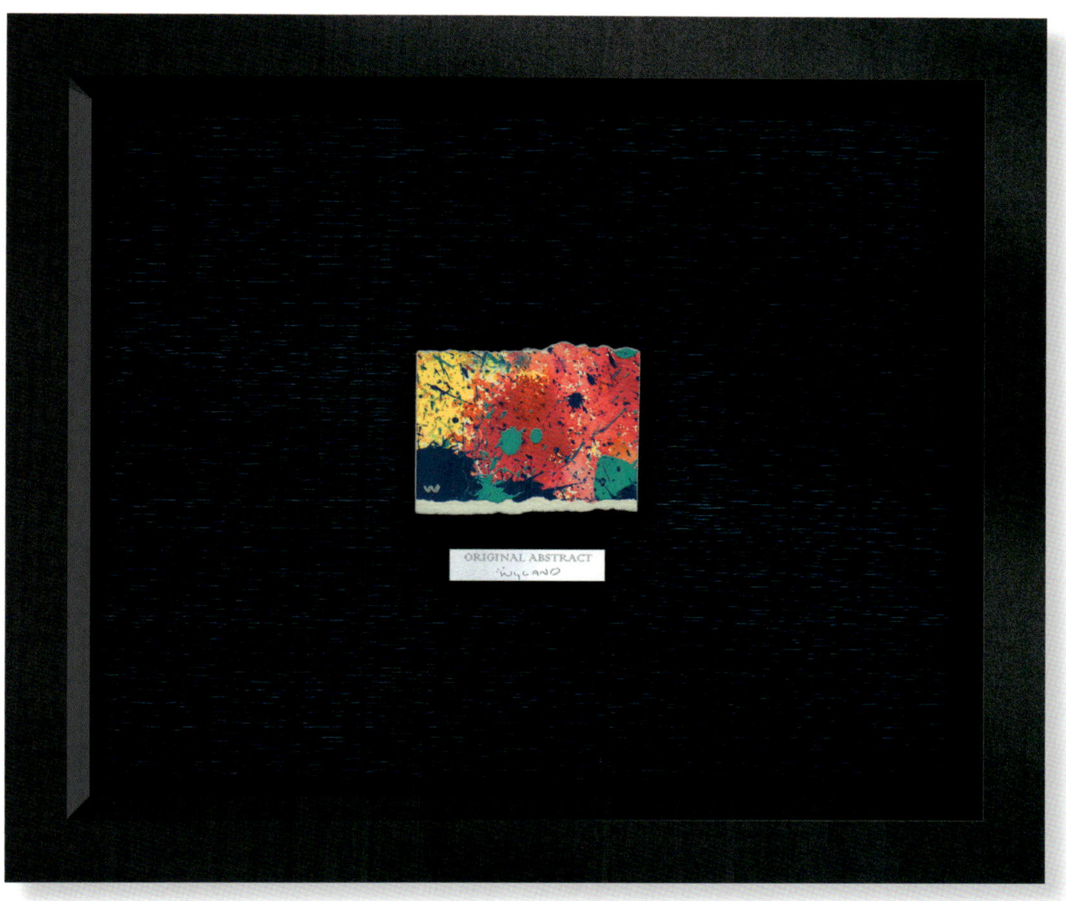

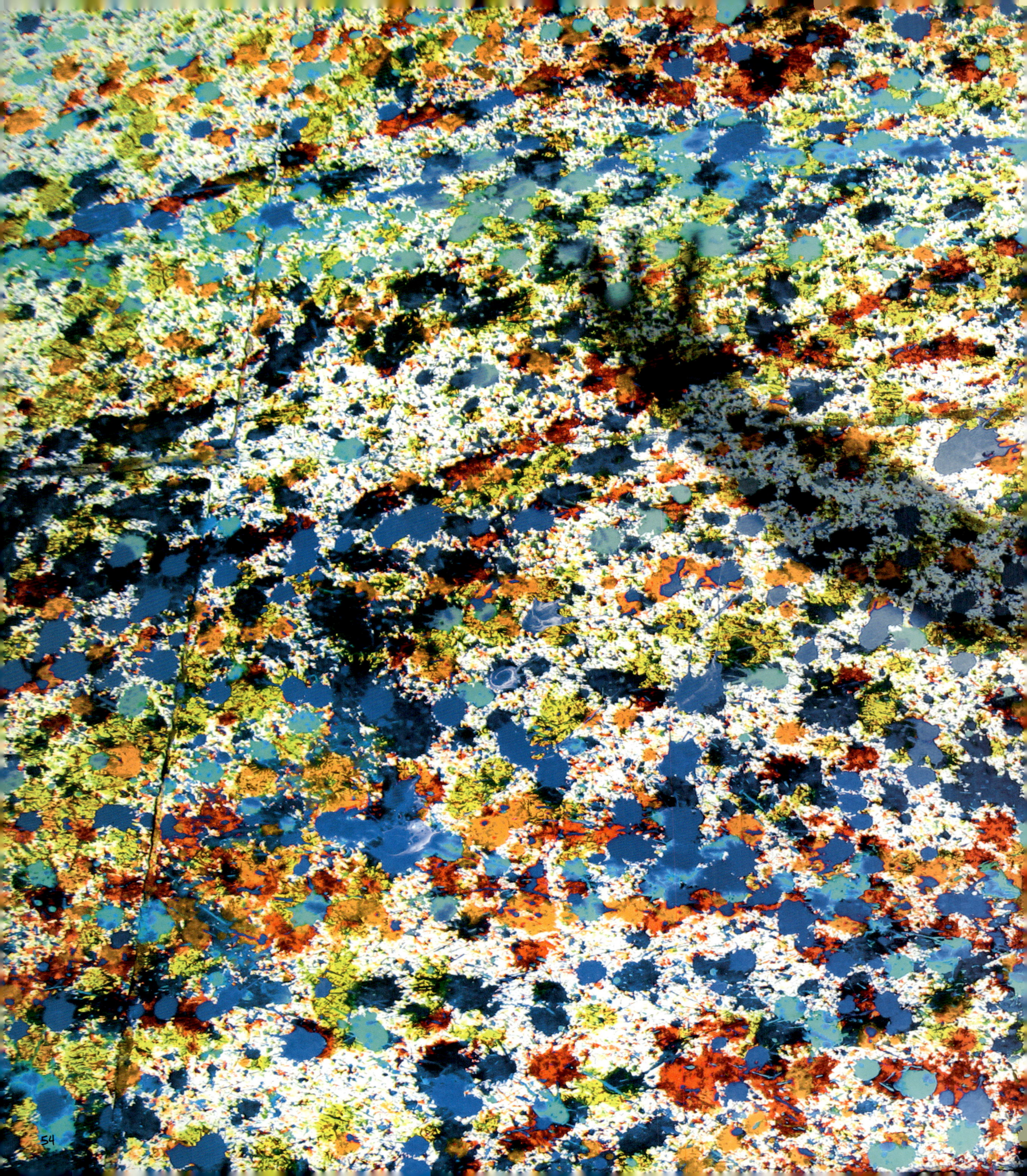

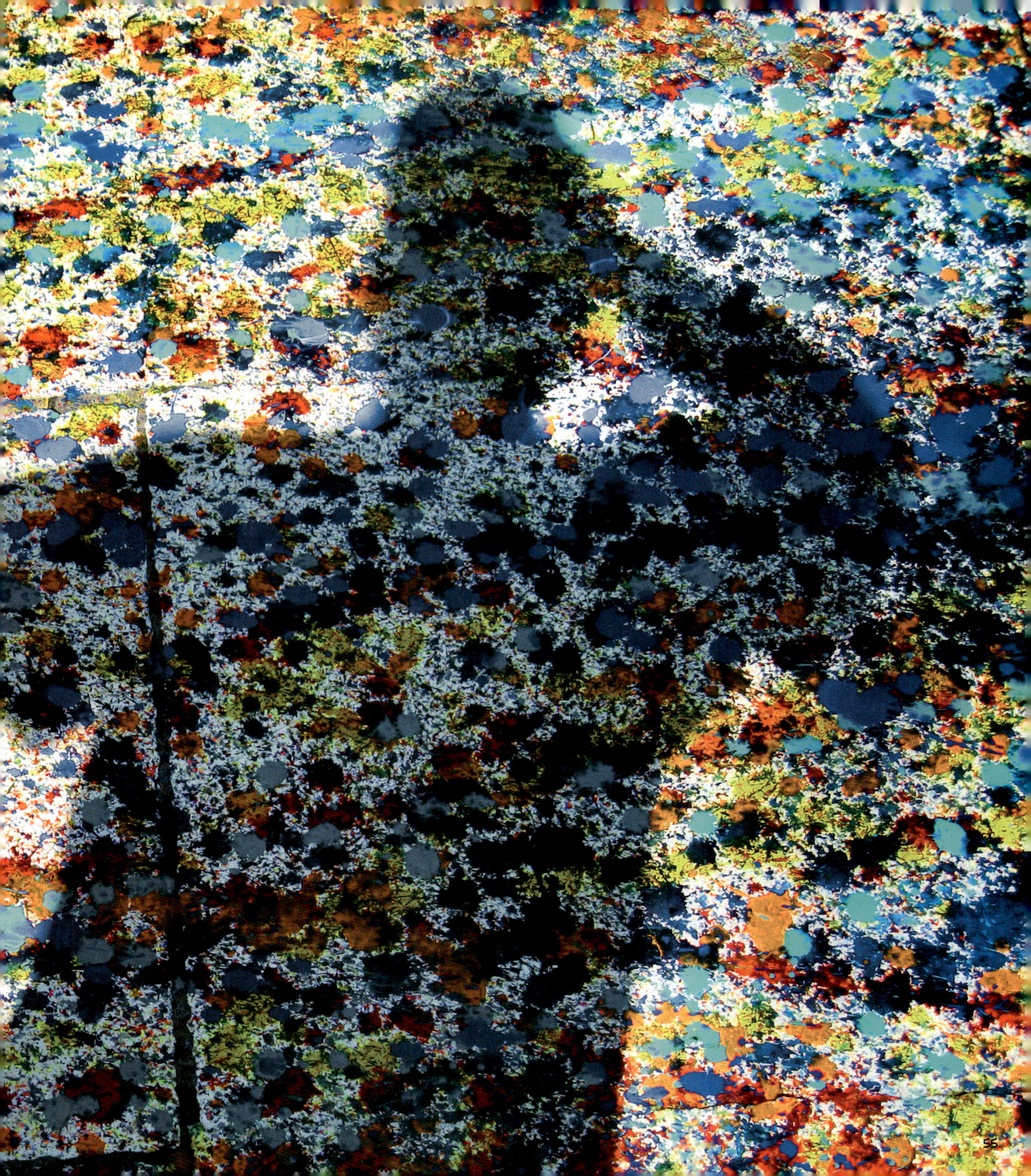

...In nature less is more, and Sumi-e brush captures its power and simplicity in a few brushstrokes...

SUMI-E BRUSH ART

Wyland brush art paintings combine the **simplicity and power of ancient Sumi-e techniques** with personal style and vision. Simple and elegant, they are a perfect medium to depict the wonder of the natural world.

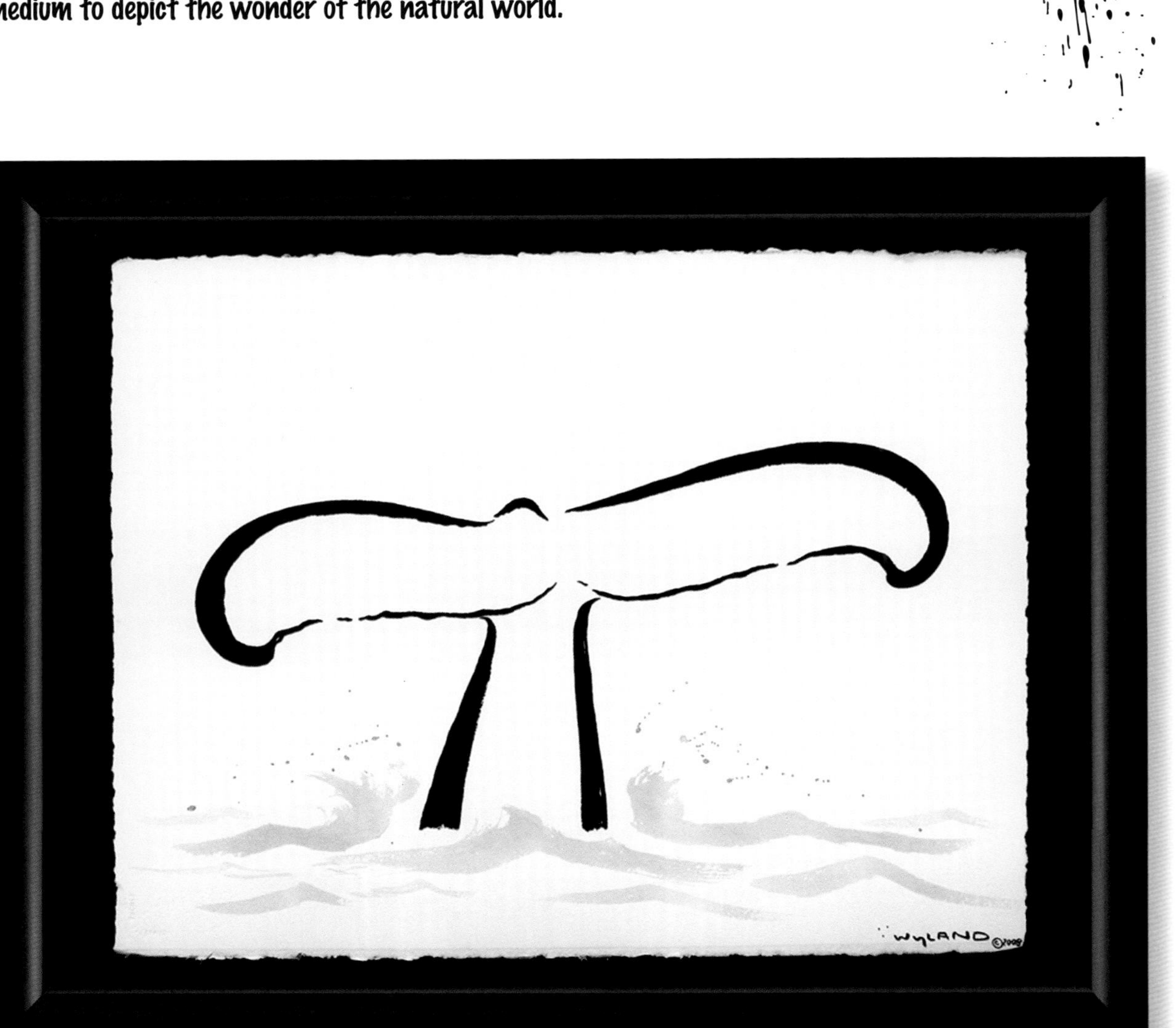

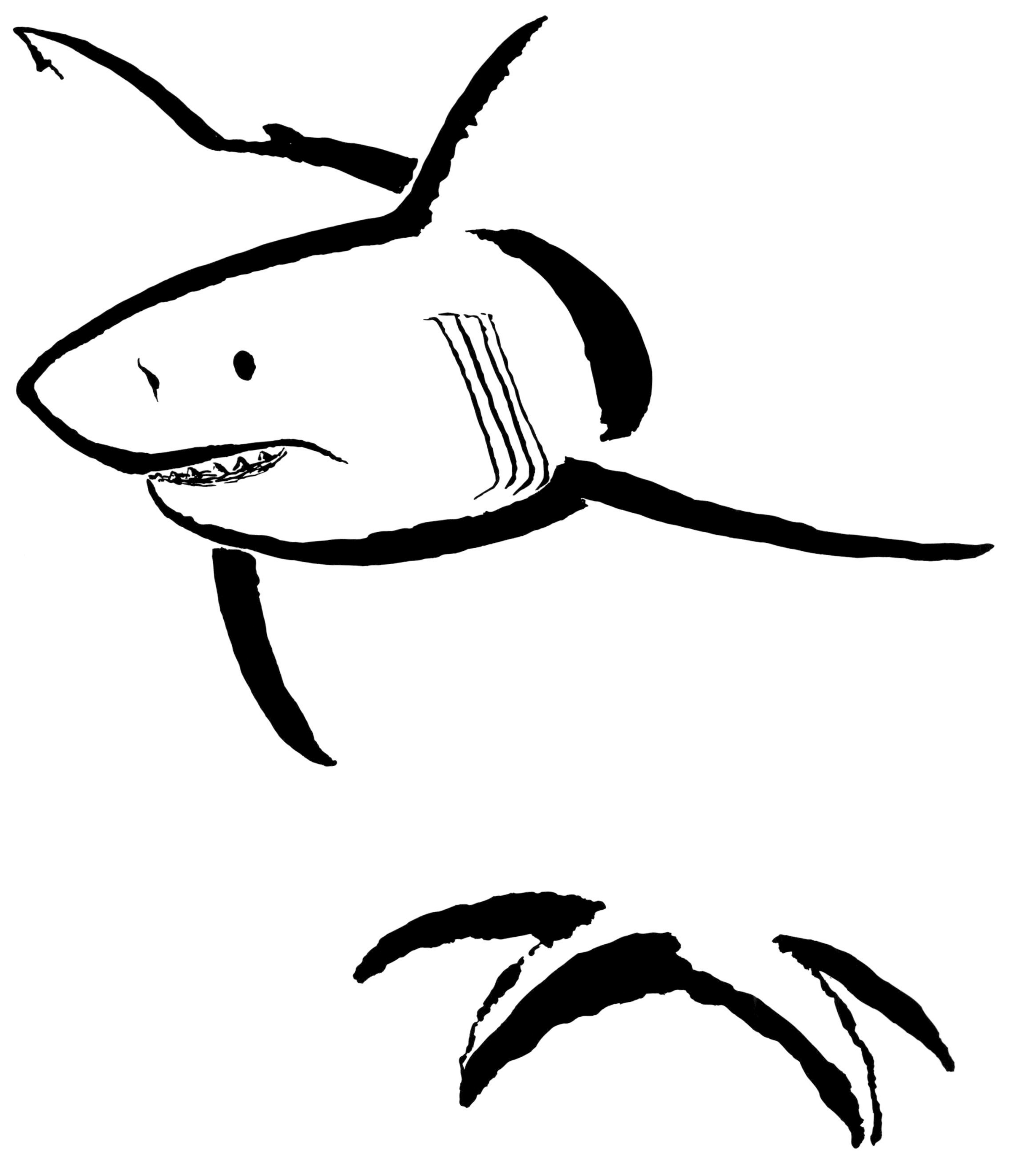

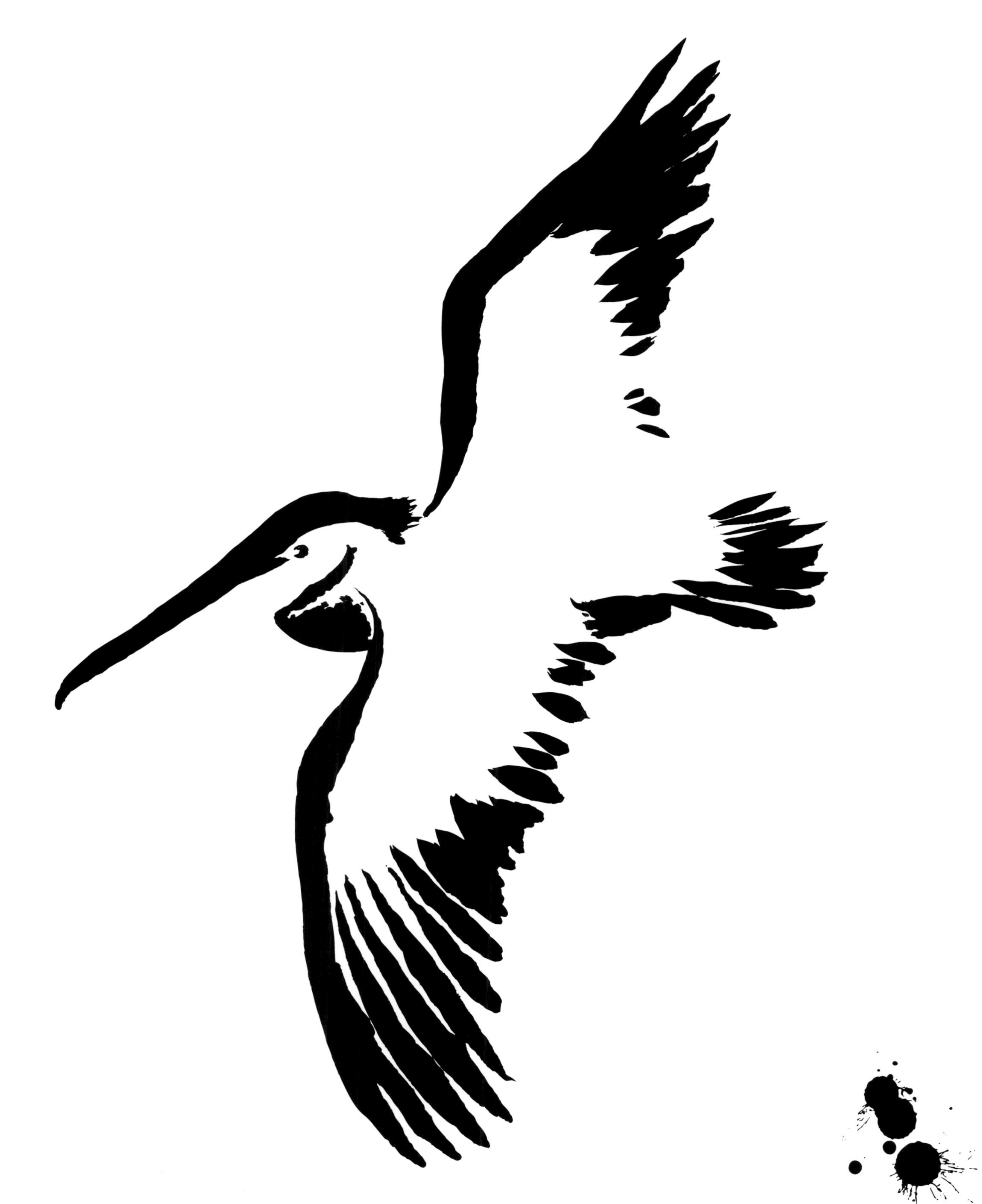

WYLAND ©

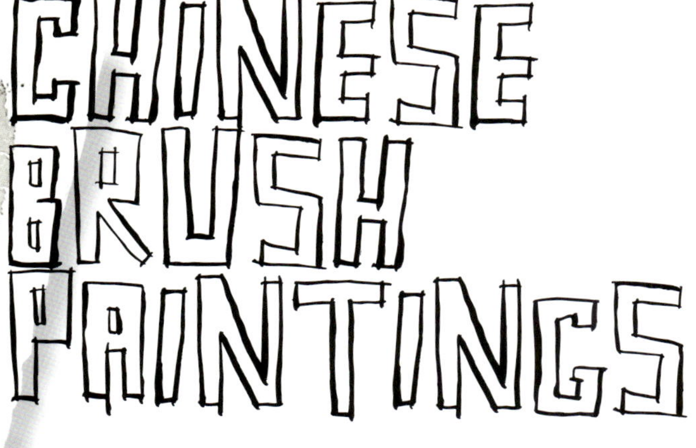

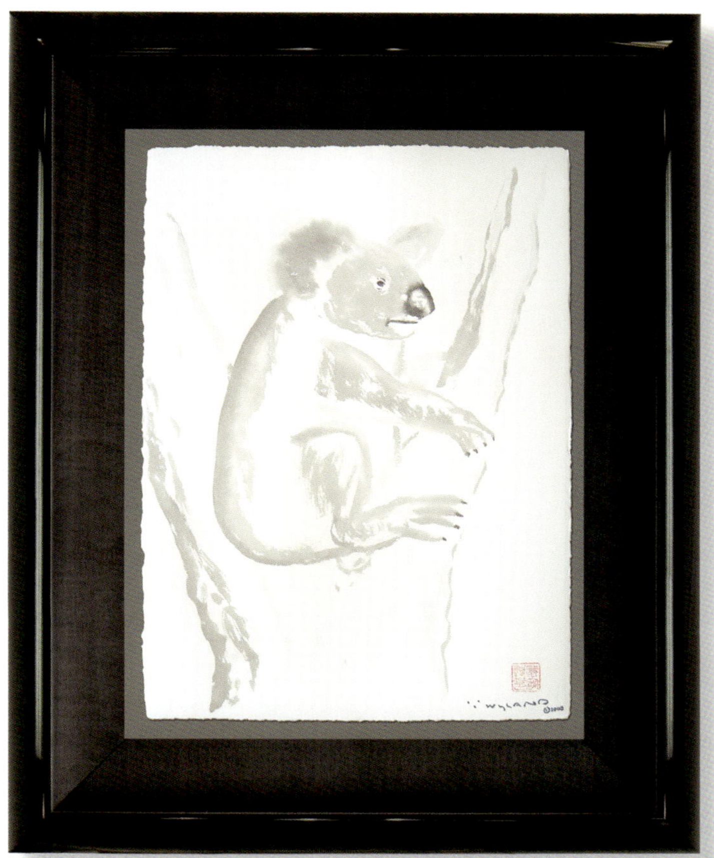

...The ancient techniques of Chinese brush create an ideal medium for painting nature and wildlife...

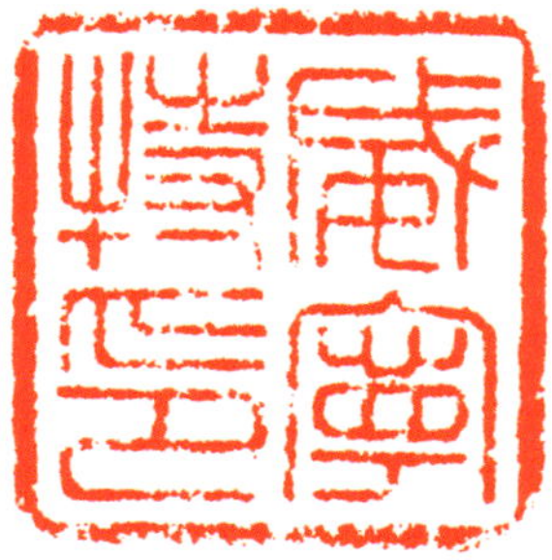

Traditional Chinese painting has evolved over six thousand years to reflect the changes of the times. Now in the 21st century, a time of environmental awareness and focus on the state of our natural world, Wyland has adapted the ancient Chinese brush techniques with his own personal style to create a series of paintings featuring wildlife from across the globe. Wyland's technique has evolved further with his recent work with renowned Chinese artist and sculptor Professor Xikun Yuan during the "Hands Across the Oceans" project in Beijing.

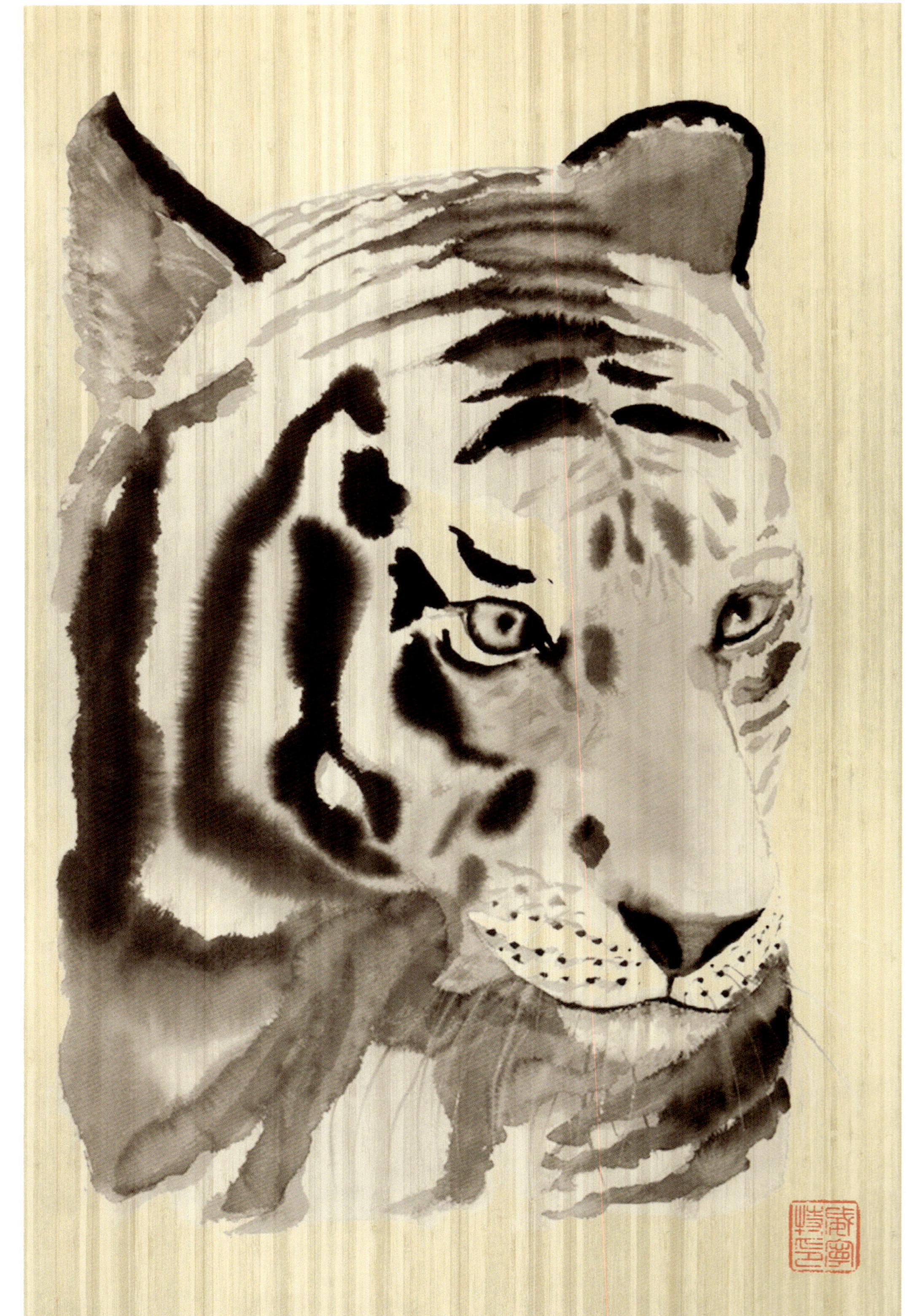

"I was influenced by great masters like Michelangelo, van Gogh, Picasso, and my favorite surrealist painter, Salvador Dali. Later, I began to appreciate artists like Andrew Wyeth and wildlife artist Robert Bateman. They inspired me to want to be a professional artist."

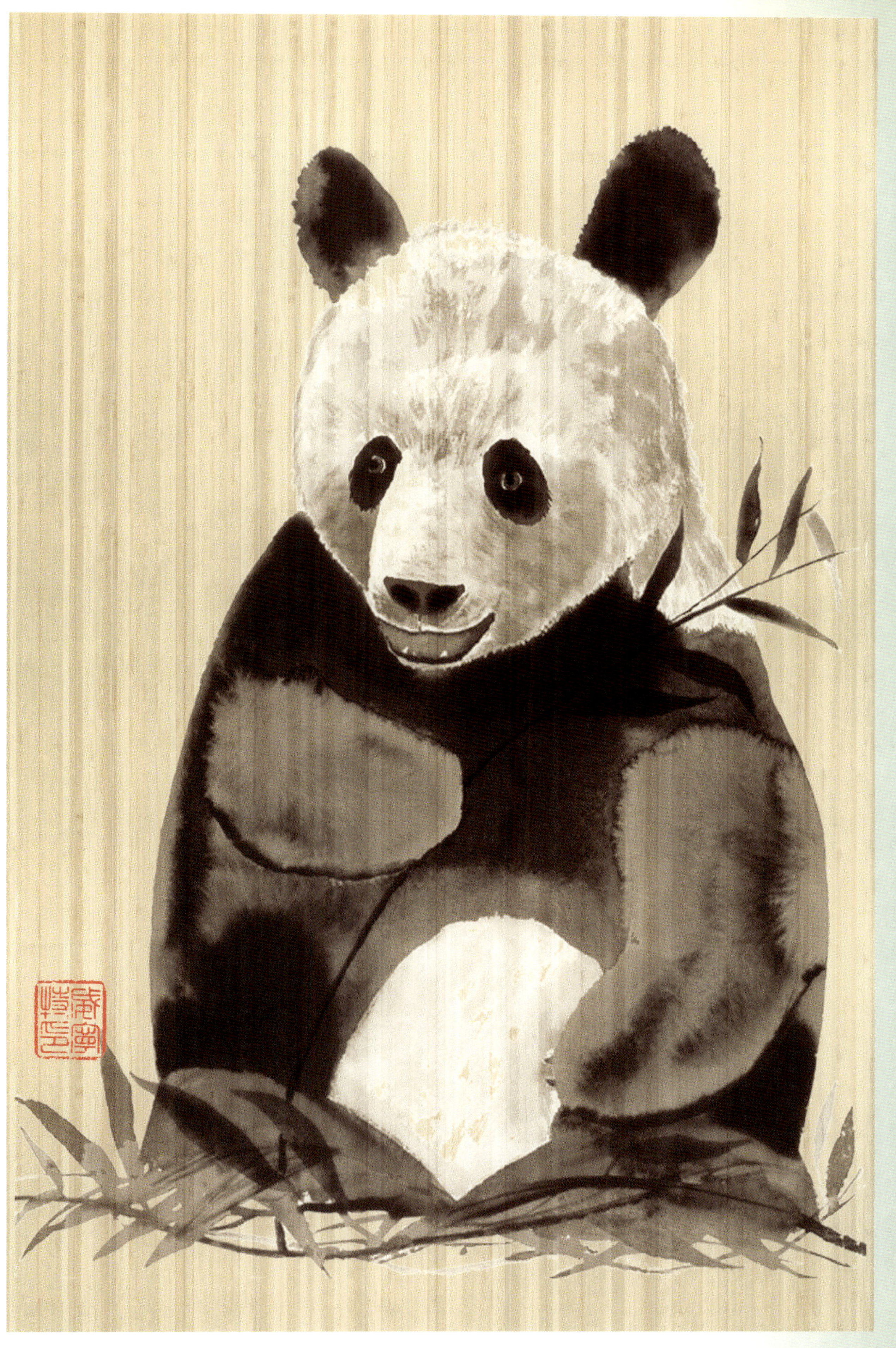

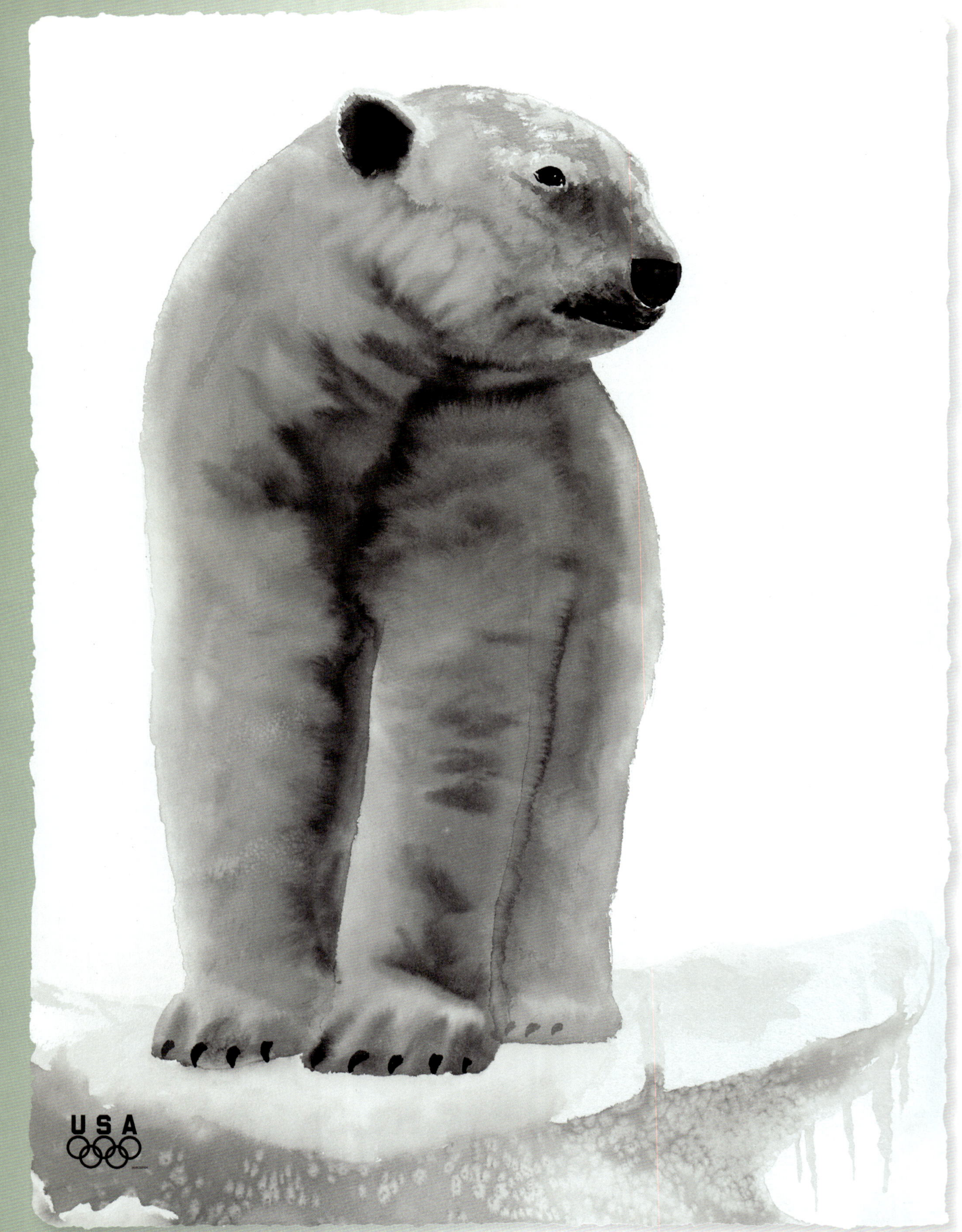
USA

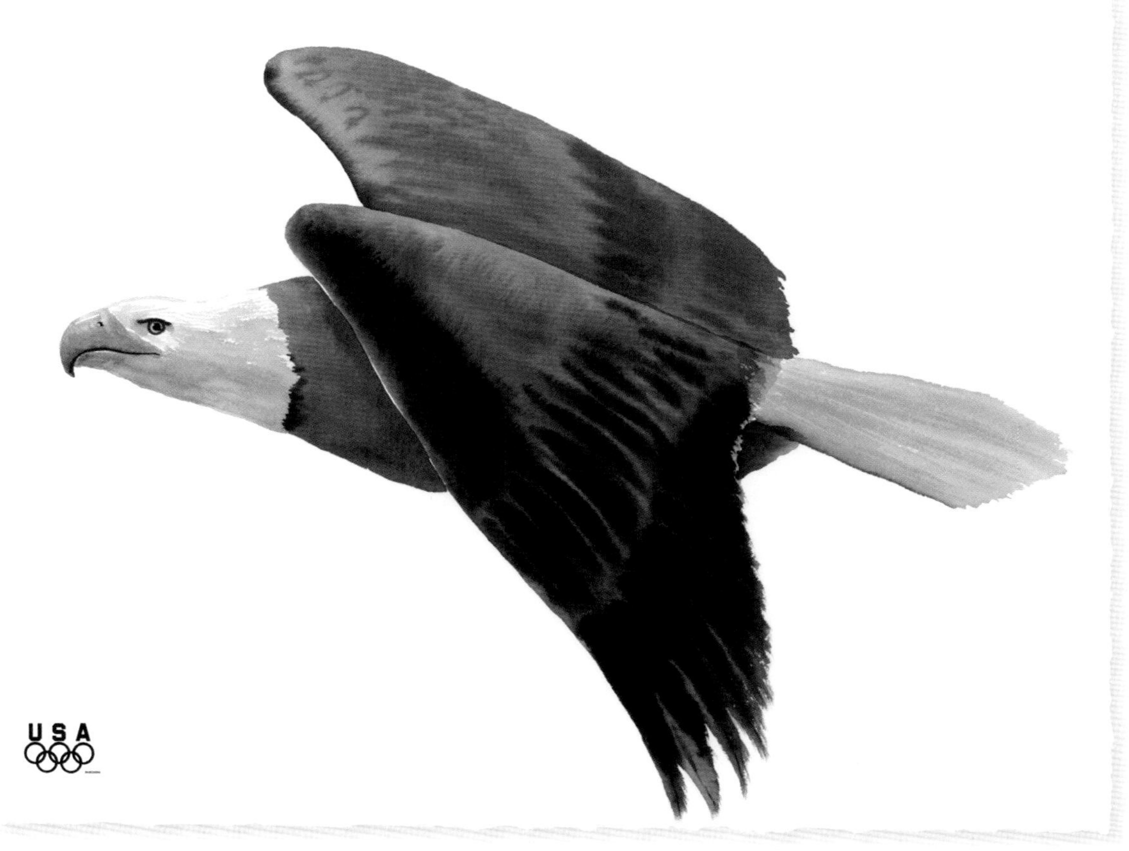
USA

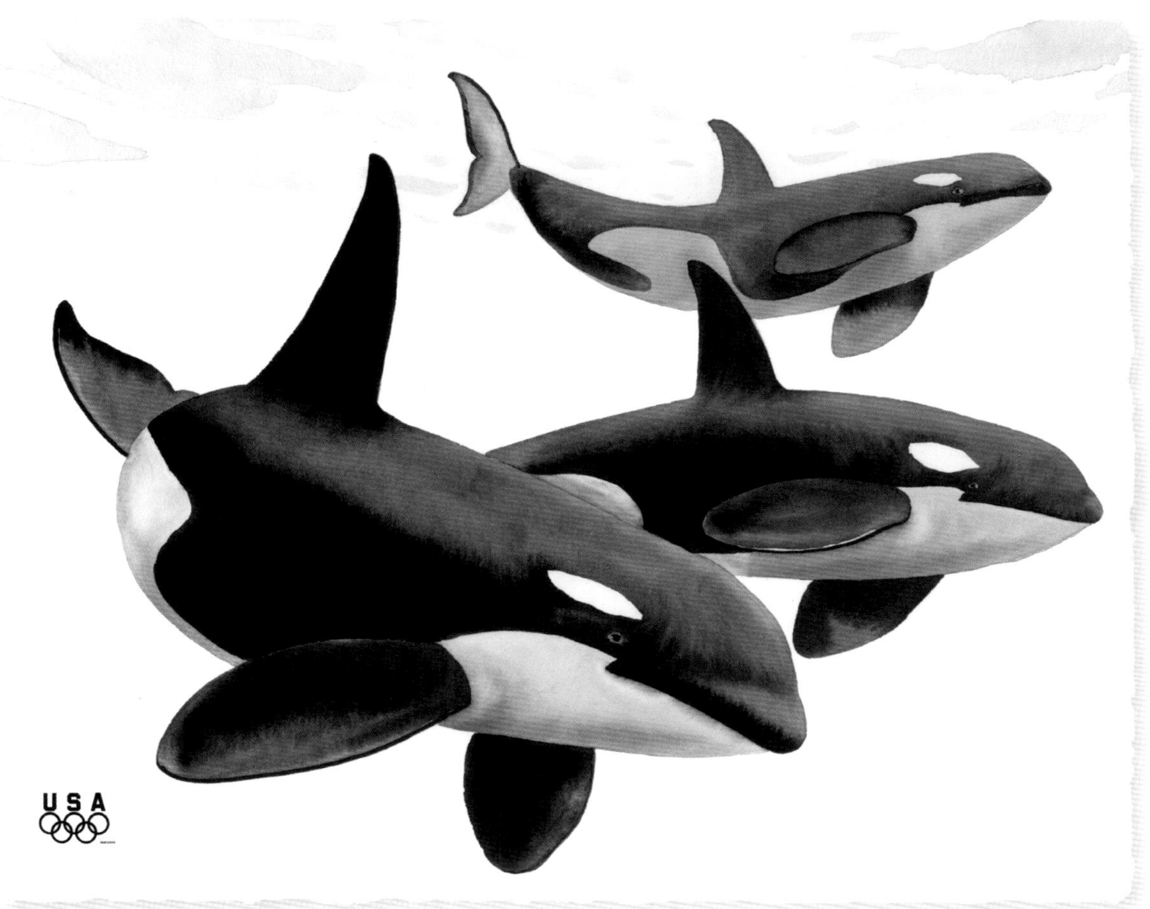
USA

FINE ART PHOTOGRAPHY

...The challenge is capturing that moment when light and motion reveal nature's beauty...

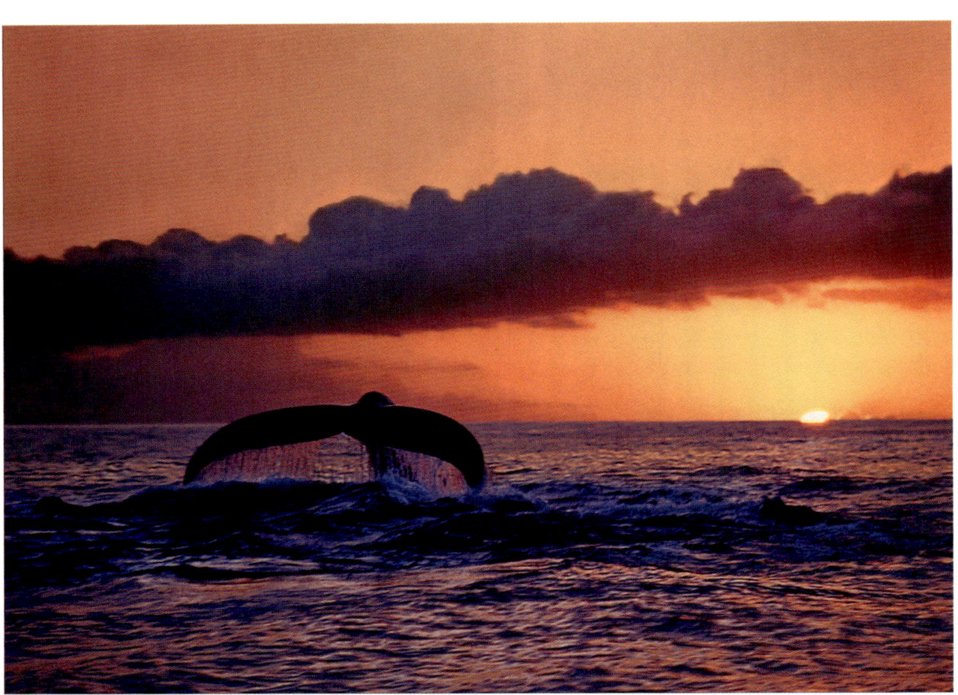

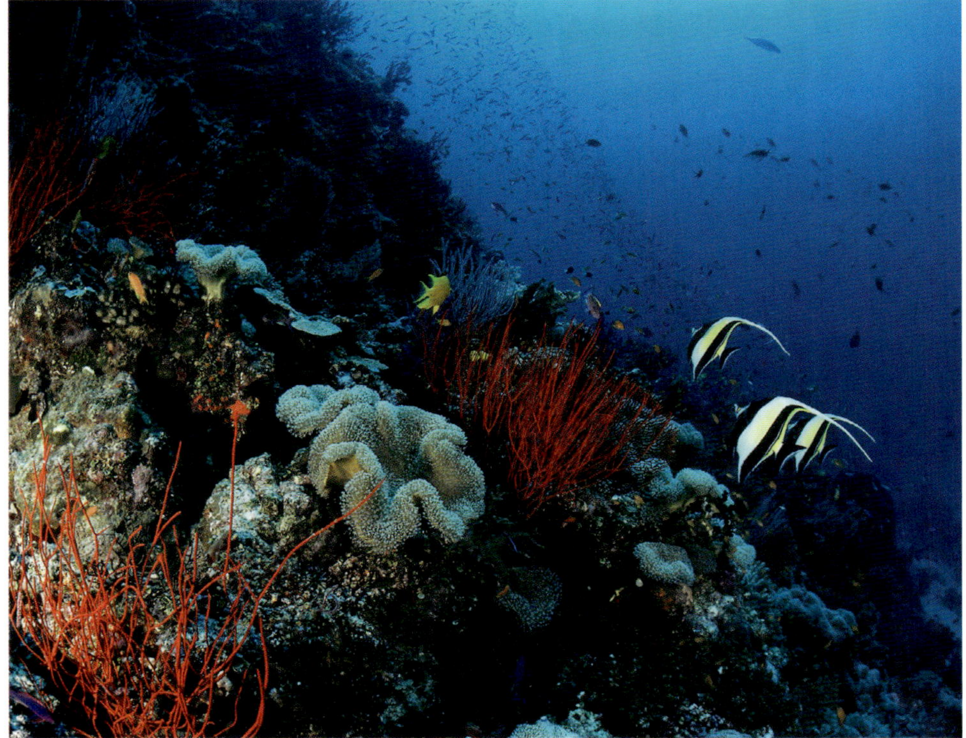

For more than a quarter century, Wyland has been traveling the world diving and photographing the most pristine habitats on the planet. His paintings, sculptures, and monumental marine-life murals are world renowned, but recently his fine art nature photography has begun to capture the attention of collectors. "For me," the artist says, "the natural world provides an endless supply of beauty and wonder and rare encounters with fantastic aquatic life that can be shared forever."

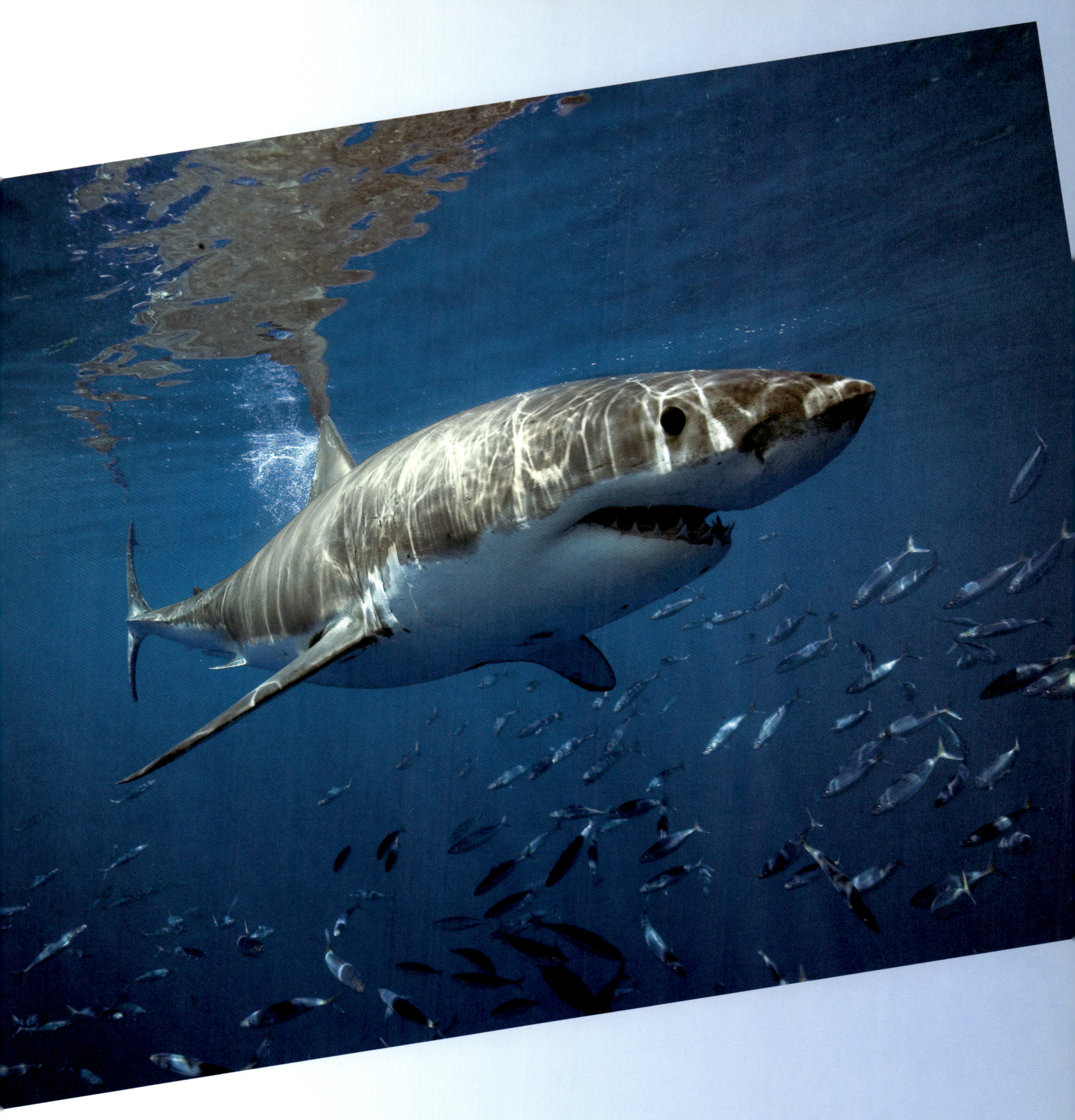

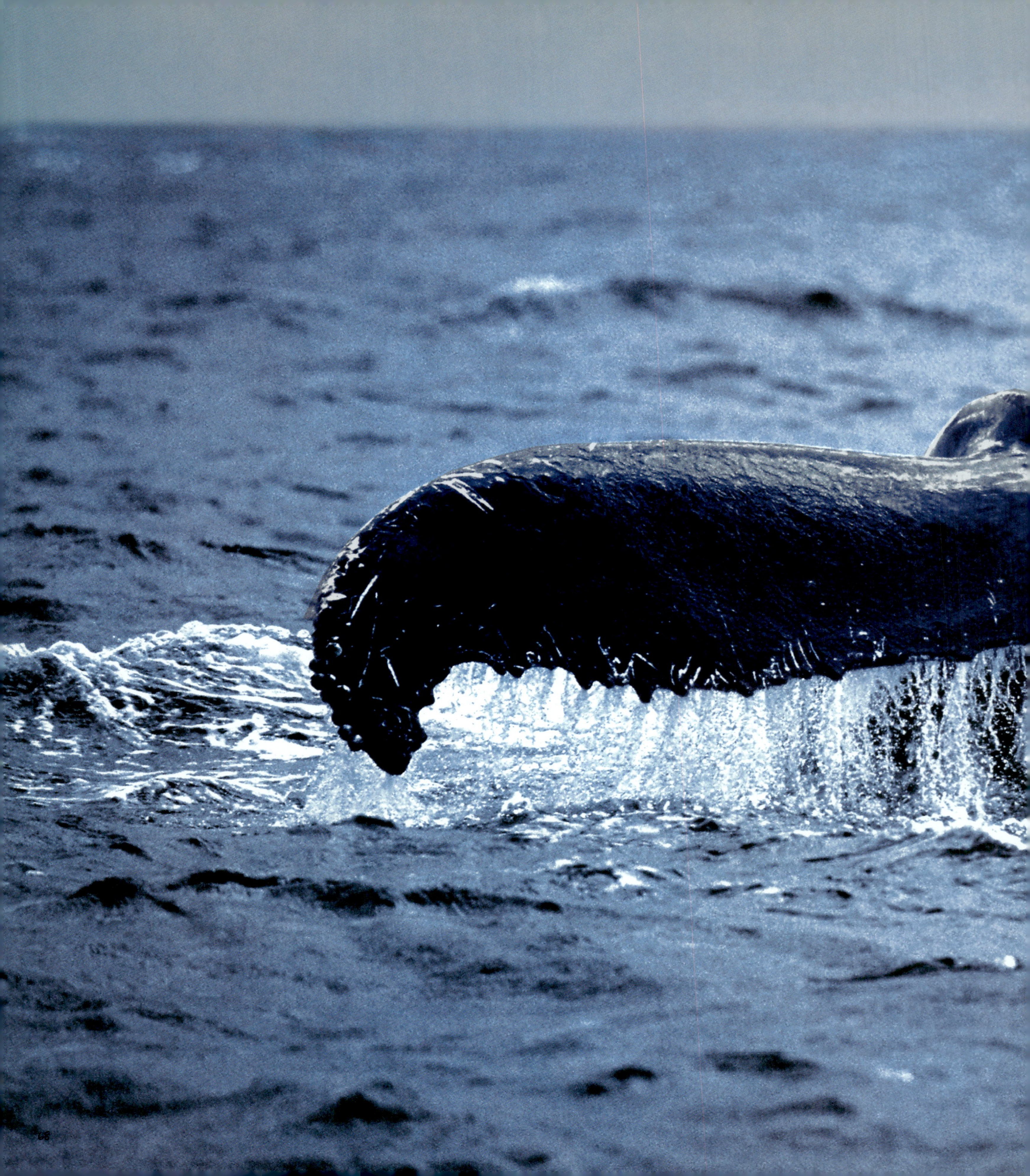

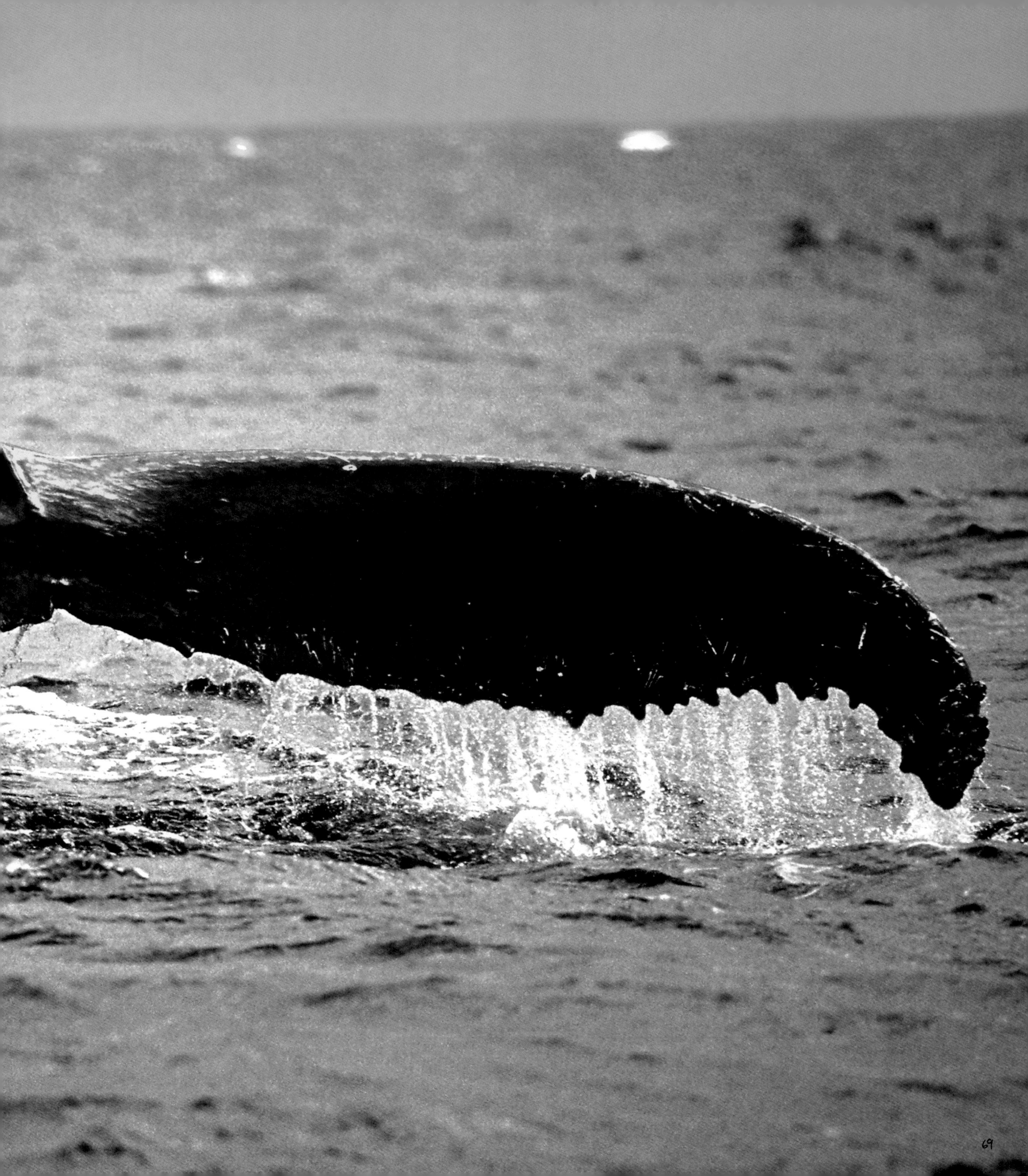

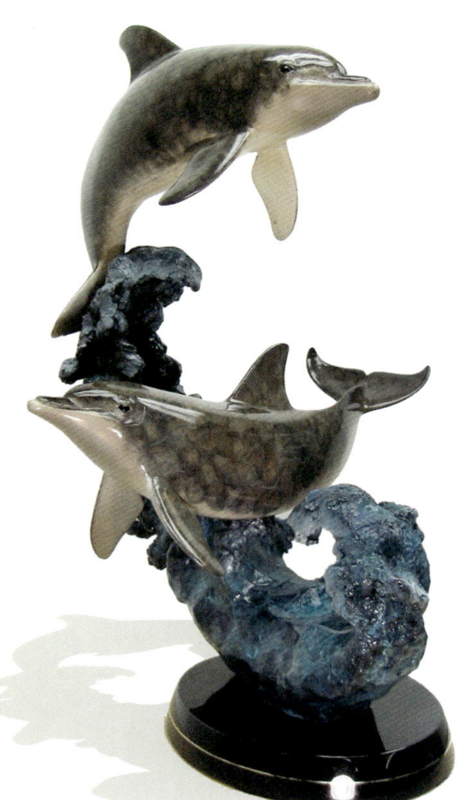

BRONZE SCULPTURE

The lifelike energy and motion of Wyland's marine-life sculpture work has made him **one of the most in-demand artists of the last twenty-five years.** Wyland attributes this, in part, to the countless hours of study he devotes to marine animals each year.

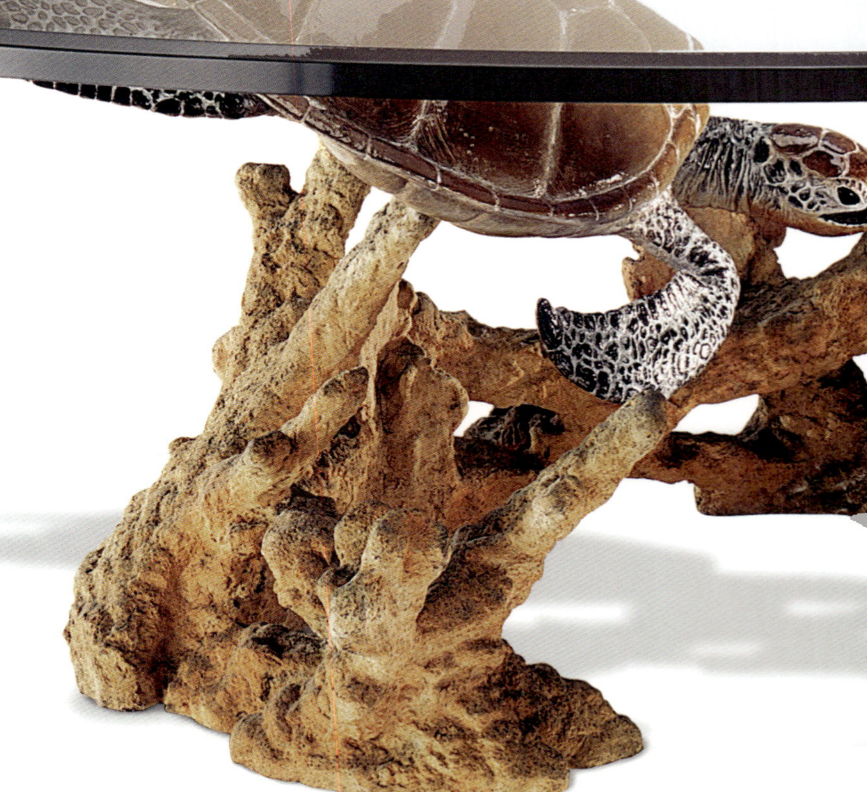

Certainly, those who stand beside a Wyland sculpture come to feel a stronger connection with the natural world. His bronze and Lucite tables are conceived as an extension of his fine art sculpture and carefully engineered to the highest standards.

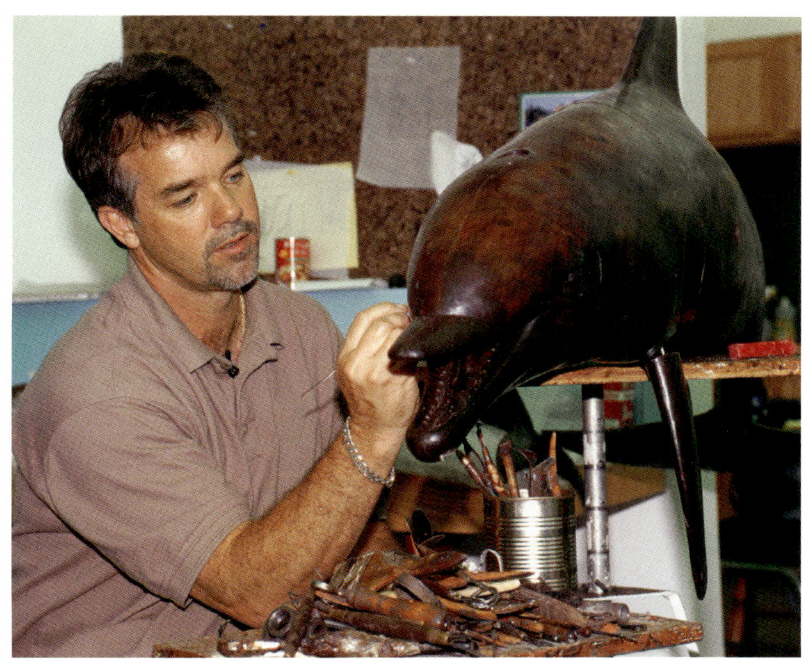

...I've always felt that I was a better sculptor than painter...

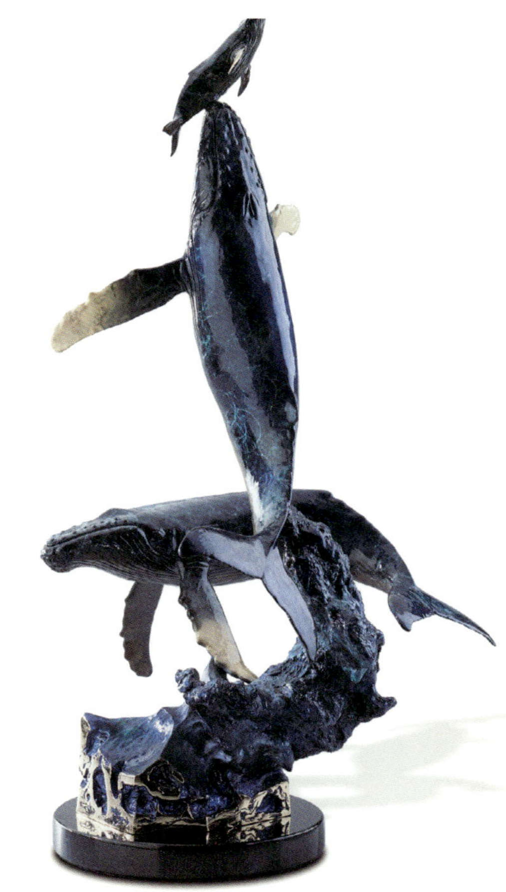

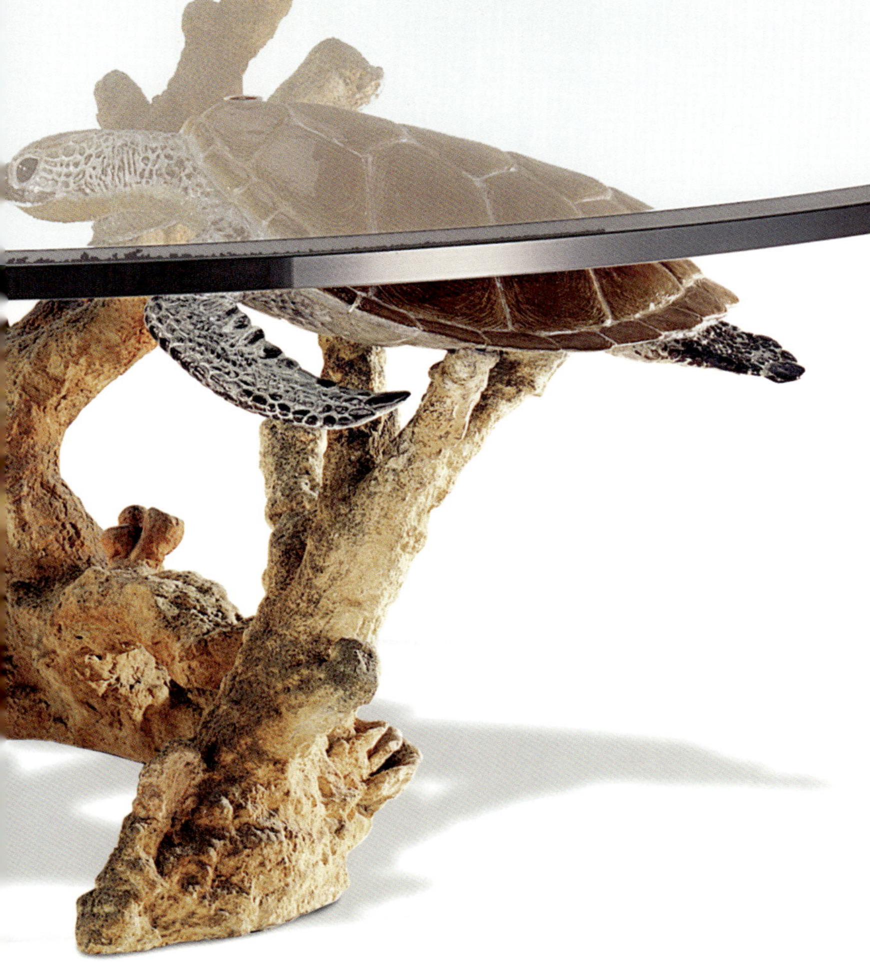

As in Wyland's art, **the spirit of environmental conservation comes through in every sculpture.** His attention to detail, dynamic motion, and use of space are all signature hallmarks.

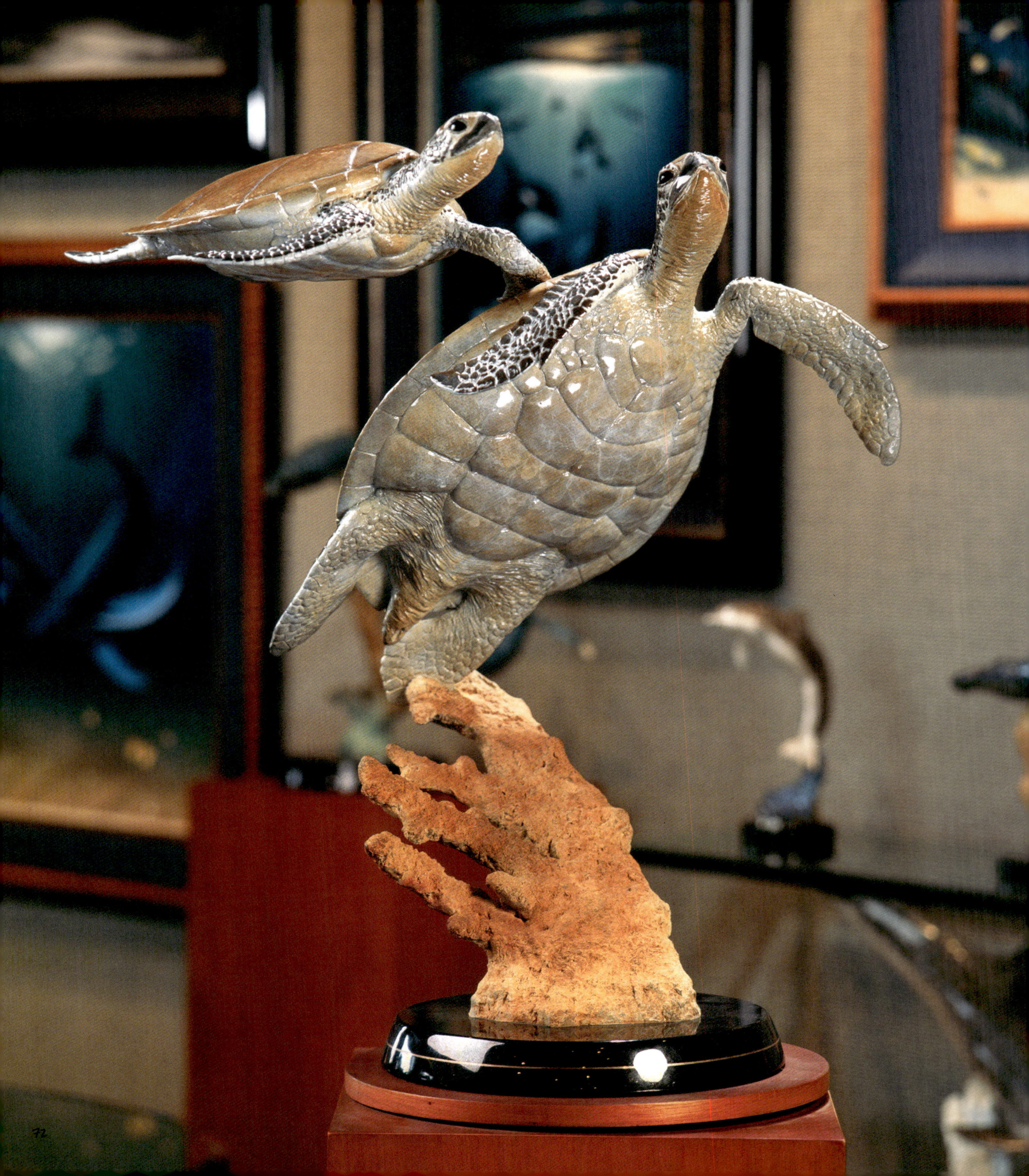

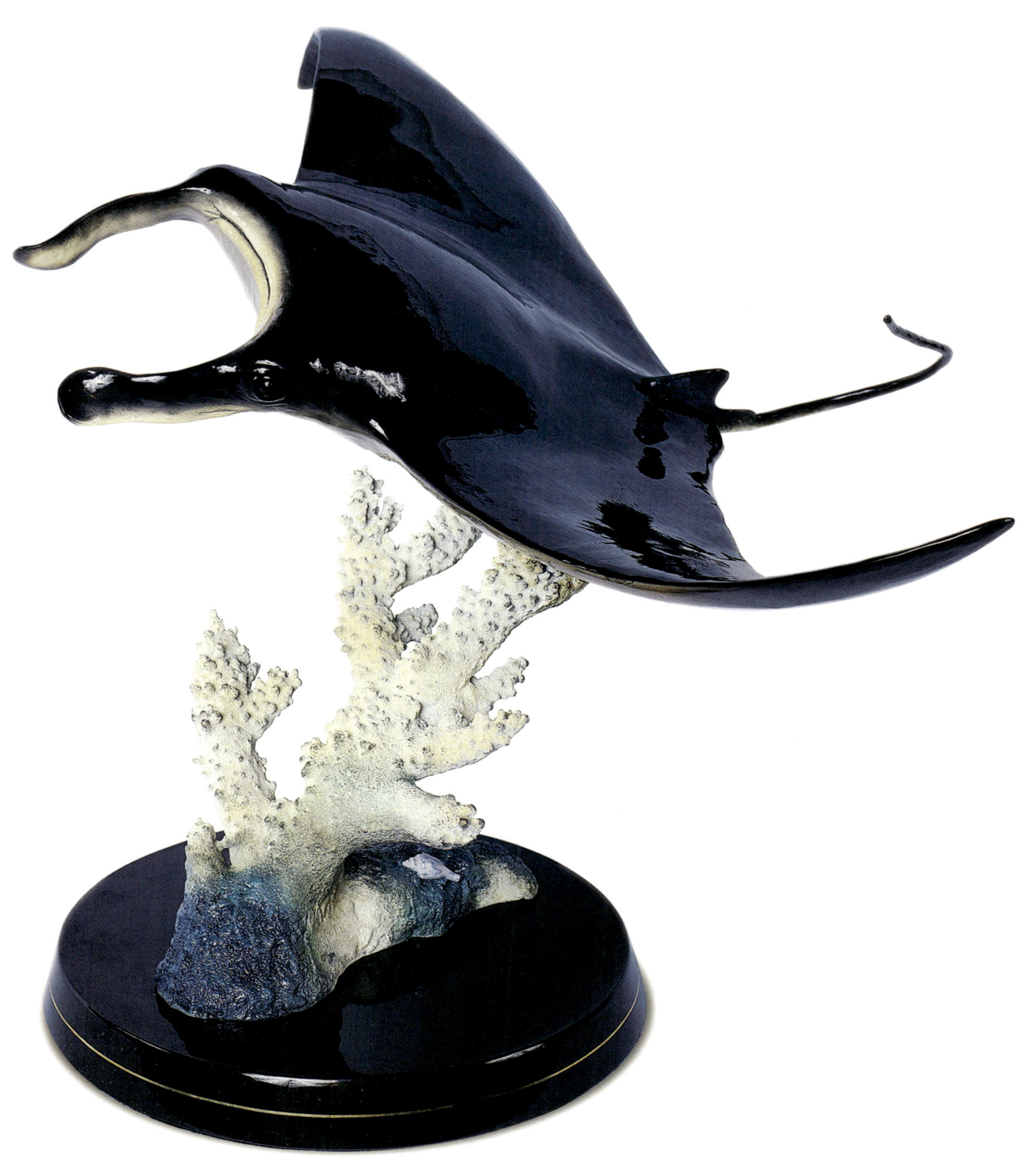

LUCITE SCULPTURE

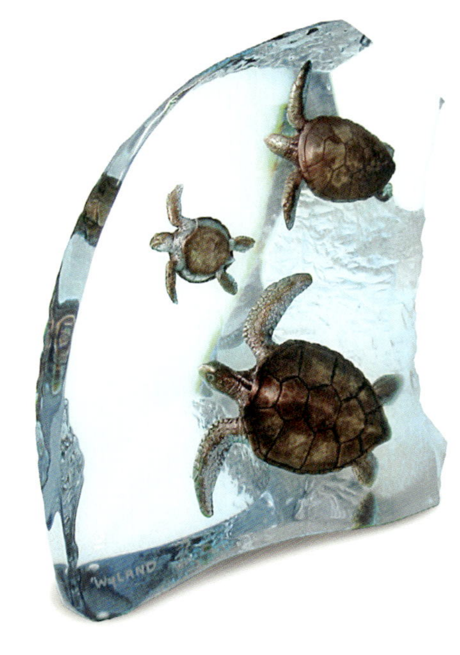

...If there ever was a perfect medium for Wyland's sculpture, it is Lucite, an underwater world suspended in time...

Wyland's sculptures in Lucite have **a luminous inner light that bathes the water elements and reflects the marine-life sculptures embedded within.** When it all comes together, the viewer becomes immersed in fine art sculpture that awakens the senses and invites the imagination.

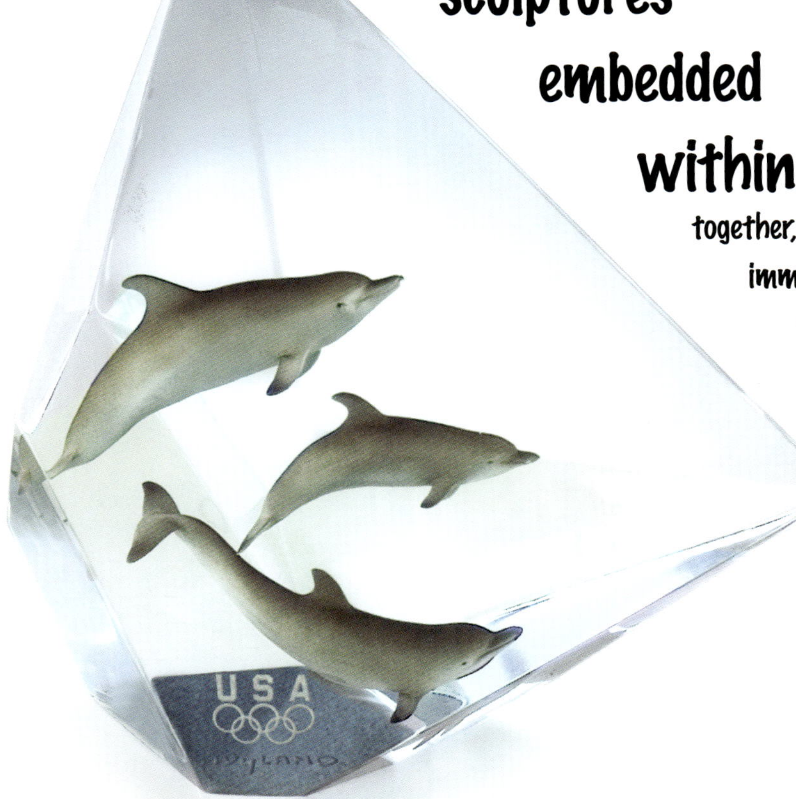

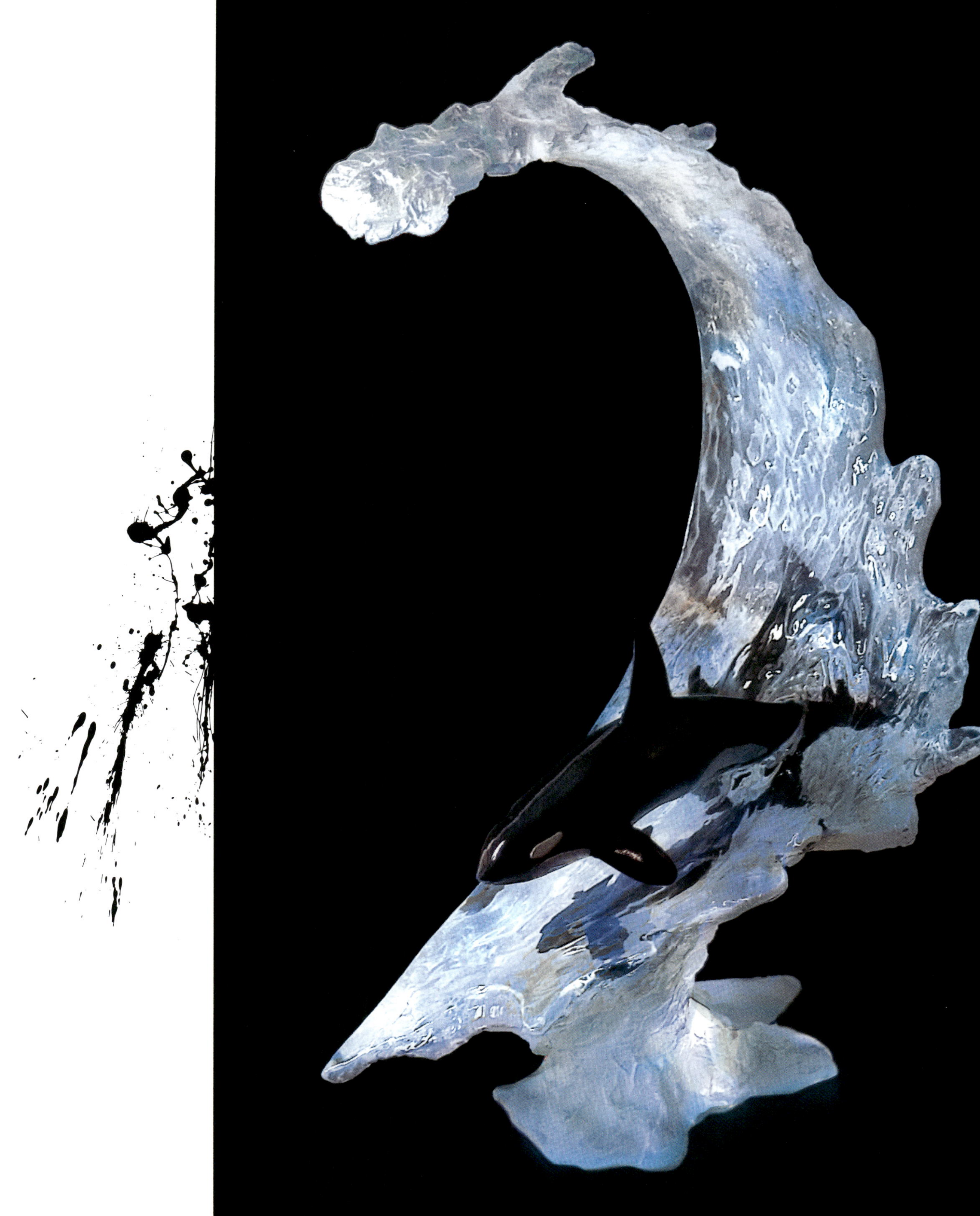

Faster, Higher, Stronger

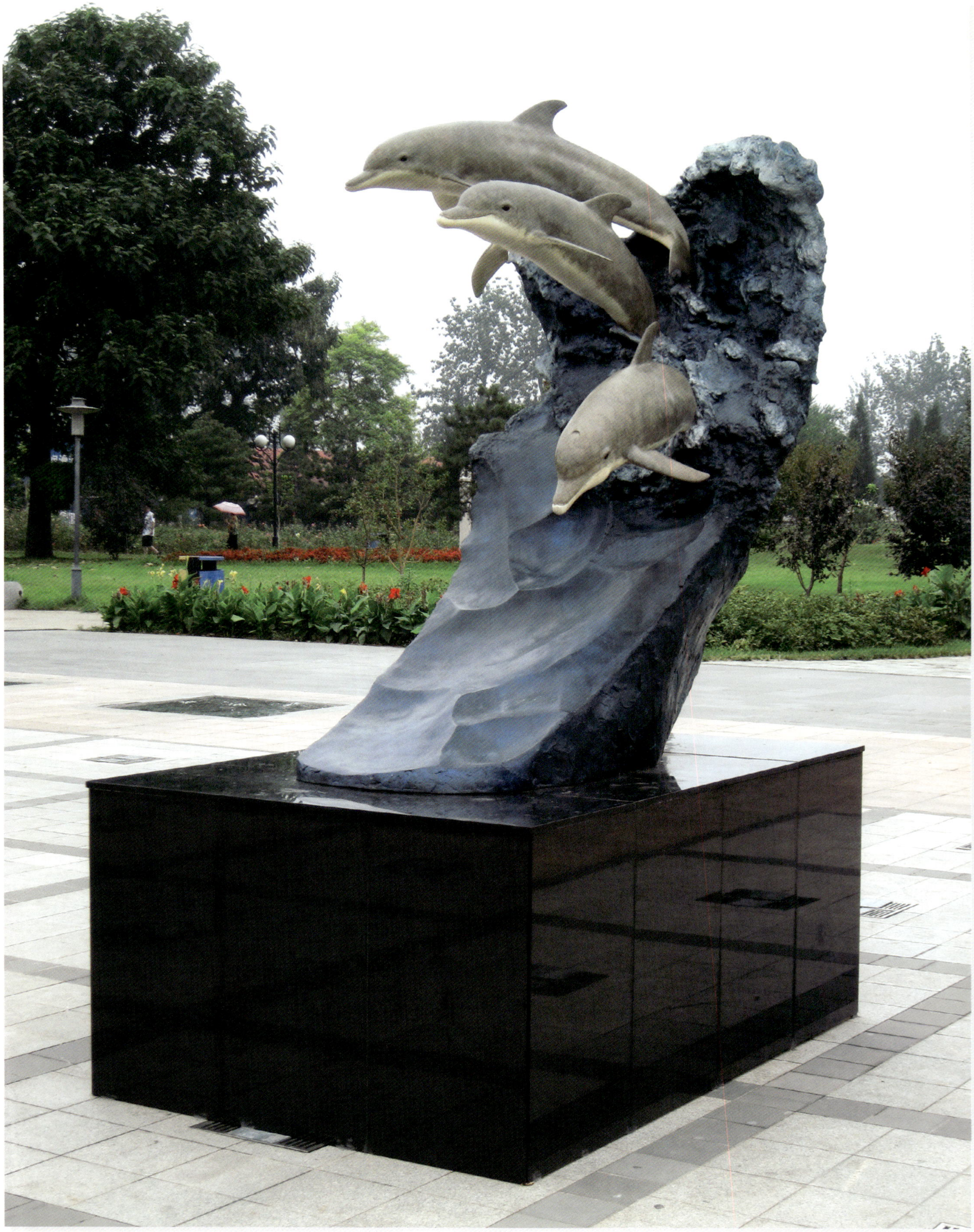

Monumental Sculpture Number One, Beijing, China

MONUMENTAL ART

"...In the next twenty-five years I am planning one hundred larger-than-life sculptures with water elements..."

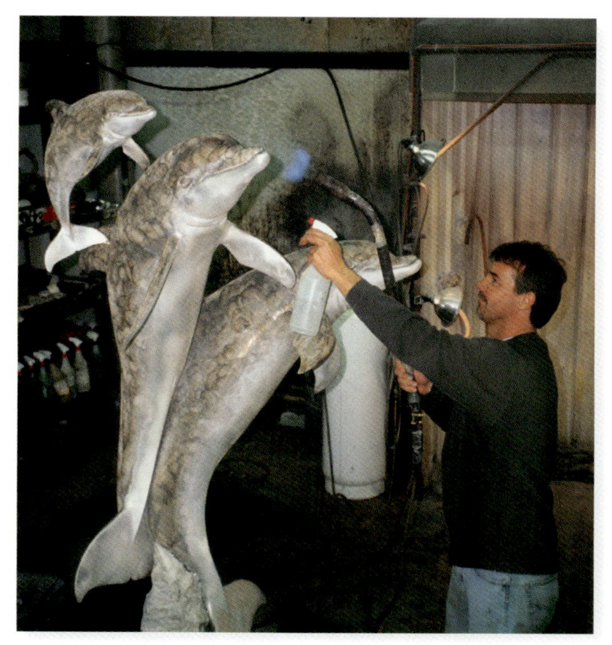

After completing his one hundred Whaling Walls, Wyland is focused on **creating monumental sculptures of great whales and other aquatic animals in bronze, Lucite, and other mediums with water feature elements for one hundred official designated cities throughout the world.** "Some of the sculptures will be life size," Wyland says. "Others will be larger than life. Again, the idea is using public art to create awareness and an emotional bond with the marine animals and conservation."

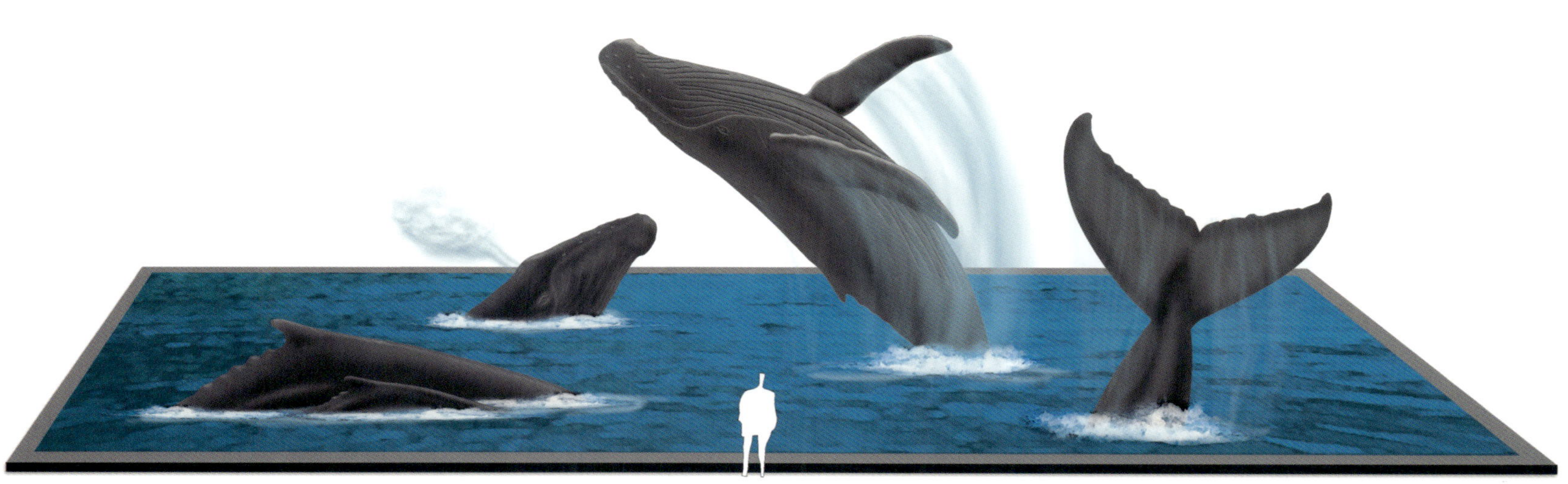

"WYLAND IS A MARINE-LIFE MICHELANGELO" – USA TODAY

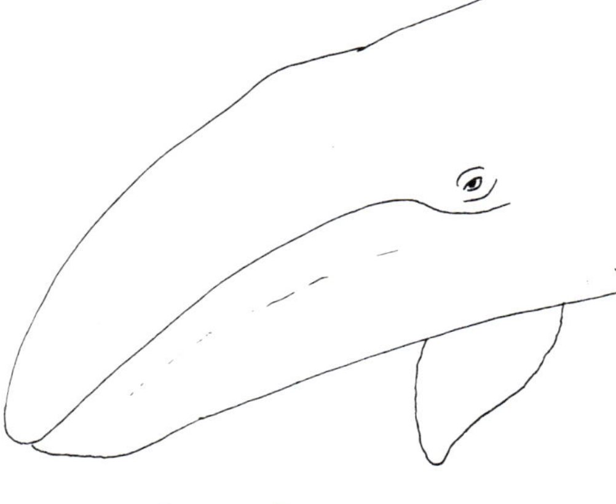

When Wyland saw his first whales during a family vacation to Laguna Beach, he knew he'd arrived at the place of his dreams.

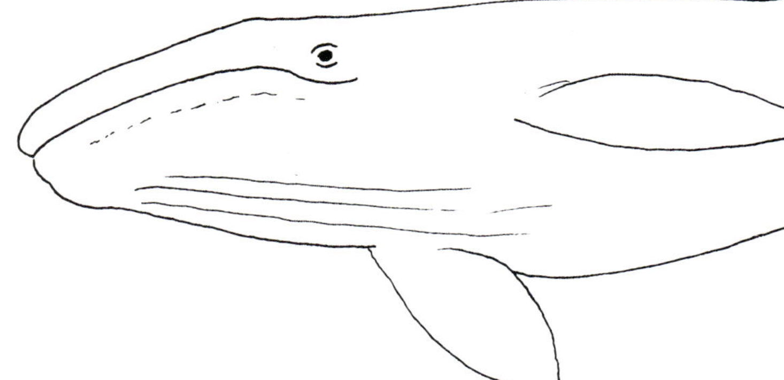

Gray Whale (*Eschrichtius robustus*)

Average Adult Length:	49 ft
Average Adult Weight:	80,000 lbs
Average Length at Birth:	16 ft
Average Weight at Birth:	1,500 lbs

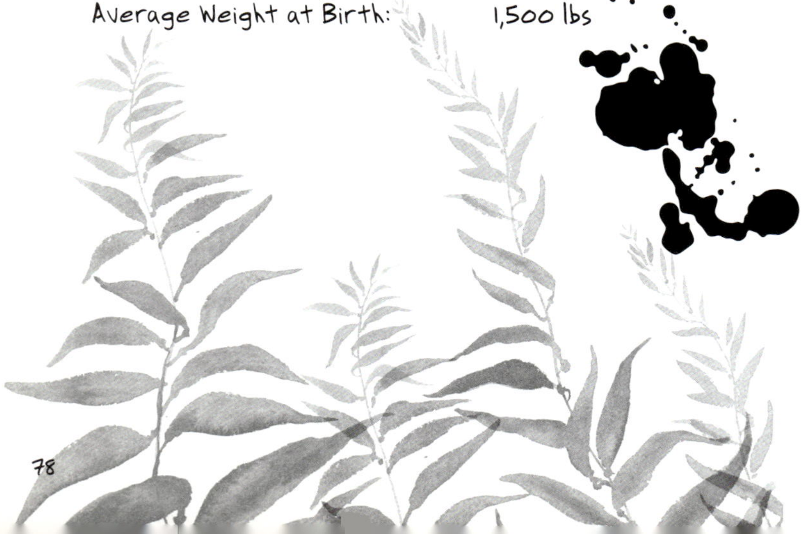

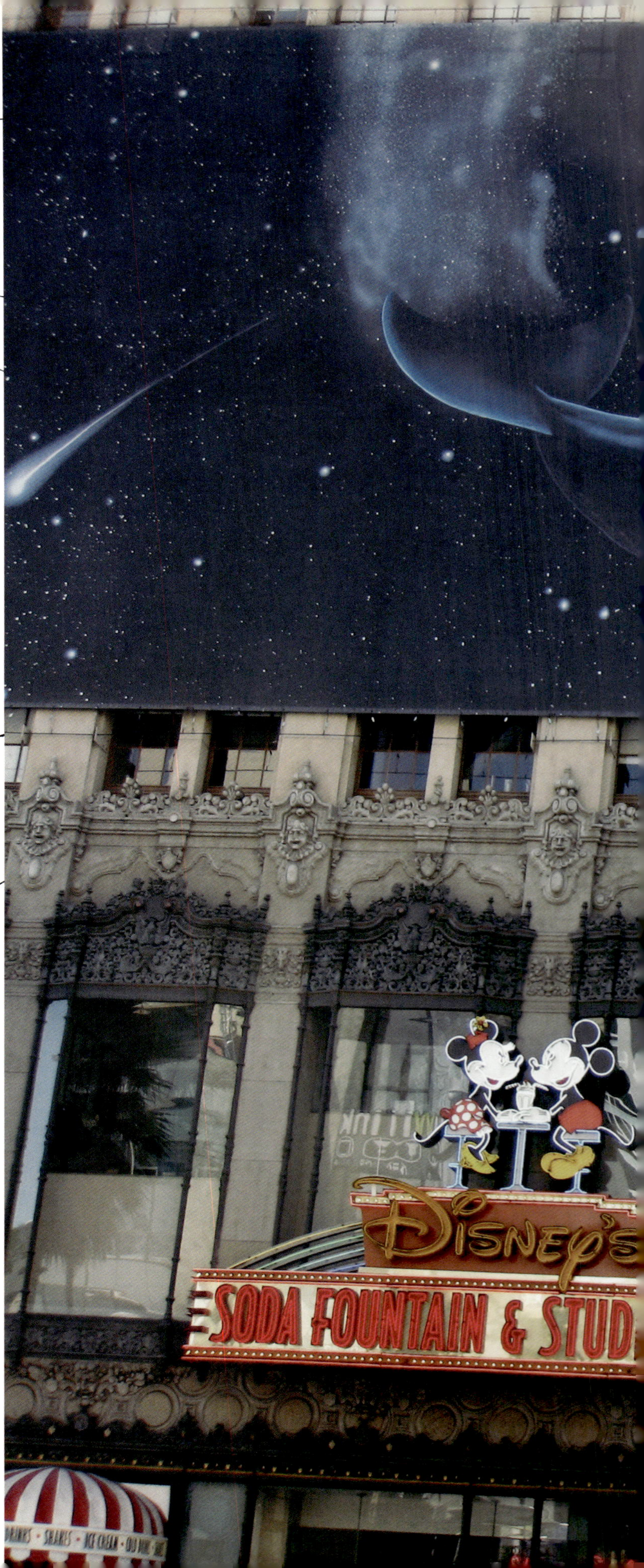

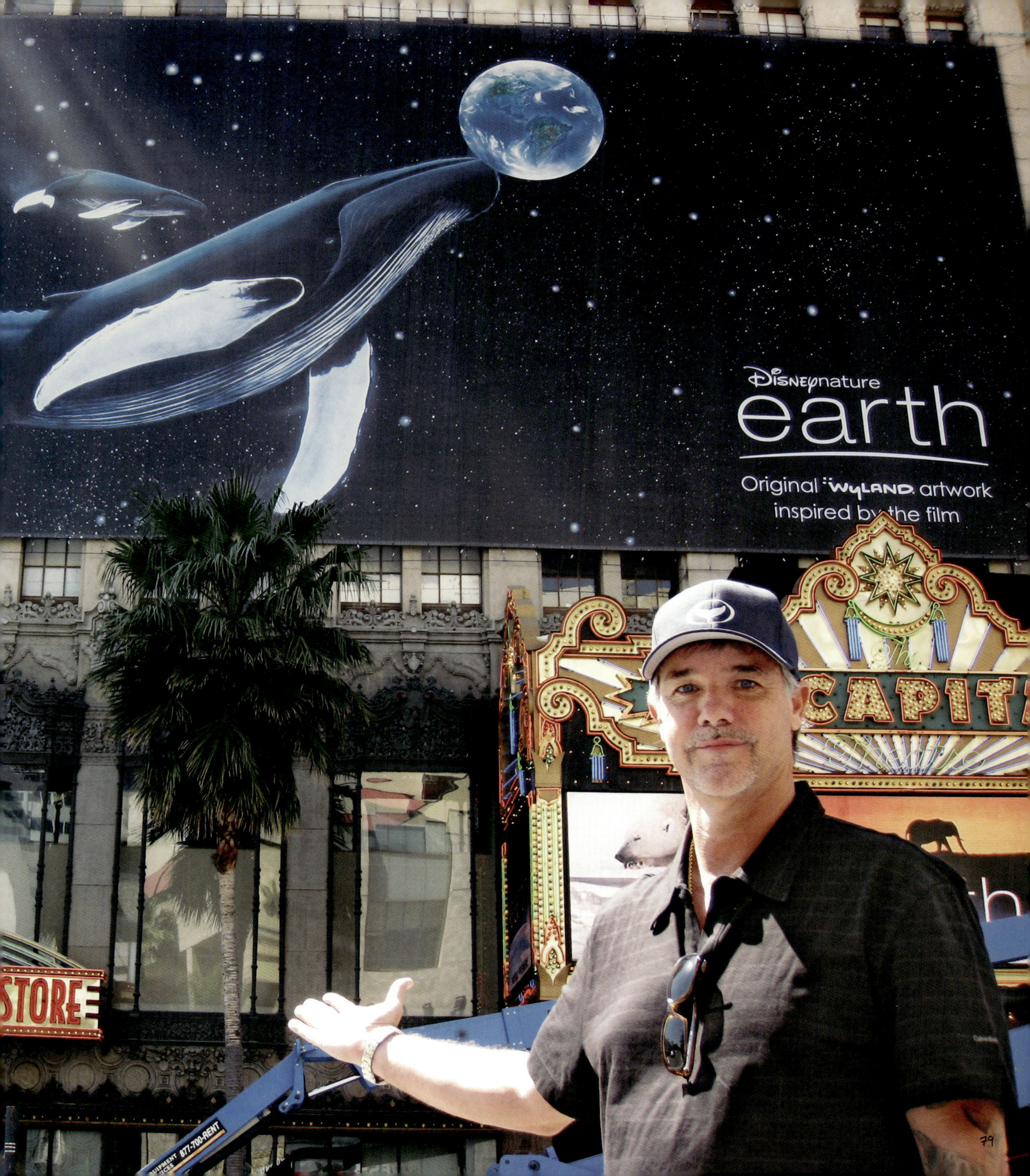
Disneynature
earth
Original Wyland artwork
inspired by the film
STORE
877-700-RENT

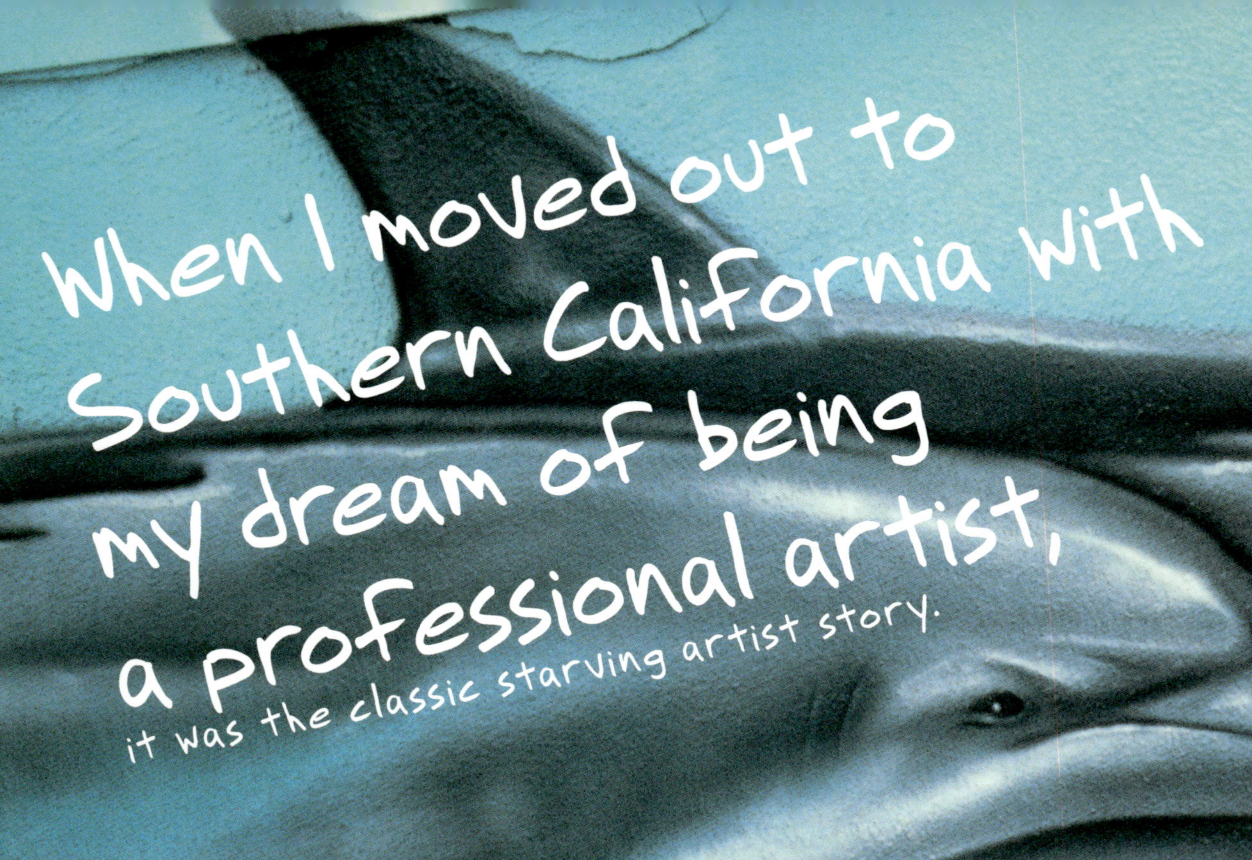

When I moved out to Southern California with my dream of being a professional artist,

it was the classic starving artist story.

The marine-life art I was creating in the 70's was not exactly popular at first, but as the environmental movement grew with organizations like Greenpeace and the Cousteau Society, so did public appreciation for my work. I remember doing small art shows and finally was accepted into the Sawdust Festival, a popular summerlong art exhibition in Laguna Beach, California. I used to paint live at the show, swapping stories with people who became early collectors. I did that show for thirteen years, and every year the demand for my art grew. Eventually, I decided to open a studio gallery where I could create new art and showcase it in a gallery setting. That was back in 1978. Today, there are more than 20 Wyland Galleries throughout the United States that feature my paintings and sculptures as well as works by other renowned artists.

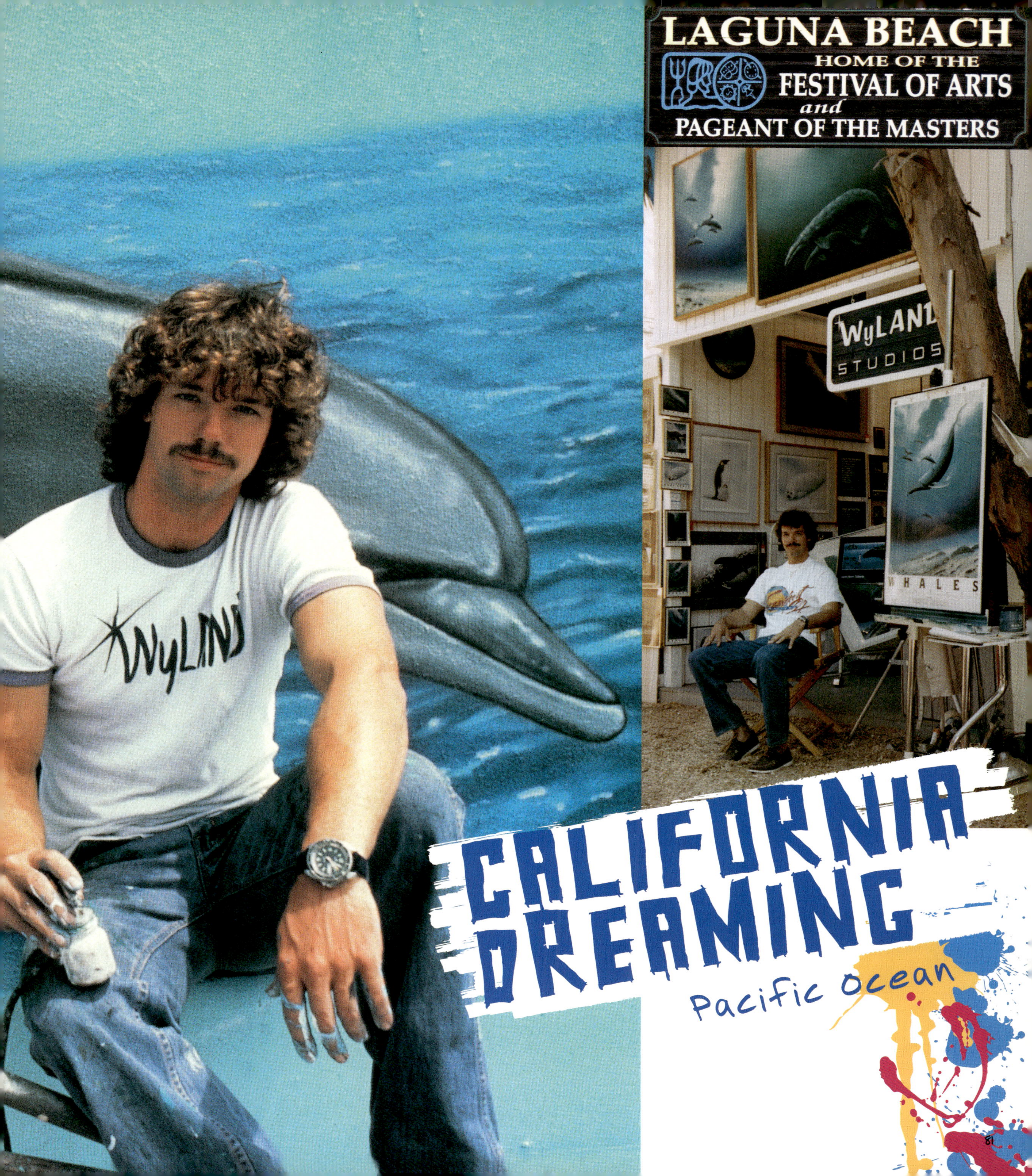

CALIFORNIA DREAMING

Pacific Ocean

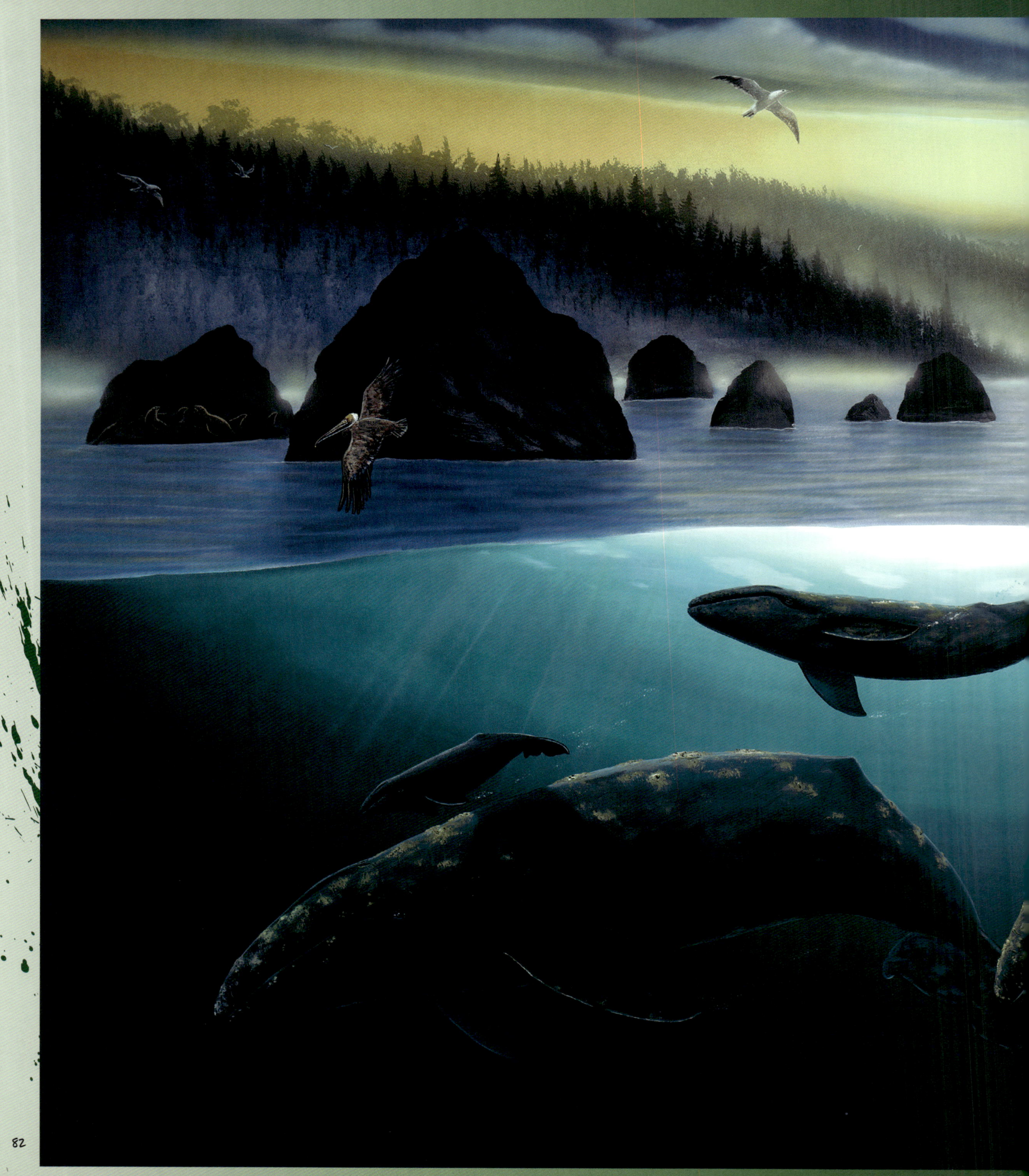

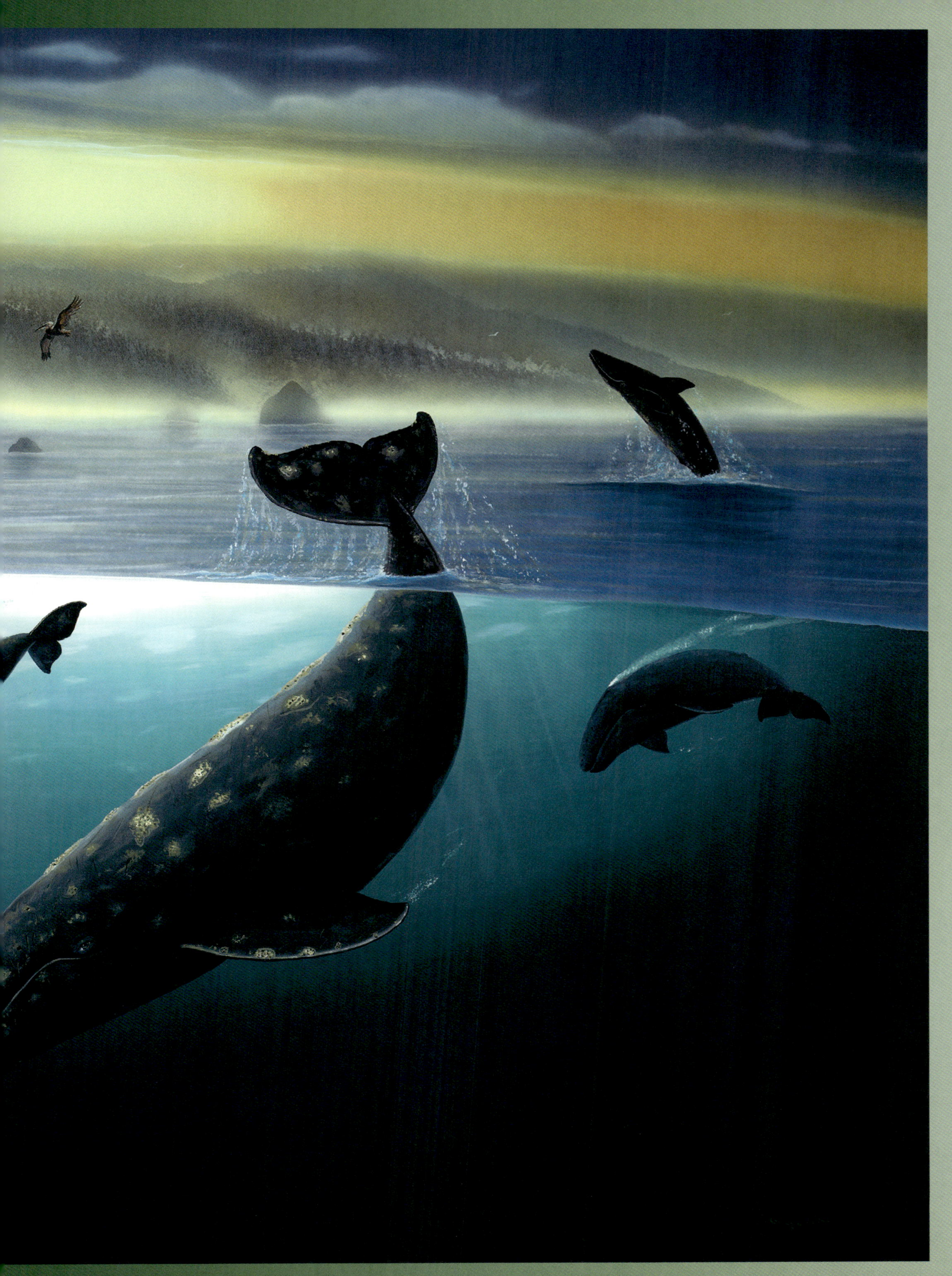

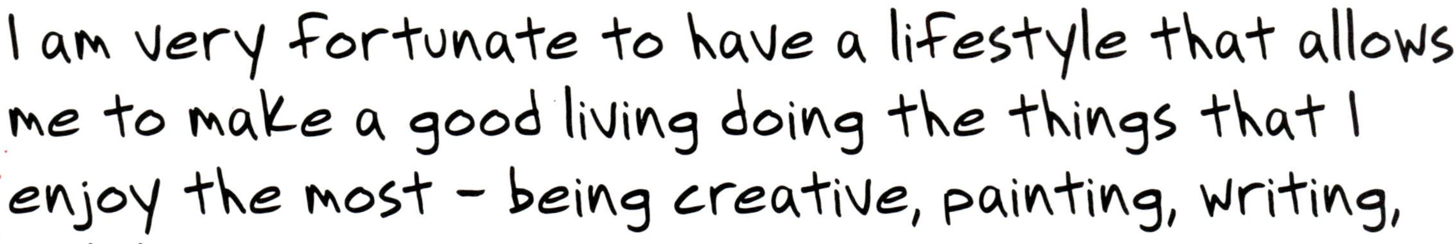

I am very fortunate to have a lifestyle that allows me to make a good living doing the things that I enjoy the most - being creative, painting, writing, and diving. I tell the young artists that it's okay to make a good living at your craft. When I grew up, it was taboo to even consider being a successful artist. But I never really liked the Bohemian starving-artist title. It didn't make sense that a basketball player could earn millions of dollars, while artists had to starve to death. I tell young artists that I don't mind taking the bullets from the art critics for being successful. Hopefully, a number of artists and I will break new ground, and it will be okay for an artist to have financial success AND live his or her dream.

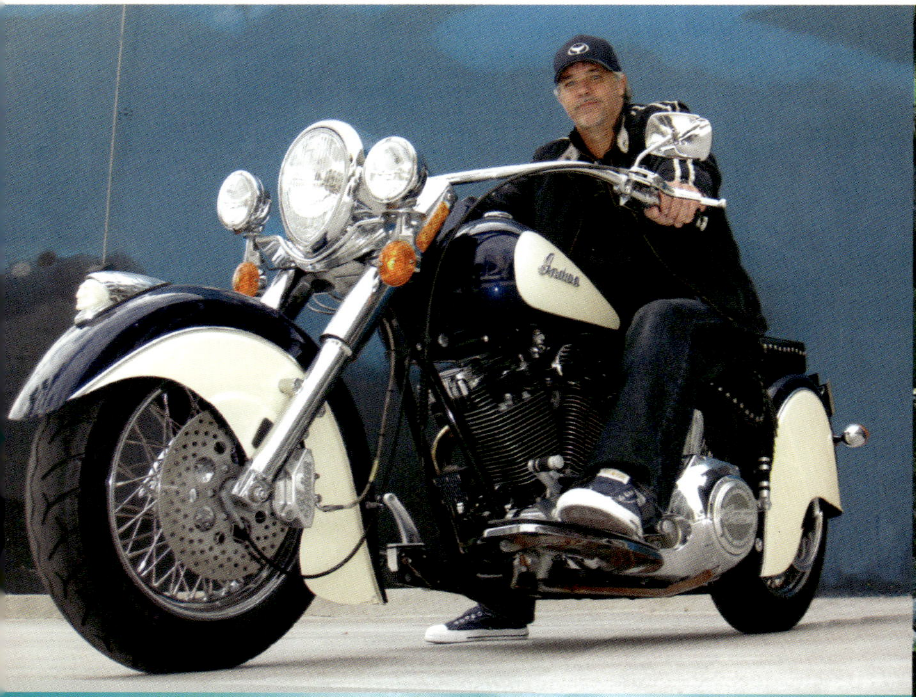

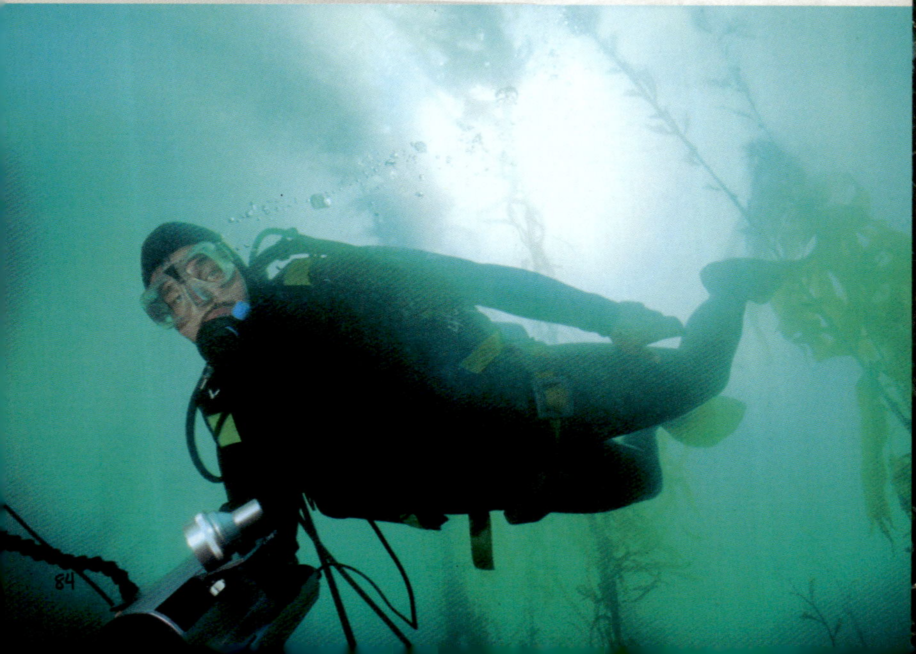

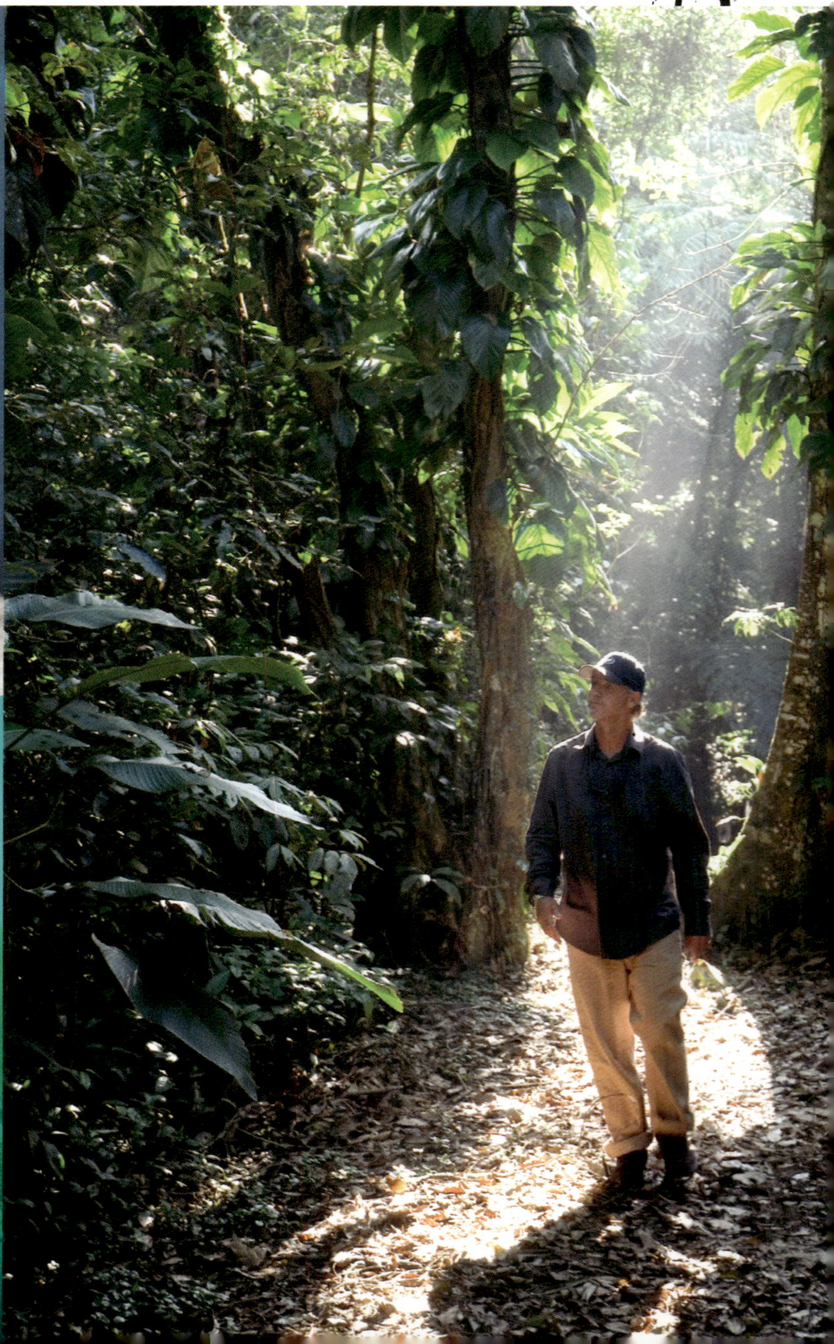

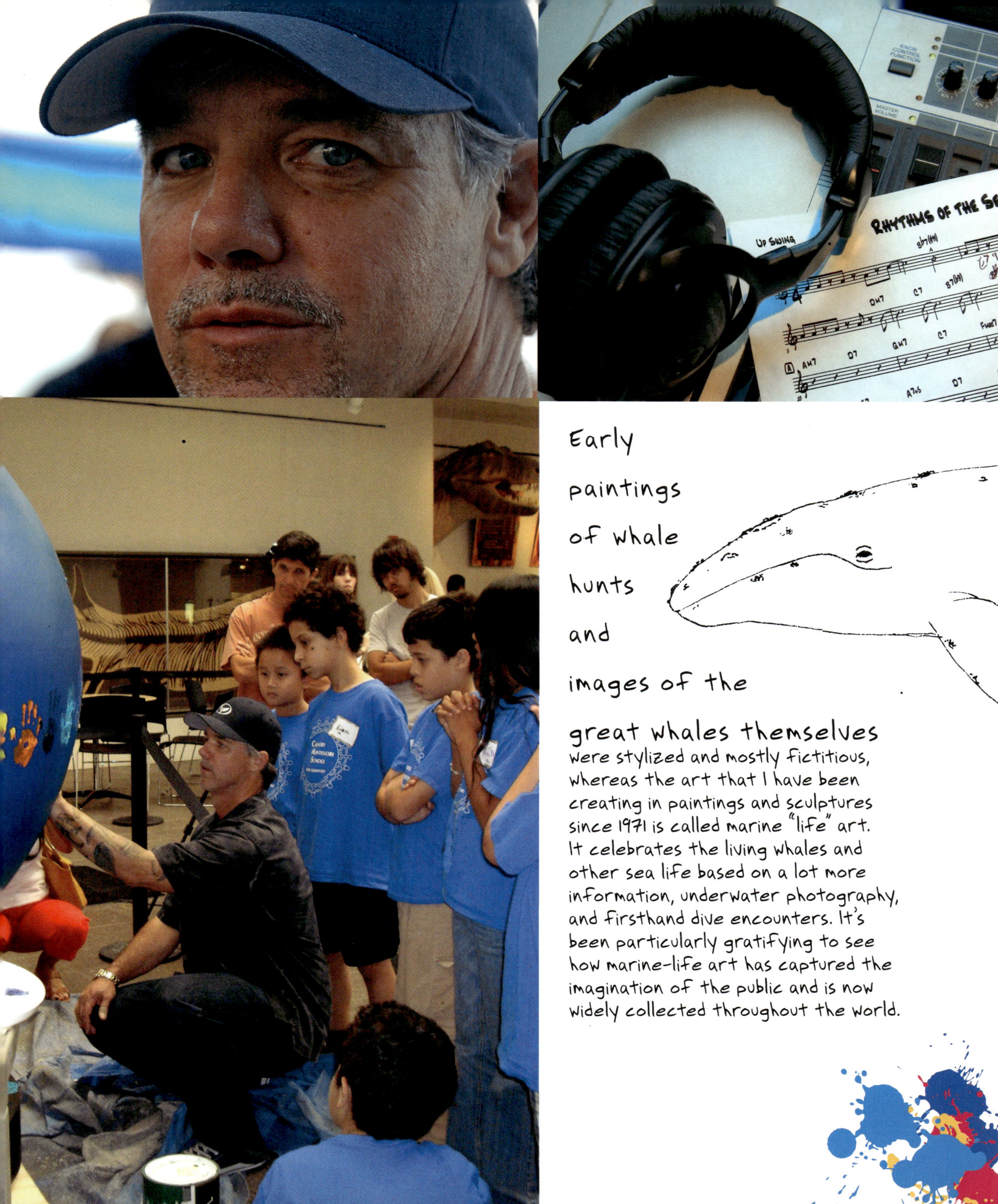

Early

paintings

of whale

hunts

and

images of the

great whales themselves were stylized and mostly fictitious, whereas the art that I have been creating in paintings and sculptures since 1971 is called marine "life" art. It celebrates the living whales and other sea life based on a lot more information, underwater photography, and firsthand dive encounters. It's been particularly gratifying to see how marine-life art has captured the imagination of the public and is now widely collected throughout the world.

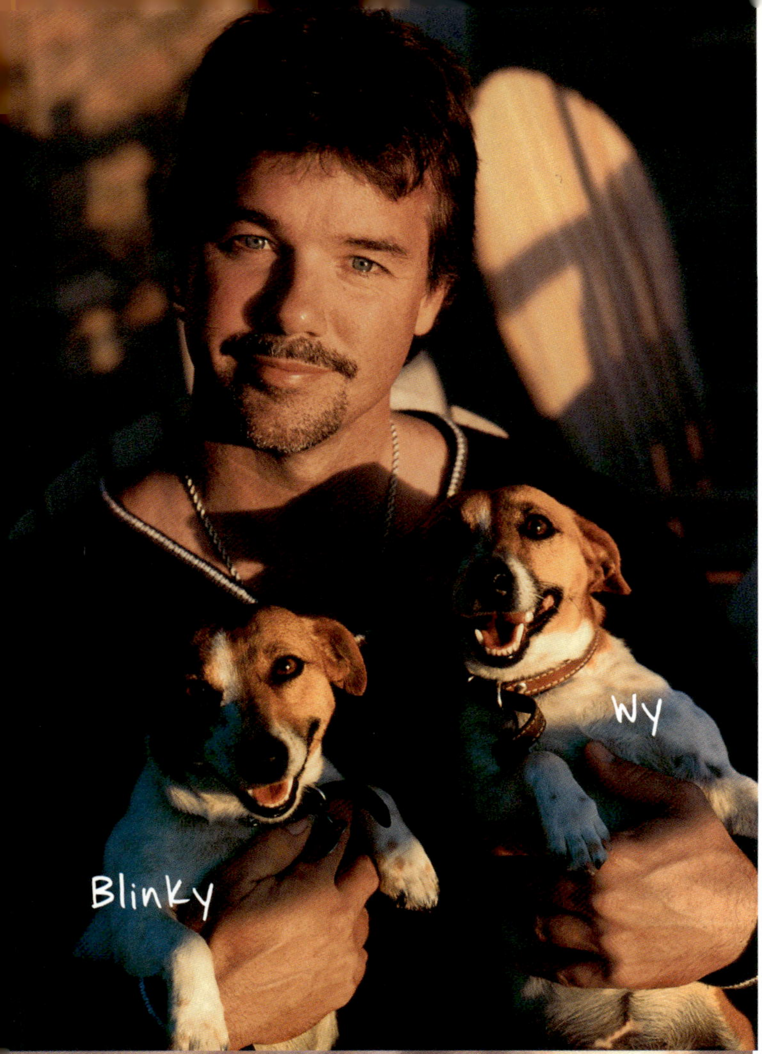

Wy

Blinky

Junior

Life

is a great

adventure

and it goes by

much more quickly

than most

of us

realize.

The only thing you can hope is to enjoy every moment and try to keep the balance by giving something back. I have been blessed with a great family, wonderful friends, and loyal supporters who continue to believe in my art and mission. I don't think you could ask for more than that.

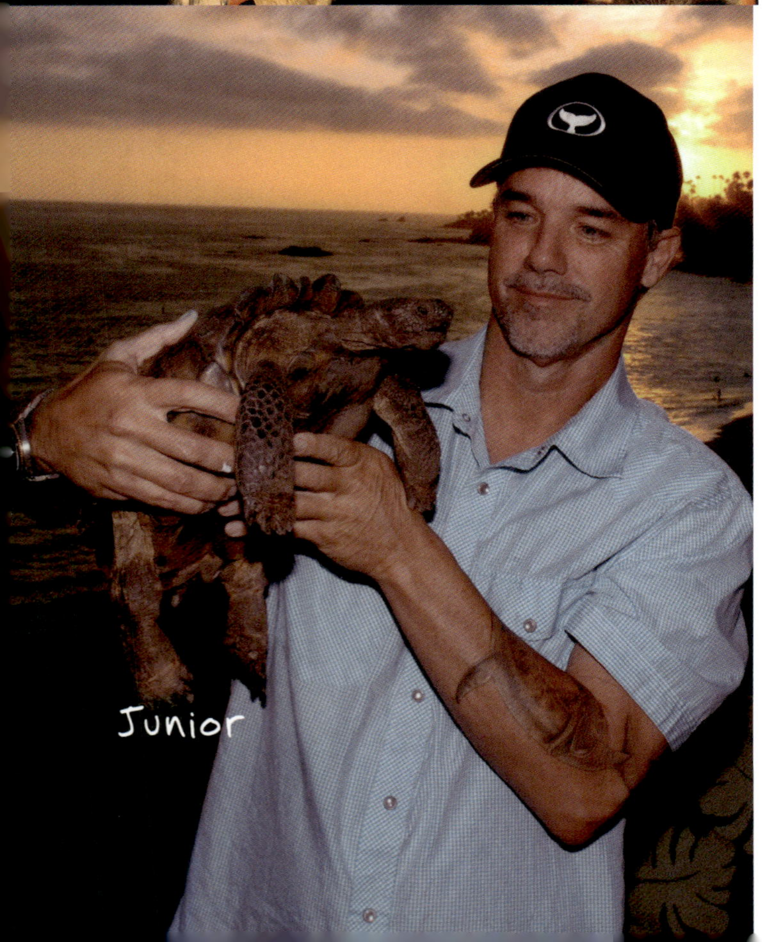

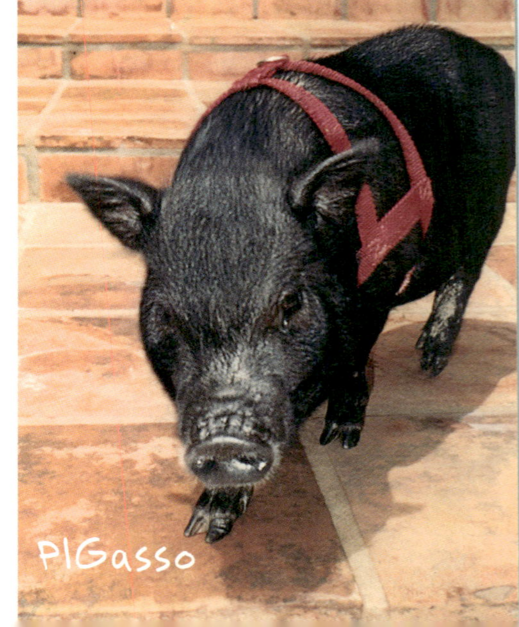

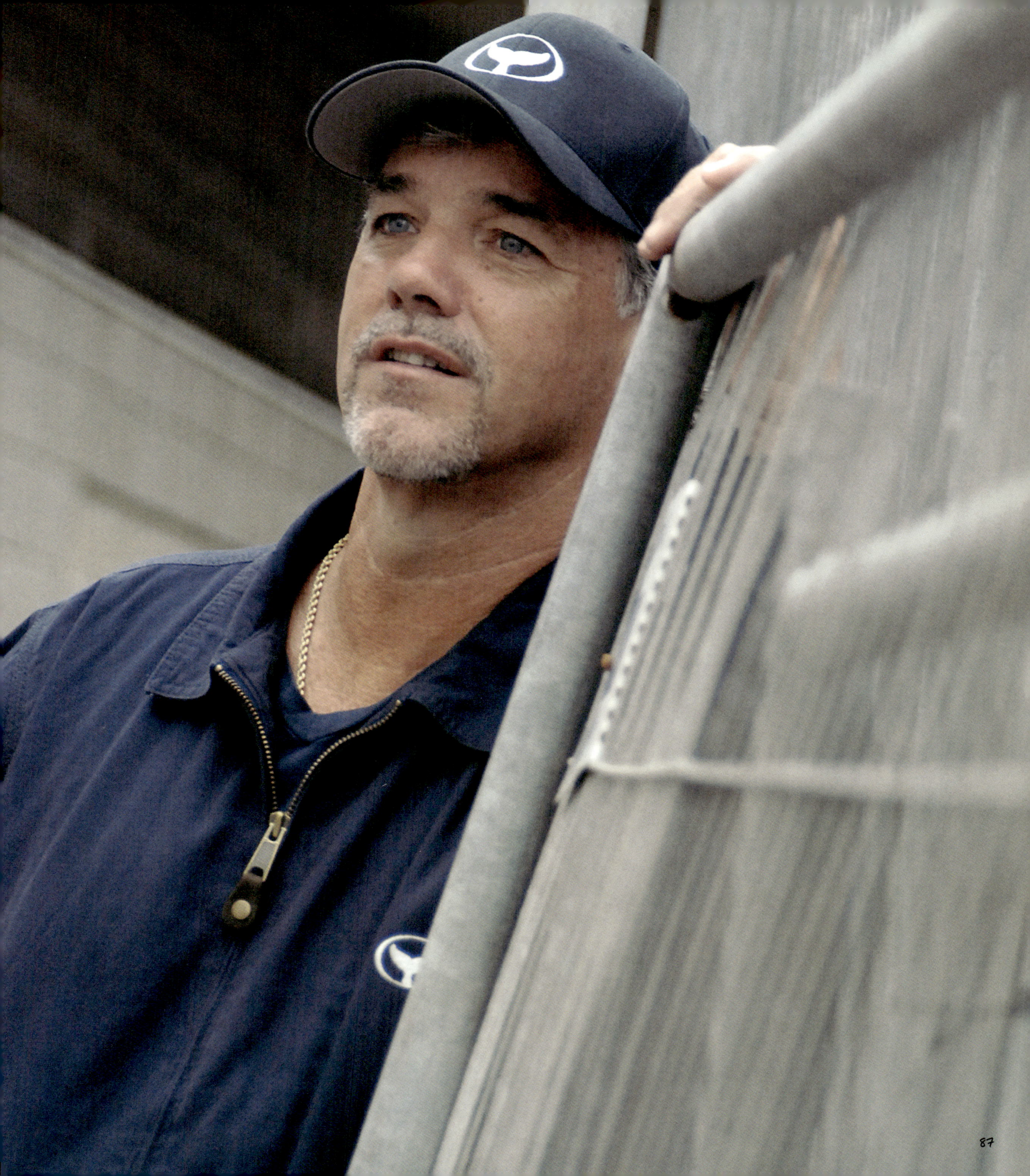

HAWAIIAN INSPIRATION

whales below

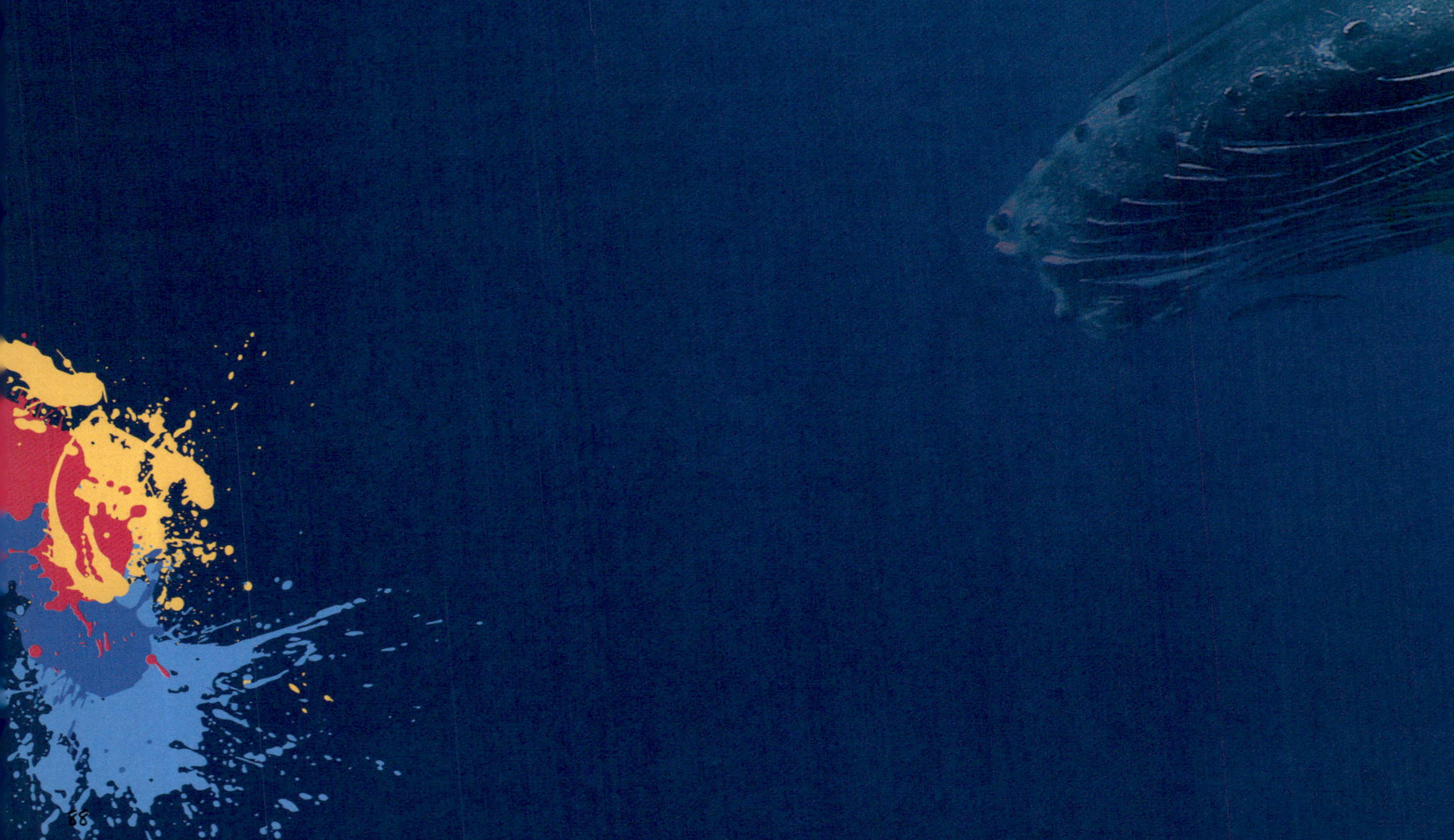

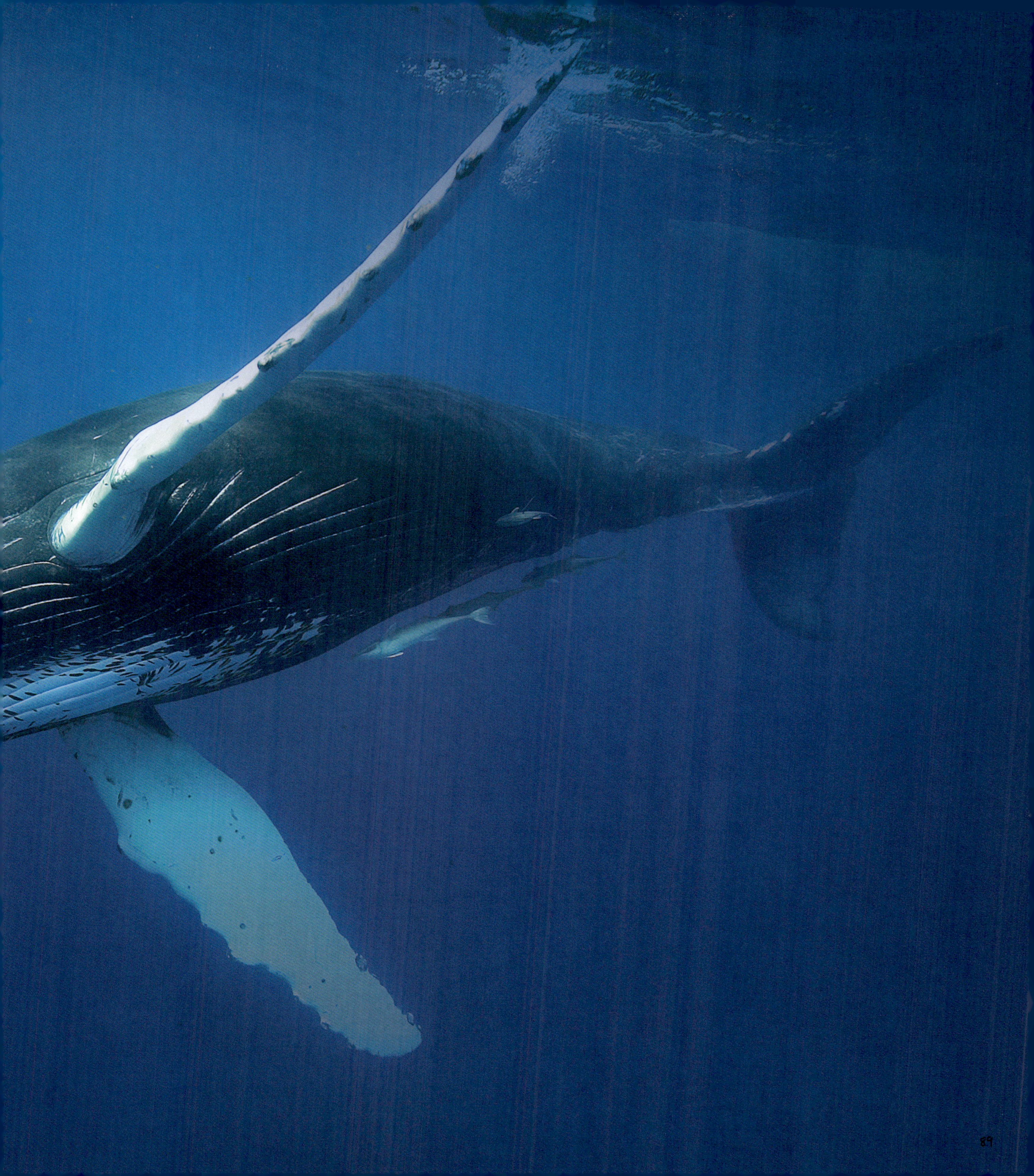

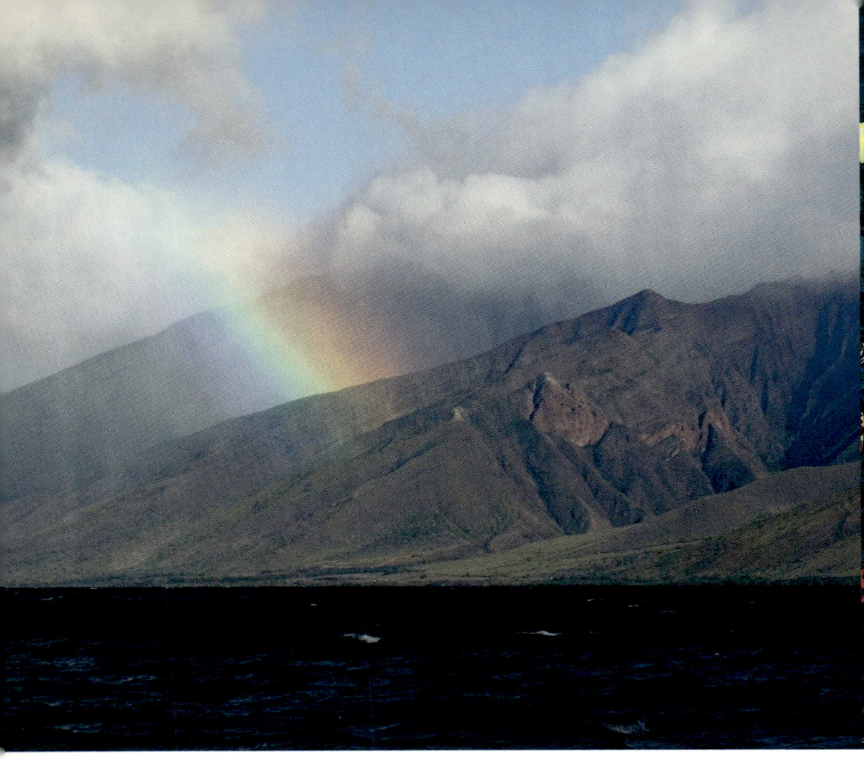

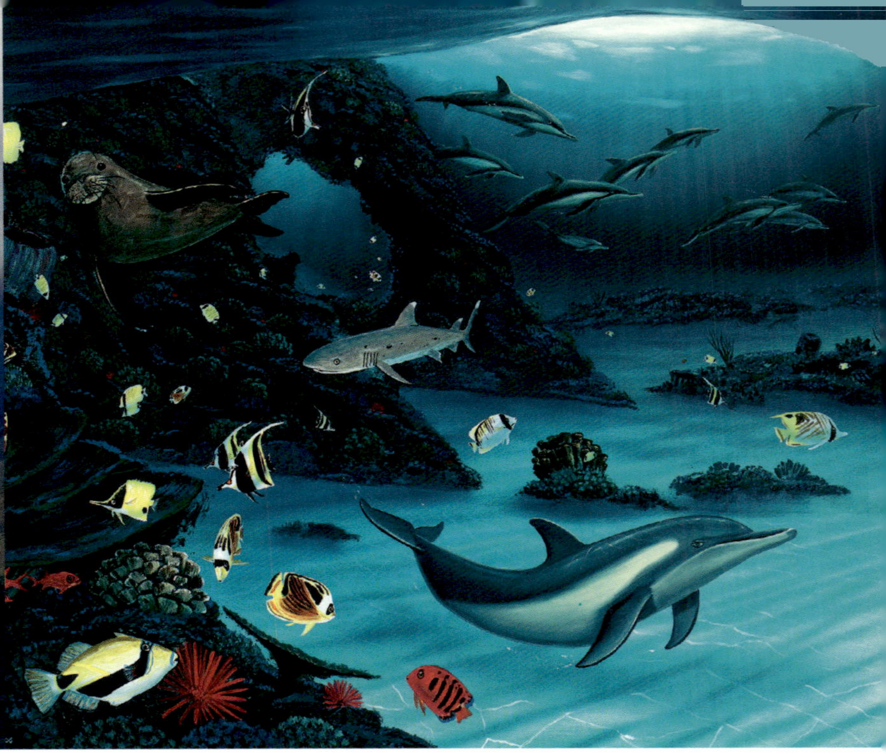

For the "man with no first name," protecting our ocean, lakes, rivers, and wetlands is pure passion.

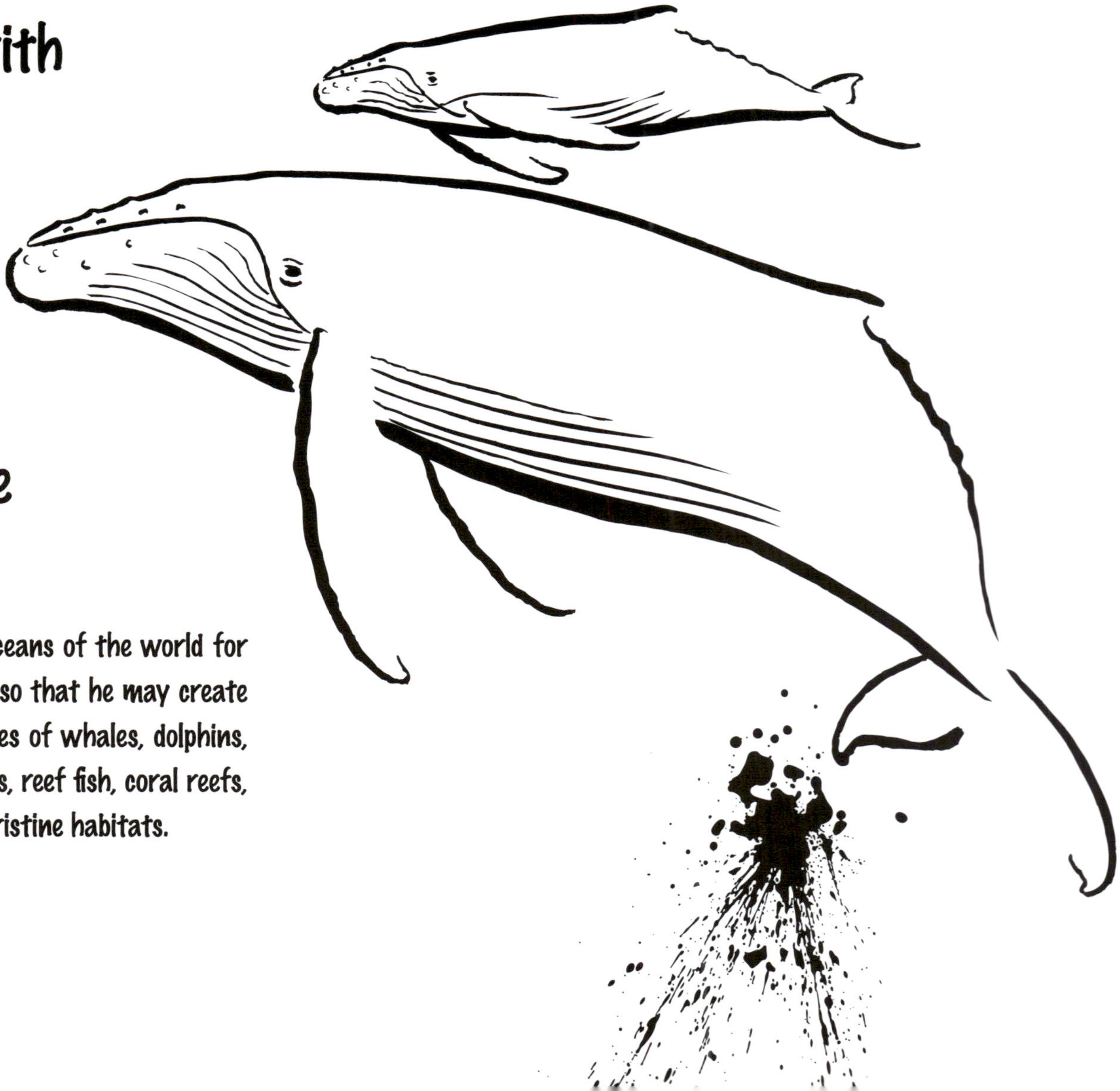

Wyland has been diving the oceans of the world for nearly a quarter of a century so that he may create realistic portrayals of all species of whales, dolphins, sharks, sea turtles, manta rays, reef fish, coral reefs, giant kelp forests, and other pristine habitats.

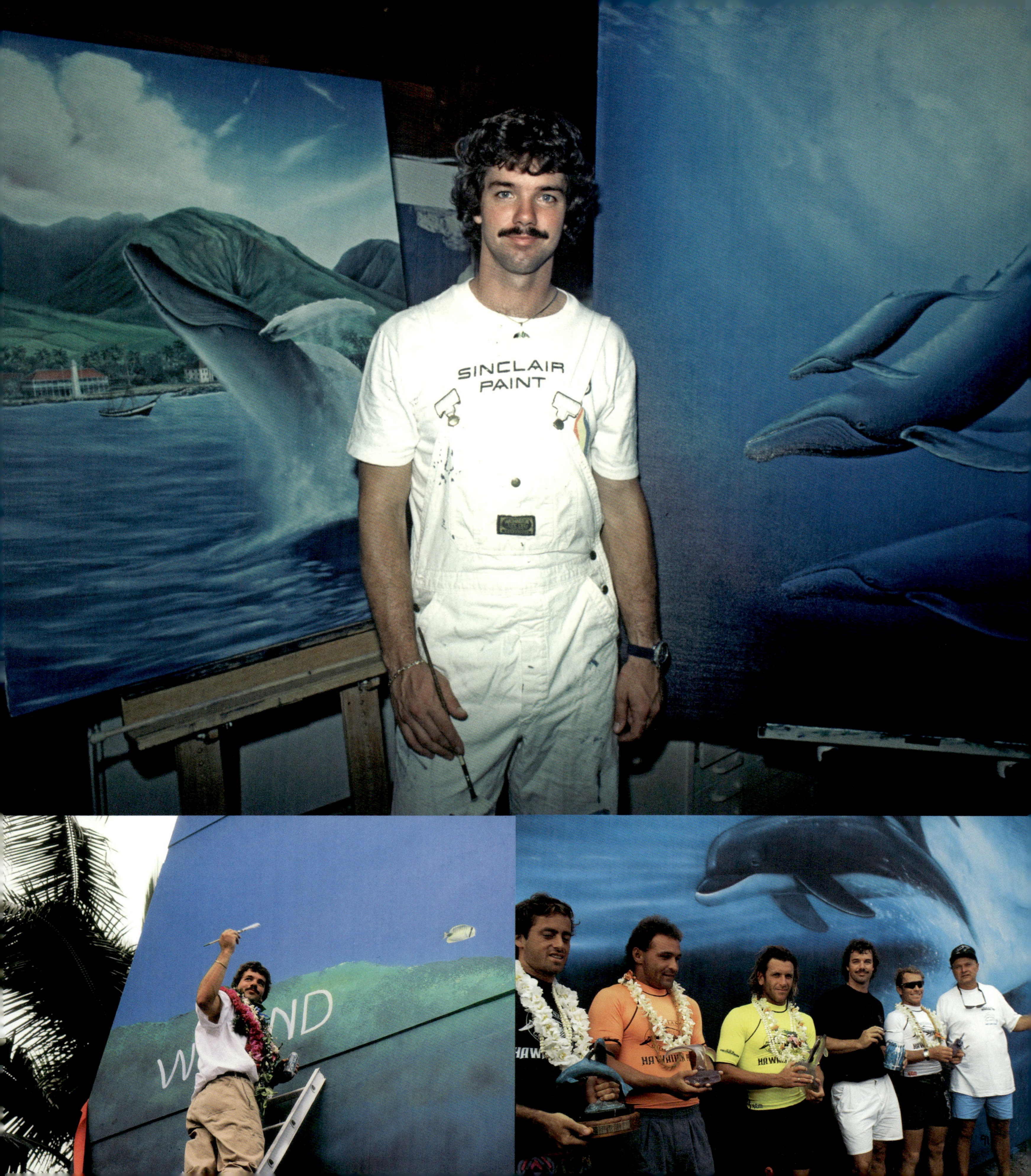
SINCLAIR
PAINT

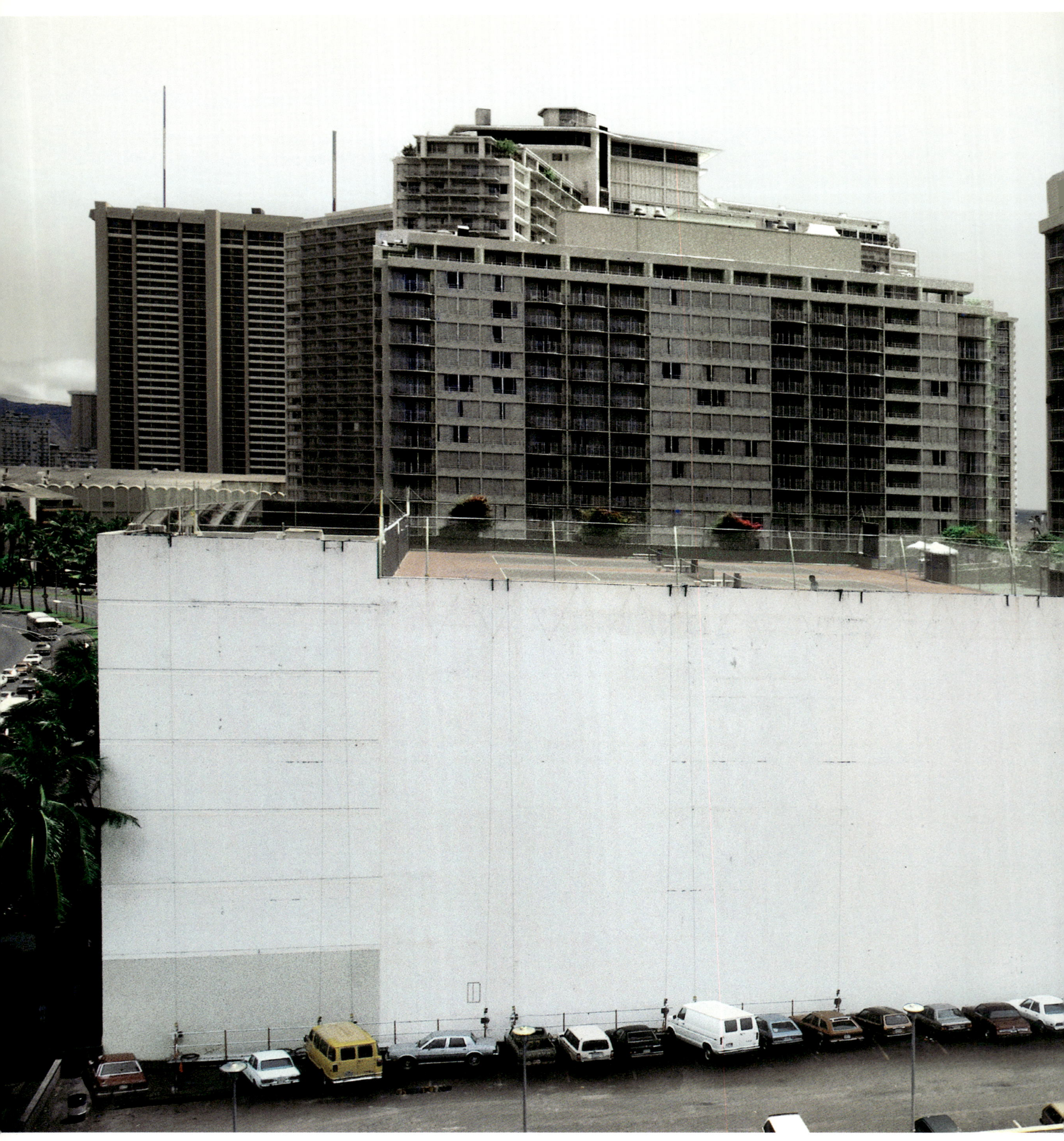

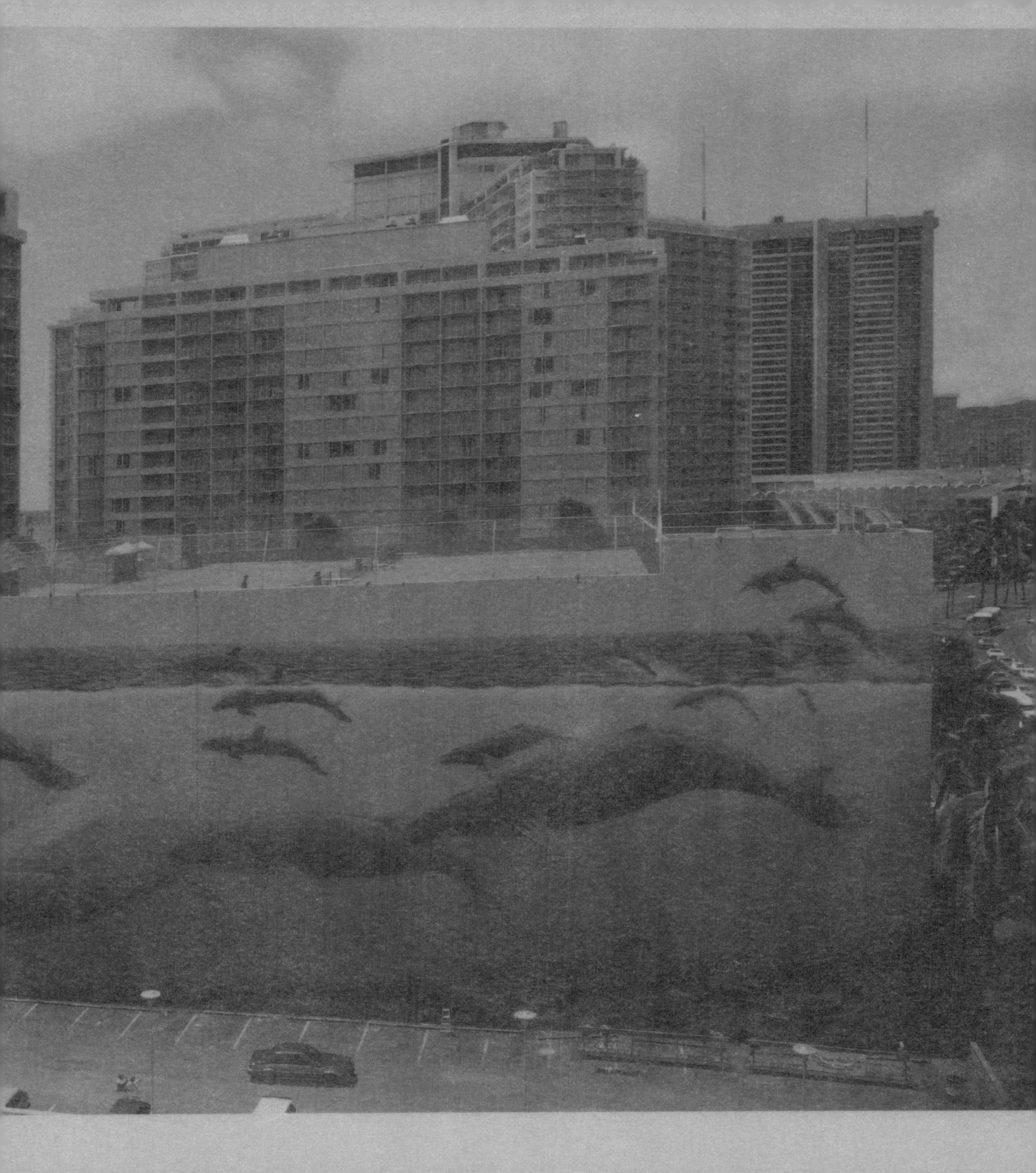

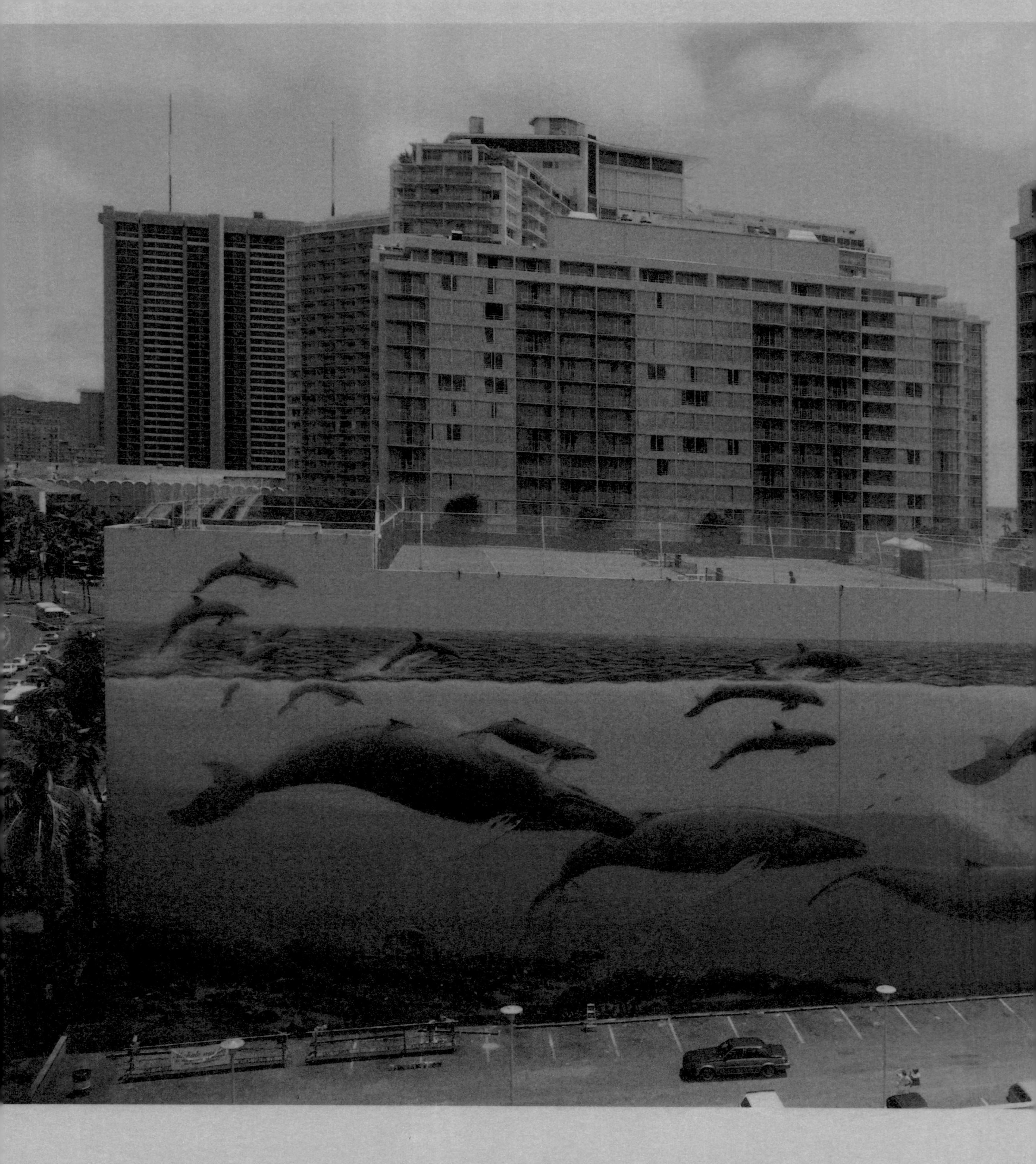

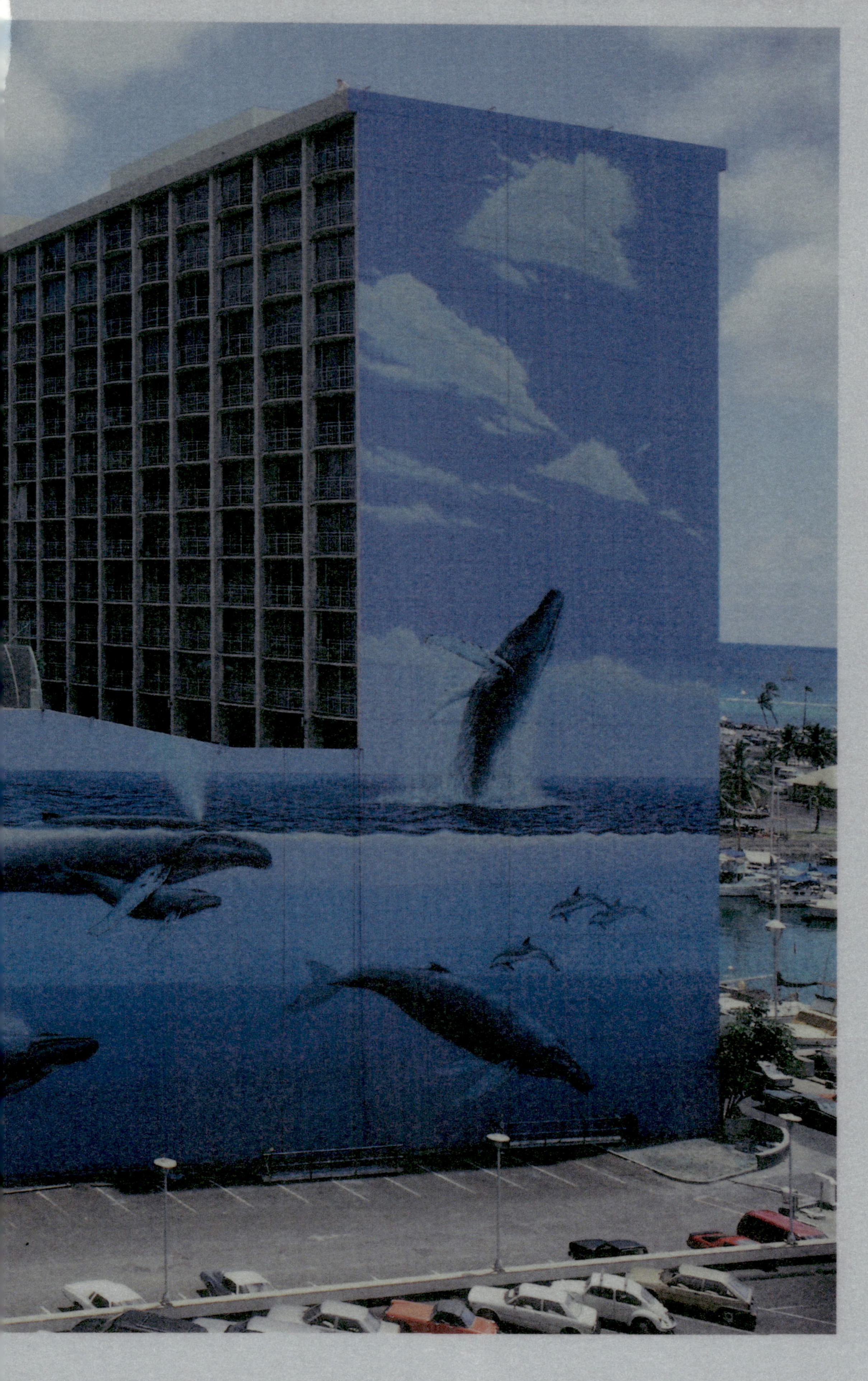

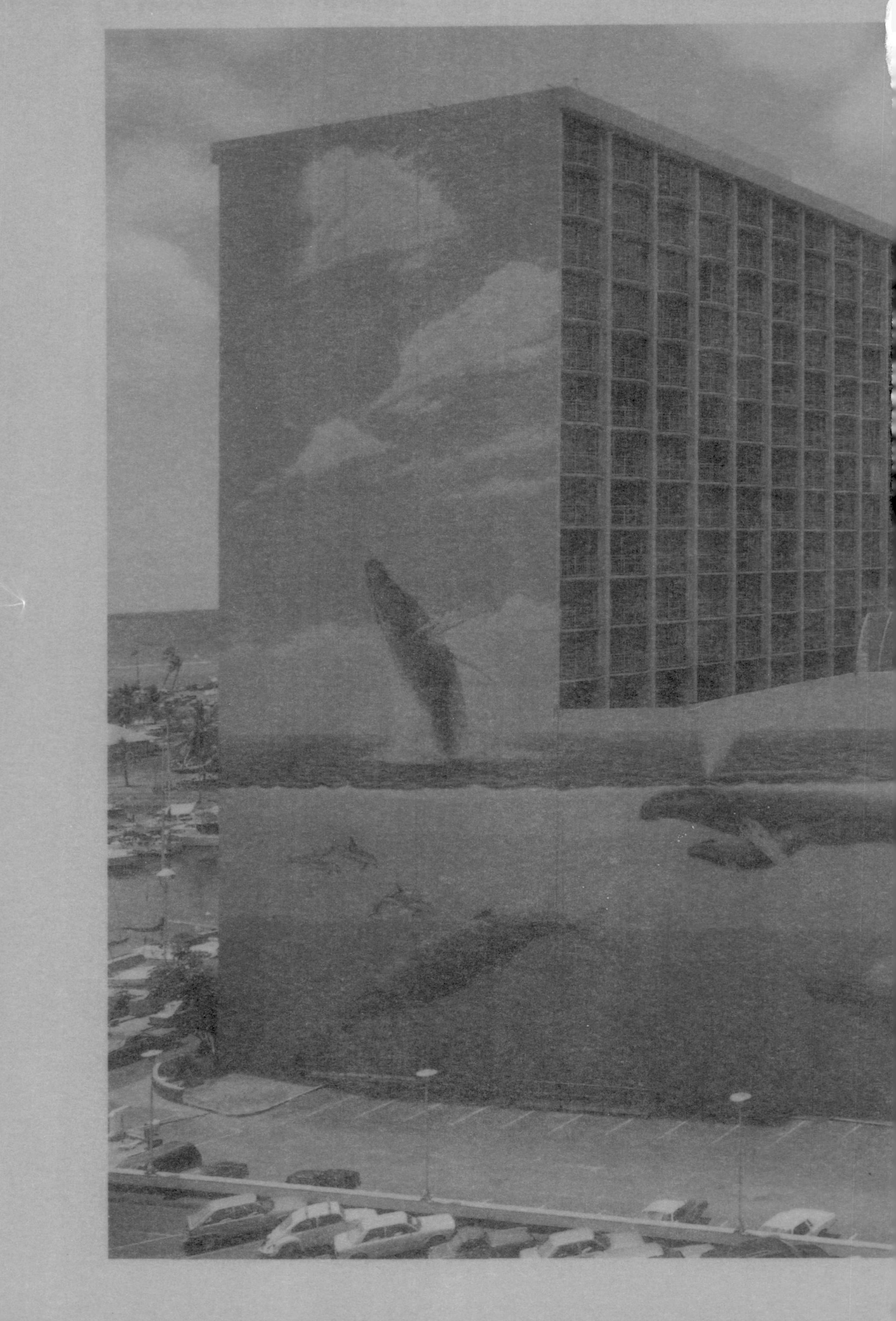

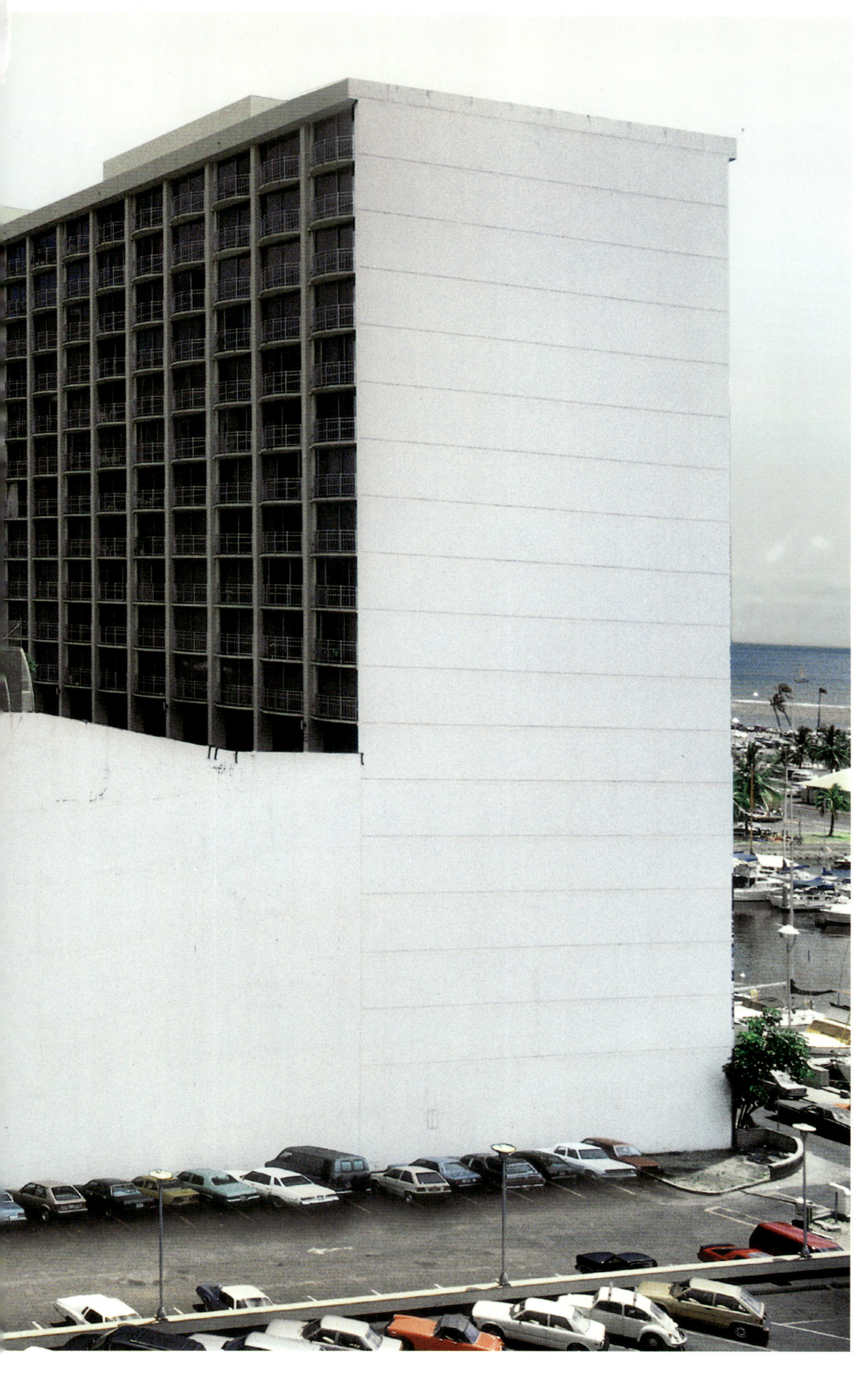

Wyland paints giant murals the way most artists paint small canvases.

He covers the entire wall with masses of paint and bands of colors that blend together to reveal the natural world. "I compare the way I paint murals to the development of a large Polaroid photograph," Wyland says. "Everything develops before your eyes. When the background is done, I simply imagine the marine life in the scene, and then I start painting it. I developed a style of painting and drawing with the same motion. First I ghost in the animals with light paint. When the proportions are correct, I add colors, then I paint in the details. Finally I add the highlights and shadows. When it's complete the wall or building disappears into the natural world. I don't use grids or even sketches," Wyland adds. "I paint primarily from what I see in my mind. What you end up seeing is drawn from years of diving and study."

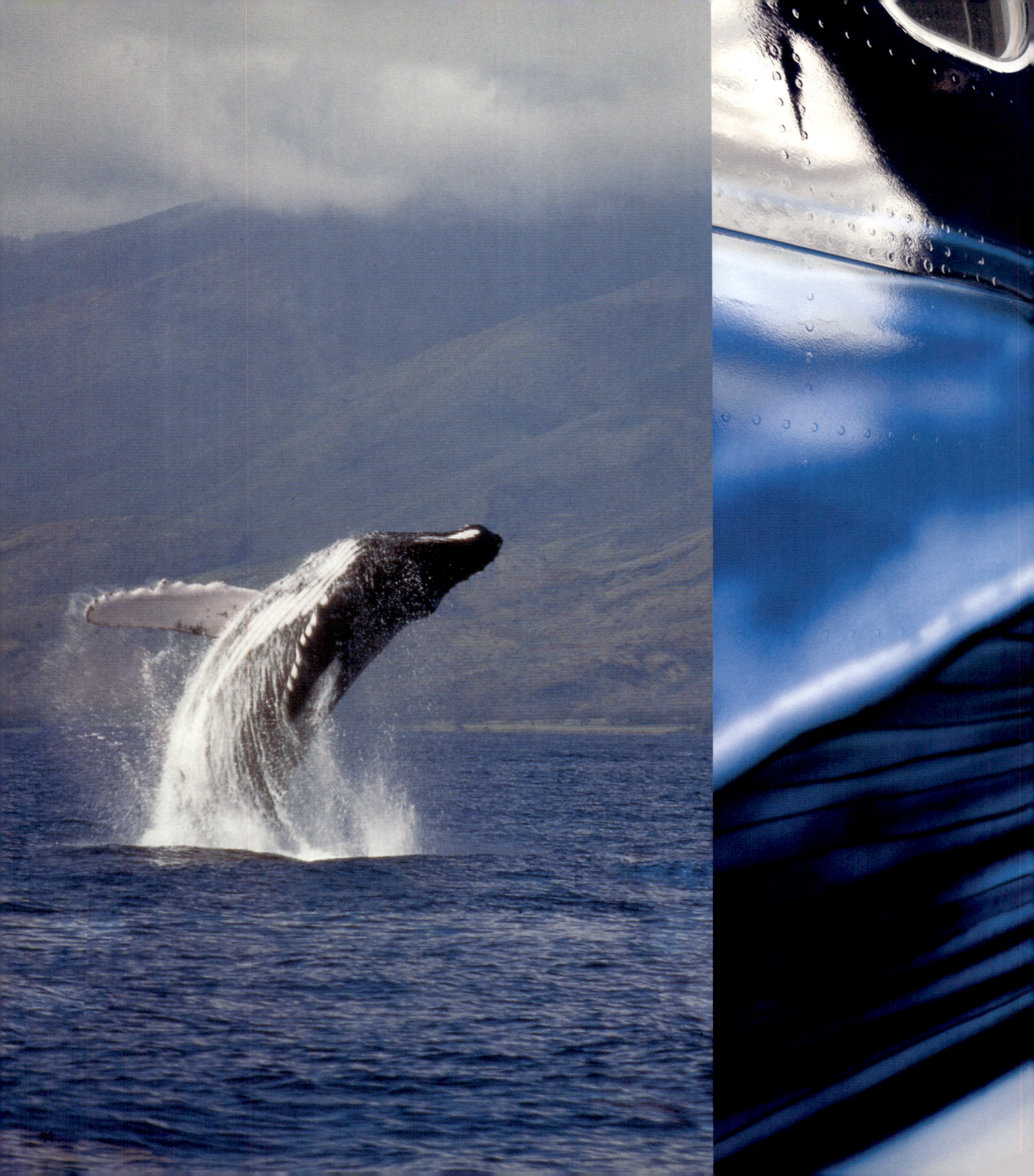

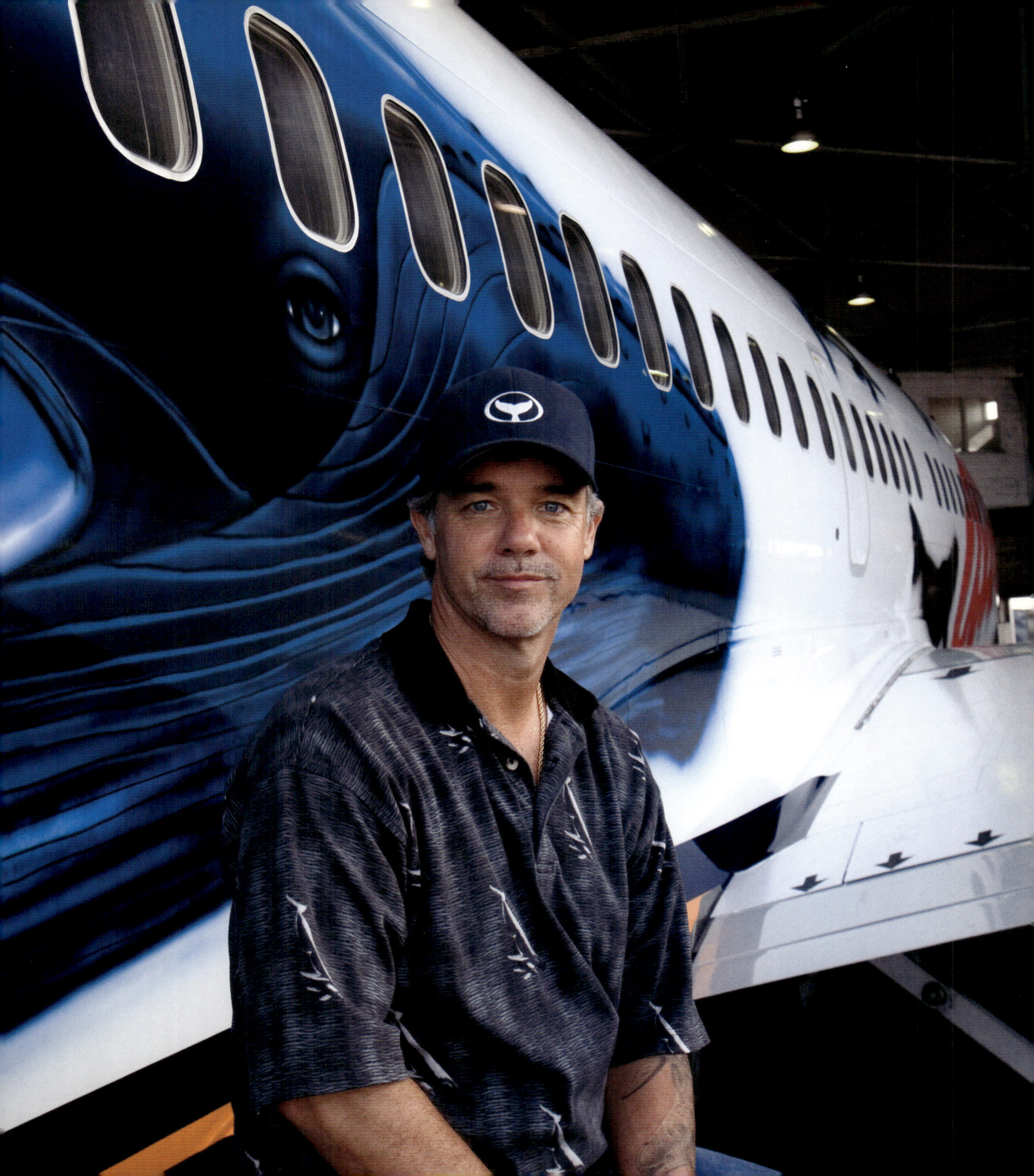

It is this never-ending quest to render the spirit, detail, and majesty of the sea

that distinguishes Wyland as the premier artist in the marine-life world, and has elevated his art to an unprecedented level.

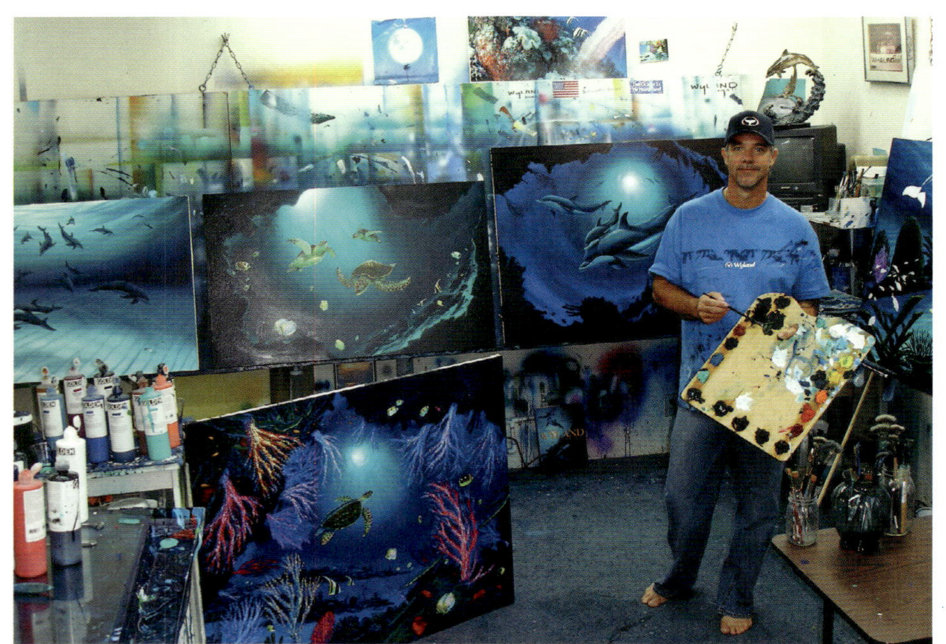

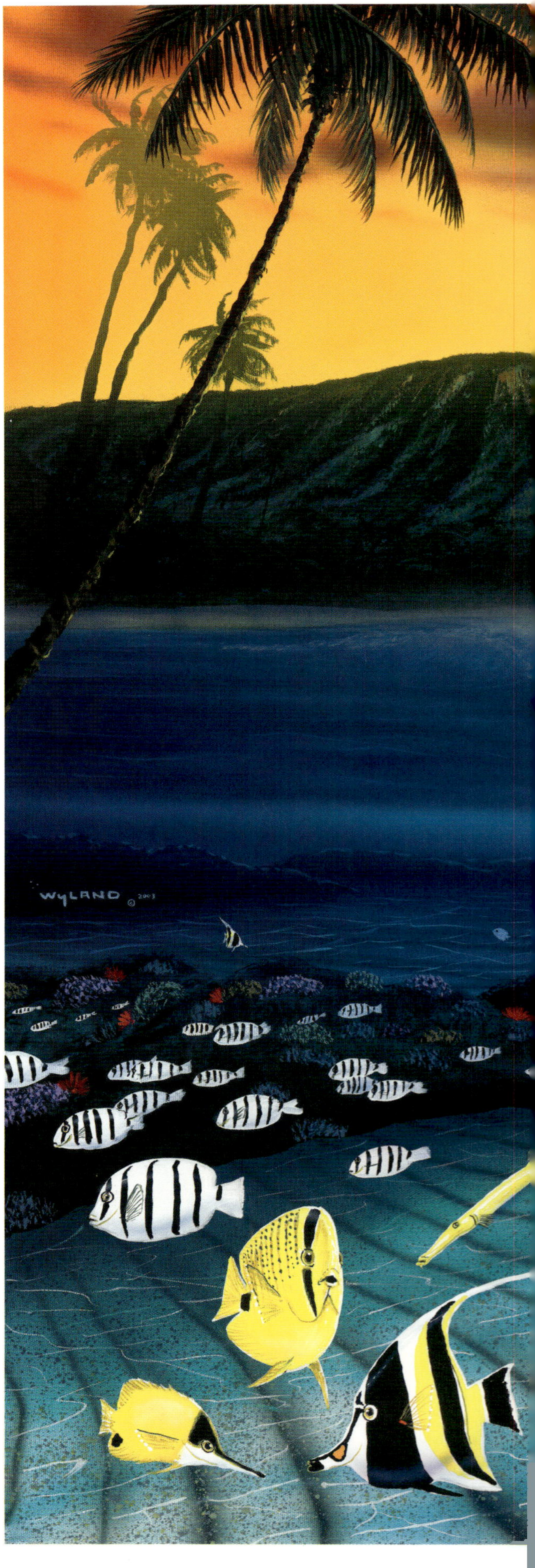

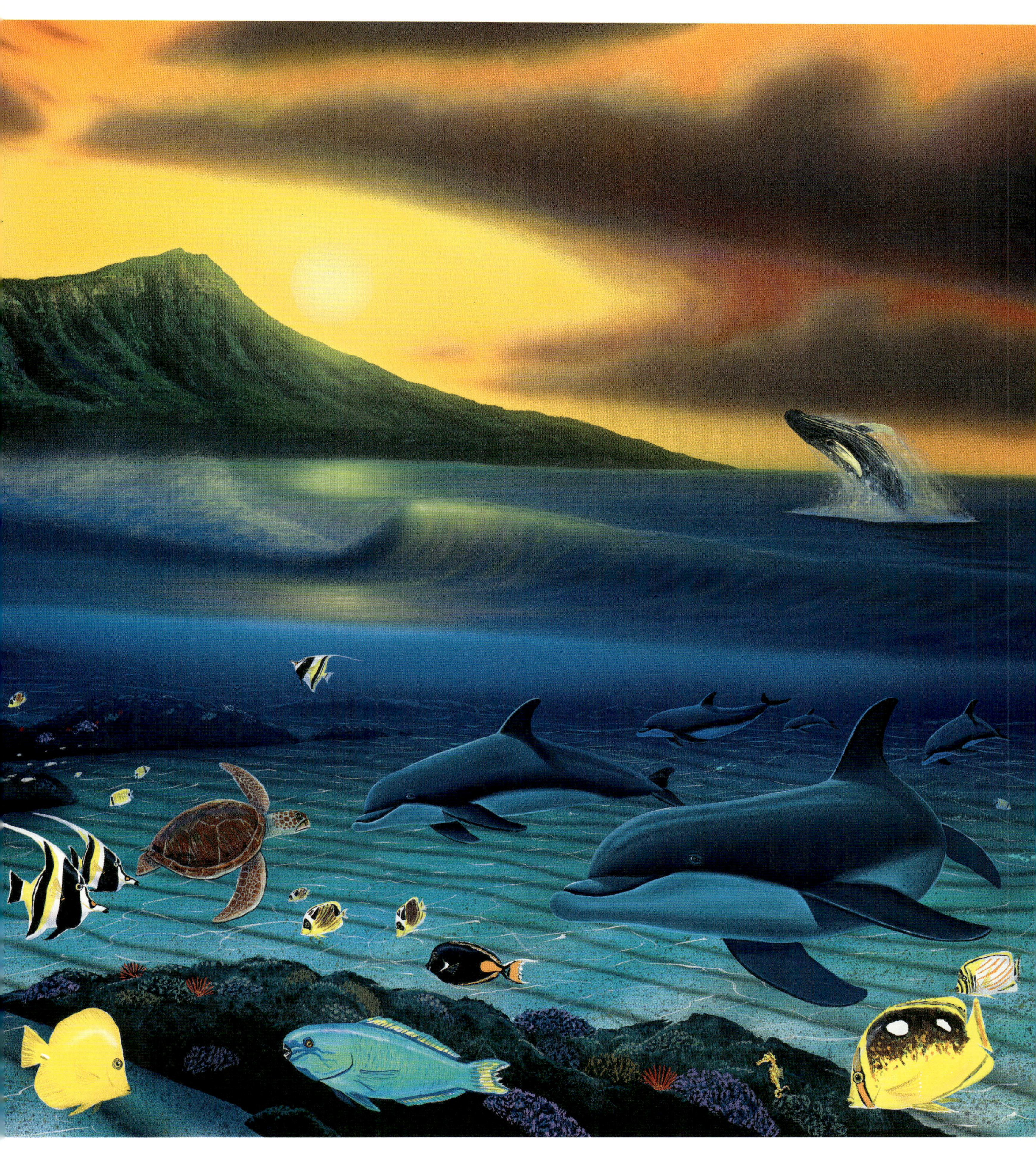

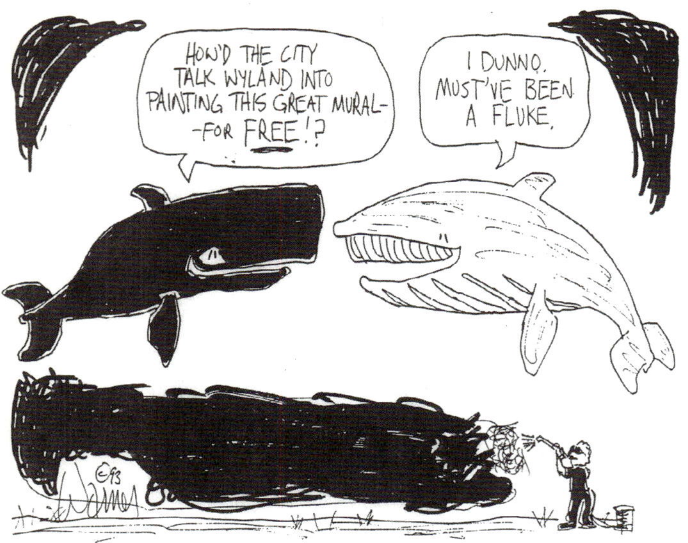

"I had already realized that research and science is great and important, but the challenge today is to make people care; affect public attitudes so voters in turn can affect government policy... Wyland's whales, large and powerful enough to demand public attention, were a sign to me that someone else felt the same way. Here was a monument as large as a building that had feeling and depth so that I felt the ocean was flooding the city, bringing the beauty and serenity of nature to the forefront of busy people's urban lives. The murals demanded attention and joined other priorities as being important to our lives."

Jim Fowler
Renowned Wildlife Expert

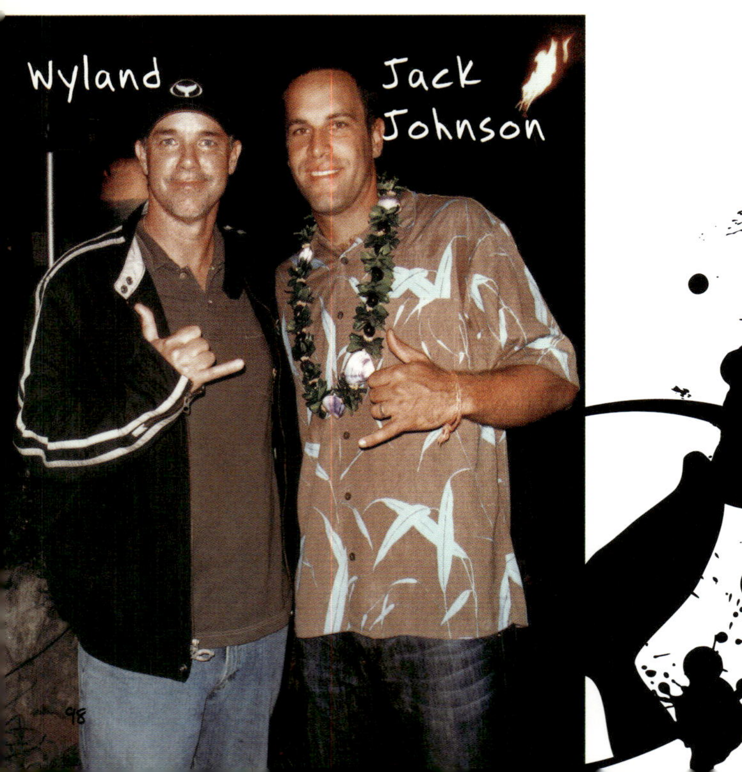

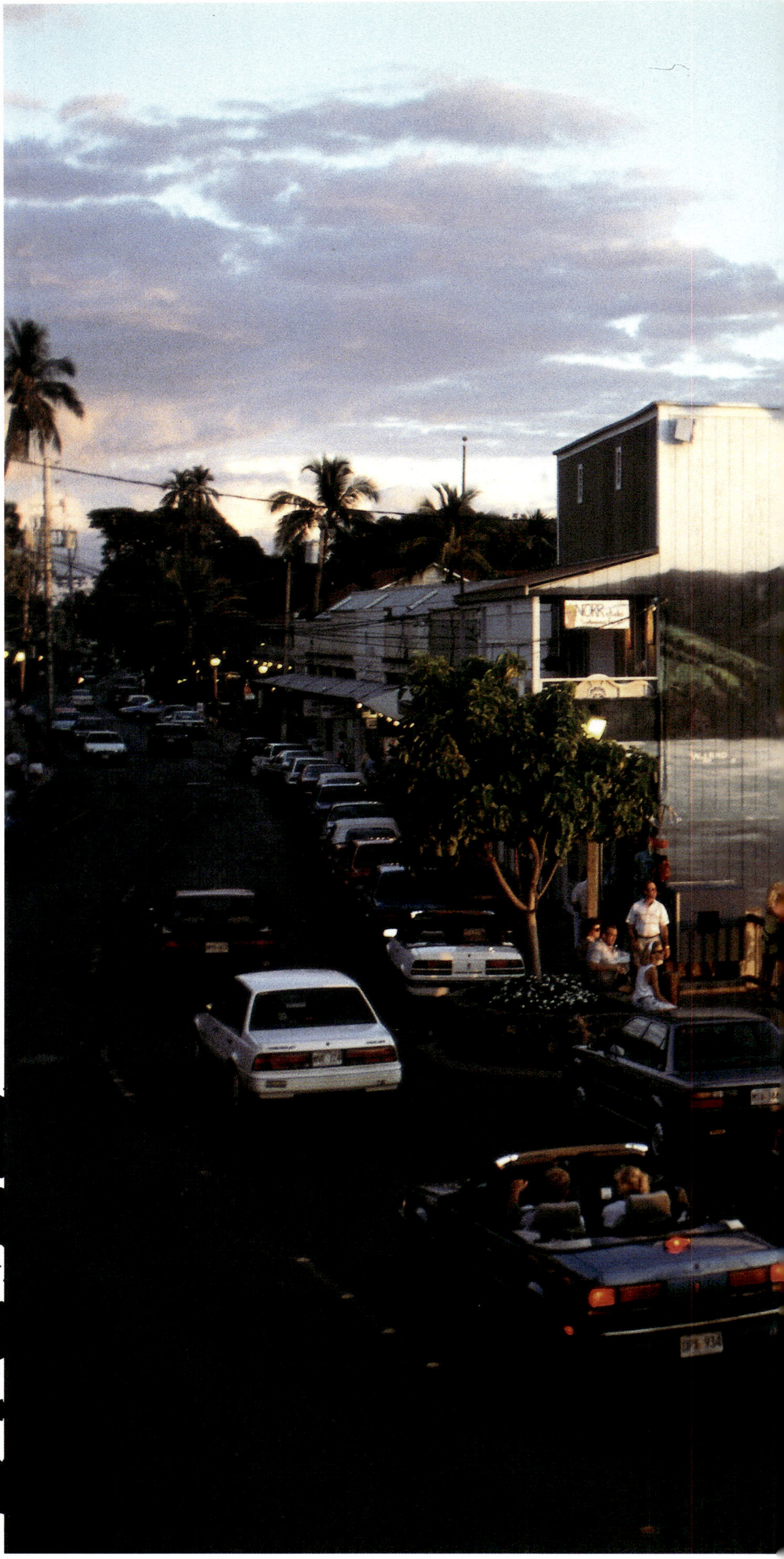

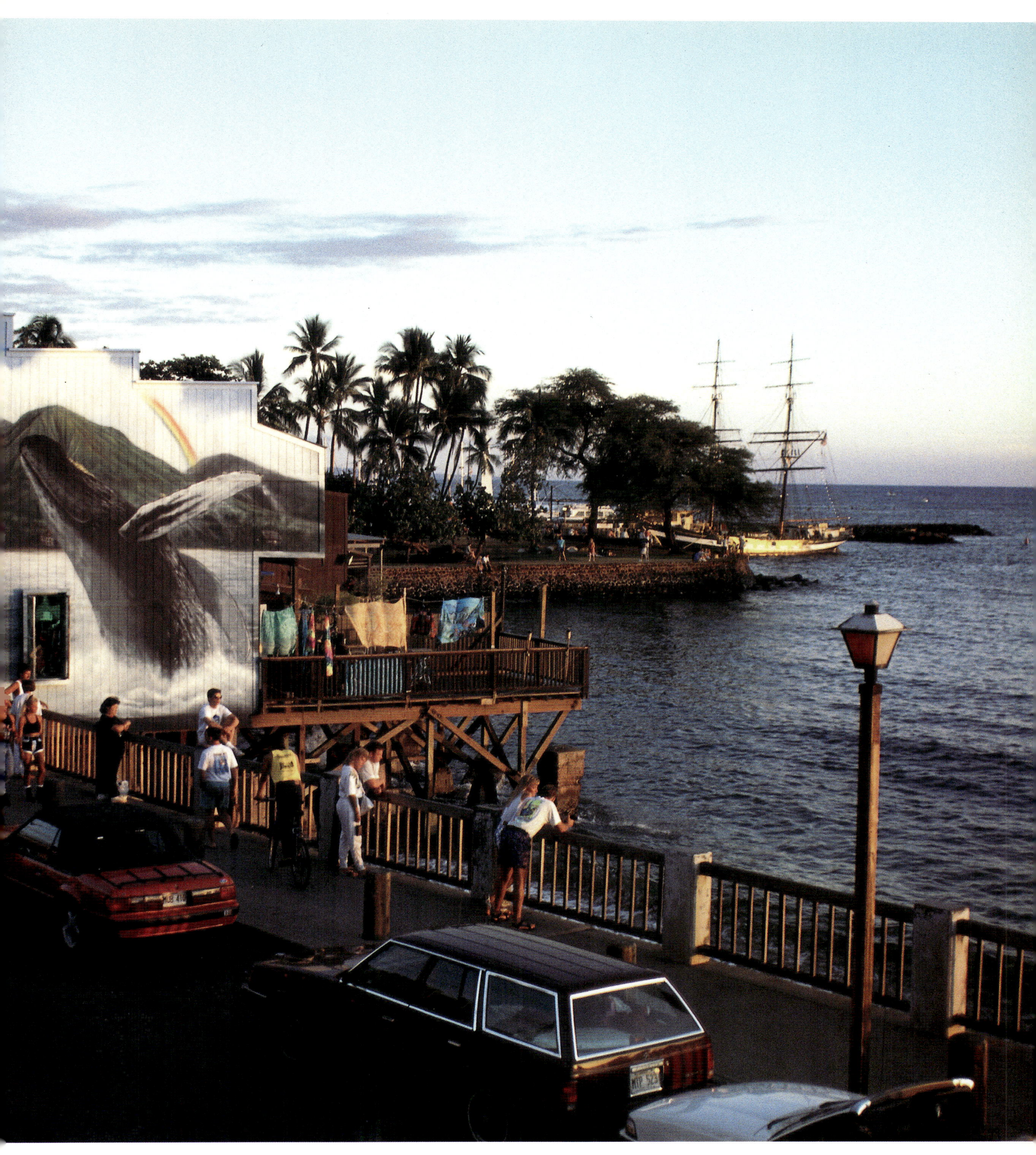

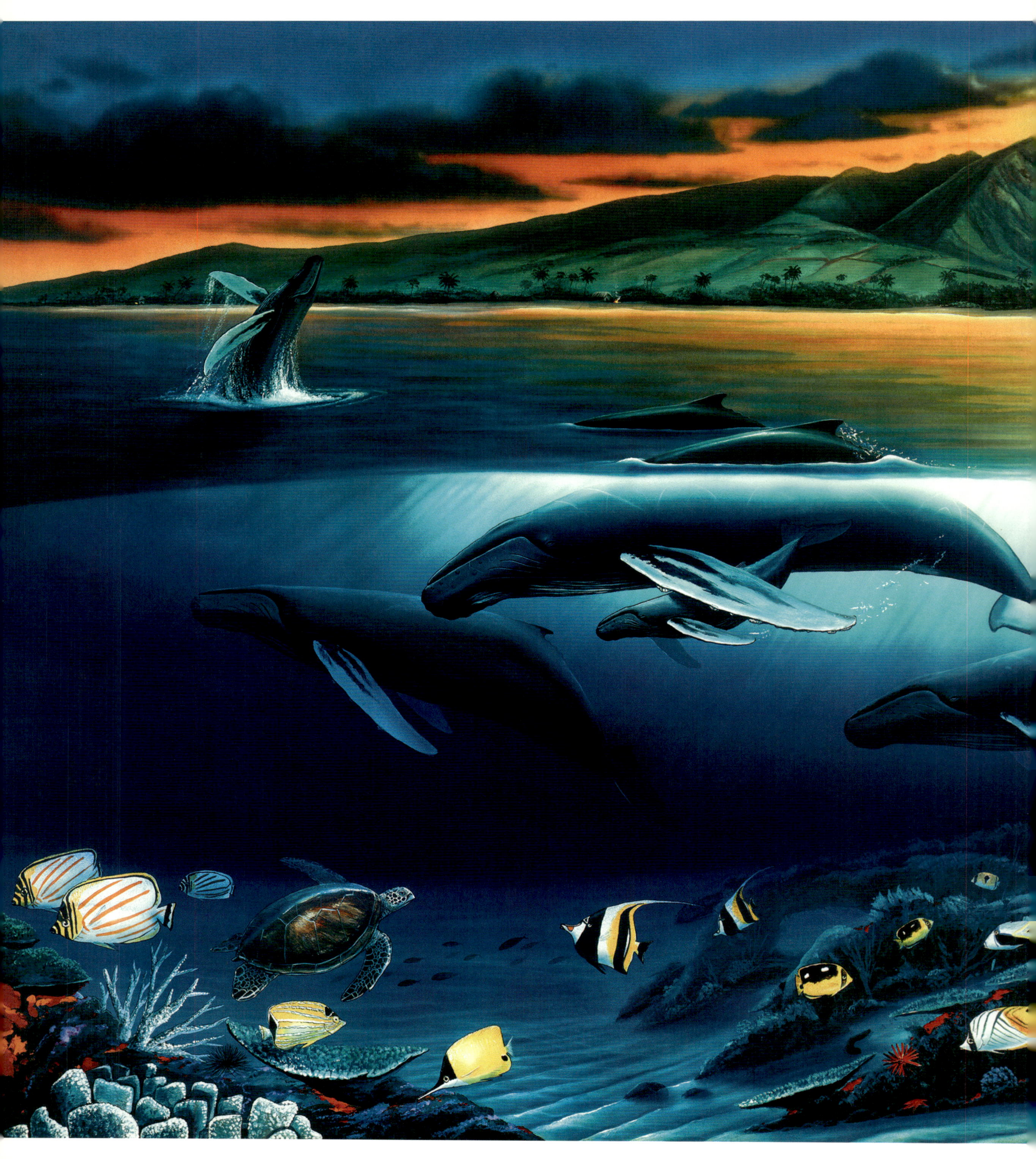

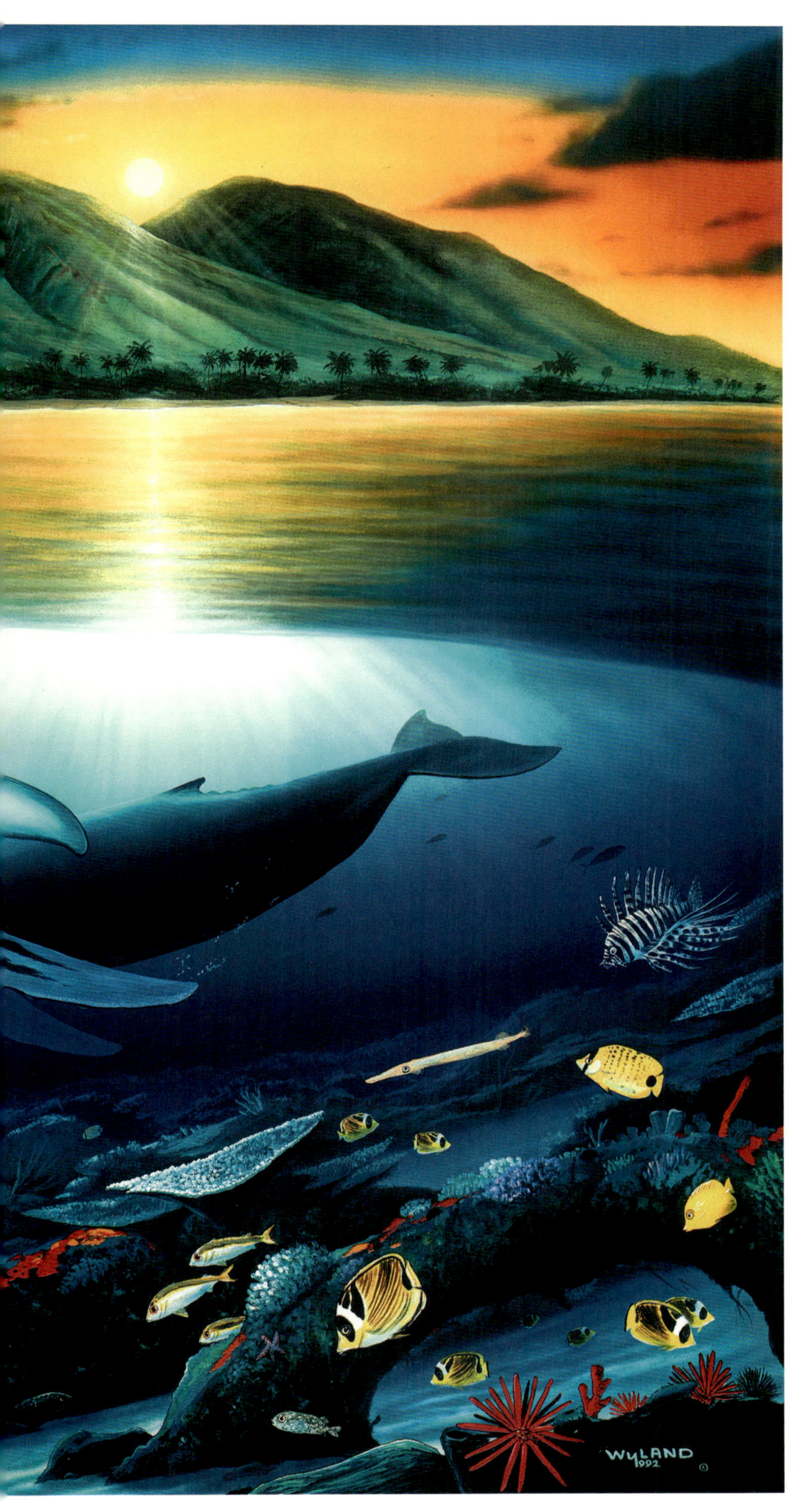

The marine art of the past that once depicted man's conquest of the sea

has evolved into
the marine-life art
of today.
The difference
is that artists now
dive the oceans ourselves
and see the wonders
of the sea firsthand.

"The strongest resource artists have is our ability to compose, but there are a lot of variables when you are floating in deep blue sea, waiting for animals to reveal themselves. This is when the magic happens - when an animal decides that it will share its world with you even for a fleeting moment. You may never see it again."

- Wyland

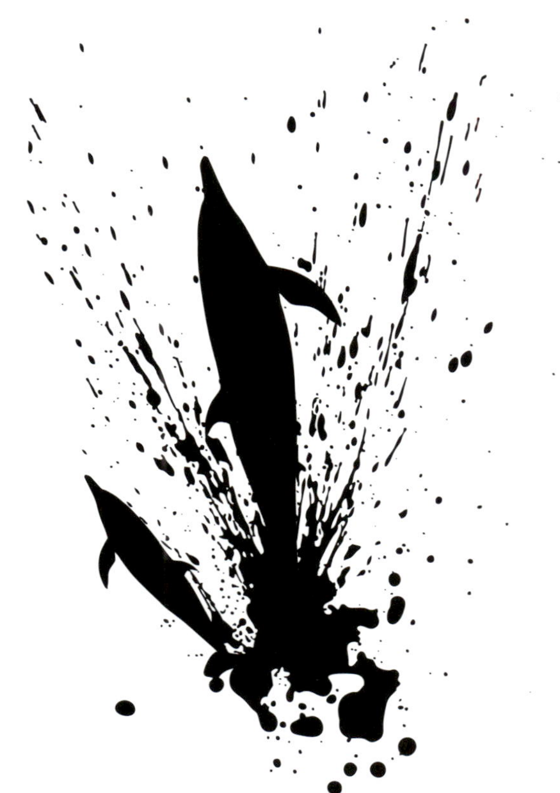

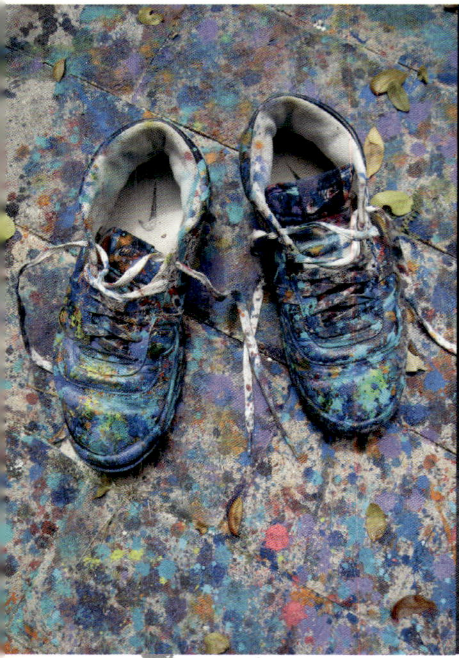

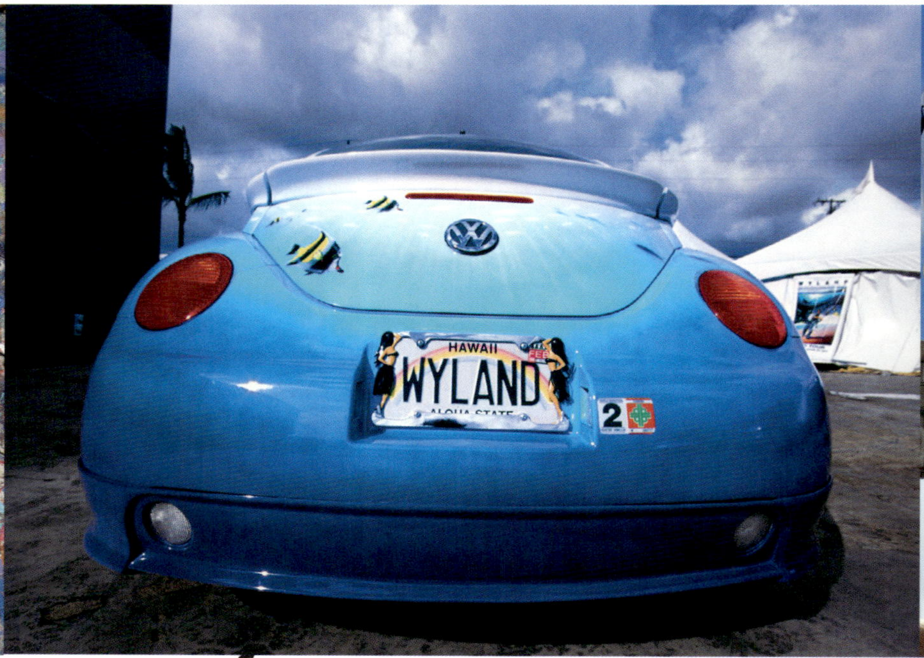

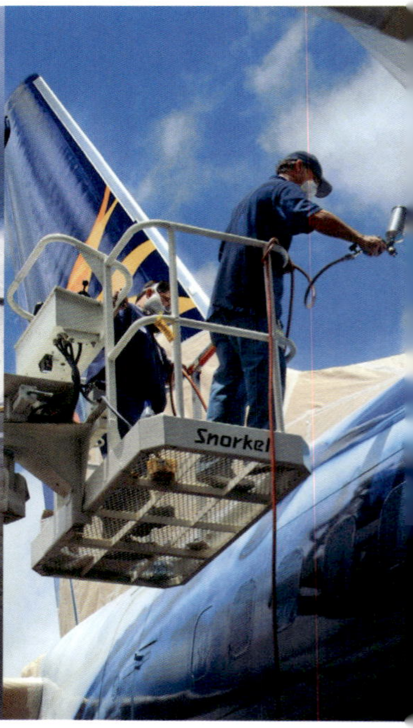

Dividing his time between the North Shore of Oahu, Hawaii; Islamorada on the Florida Keys; and the sleepy seaside town of Laguna Beach, California, Wyland is never far from the ocean.

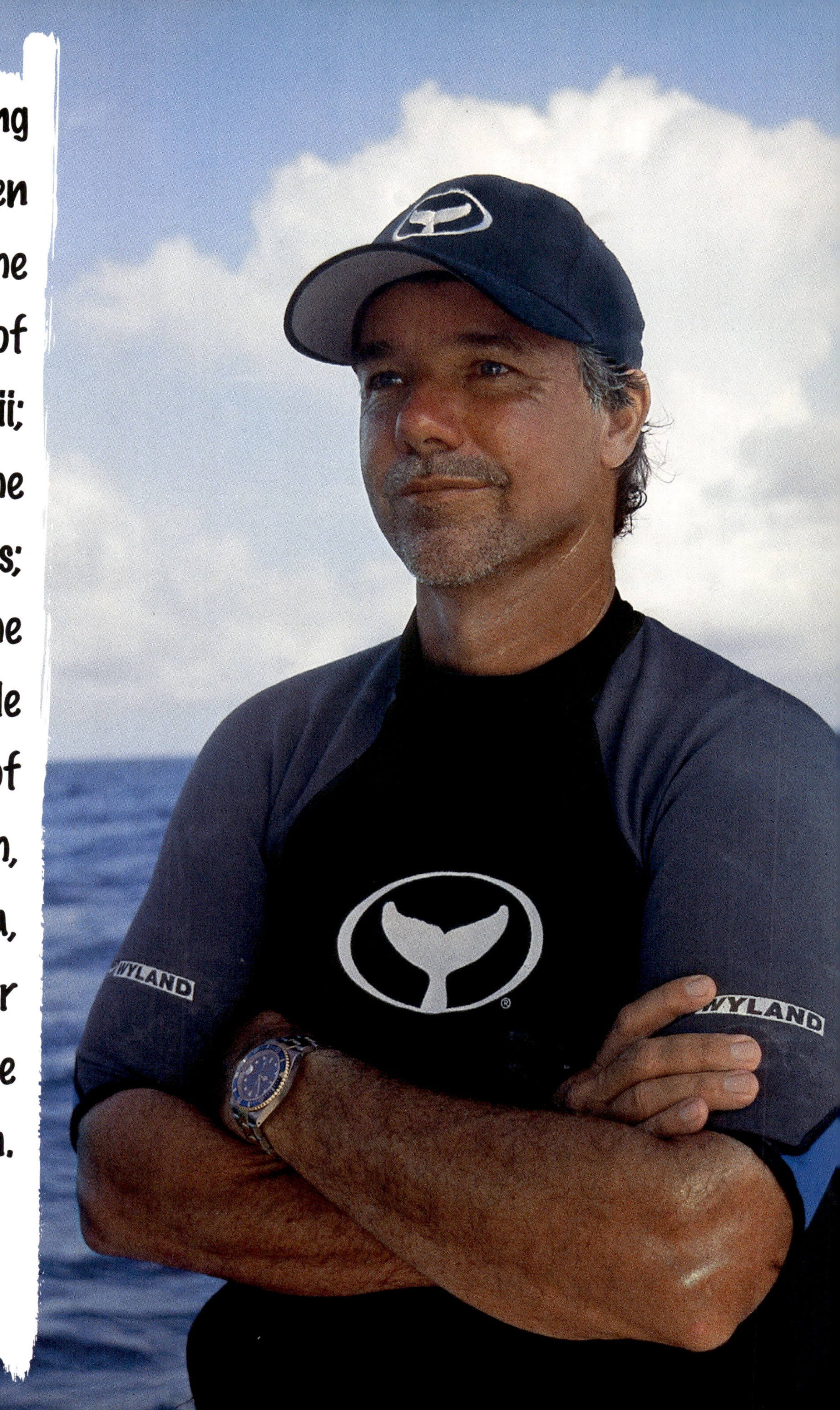

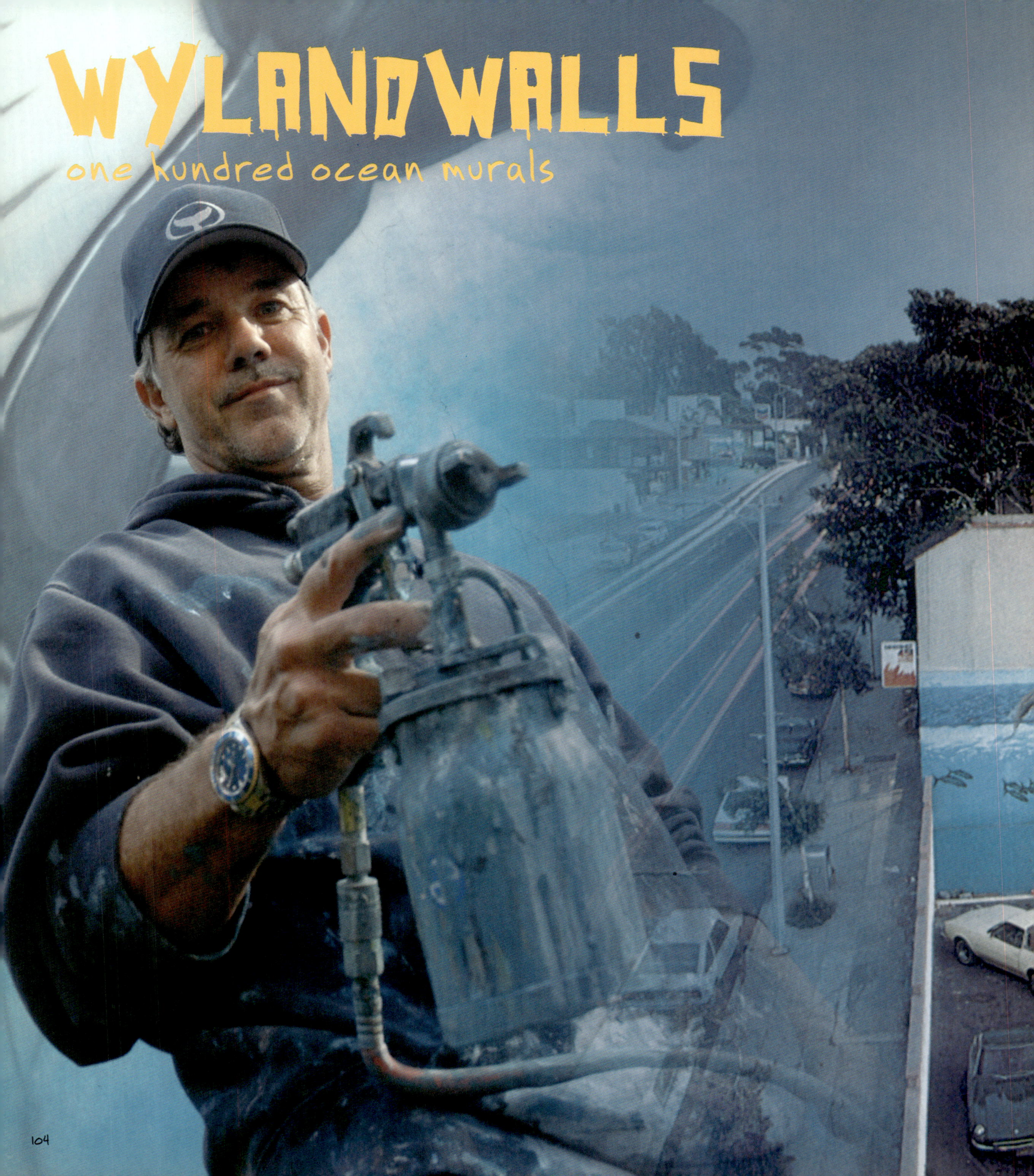
WYLANDWALLS
one hundred ocean murals

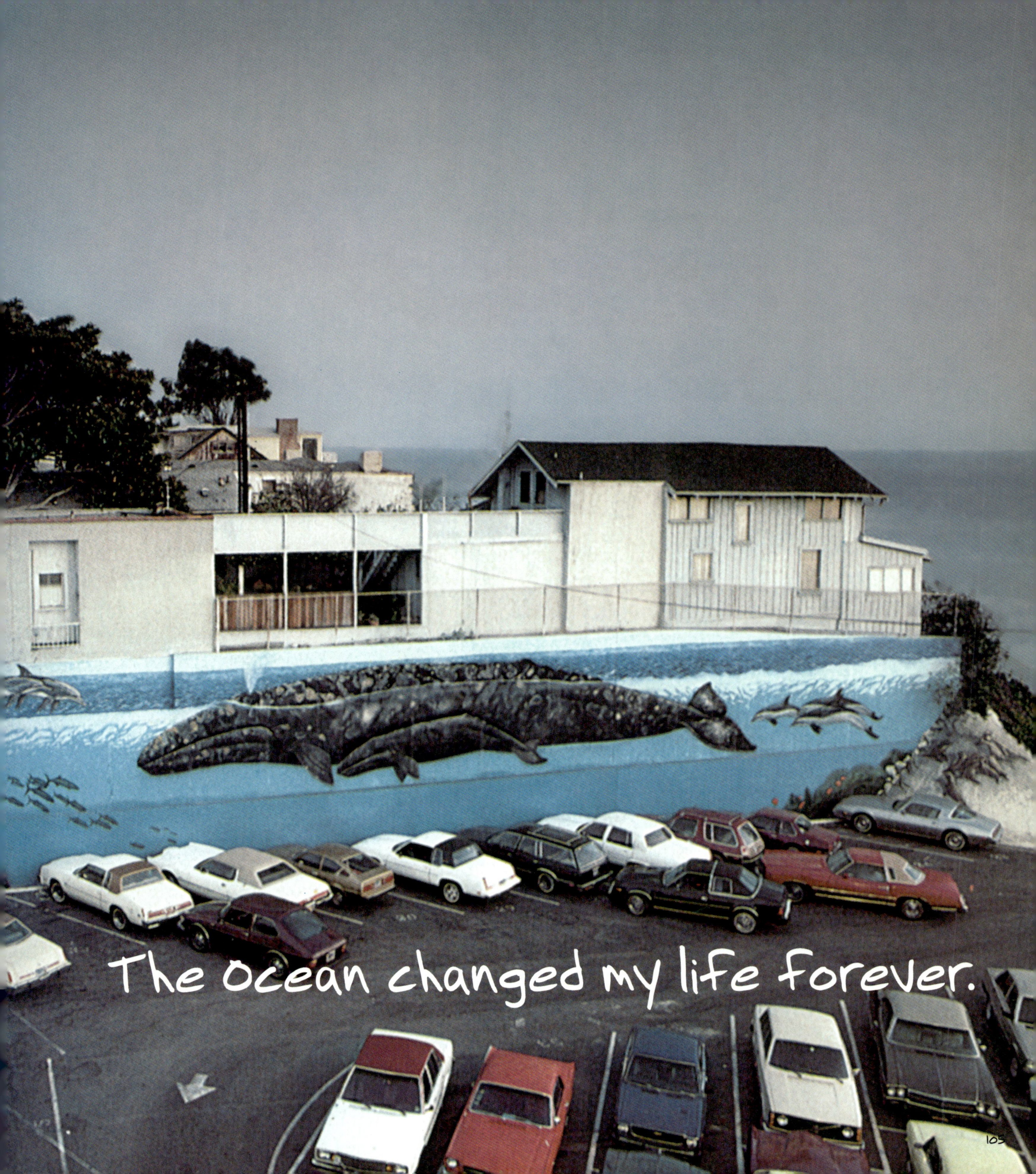

The Ocean changed my life forever.

"Wyland is considered by many to be the finest environmental artist in the world." Congressional Record

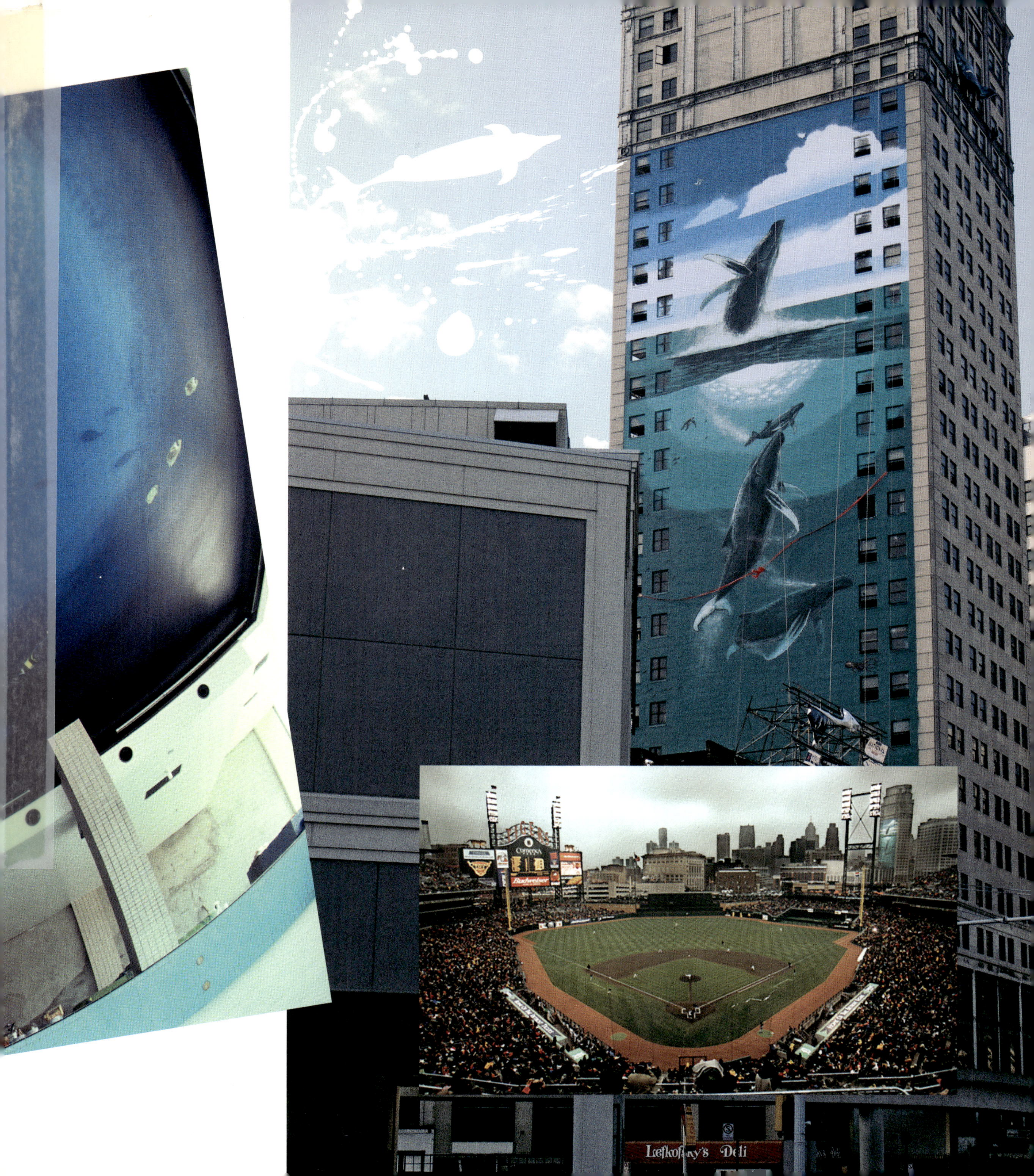
Budweiser
Deli

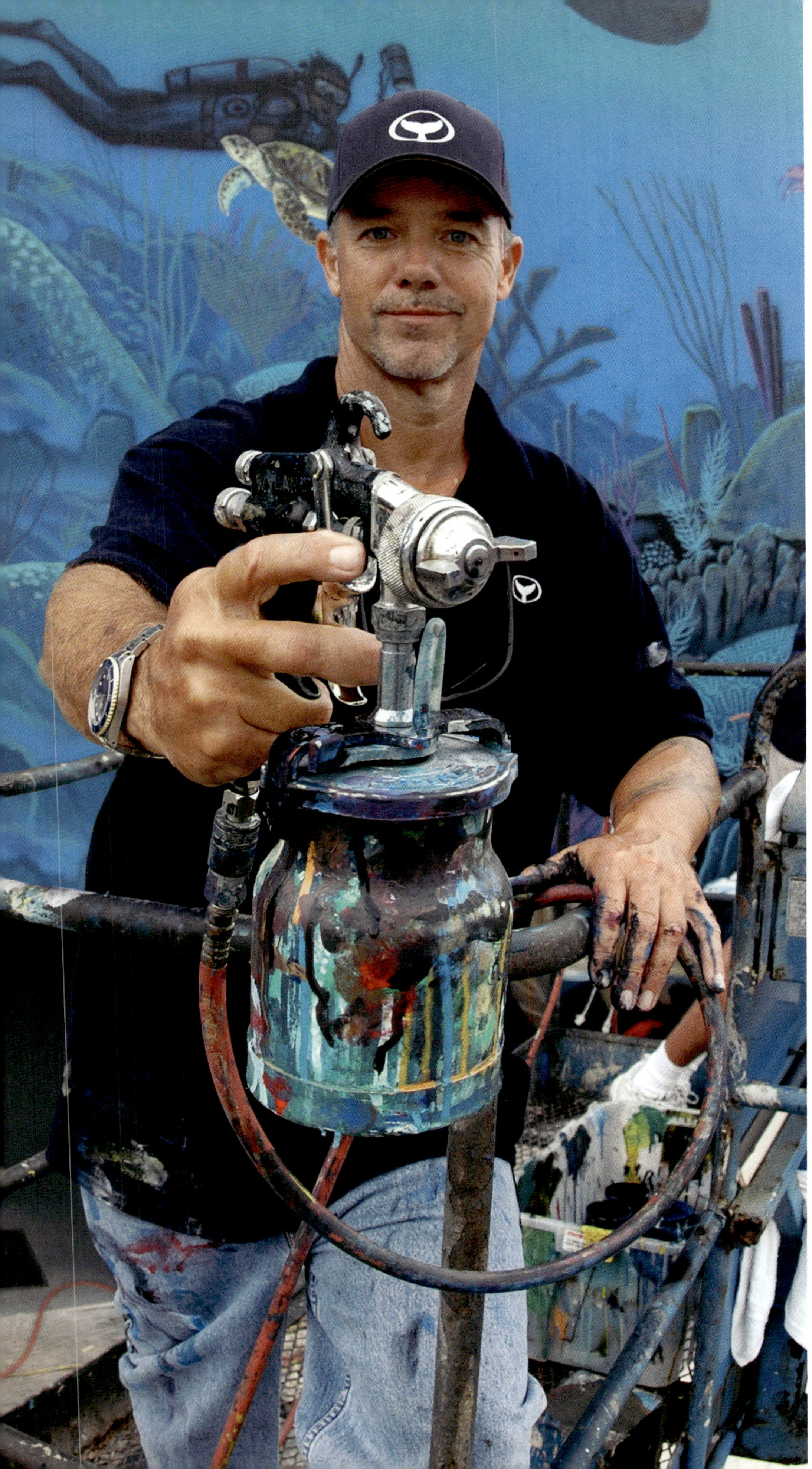

"Cousteau made films and wrote books. Others take photographs. Some write, or sing or conduct research. Wyland paints, but he also conveys to an ever-widening audience his concern and passion for taking care of the natural systems that take care of us by involving us in spectacular, engaging, moving ways."

Dr. Sylvia A. Earle,
Founder, DOER
Explorer in Residence
National Geographic Society

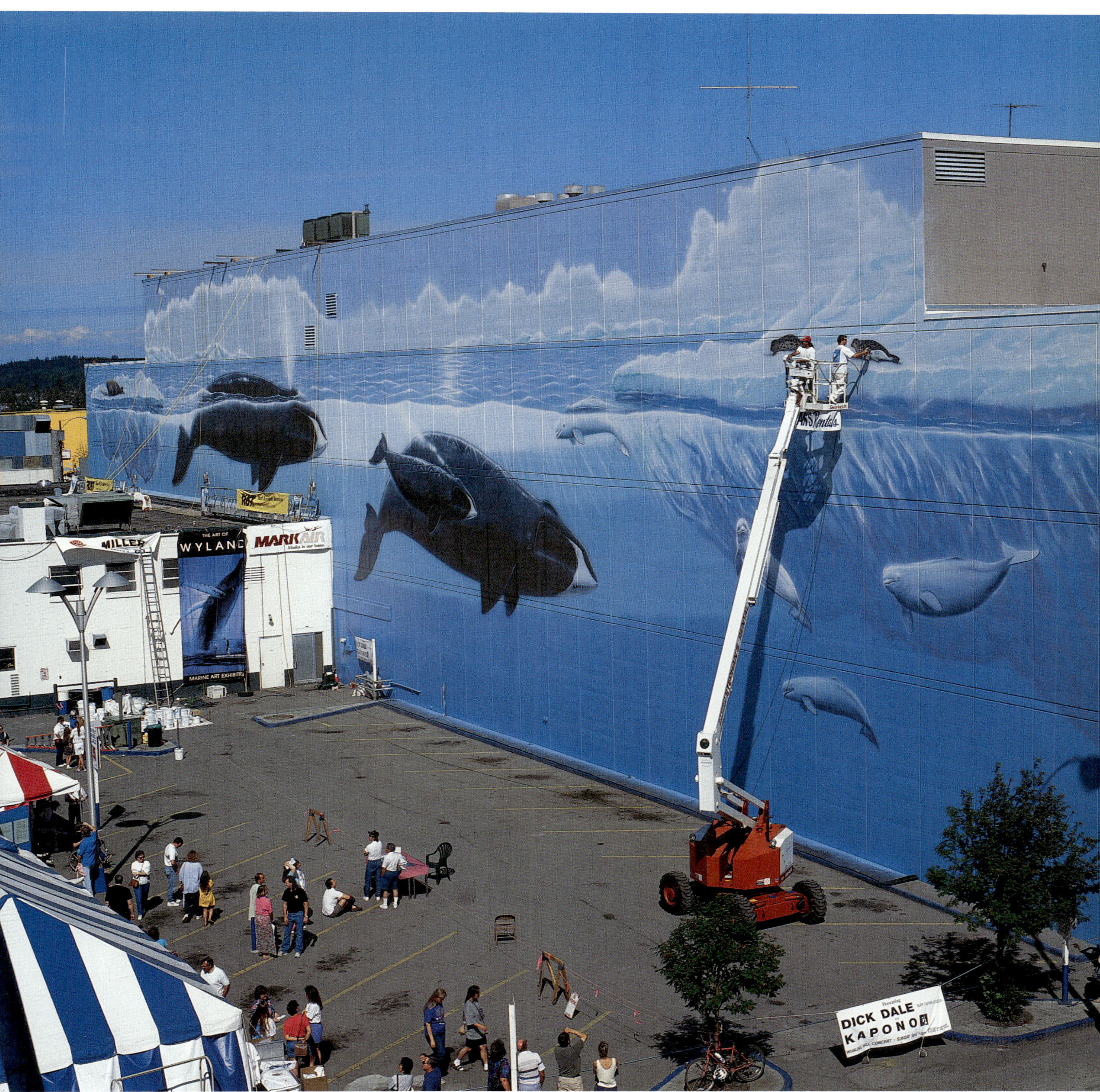
MILLER
THE ART OF
WYLAND
MARINE ART EXHIBITION
MARKAIR
Alaska is our home.
Presenting
DICK DALE
KAPONO
WHALING WALL CONCERT – SUNDAY

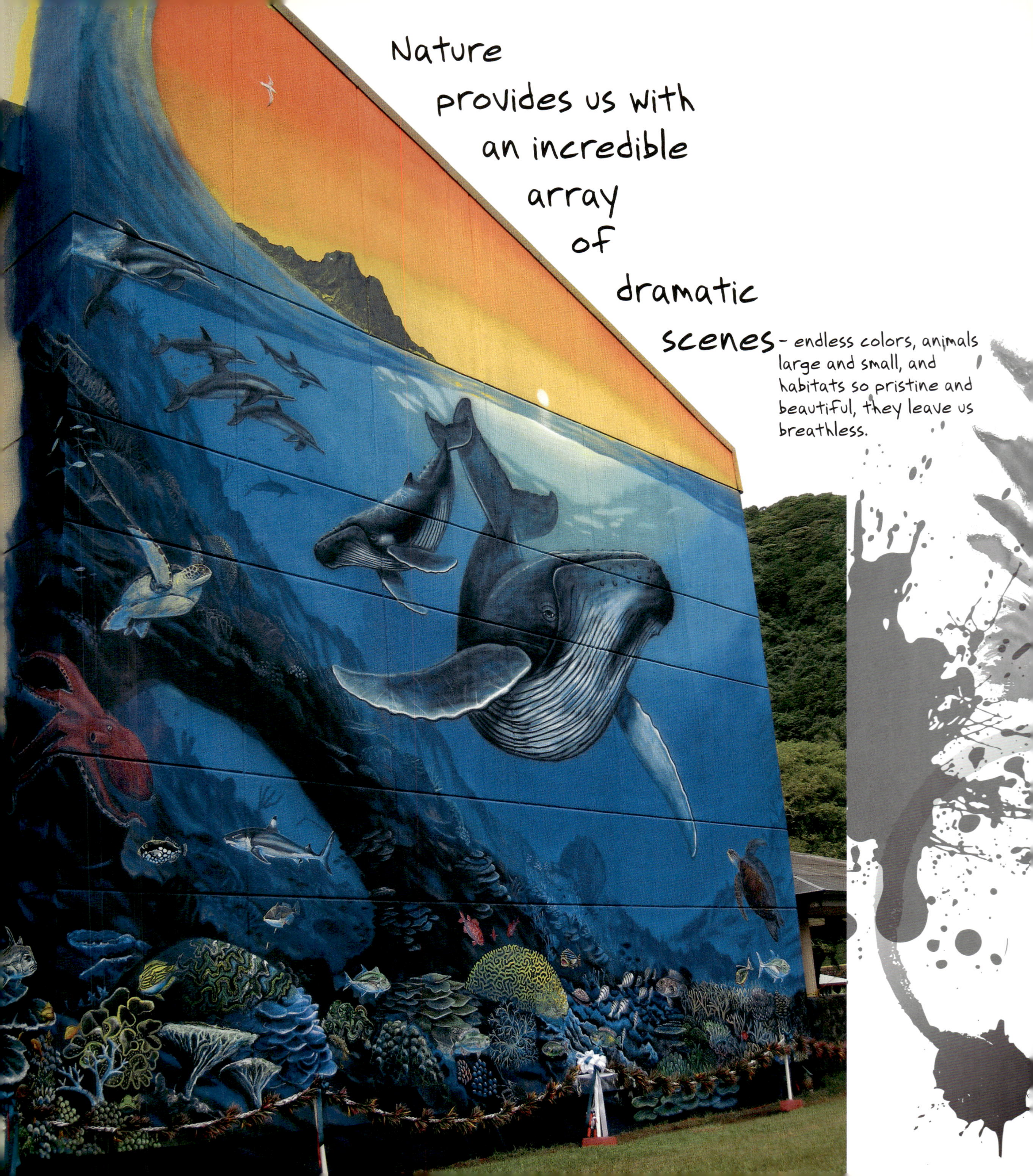

Nature provides us with an incredible array of dramatic scenes - endless colors, animals large and small, and habitats so pristine and beautiful, they leave us breathless.

“Your creative talents and your ongoing endeavors to inspire and educate young people about marine life and the beauty and fragility of the ocean are deeply appreciated. Through your paintings and murals, your public art, your research and teaching programmes you have encouraged thousands to join in respecting and preserving this precious resource. I also share and commend you on your theme: ‘One person can make a difference’ — a phrase I often use in my own public remarks.”

Kofi A. Annan,
Former Secretary-General
United Nations

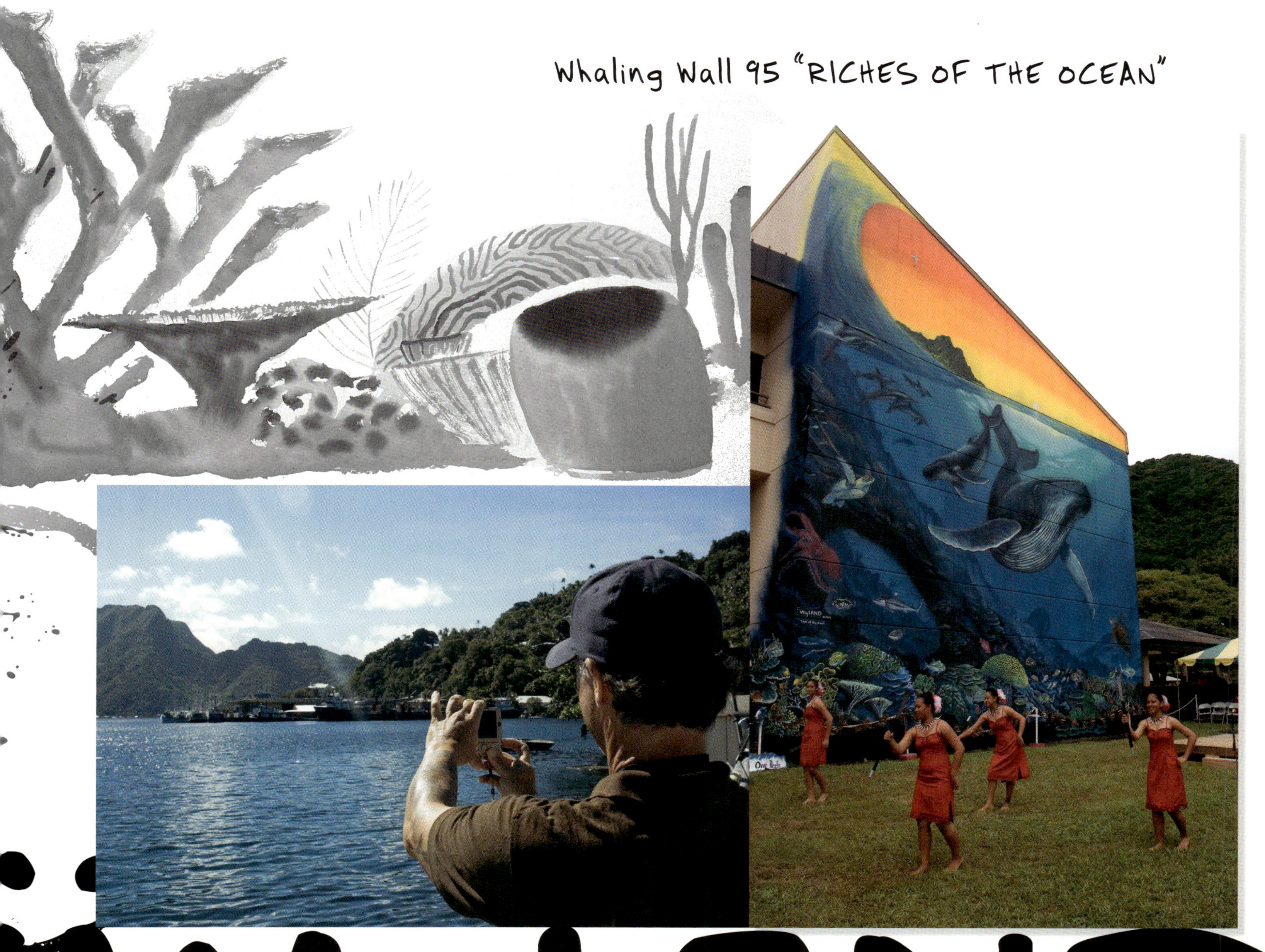

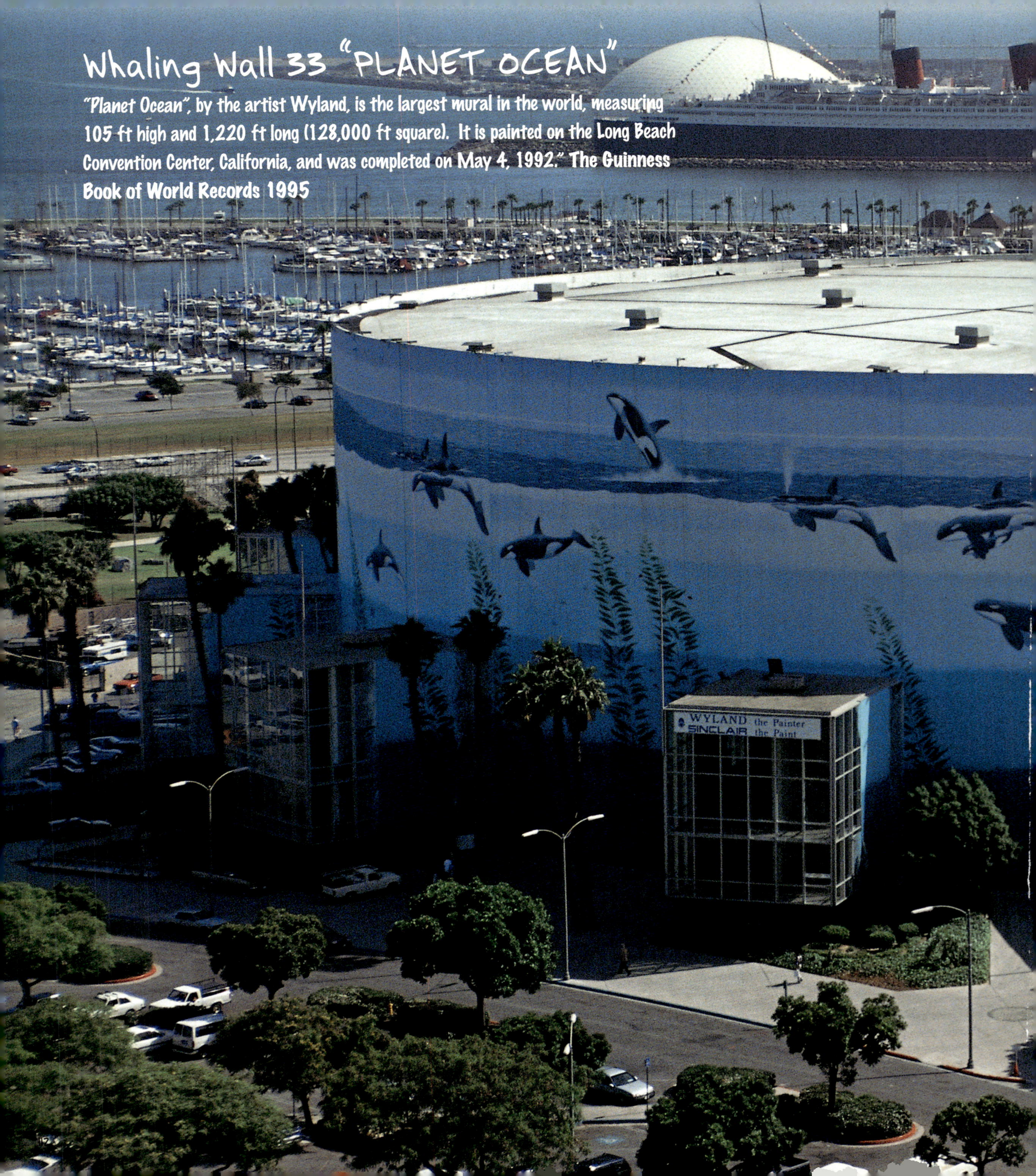

Whaling Wall 33 "PLANET OCEAN"

"Planet Ocean", by the artist Wyland, is the largest mural in the world, measuring 105 ft high and 1,220 ft long (128,000 ft square). It is painted on the Long Beach Convention Center, California, and was completed on May 4, 1992." The Guinness Book of World Records 1995

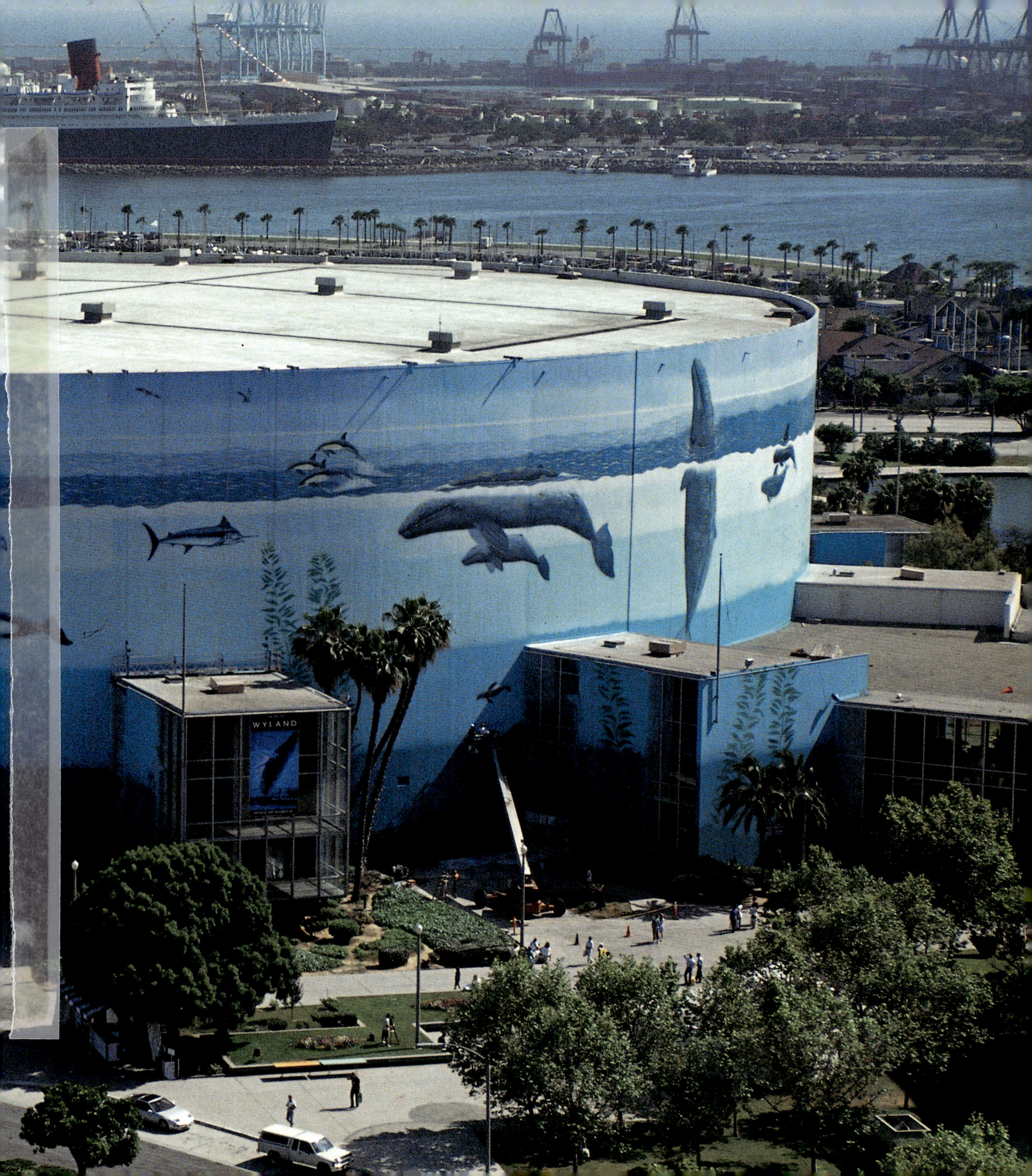
WYLAND

Whaling Wall 99 "Water for Life" From the mangroves ...

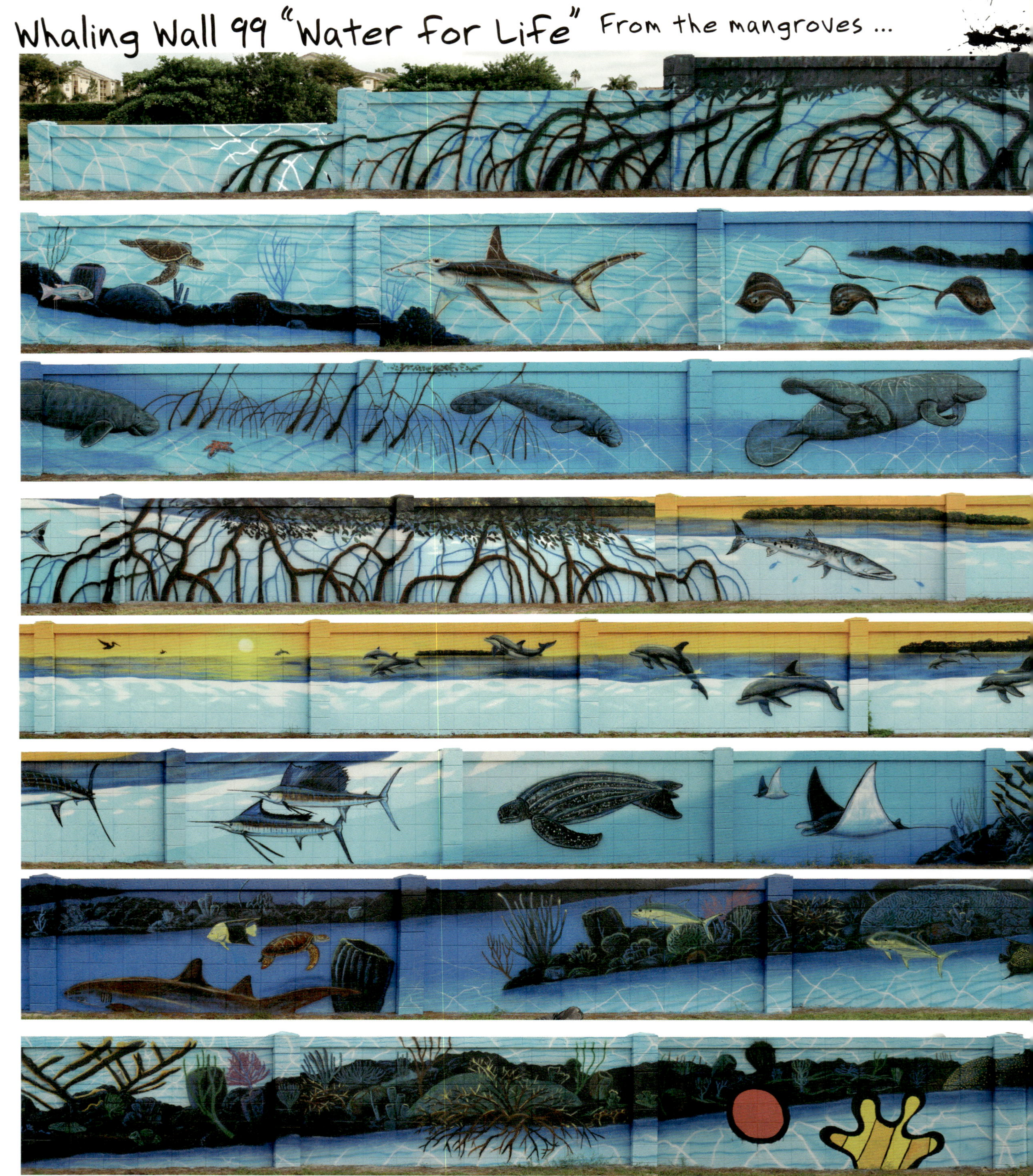

Painted by Wyland, with Guy Harvey, Romero Britto, and Deano Cook
1,000' long by 10' high

...to the reefs

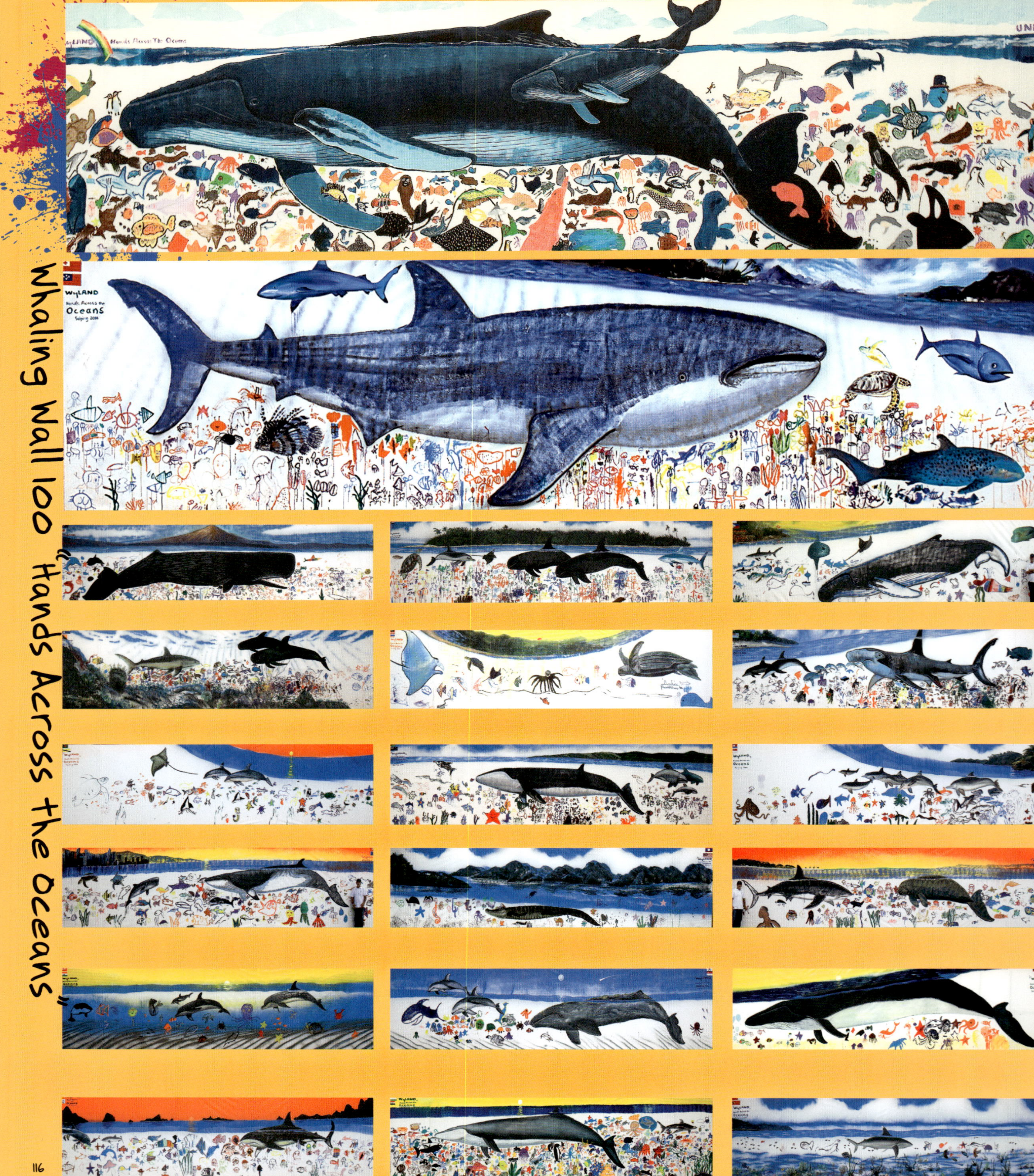

Whaling Wall 100 "Hands Across the Oceans"

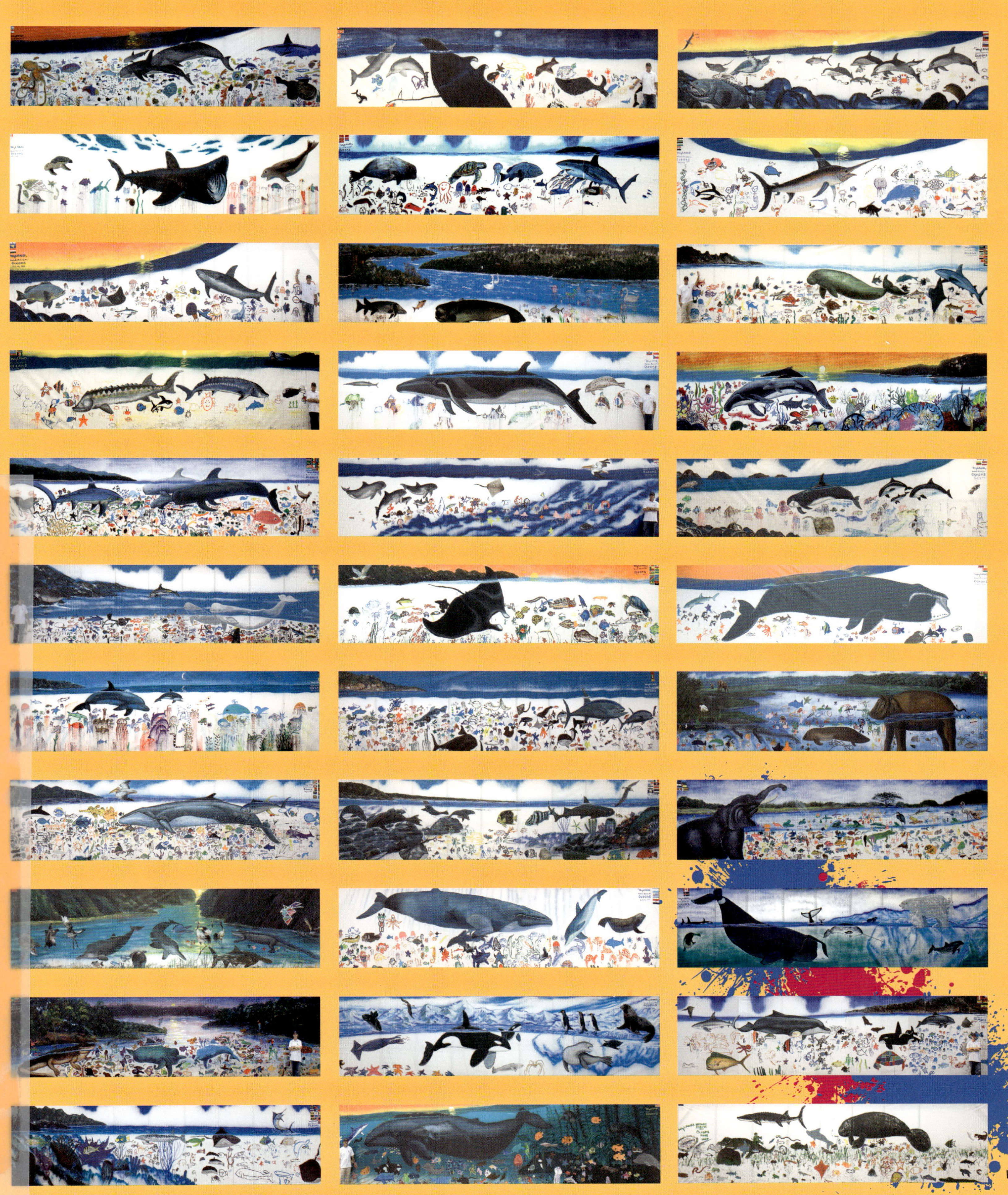

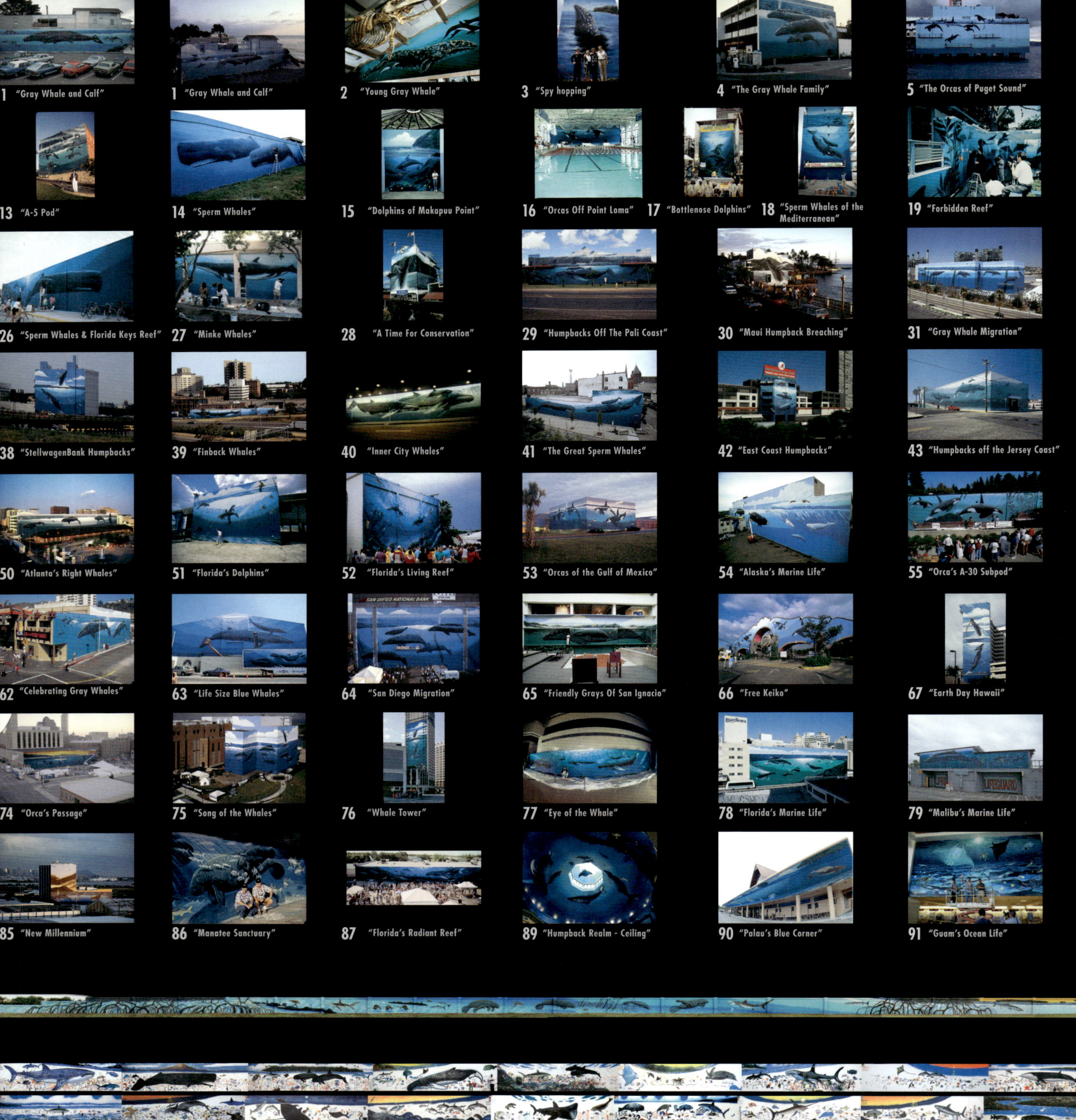

1 "Gray Whale and Calf"
1 "Gray Whale and Calf"
2 "Young Gray Whale"
3 "Spy hopping"
4 "The Gray Whale Family"
5 "The Orcas of Puget Sound"
13 "A-5 Pod"
14 "Sperm Whales"
15 "Dolphins of Makapuu Point"
16 "Orcas Off Point Loma"
17 "Bottlenose Dolphins"
18 "Sperm Whales of the Mediterranean"
19 "Forbidden Reef"
26 "Sperm Whales & Florida Keys Reef"
27 "Minke Whales"
28 "A Time For Conservation"
29 "Humpbacks Off The Pali Coast"
30 "Maui Humpback Breaching"
31 "Gray Whale Migration"
38 "StellwagenBank Humpbacks"
39 "Finback Whales"
40 "Inner City Whales"
41 "The Great Sperm Whales"
42 "East Coast Humpbacks"
43 "Humpbacks off the Jersey Coast"
50 "Atlanta's Right Whales"
51 "Florida's Dolphins"
52 "Florida's Living Reef"
53 "Orcas of the Gulf of Mexico"
54 "Alaska's Marine Life"
55 "Orca's A-30 Subpod"
62 "Celebrating Gray Whales"
63 "Life Size Blue Whales"
64 "San Diego Migration"
65 "Friendly Grays Of San Ignacio"
66 "Free Keiko"
67 "Earth Day Hawaii"
74 "Orca's Passage"
75 "Song of the Whales"
76 "Whale Tower"
77 "Eye of the Whale"
78 "Florida's Marine Life"
79 "Malibu's Marine Life"
85 "New Millennium"
86 "Manatee Sanctuary"
87 "Florida's Radiant Reef"
89 "Humpback Realm - Ceiling"
90 "Palau's Blue Corner"
91 "Guam's Ocean Life"

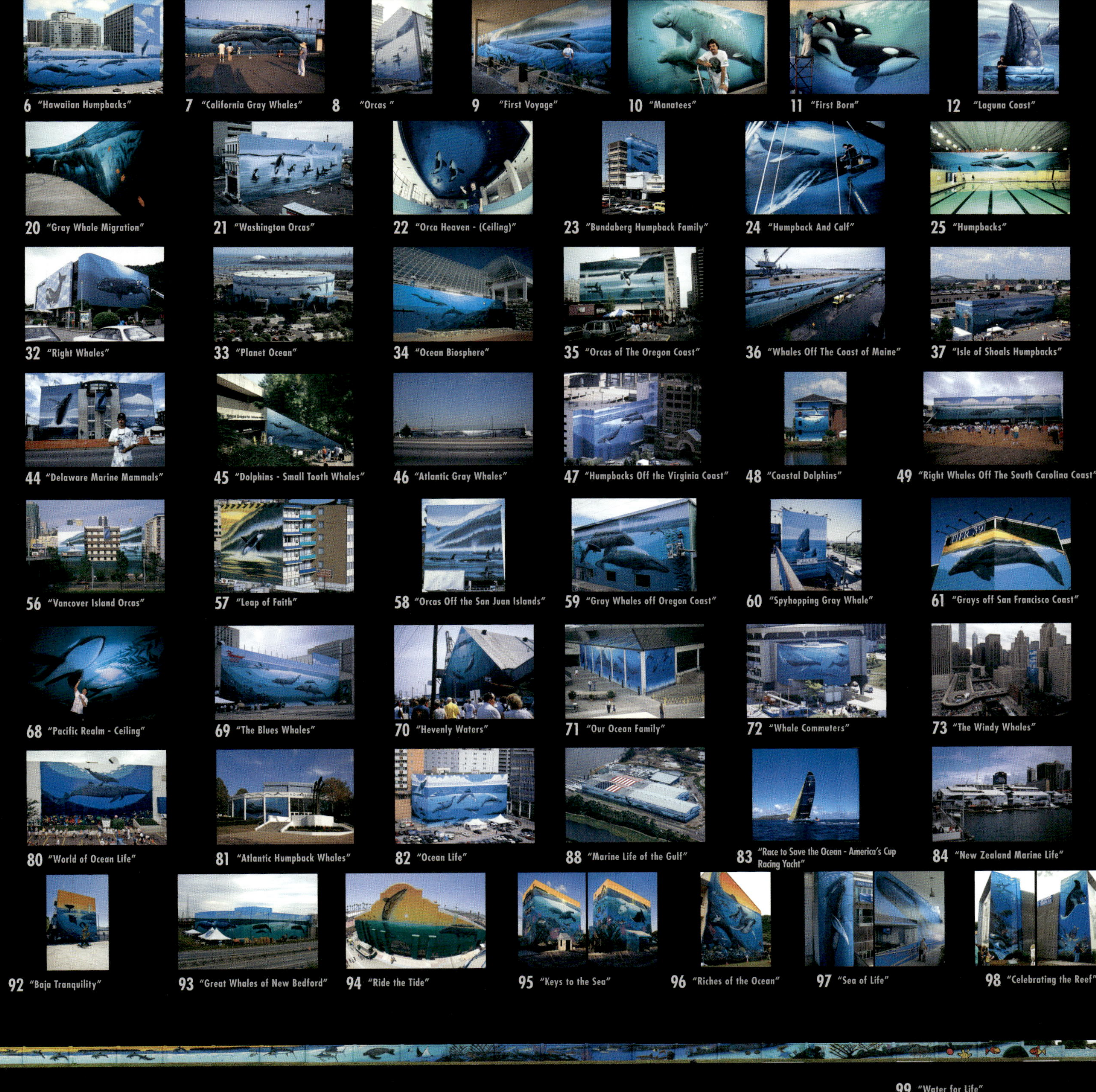
6 "Hawaiian Humpbacks"
7 "California Gray Whales"
8 "Orcas"
9 "First Voyage"
10 "Manatees"
11 "First Born"
12 "Laguna Coast"
20 "Gray Whale Migration"
21 "Washington Orcas"
22 "Orca Heaven - (Ceiling)"
23 "Bundaberg Humpback Family"
24 "Humpback And Calf"
25 "Humpbacks"
32 "Right Whales"
33 "Planet Ocean"
34 "Ocean Biosphere"
35 "Orcas of The Oregon Coast"
36 "Whales Off The Coast of Maine"
37 "Isle of Shoals Humpbacks"
44 "Delaware Marine Mammals"
45 "Dolphins - Small Tooth Whales"
46 "Atlantic Gray Whales"
47 "Humpbacks Off the Virginia Coast"
48 "Coastal Dolphins"
49 "Right Whales Off The South Carolina Coast"
56 "Vancover Island Orcas"
57 "Leap of Faith"
58 "Orcas Off the San Juan Islands"
59 "Gray Whales off Oregon Coast"
60 "Spyhopping Gray Whale"
61 "Grays off San Francisco Coast"
68 "Pacific Realm - Ceiling"
69 "The Blues Whales"
70 "Hevenly Waters"
71 "Our Ocean Family"
72 "Whale Commuters"
73 "The Windy Whales"
80 "World of Ocean Life"
81 "Atlantic Humpback Whales"
82 "Ocean Life"
88 "Marine Life of the Gulf"
83 "Race to Save the Ocean - America's Cup Racing Yacht"
84 "New Zealand Marine Life"
92 "Baja Tranquility"
93 "Great Whales of New Bedford"
94 "Ride the Tide"
95 "Keys to the Sea"
96 "Riches of the Ocean"
97 "Sea of Life"
98 "Celebrating the Reef"
99 "Water for Life"
100 "Hands Across the Ocean"

WYLAND FOUNDATION

water is life

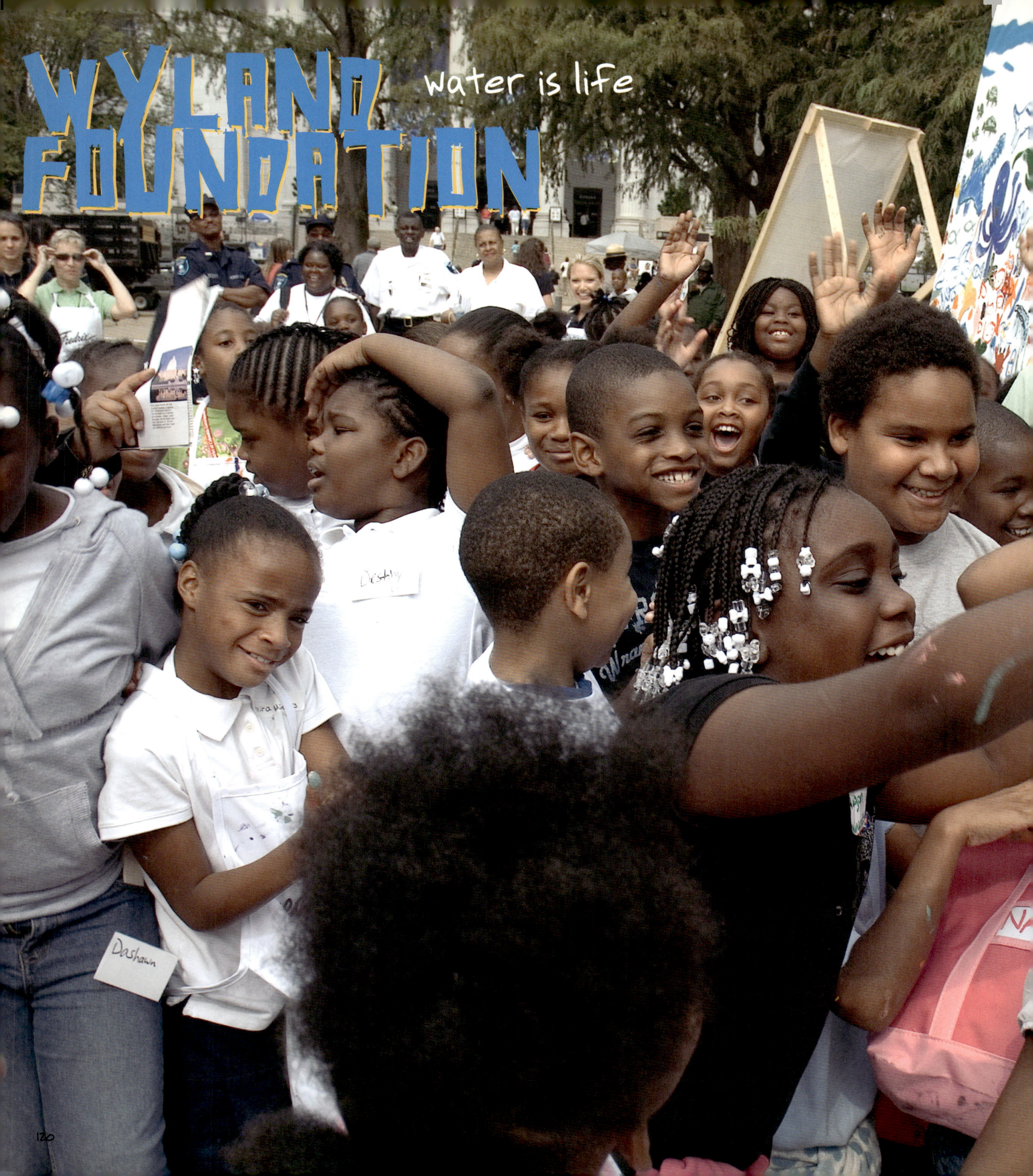

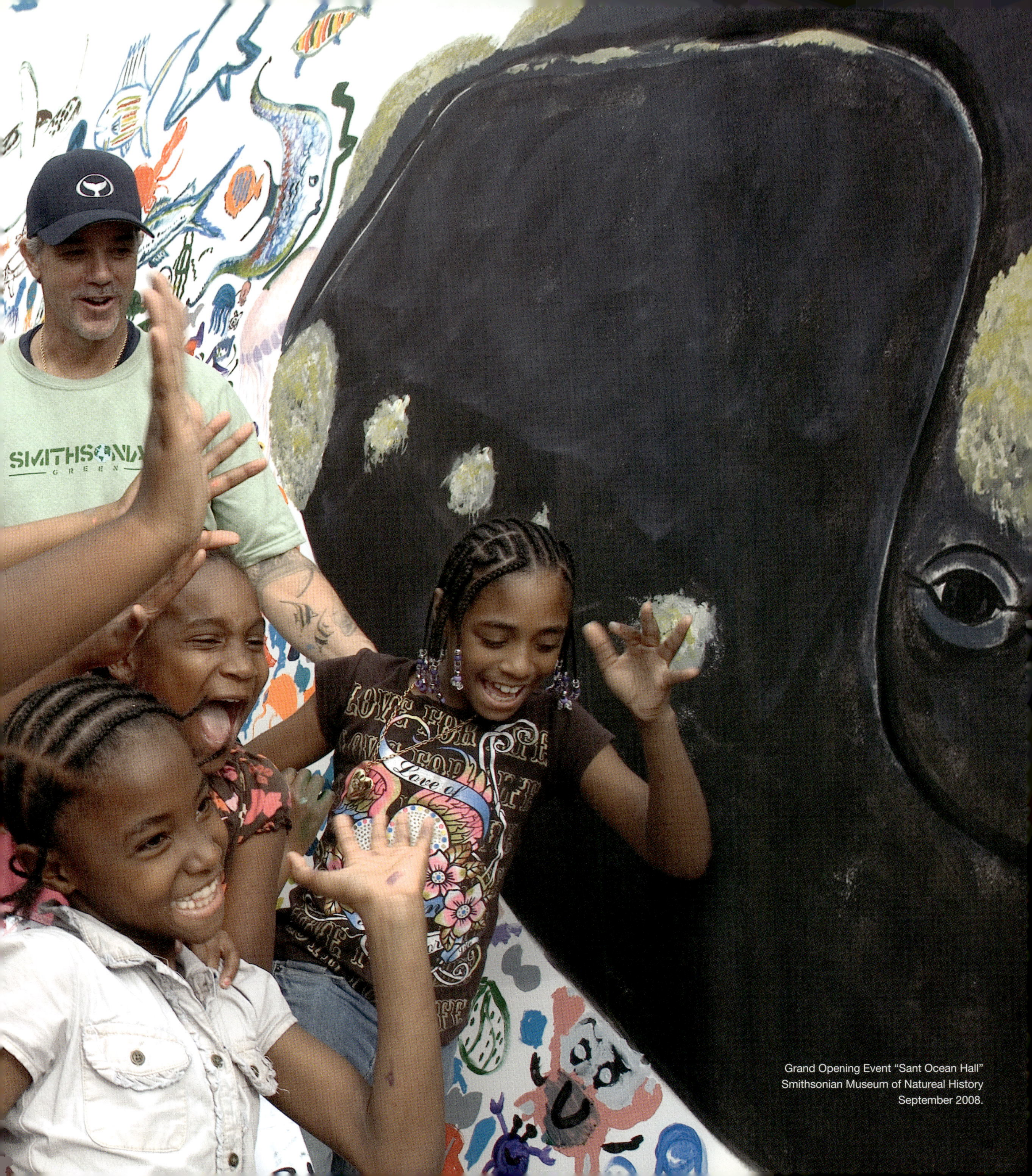

Grand Opening Event "Sant Ocean Hall"
Smithsonian Museum of Natureal History
September 2008.

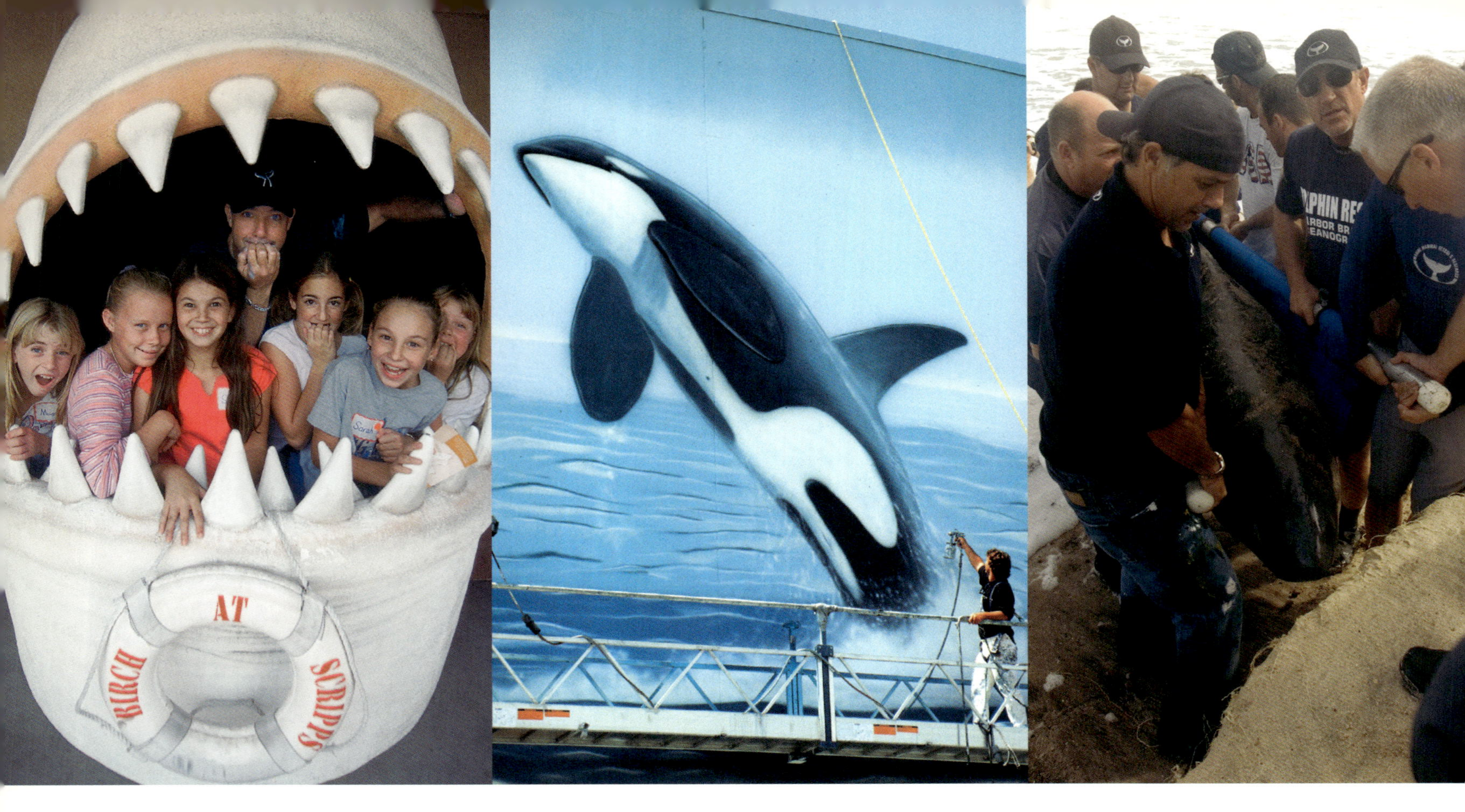

The nonprofit Wyland Foundation was founded in 1993 to further the artist's vision of programs that educate and inspire a new generation to become stewards of our planet's oceans. The foundation has since expanded its efforts for conservation of our ocean, lakes, rivers, streams, and wetlands.

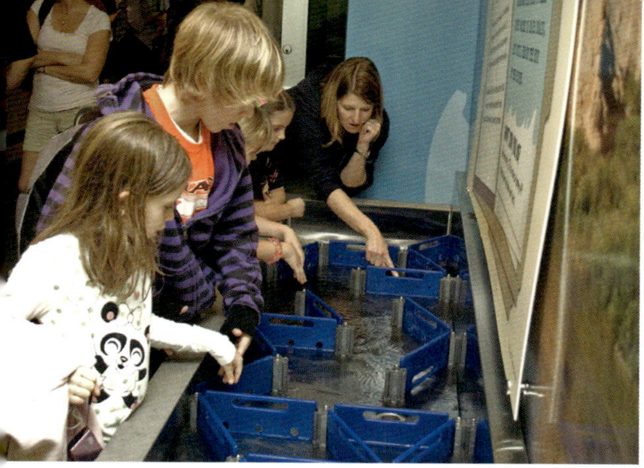

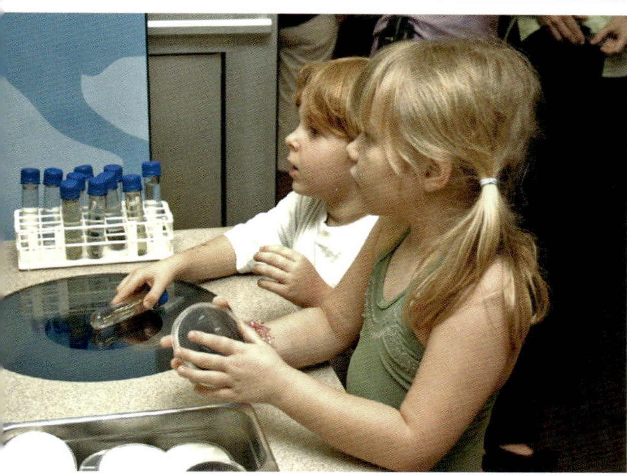

"Your organization is making an invaluable contribution to the effort to promote environmental awareness among our youth and to encourage them to continue their own efforts.... Please accept my congratulations on your success and my best wishes for the future."

Al Gore
Former Vice President
of the United States

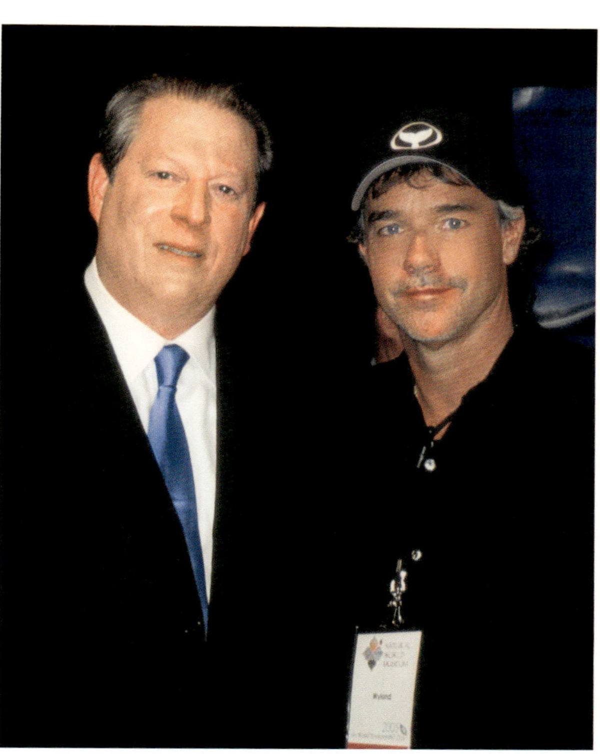

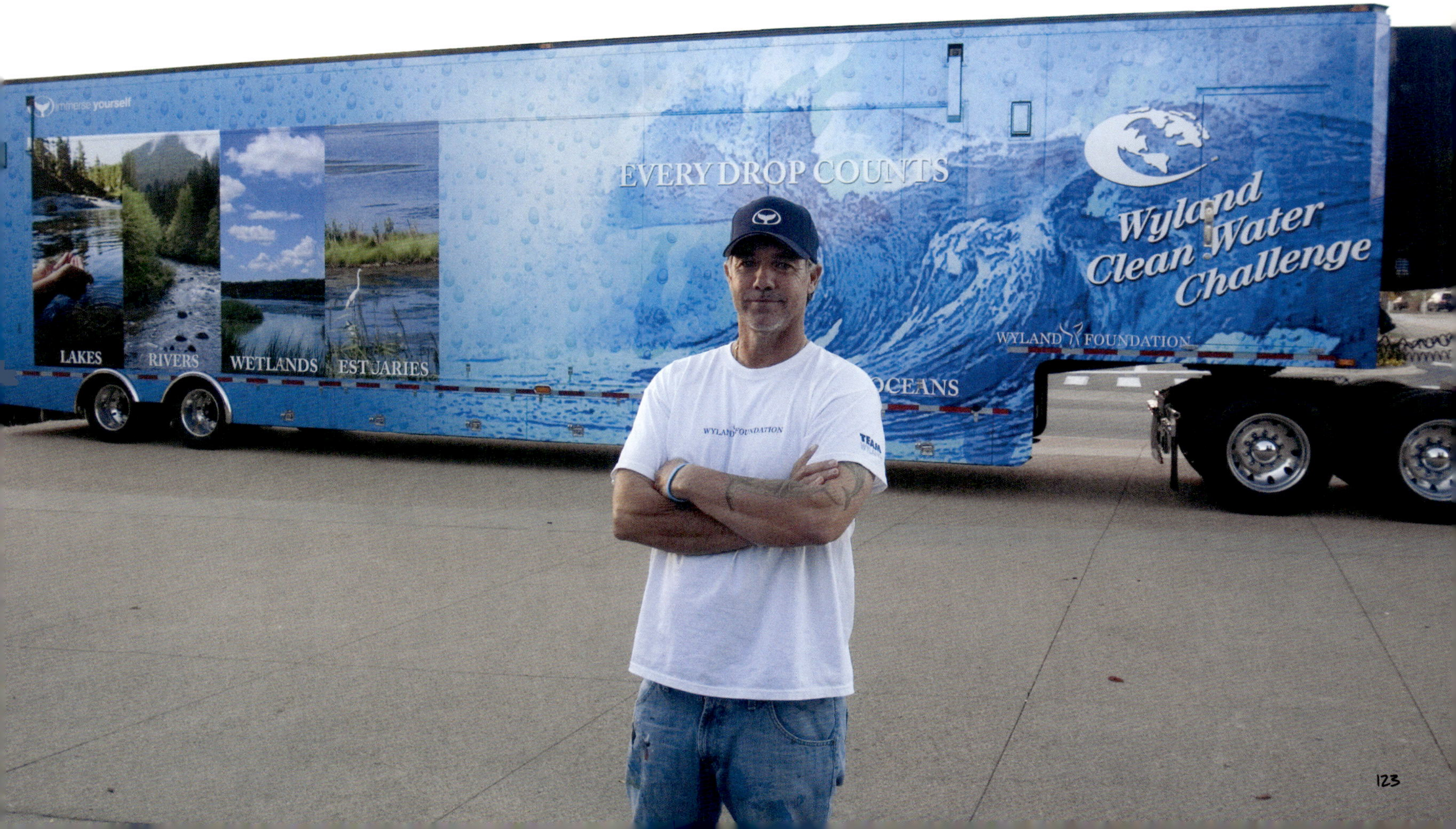

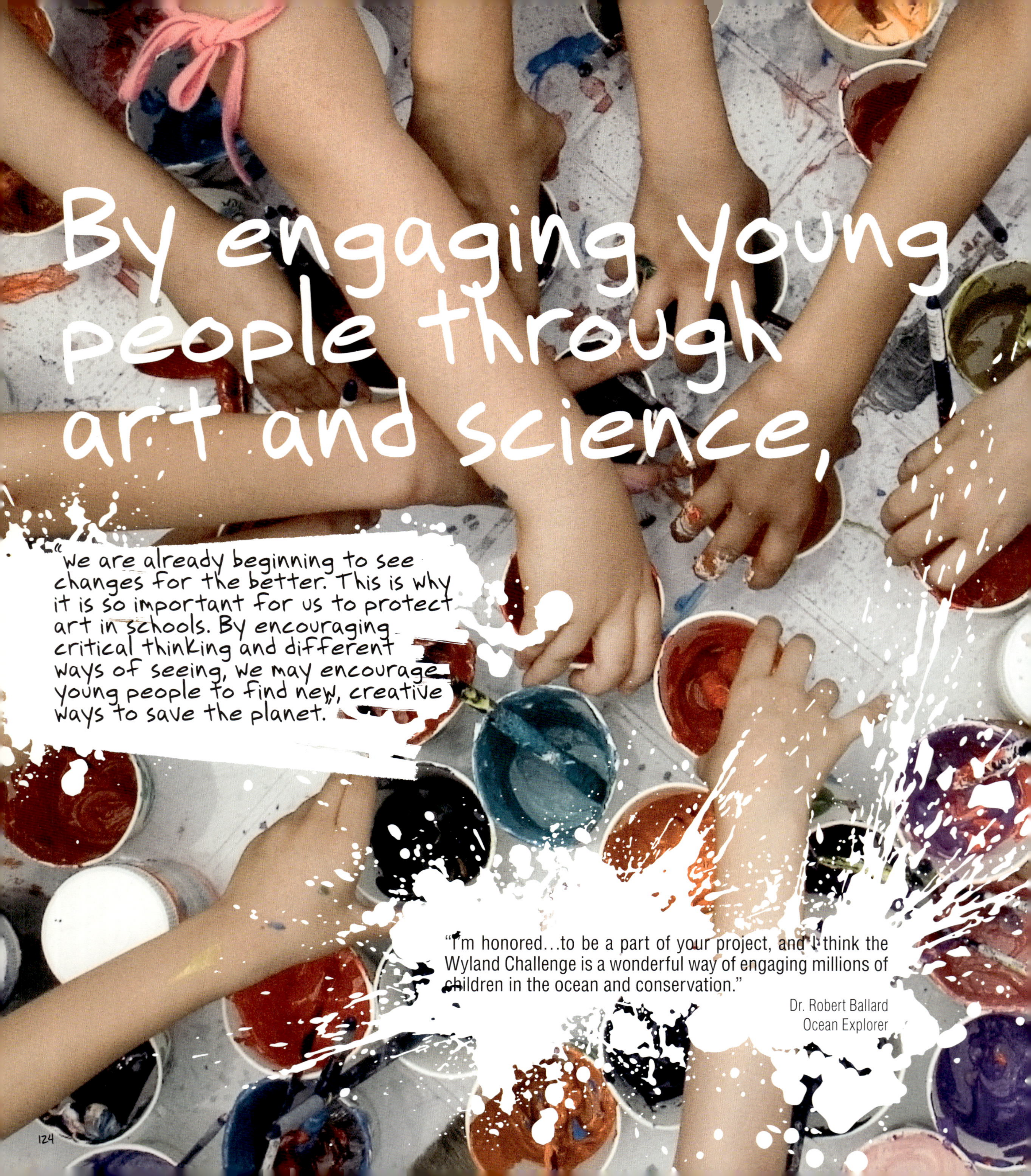
By engaging young people through art and science,
"we are already beginning to see changes for the better. This is why it is so important for us to protect art in schools. By encouraging critical thinking and different ways of seeing, we may encourage young people to find new, creative ways to save the planet."
"I'm honored…to be a part of your project, and I think the Wyland Challenge is a wonderful way of engaging millions of children in the ocean and conservation."
Dr. Robert Ballard
Ocean Explorer

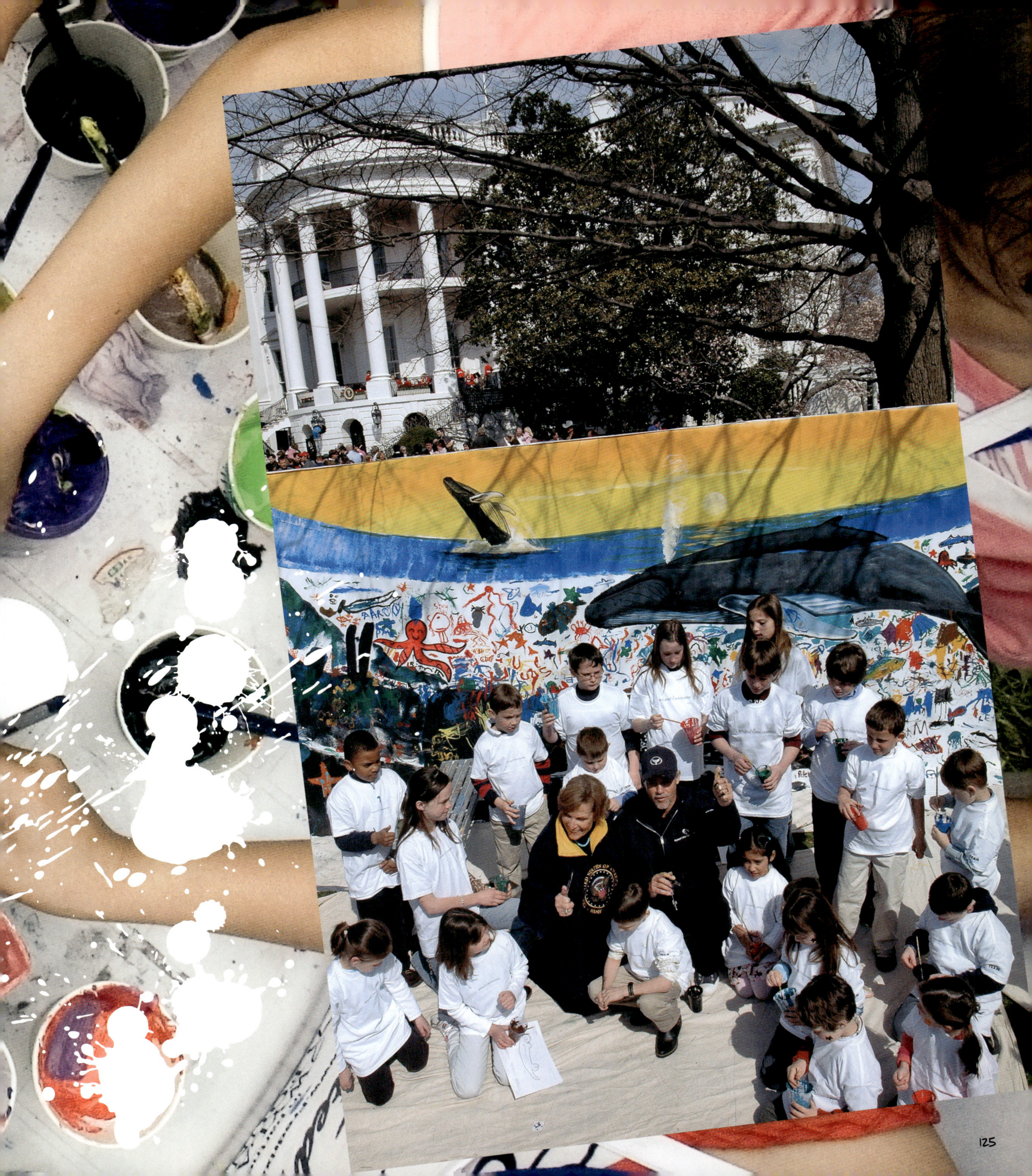

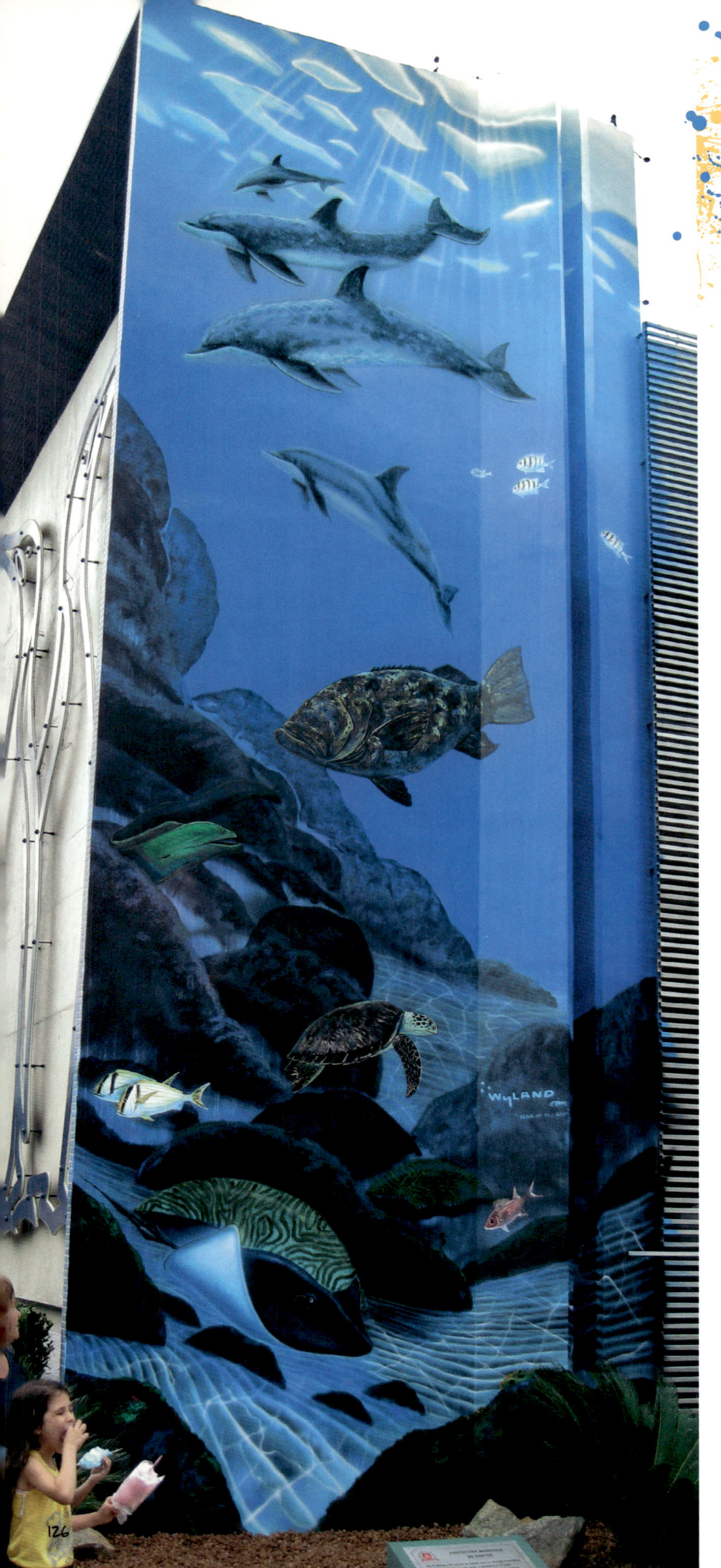

Whaling Wall 98

"Celebrating the Reef"

Location: Santos Municipal Aquarium
Santos, Brazil
Size: 30' w x 40' h
Gallons of Paint Used: 50 gallons
Sea life depicted: Manta ray, hawksbill sea turtle, green sea turtle, Goliath grouper, reef fish, spotted dolphins, black tip reef shark, soft and hard coral
Dedicated: May 17, 2008 by Mayor of Santos, Joao Paulo Tavares Papa

One of my dreams is to design a world-class Wyland art and science museum.

I love museums and believe they play an important role in inspiring and educating each new generation. I love the museums of the Smithsonian; the Museum of Modern Art; the Louvre, the Picasso Museum in Barcelona; the Norman Rockwell Museum in Stockbridge, Massachusetts; and new museums like the Dali Museum in St. Petersburg, Florida. My personal favorite has to be the Salvador Dali museum in Cadaqués, Spain. It encompasses all of Dali's mediums – painting, sculpture, and a fantastic ceiling mural – and truly reflects his surrealistic art. I envision a Wyland museum near the ocean that will display all of my original paintings in oil and watercolor, as well as my bronze sculptures. Of course, I would hope to still be young enough to paint a number of monumental murals on the ceiling and throughout the museum. I would also like to have many of the great whales and other marine life represented on giant canvases and in life-size sculptures with water elements. The idea would be similar to my plan for a traveling Wyland "Life-Size Exhibition." Sculptures would be suspended from the ceiling against a background of giant canvases to give viewers a sensation of standing next to the great mammals of the sea. There would be an IMAX film, interactive exhibits, and other educational opportunities. Art is such a great way to get people involved in learning, and over the millennium it has shaped the history of mankind. In the 21st century I believe the environment will be the most important issue we face, affecting every facet of our lives. My goal is to use art as a way to raise awareness about these environmental issues. The Wyland Museum will showcase people and groups who are on the forefront of marine conservation. It would also showcase renowned artists, scientists, and organizations that are contributing to the humanities. The ultimate goal is to leave future generations with a sense of wonder and hopefully a greater appreciation of the marine world.

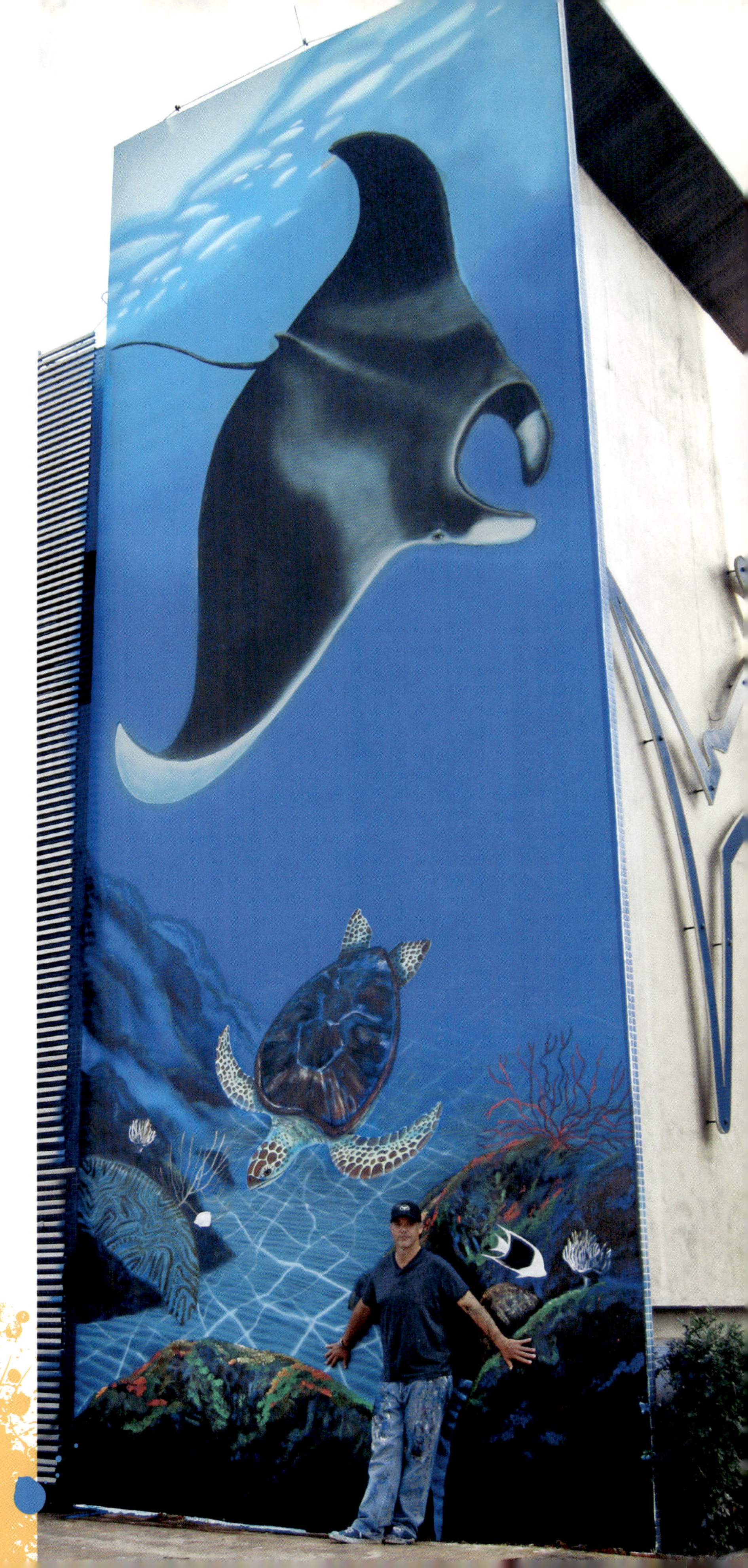

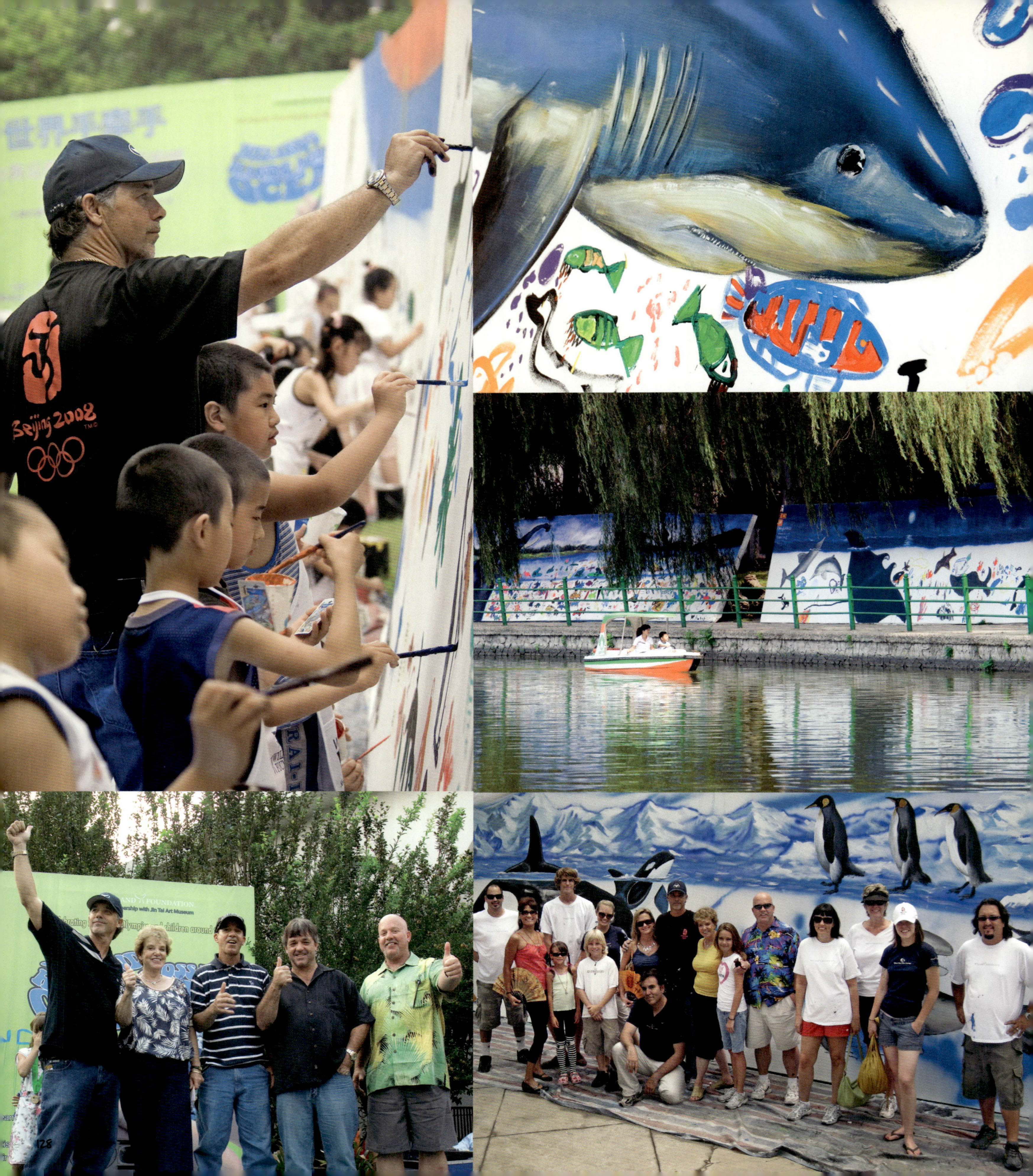
Beijing 2008

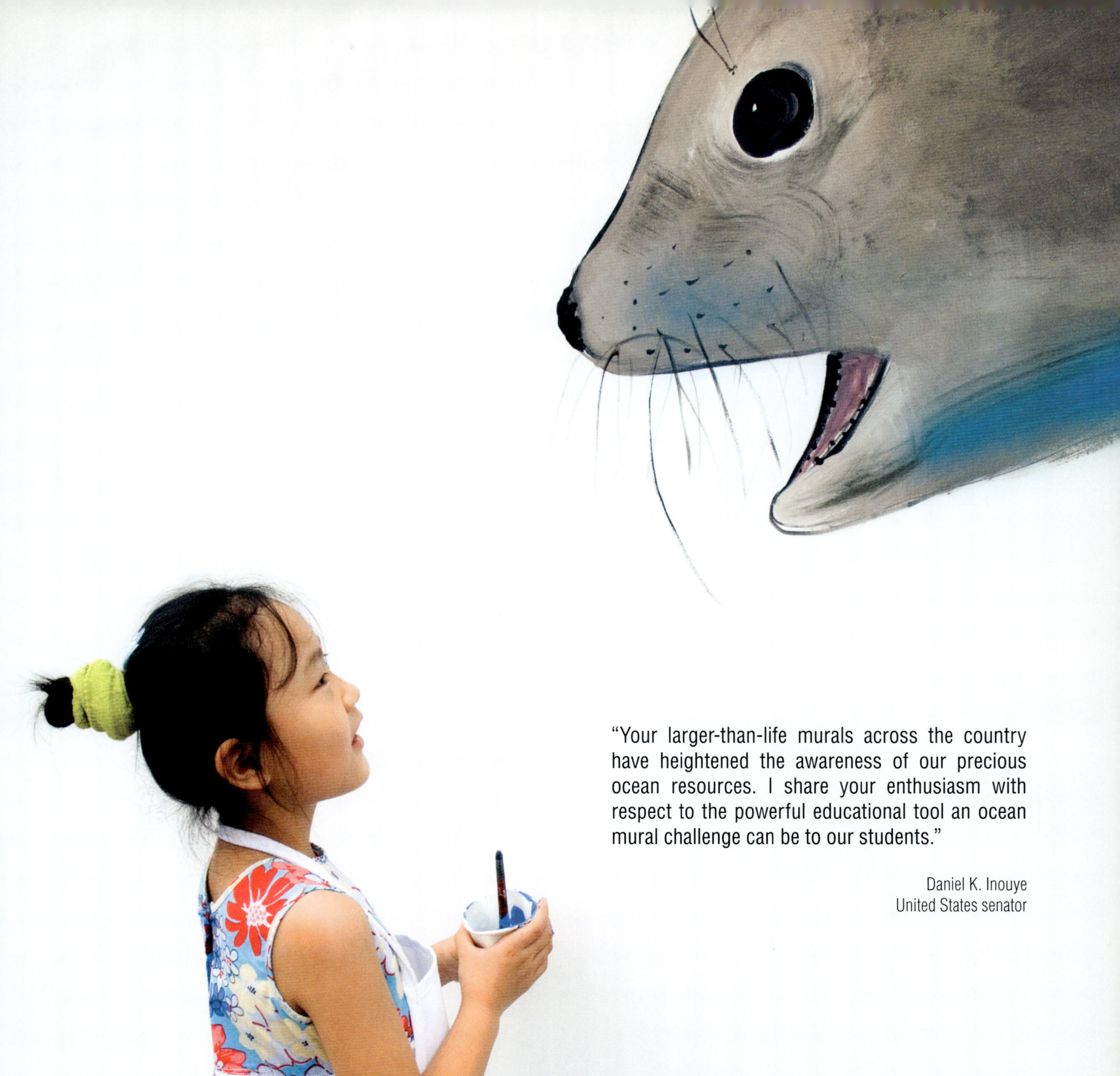

"Your larger-than-life murals across the country have heightened the awareness of our precious ocean resources. I share your enthusiasm with respect to the powerful educational tool an ocean mural challenge can be to our students."

Daniel K. Inouye
United States senator

"Teaching our children to care about

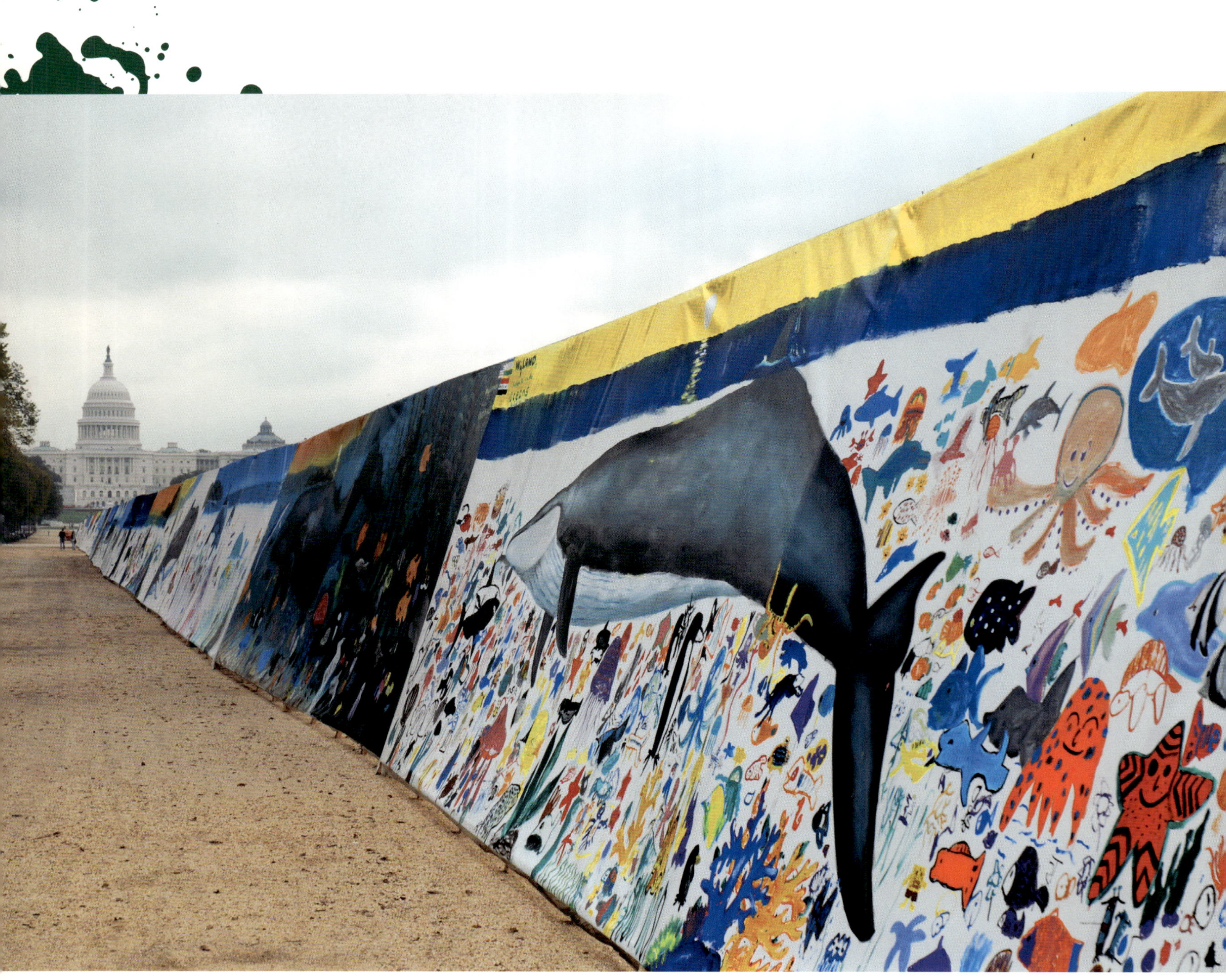

the planet may be our greatest mission..."

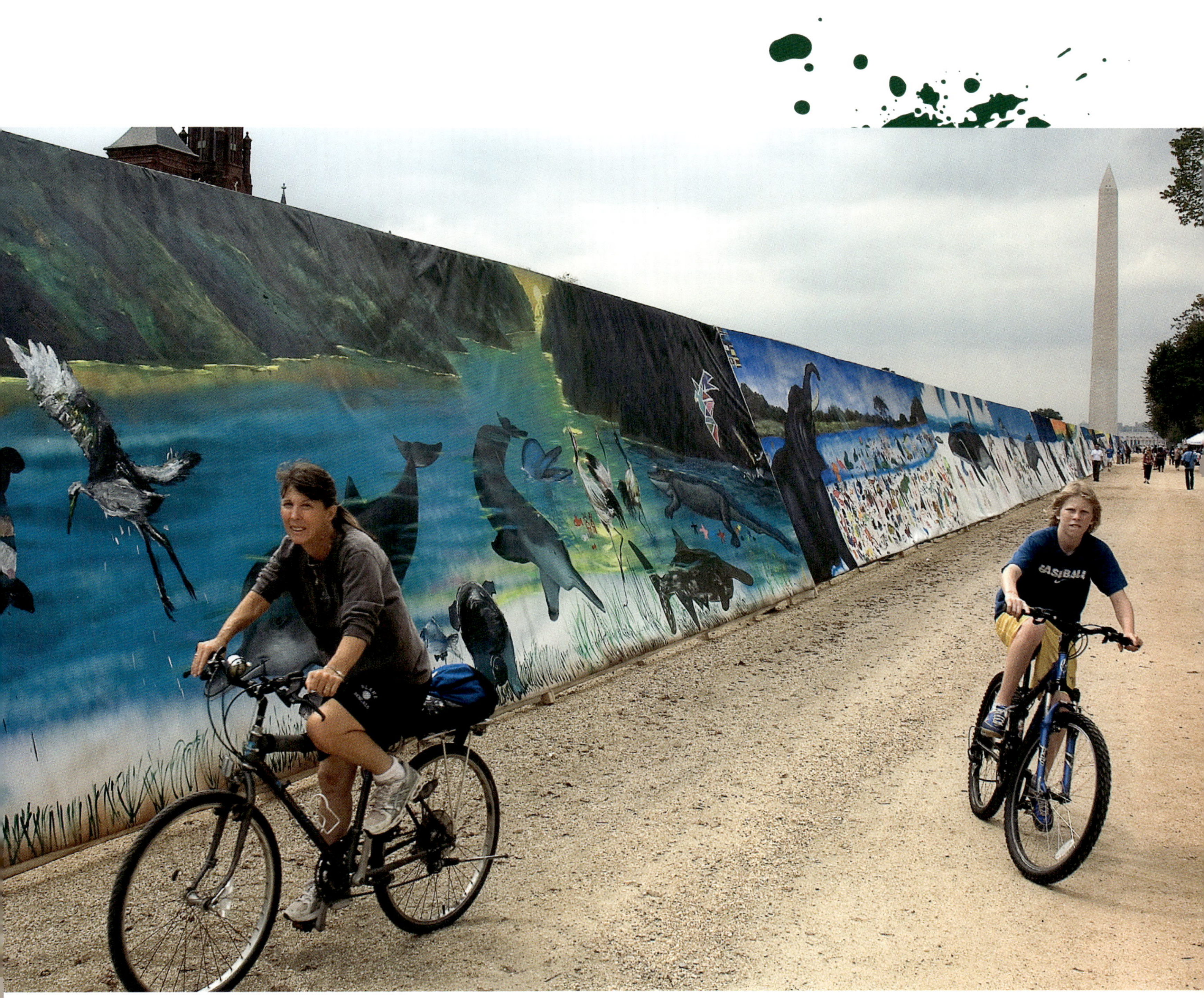

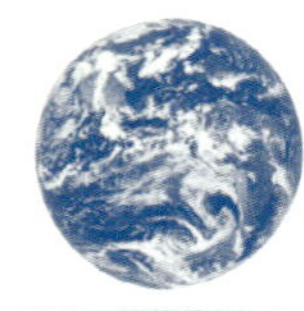

OCEAN ARTISTS SOCIETY™

Michael Aw
Franco Banfi
Al Barnes
Gary Bell
Jennifer Belote
Jonathan Bird
Ernie Brooks
James Cameron
Tom Campbell
Eric Cheng
Cathy Church
Ian Coleman
Mark Conlin
Deano Cook
Annie Crawley

Bill Curtsinger
Ned DeLoach
David Doubilet
Richard Ellis
Todd Essick
Bob Evans
Beverly Factor
Chris & Monique Fallows
David Fleetham
Stephen Frink
Al Giddings
Howard Hall
Michele Hall
Eric Hanauer

Bill Harrigan
Guy Harvey
Jennifer Hayes
Richard Herrmann
Carlos Hiller
Paul Humann
Pascal Jagut
Denis Lagrange
Pascal Lecocq
Greg MacGillivray
Stanley Meltzof
Hiroya Minakuchi
Jeff Mondragon
Simon Morris
Amos Nachoum

Chris Newbert
Charles "Flip" Nicklin
Chuck Nicklin
Michael S Nolan
Phil Nuytten
Doug Perrine
Tim Rock
BJ Royster
Andre Seale
Douglas David Seifert
Marty Snyderman
Roland St. John
John Steel
Ronald G. Steven

Bob Talbot
Ron & Valerie Taylor
Danny Van Belle
Viktor
Ingrid Visser
Stan Waterman
James D. Watt
Berkley White
Birgitte Wilms
David Wrobel
Wyland
Mirko Zanni
Vadim Zverev

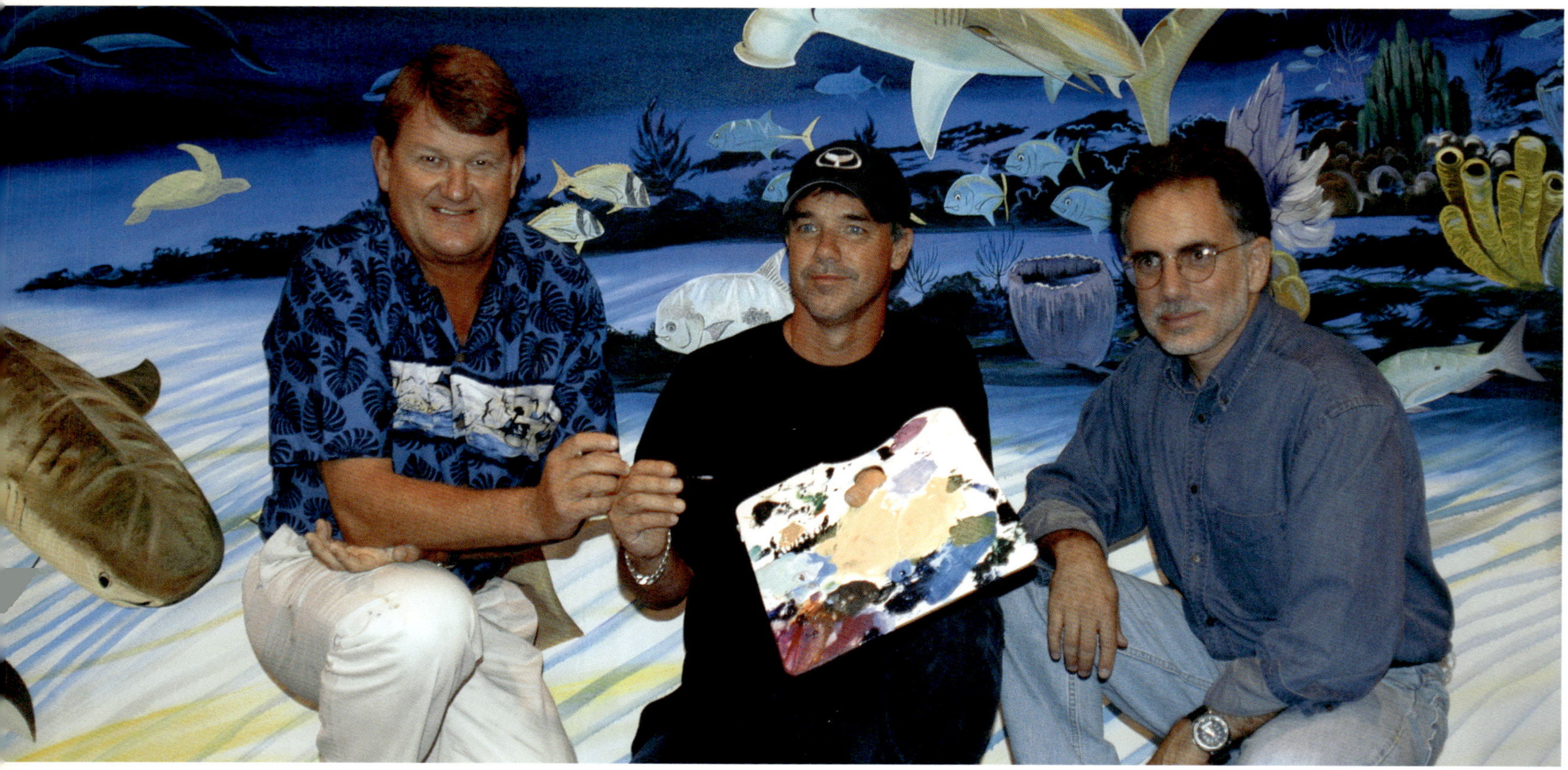

Founding members Left to right: Guy Harvey, Wyland, and Bob Talbot

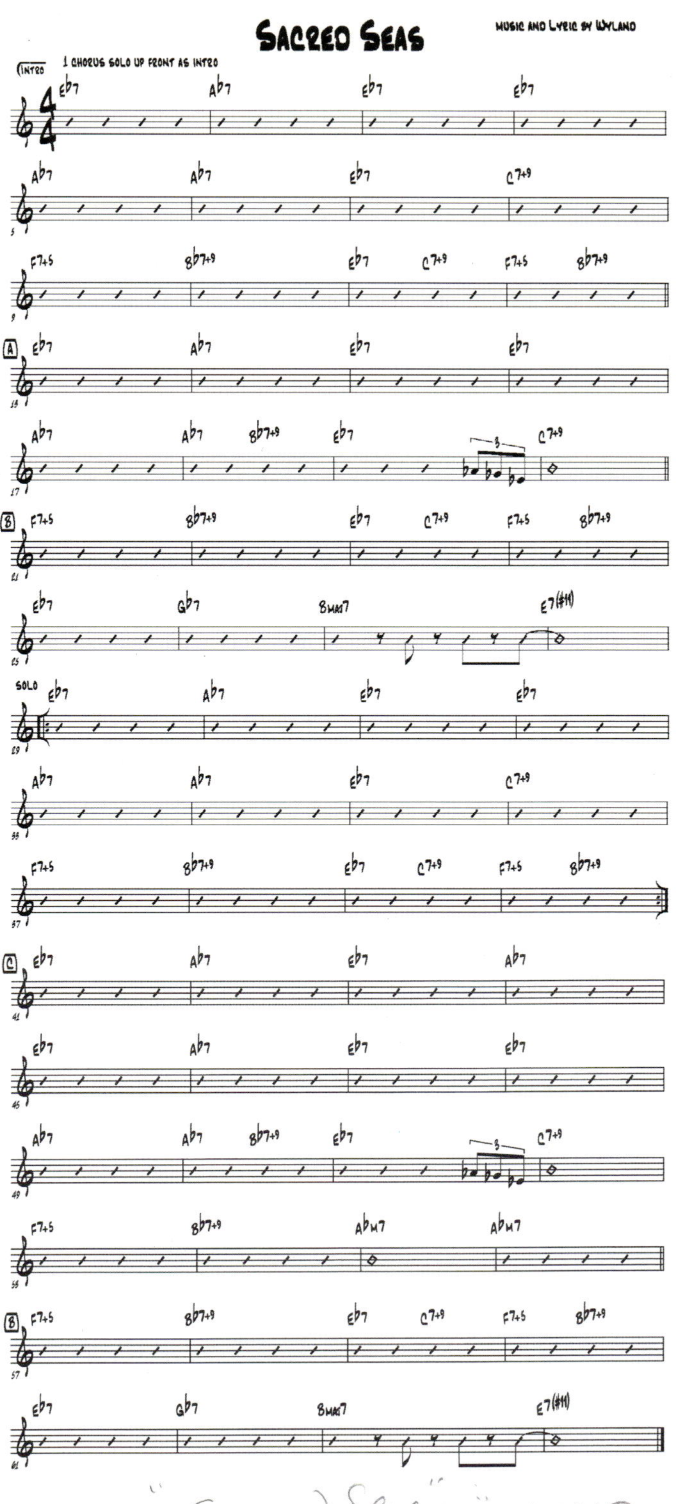

"Sacred Seas" by Wyland ©2005

SACRED SEAS – RHYTHM – 2

The sky on fire
ooting star above
us to her warmth
live and moving
Rythms we feel Give
us inspiration
o keep us full of love

it inspiration you are
providing
are a sea of beauty
warm and inviting
ngs a smile to me
ever in my life

you will always be
our sacred seas are calling
we all can hear
we need to help protect her
and never shed a tear
if we listen closely
the voice of mother ocean calls
upon us
now the message is so clear
there's nothing to fear

what inspiration you are providing
you are a sea of beauty
so warm and inviting
bring a smile to me
forever in my life
you will always be

CD COVER/MUSIC CHIP HERE

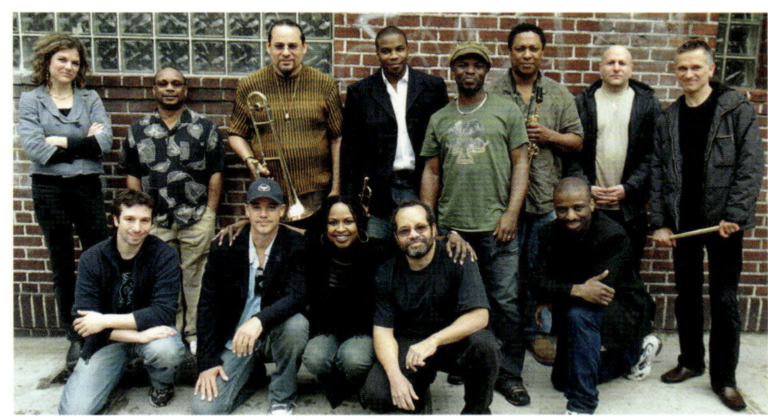

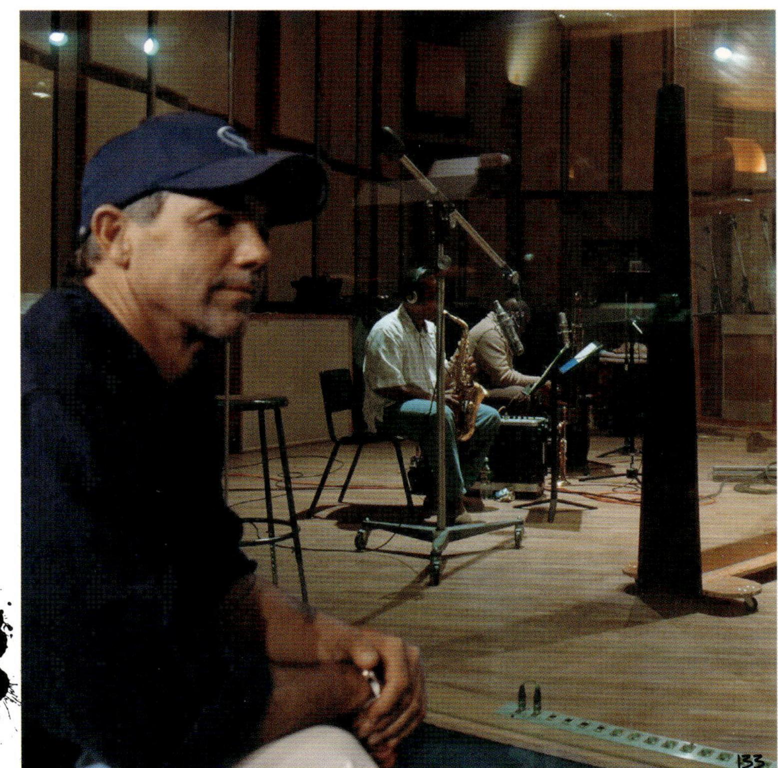

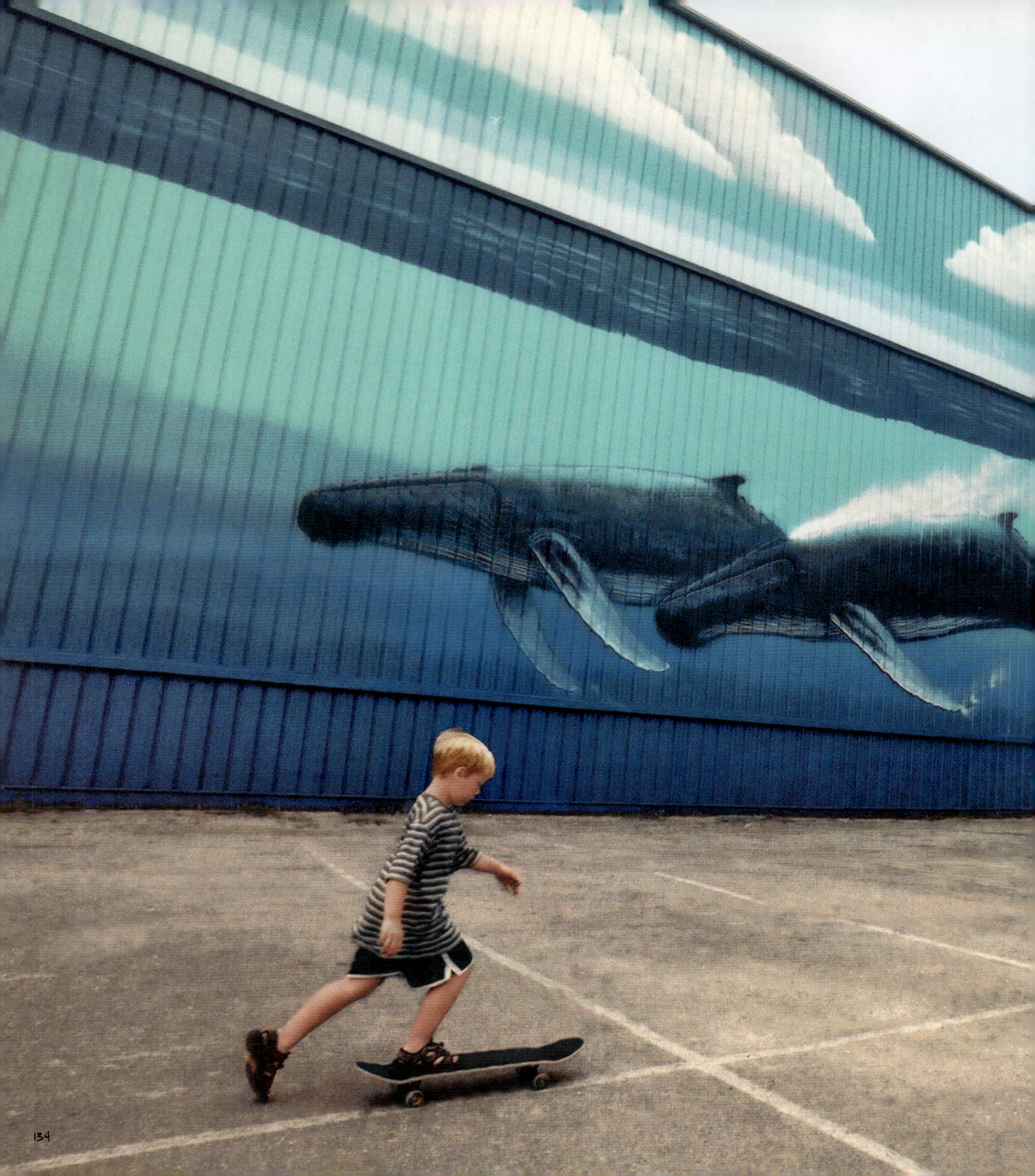

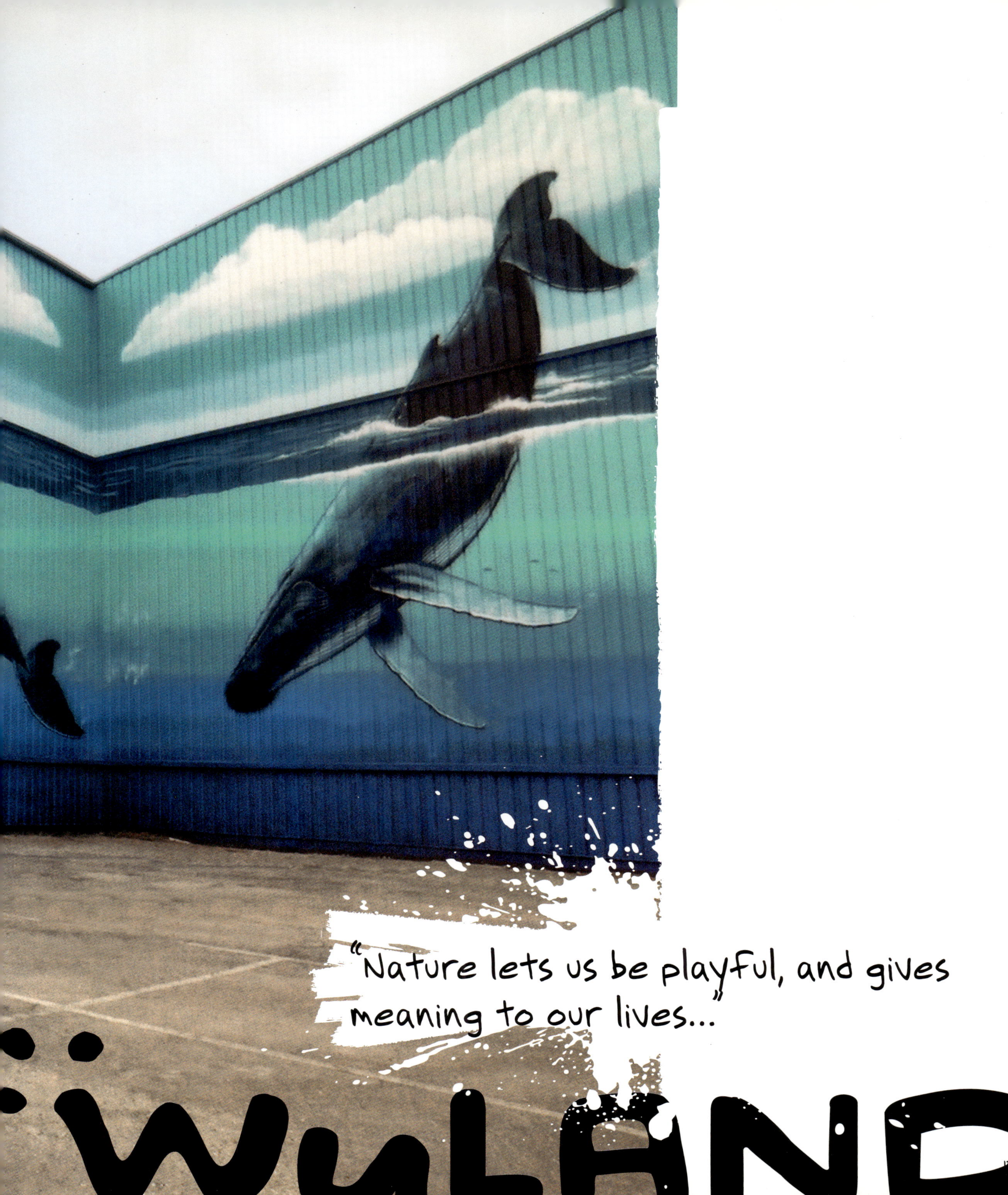
"Nature lets us be playful, and gives meaning to our lives..."
WYLAND

GREEN FUTURE

environmental renaissance

"The 21st century must be an environmental renaissance..."

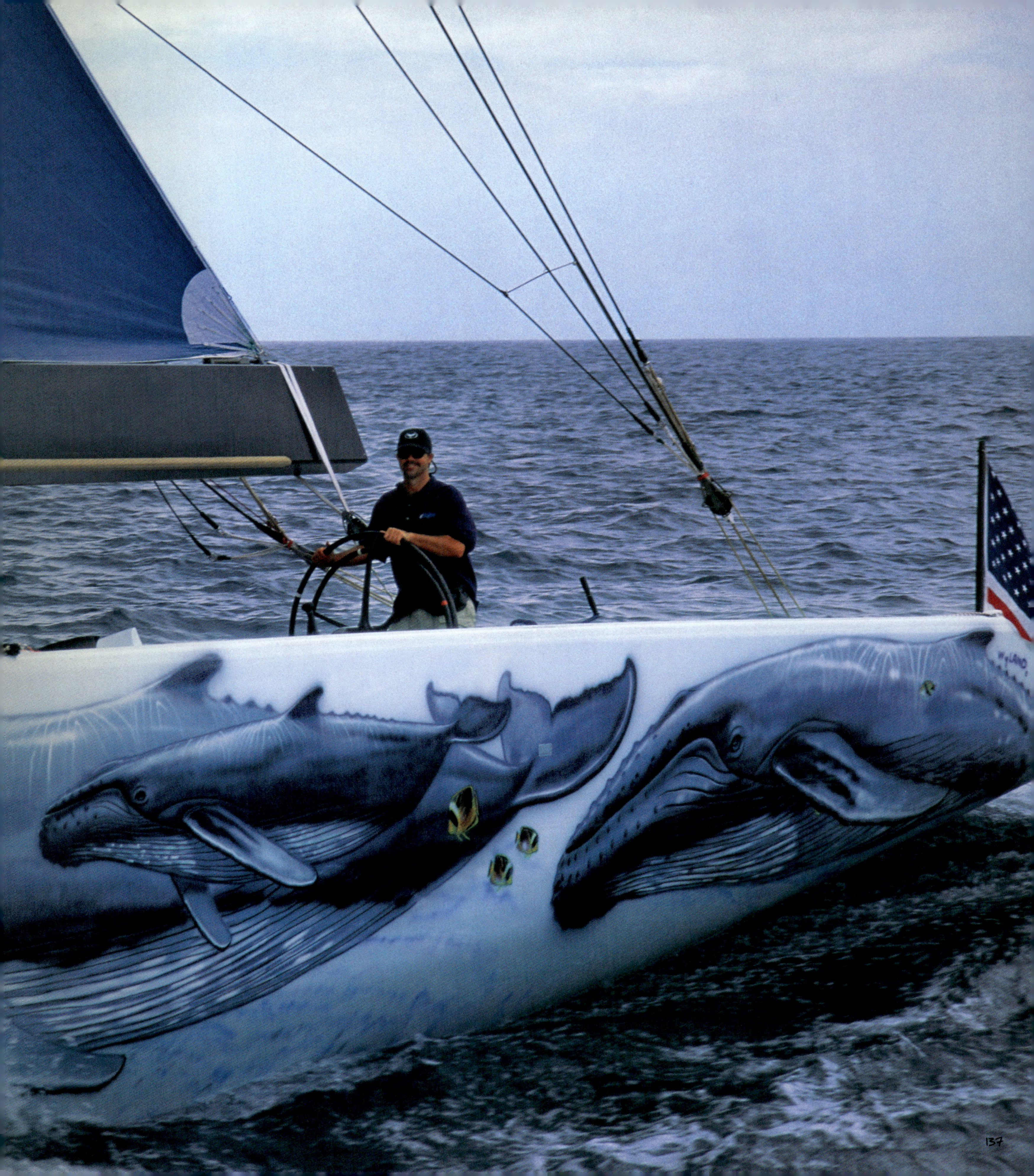

"If we can pass along our knowledge and appreciation for our planet's natural resources to the next generation, we can leave a legacy that will make all the difference."

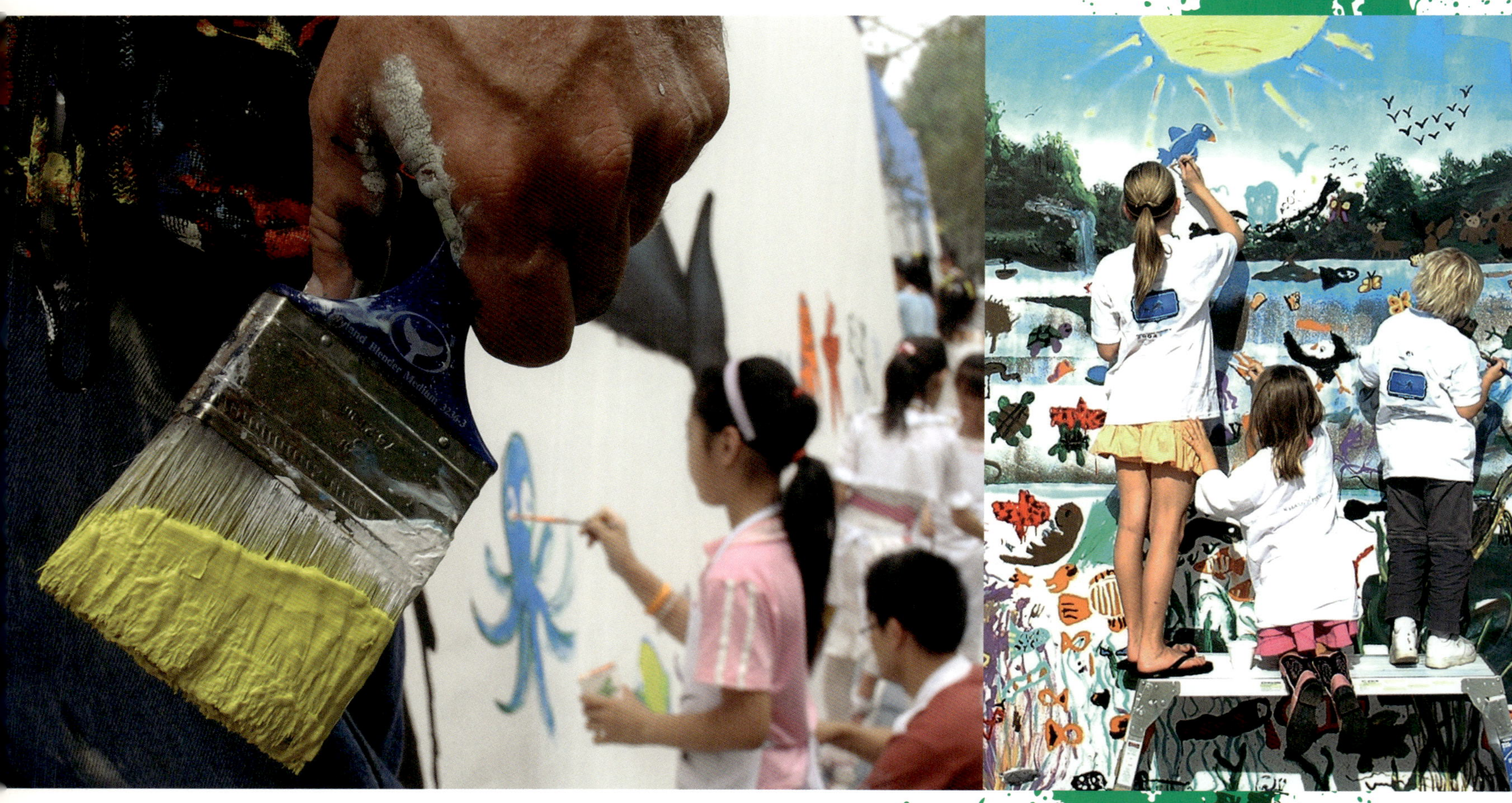

Amazing, isn't it, how Wyland can talk about a world tour the way most people talk about going to the grocery store. But Wyland wants nothing less than the world, and he's getting there millions of people at a time. "Out of the earth's seven billion people, we probably have five billion to go, but that's the goal. I'd like nothing better than to have six billion people talking and thinking about protecting our planet, and I see no reason to stop trying." His blue eyes blaze. "It's doable. We're doing it. We are making a difference. I can see it firsthand, and I'm totally energized about it."

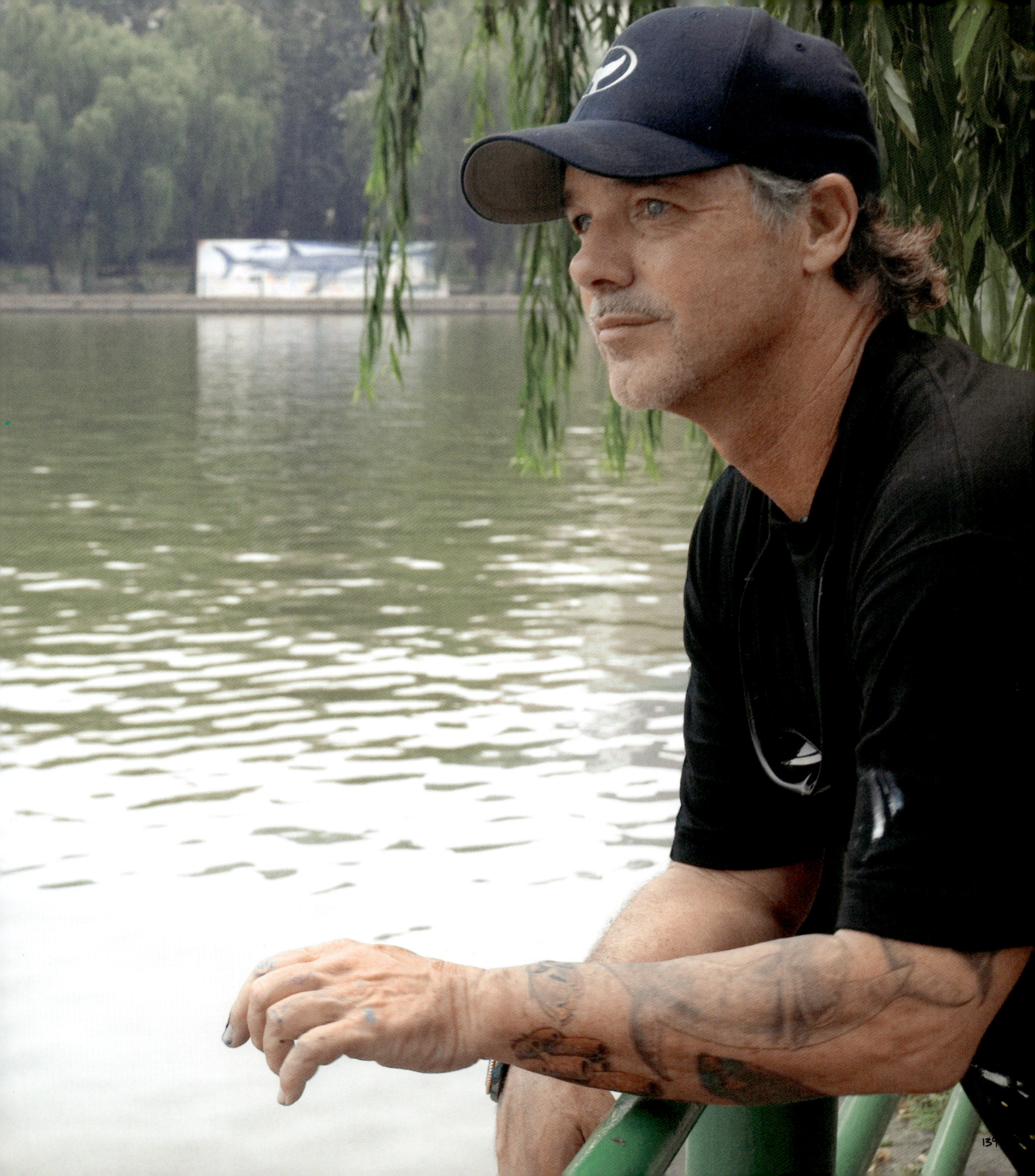

From the beginning, Wyland's vision for the Foundation was simple: to be able to wake up every morning and know that what you are doing today will make the world a better place tomorrow.

"I want to be one of the people who actually contributed to protecting water for future generations."

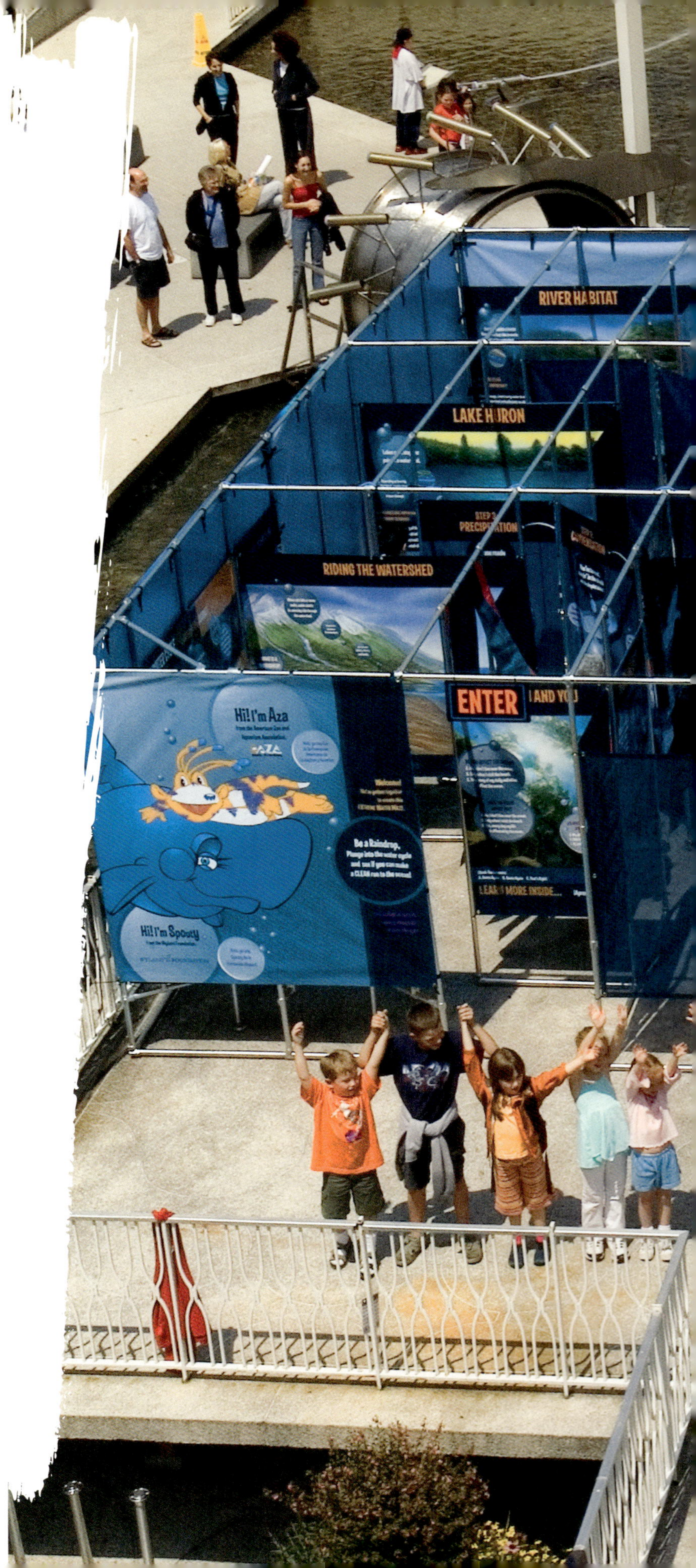

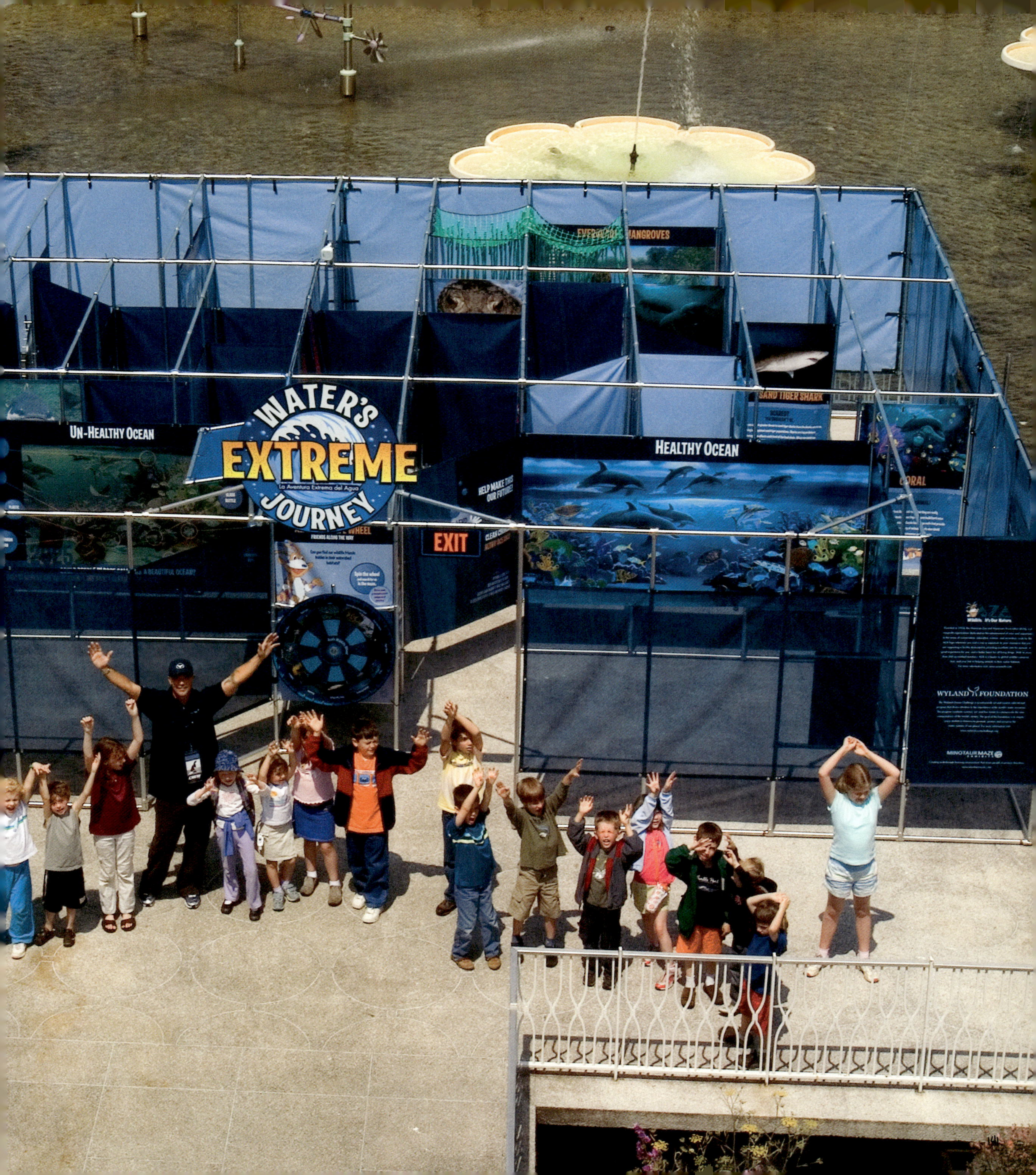

WATER'S EXTREME JOURNEY
La Aventura Extrema del Agua
UN-HEALTHY OCEAN
HEALTHY OCEAN
EXIT
HELP MAKE THIS OUR FUTURE!
MANGROVES
SAND TIGER SHARK
CORAL
WYLAND FOUNDATION
MINOTAUR MAZES

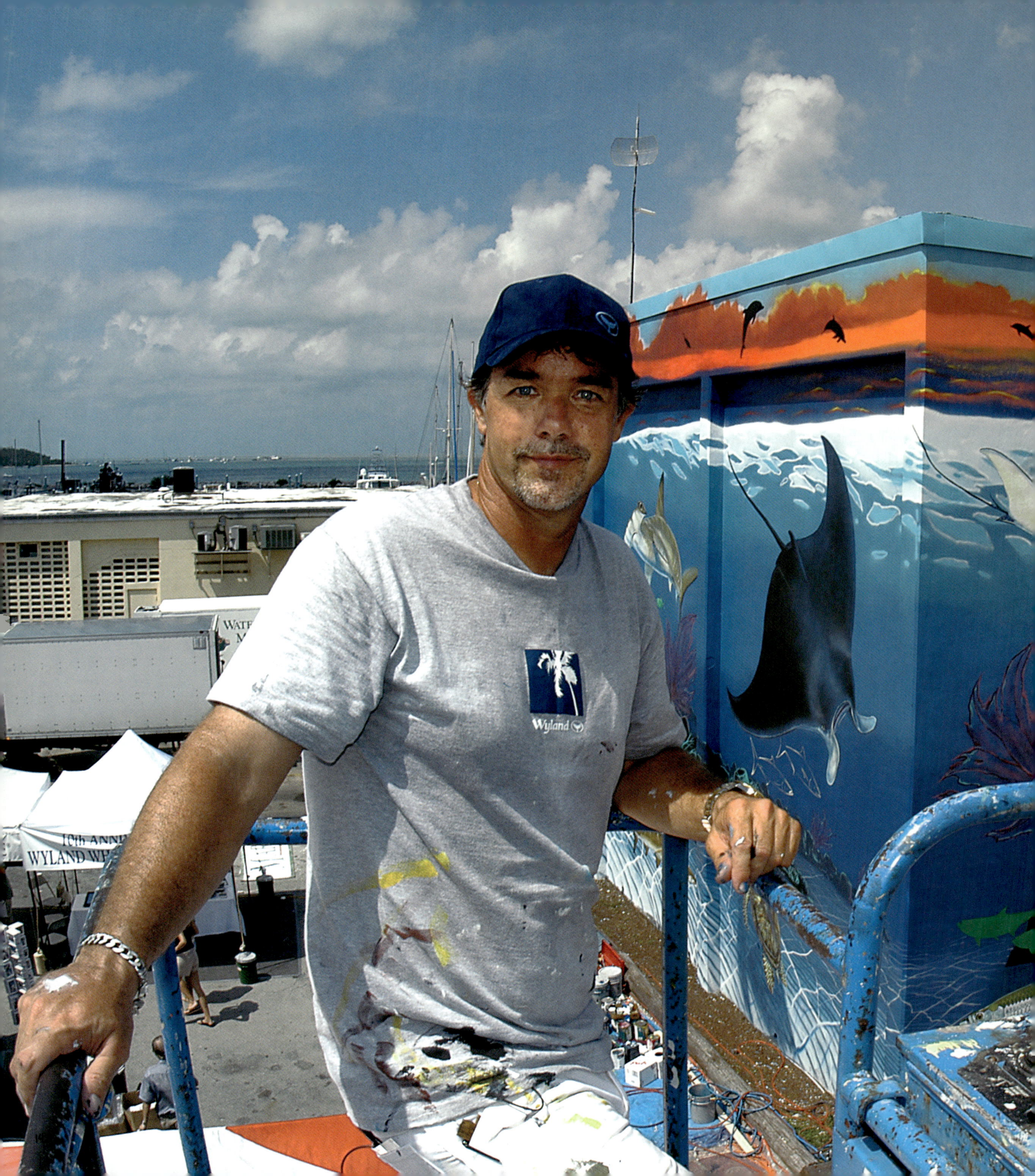
Wyland

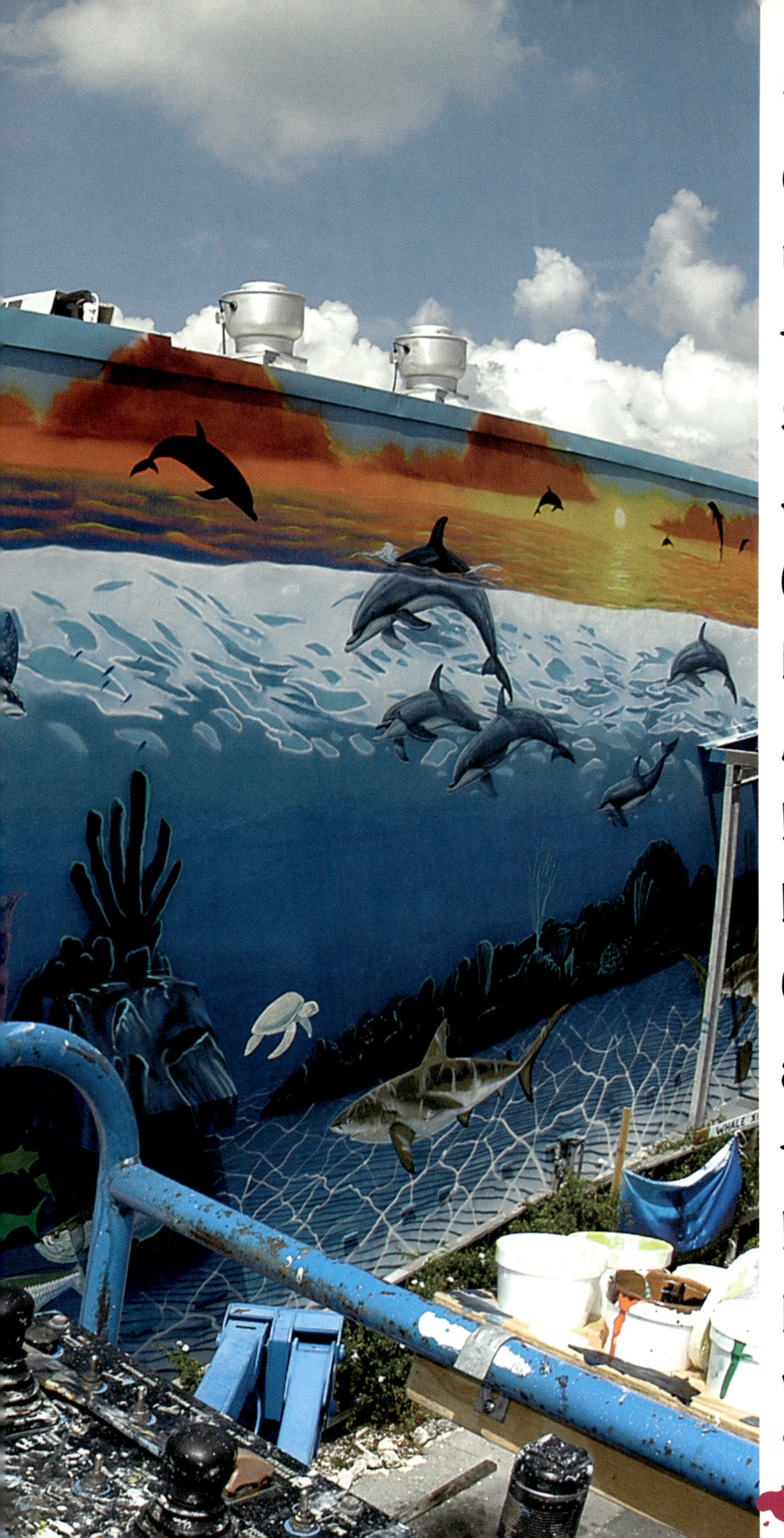

He has completed
over one hundred
monumental murals
throughout the United
States, Canada,
Japan,
China,
France,
Australia,
New Zealand,
Palau,
Guam,
and Mexico,
to name a few.
It is estimated that a
billion people annually view
Wyland's art.

"When I'm physically up against the wall painting a life-size whale, I simply imagine how the entire wall would look from several blocks away. It's visualization, pure and simple. I simply imagine the whale swimming across the wall and I paint it as it goes by.

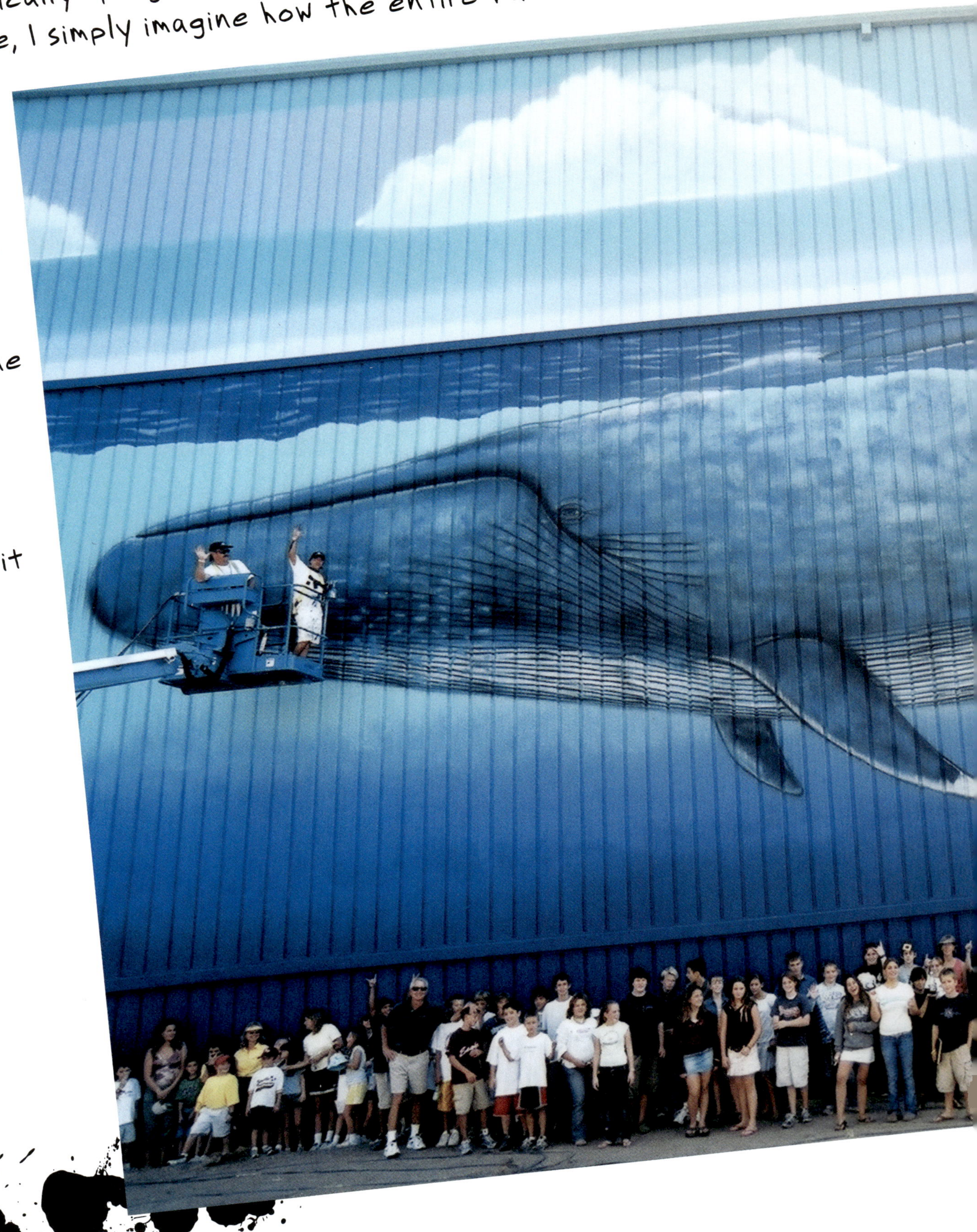

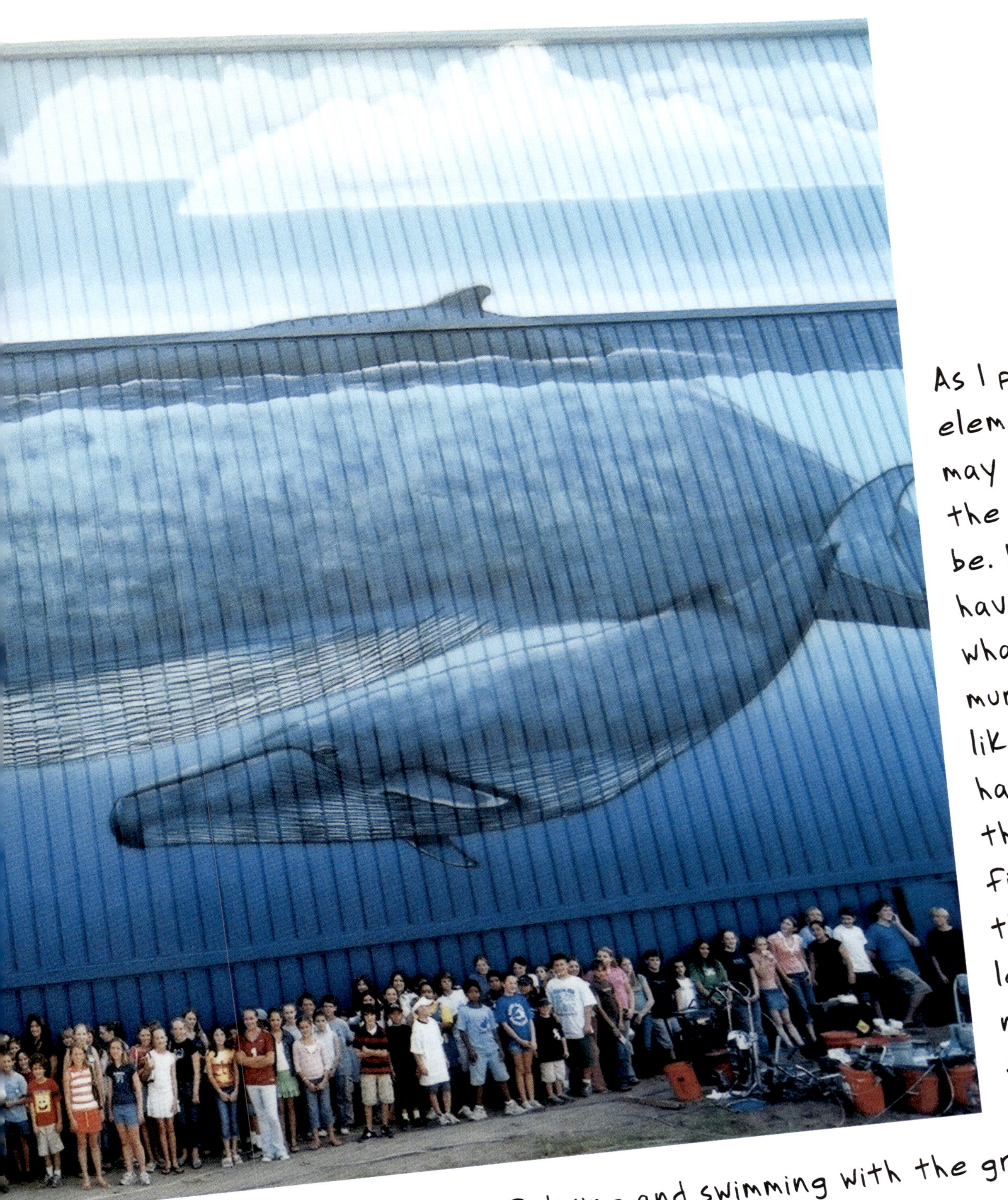

As I paint one element, that may tell me what the next one will be. I really don't have an idea of what the finished mural will look like. However, I have spent more than twenty-five years diving the oceans and looking at the natural world from an artist's perspective.

All the years of diving and swimming with the great whales and other aquatic life have helped me visualize my subject and put it on a wall or canvas or in a monumental sculpture."

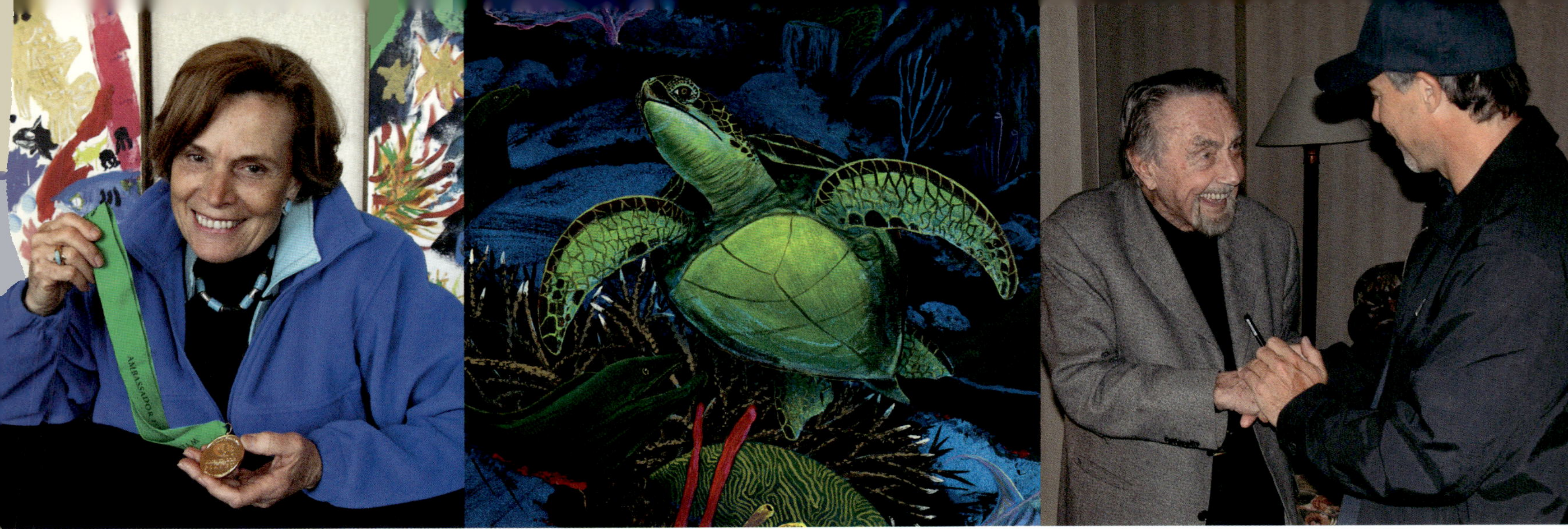

Dr. Sylvia Earle

"I have admired the great underwater photography of Hans Hass, who created some of the first underwater images using the cameras he invented. His images still hold up. I had a chance to meet him a few years ago and tell him how much his photography inspired my art. We immediately became fast friends."

"The Ocean is a world without nations..."

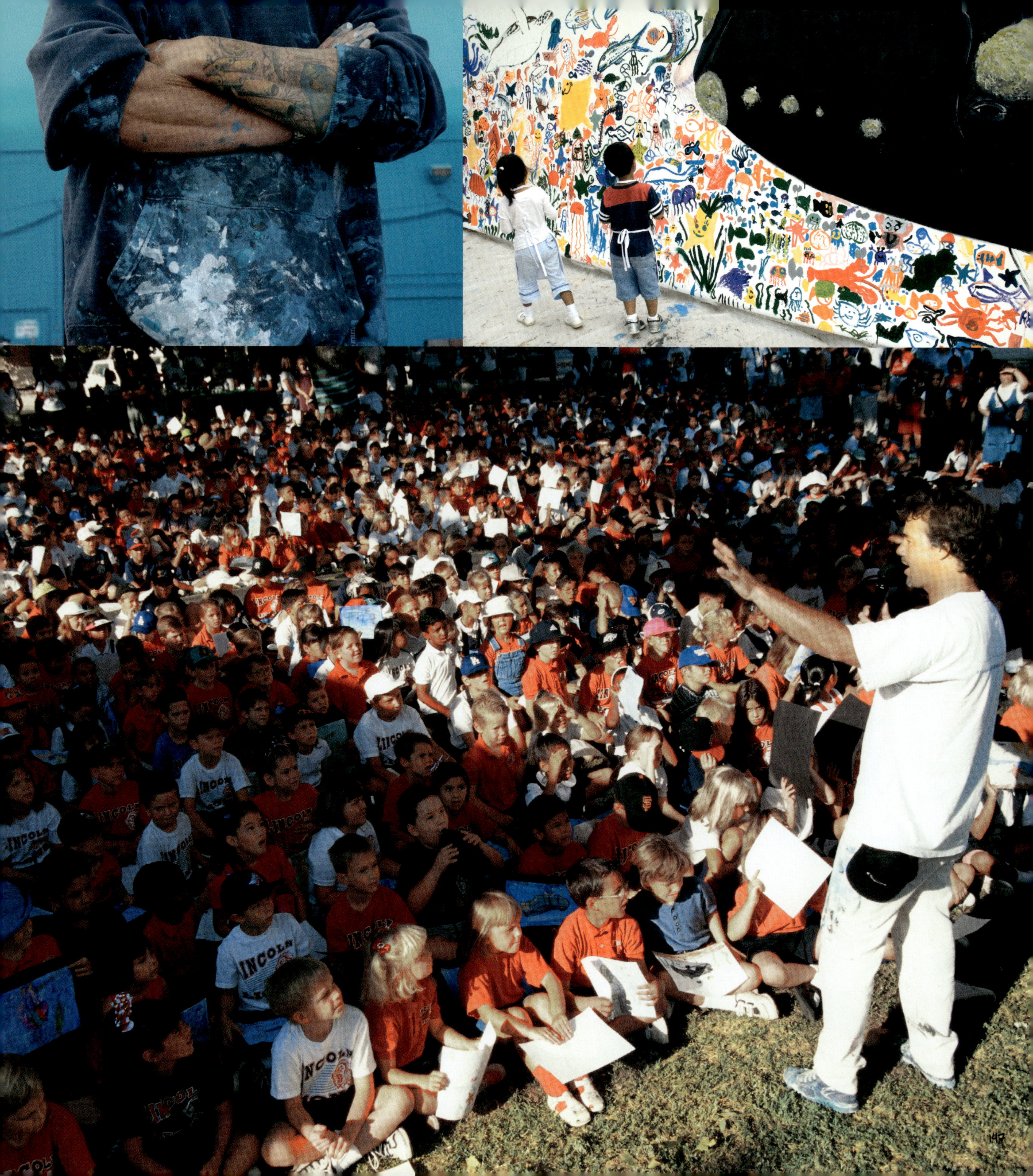

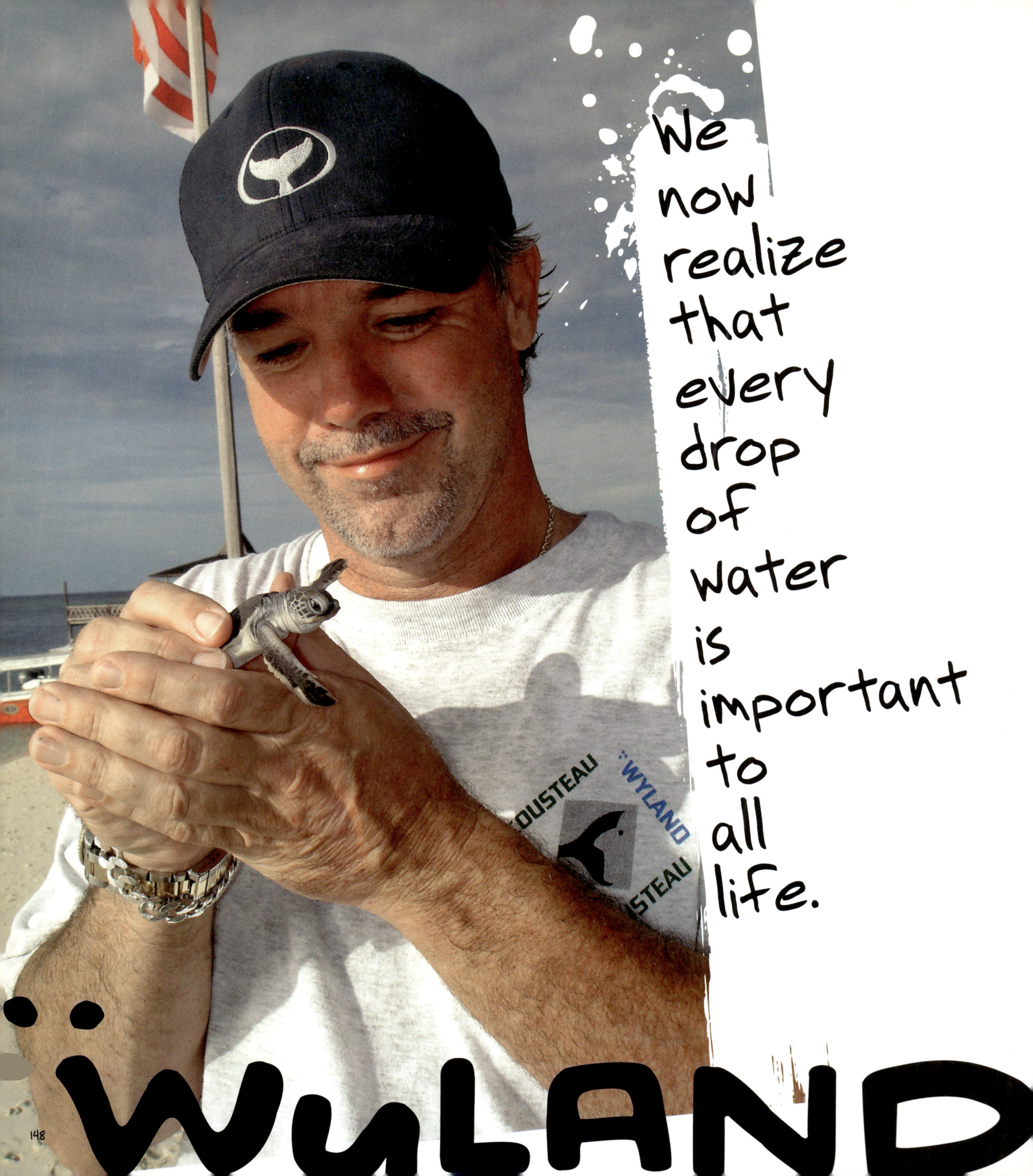
We now realize that every drop of water is important to all life.
WYLAND

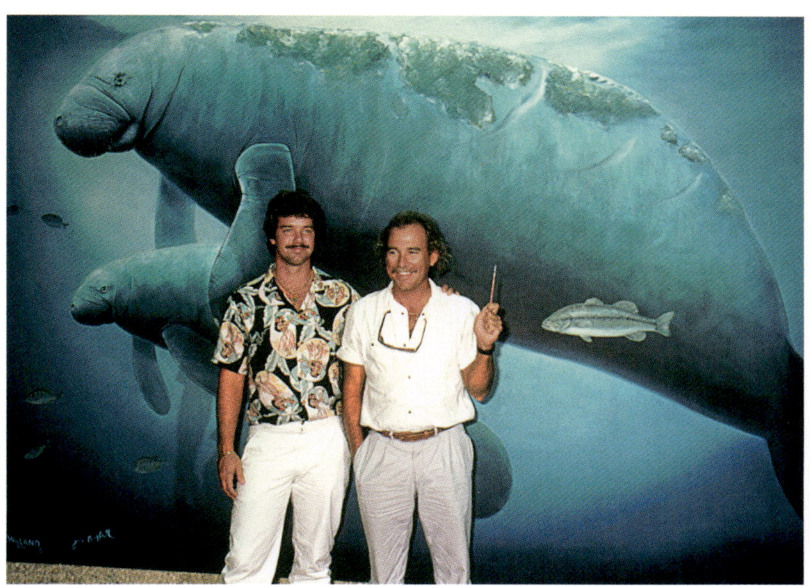

Wyland with Jimmy Buffett
"Save the Manatees"

"We can't protect one body of water without thinking about the next. To protect our oceans and reefs, we must protect our lakes, rivers, streams, and wetland habitats. Climate change, over-fishing, pollution, over-development, and other human activities have wreaked havoc on our aquatic systems. We are seeing the effects today throughout the world."

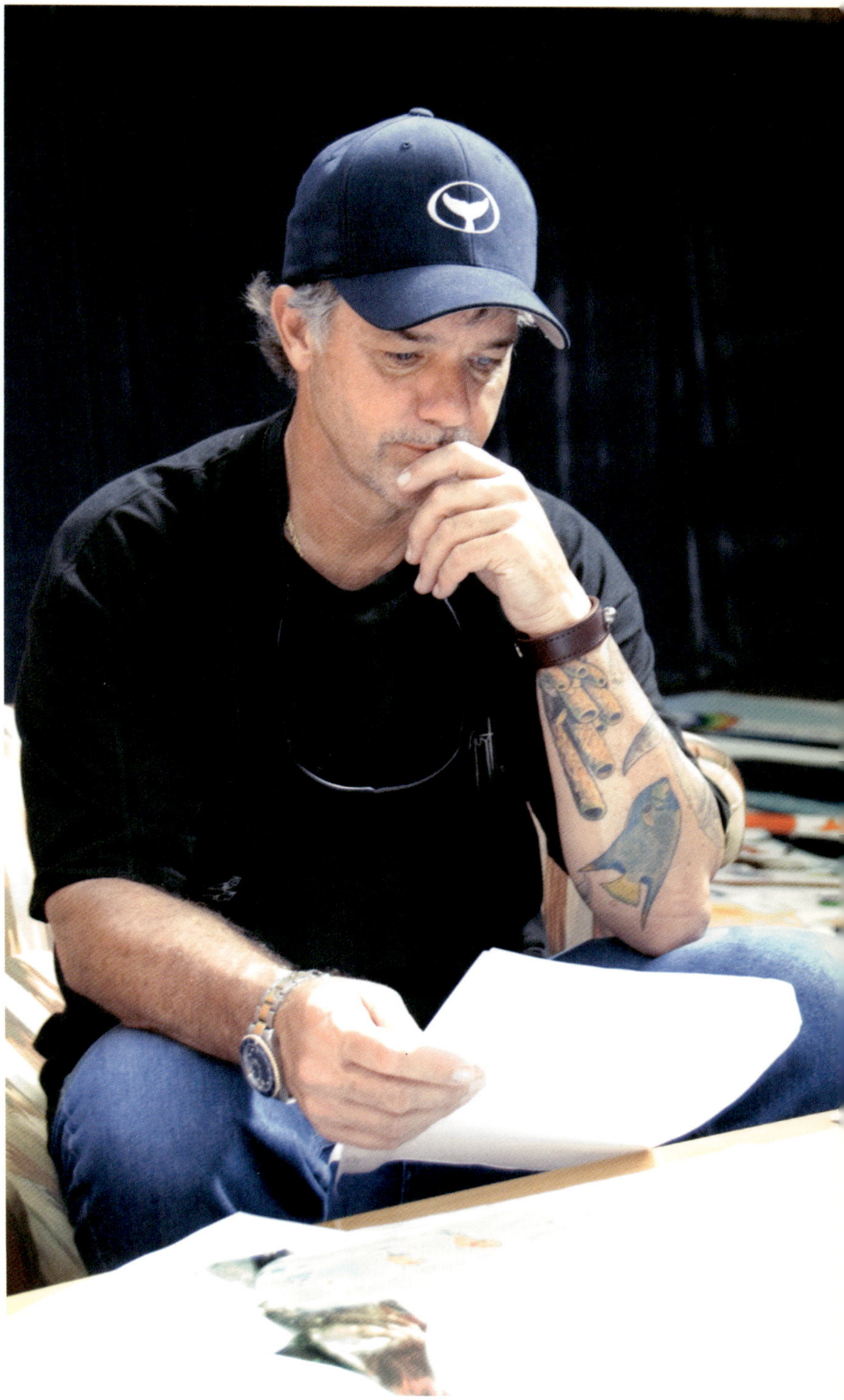

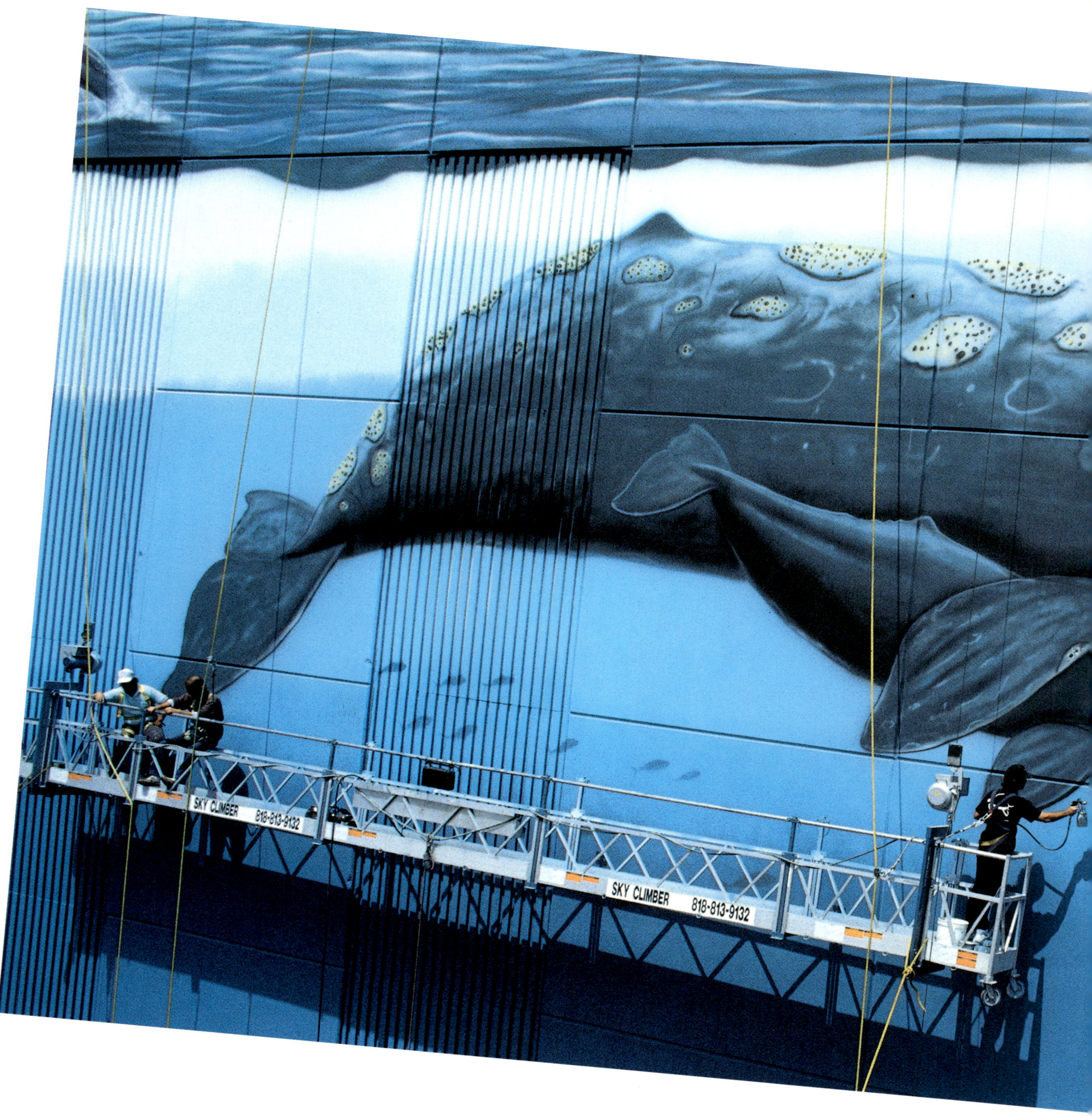
SKY CLIMBER 818-813-9132
SKY CLIMBER 818-813-9132

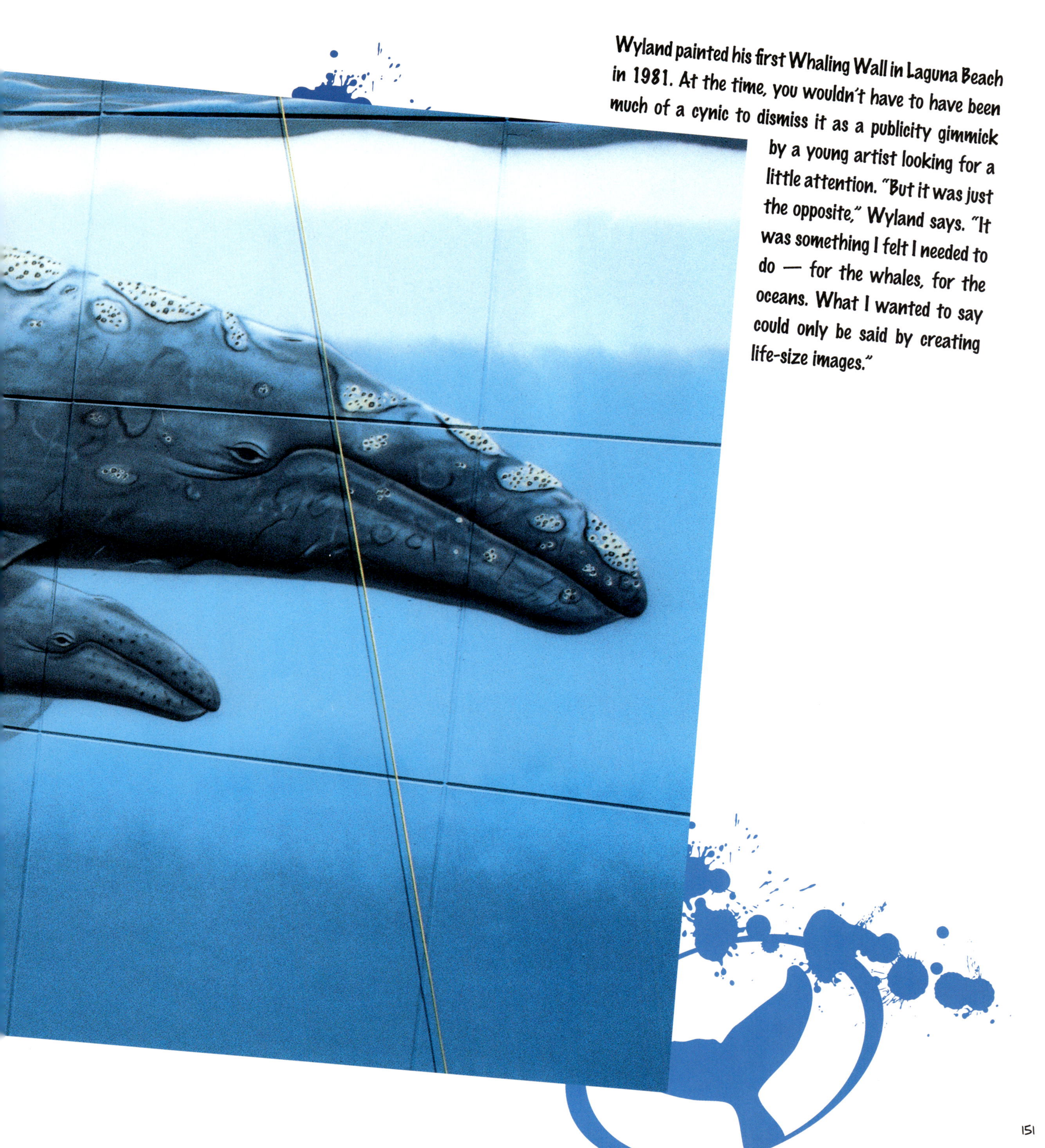

Wyland painted his first Whaling Wall in Laguna Beach in 1981. At the time, you wouldn't have to have been much of a cynic to dismiss it as a publicity gimmick by a young artist looking for a little attention. "But it was just the opposite," Wyland says. "It was something I felt I needed to do — for the whales, for the oceans. What I wanted to say could only be said by creating life-size images."

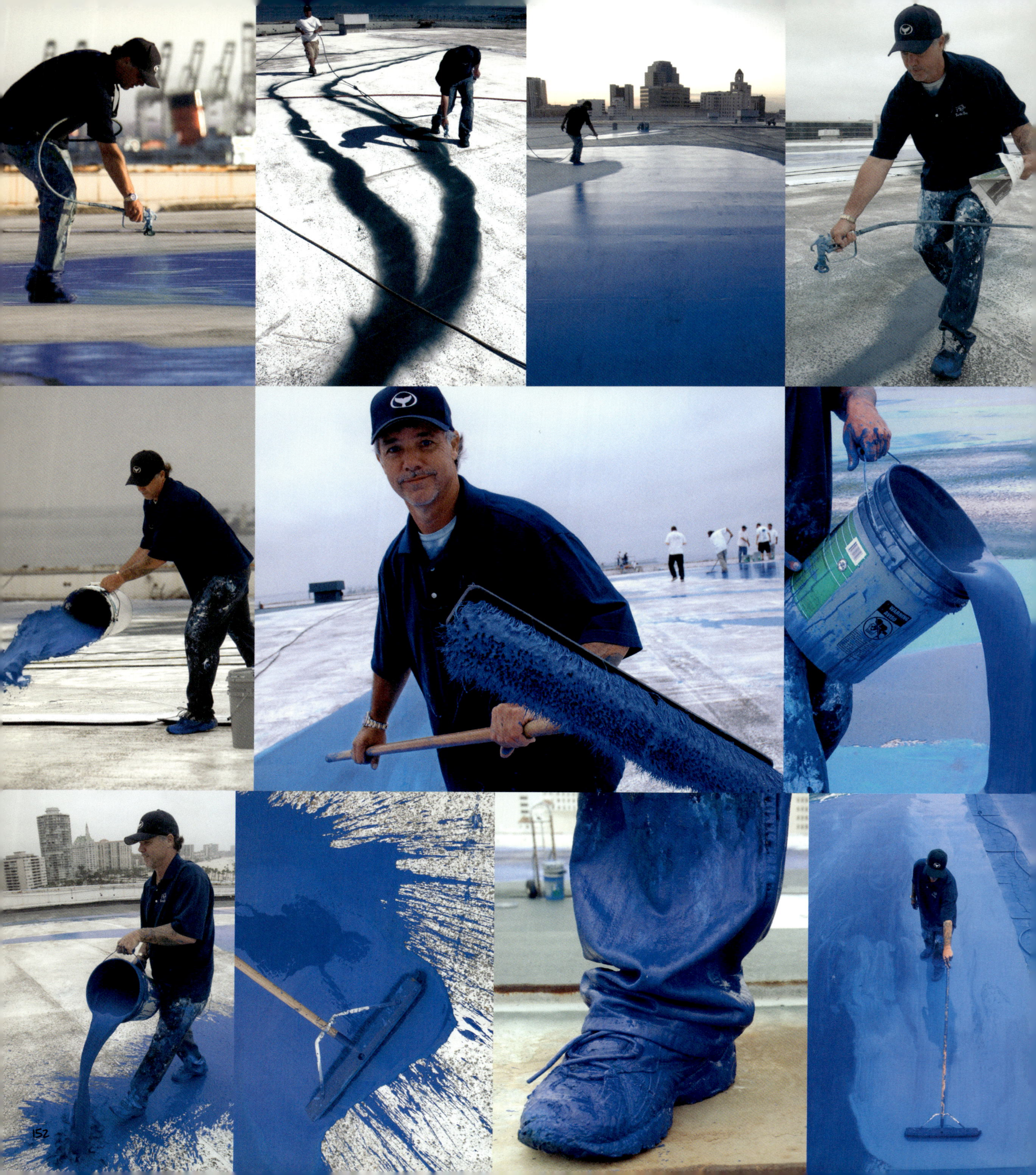

“I was thinking of the many people in the City of Angels that have done great things for the world and environment — and Wyland stands right at the top.”

John McConnell
Founder of Earth Day
and the Earth Society

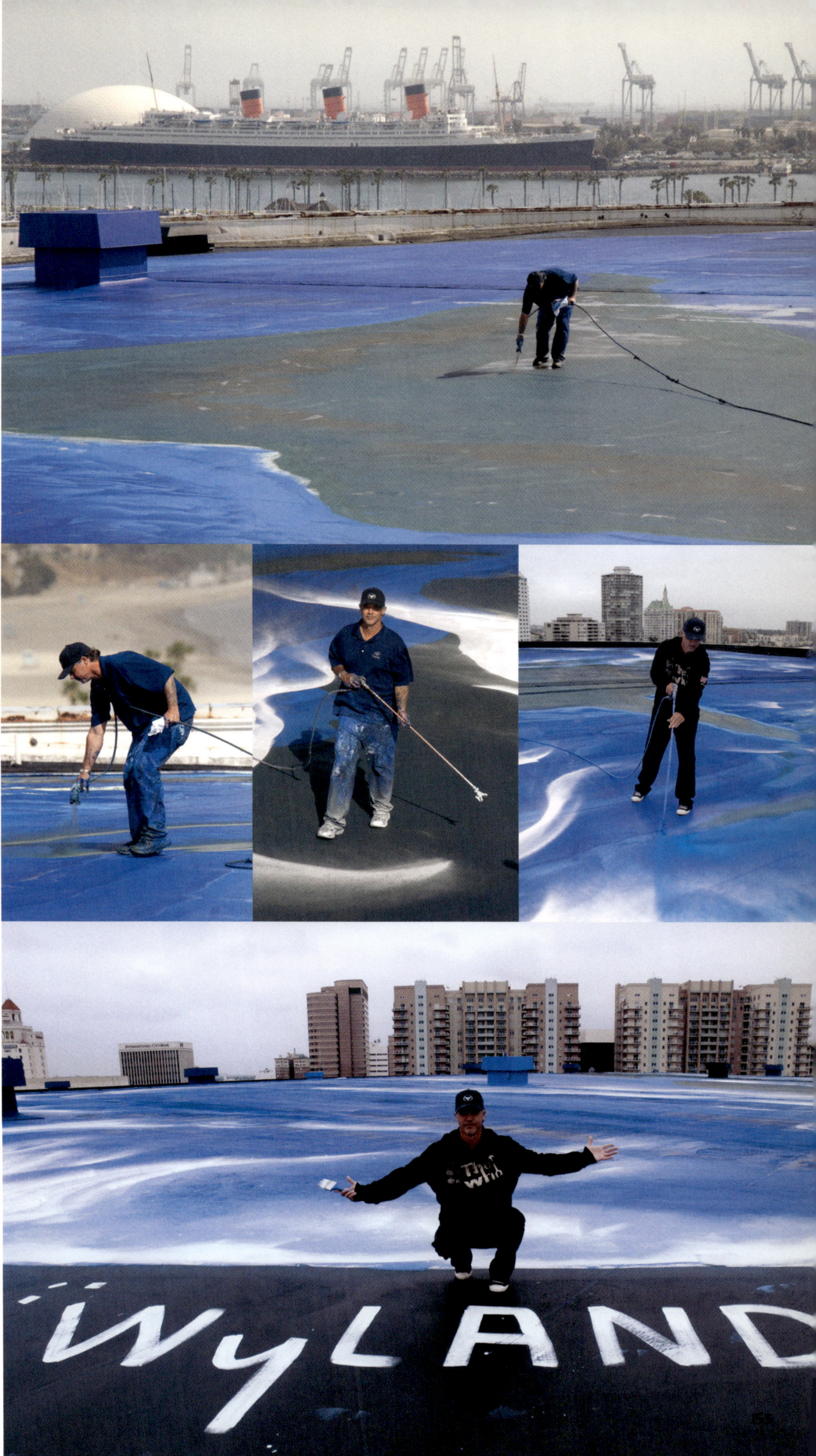

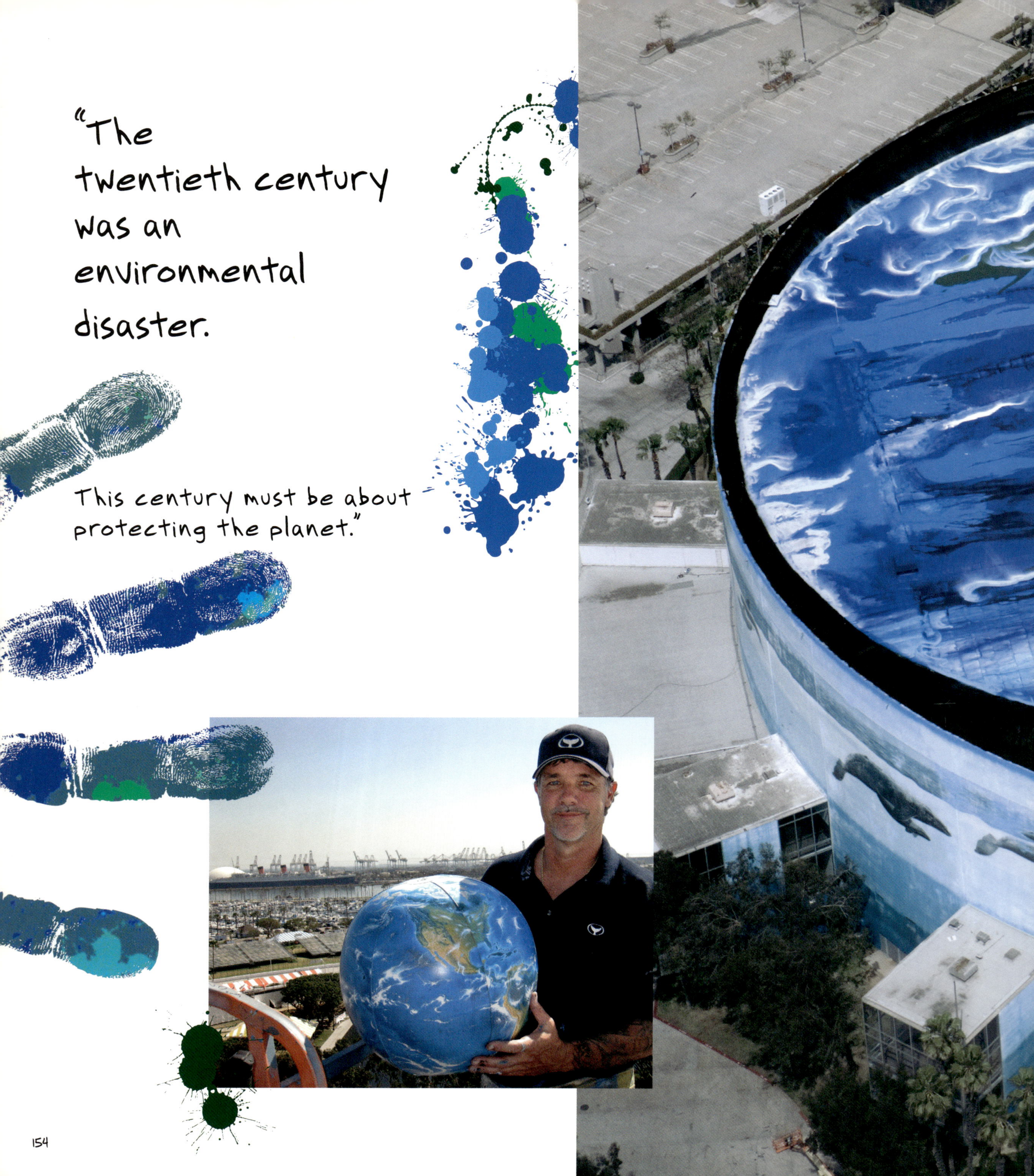

"The twentieth century was an environmental disaster.

This century must be about protecting the planet."

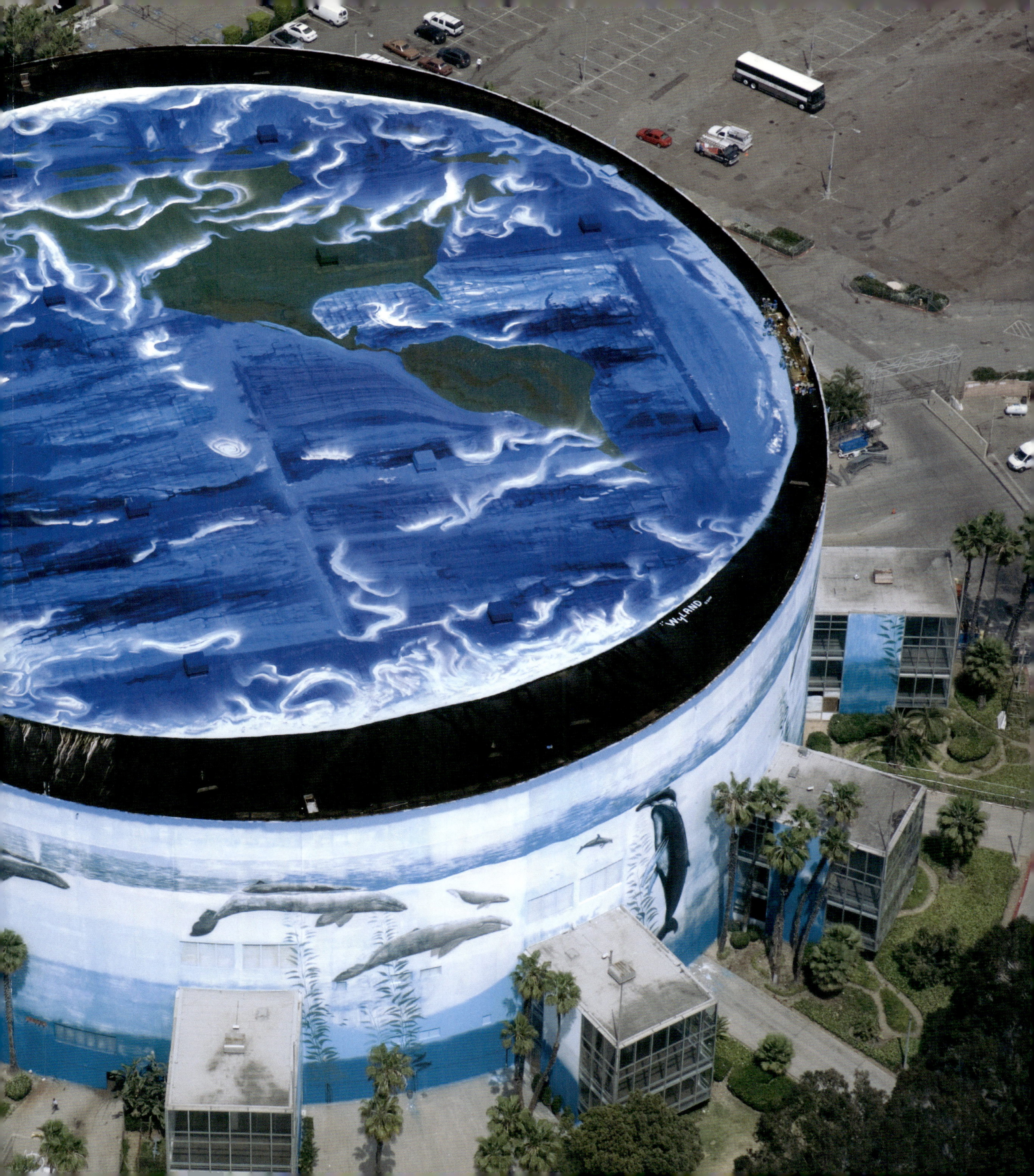
WyLAND

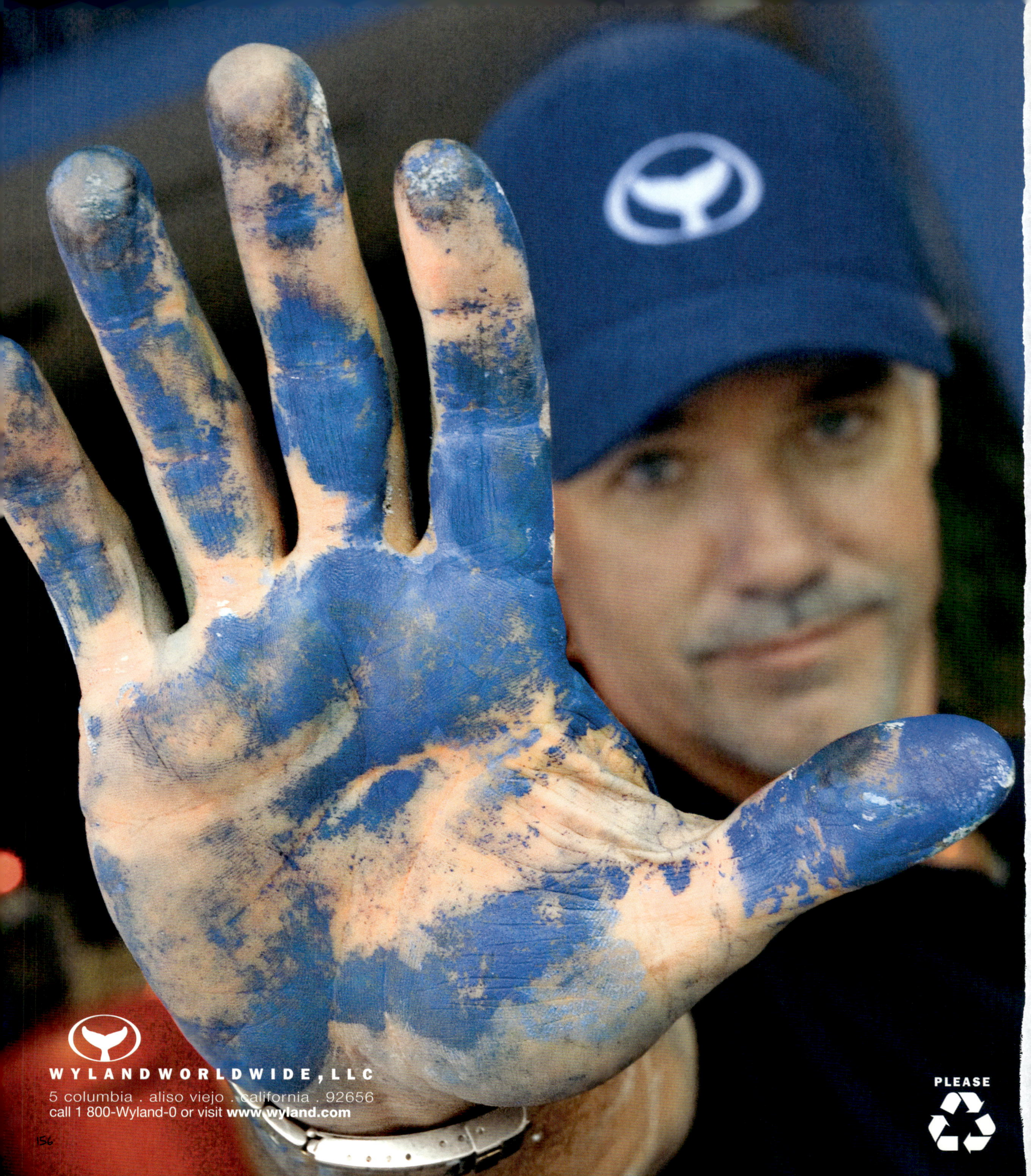
WYLAND WORLDWIDE, LLC
5 columbia . aliso viejo . california . 92656
call 1 800-Wyland-0 or visit www.wyland.com
PLEASE

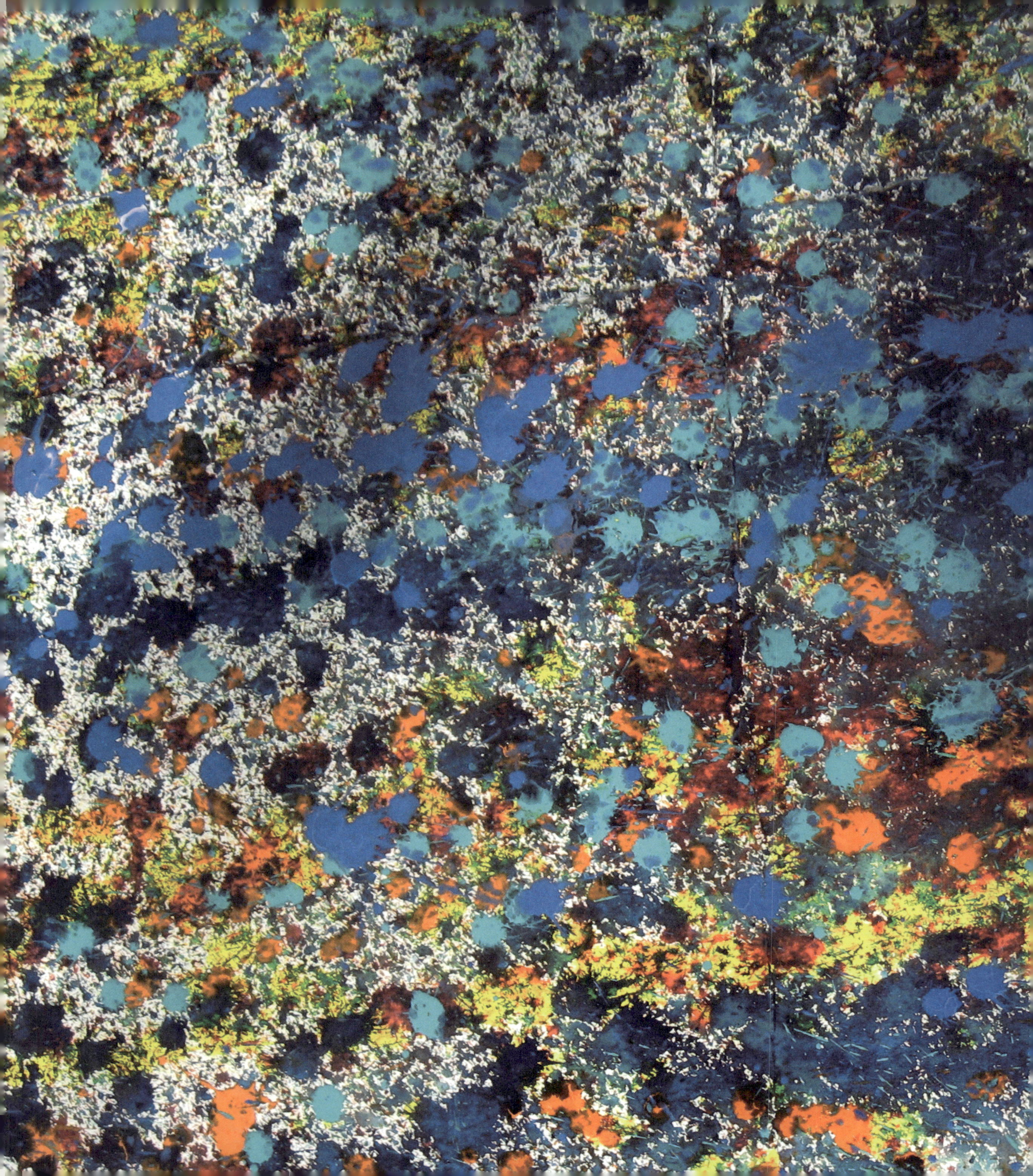